Nonprescription Drugs

By Thomas A. Gossel, R.Ph., Ph.D.,
Donald W. Stansloski, R.Ph., Ph.D.,
and the Editors of CONSUMER GUIDE®

Beekman House
New York

Contents

You can treat many minor ailments safely and effectively with nonprescription drugs. But you must buy and use these products responsibly. You should learn to select the correct product and to follow label directions exactly. Misused, over-the-counter (OTC) drugs can be ineffective or dangerous.

These guidelines for buying, storing, and using drugs will help you use OTC products economically. Purchasing the correct amount of the medication will avoid waste; storing a drug properly will maintain its effectiveness; and proper administration assures that you will get the drug's full benefit.

There may be as many as half a million OTC items from which to choose. Trying to select a remedy from the scores of items intended for treating any one condition can be confusing. These introductions to specific types of OTC drugs will guide you in choosing nonprescription medications. You will find that many of the most effective OTC drugs are sold generically (without brand names), and buying generically can mean saving money.

The drug profiles tell you what to expect from specific nonprescription drugs, when to be concerned about possible side effects or drug interactions, and how to take the medication to achieve maximum benefit, as well as other important and useful information. Here, arranged alphabetically, are profiles on hundreds of the most commonly used OTC drugs.

ABOUT THE AUTHORS

Drs. Gossel and Stansloski are on the faculty of Ohio Northern University, College of Pharmacy and Allied Health Sciences, in Ada, Ohio. Dr. Gossel is Associate Professor of Pharmacology and Chairman of the Department of Pharmacology and Biomedical Sciences. Dr. Stansloski is Associate Professor of Pharmacy and Chairman of the Department of Pharmacy and Health Care Administration. Both men are active participants in many local, state, and national health and pharmacy groups and committees. They firmly believe that an informed consumer is a healthier consumer.

Manufactured in the United States of America
1 2 3 4 5 6 7 8 9 10

Library of Congress Catalog Card Number 81-83990
ISBN: 0-517-292904

This edition published by
Beekman House
Distributed by Crown Publishers, Inc.
One Park Avenue
New York, N.Y. 10016

Note: Neither the authors nor the Editors of CONSUMER GUIDE® and PUBLICATIONS INTERNATIONAL, LTD. take responsibility for any possible consequences from any treatment, action, or application of medication or preparation by any person reading or following the information in this book. The publication of this book does not constitute the practice of medicine, and this book does not attempt to replace your physician or your pharmacist. The authors and publisher advise the reader to check with a physician before administering or consuming any medication or using any health care device.

Introduction

Sometime within the next two weeks, you will probably purchase a medical product without a prescription. You will probably buy it without thinking too much about what it is really supposed to do. You will choose it without knowing anything about its ingredients or its possible side effects. Most likely, you will buy the product because the ads on television or in magazines promise relief of your symptoms. And you will not worry about its ingredients or possible side effects because you believe that nonprescription medications must be safe or they would not be on the market.

When people have any major health problems, they should seek professional help. However, most of us feel confident enough to treat our minor ailments. In fact, three out of every four Americans treat many of their own maladies. And most often, people choose to treat themselves with over-the-counter (OTC) drugs.

Yet medical products sold over the counter can be dangerous. In one three-year period, nearly 18 percent of the people admitted to a hospital for a problem related to drugs had a toxic or allergic reaction to an OTC medication, took an overdose, or experienced an unanticipated and dangerous interaction between a prescription drug and an OTC drug. OTC medications are safe as long as they are used as *directed*, and the authors of this book and the editors of CONSUMER GUIDE® magazine believe that the use of OTC medications is an important part of your health care.

But we also believe that you must learn how to use OTC medications correctly. You must know how to choose among OTC products. You must be aware of what to look for on labels and what questions to ask. Above all, you must understand when to use OTC drugs and when *not* to use them.

This book is intended to guide you in your decisions on health care and on the safe, effective, and economical use of OTC drugs. It provides valuable information on the most popular OTC medications, listing for each drug the name of its manufacturer, its ingredients, possible side effects, and any warnings or special comments about its use. Furthermore, our product evaluations will guide you in choosing drug products to treat your minor physical ailments.

Nonprescription Drugs and Self-Treatment

Over-the-counter drugs; nonprescription medications; proprietary, patent, and family medicines—what are they? They are drugs that can be purchased without a doctor's prescription. They sit on shelves in supermarkets, discount stores, and hotel lobbies. They crowd displays in drugstores. They are the antacids and the first aid creams, the cough syrups and the cold tablets, the laxatives and the vitamins.

As many as 75 percent of all Americans who have a minor illness choose to buy and use OTC drugs. Most American adults will experience some sort of discomfort within the next two weeks. In many cases, they will decide what's wrong and then prescribe their own drug therapy, basing their choice perhaps on an ad they read in a magazine or heard on television. They may ask a pharmacist or a friend for advice, but they alone will make the final decision on what to do for their toothache or stomachache, their dizziness or sore feet.

How many OTC medical products can Americans choose from? No one knows for sure, but some people estimate that there are between 100,000 and 500,000, or even more. What do these drugs contain? Surprisingly, all OTC medical products are made from only 300 to 500 significantly active ingredients. And how much do we spend on them? As much as $5 billion per year. Obviously, the making and selling of OTC drugs is big business in the United States.

Are OTC drugs considered effective? Yes. As a matter of fact, doctors consider many OTC drugs the treatment of choice for certain severe diseases. Aspirin, for example, is still the best way to treat rheumatoid arthritis, and antacids have long been considered the most useful drugs for relieving the pain from a peptic ulcer. Many of the ingredients found in OTC drugs today have been used successfully to treat minor health problems for centuries.

6

However, some doctors and pharmacists feel that professional help should be sought before taking any drug. They argue that if OTC drugs are permitted to exist, they should be sold only in pharmacies. And it is true that the purchase of drugs in supermarkets, discount houses, gas stations, or hotel lobbies does prevent people from getting professional assistance. However, the intent of OTC therapy is clear: *OTC drugs are intended to be used by consumers without assistance.*

Treating Your Health Problems with OTC Products

Of course, you should seek professional assistance to diagnose and treat serious health problems. But by following a few simple steps, you can use OTC drugs to treat most of your minor ailments.

• *Study the label* on the OTC drug before you purchase it. Be sure the label includes the name and type of the drug, its purpose, dosage, special warnings, and the directions for its use. The label should include the drug's expiration date, the date beyond which the drug should not be used. Look for an explanation of the maximum safe dosage, any possible side effects, drug interactions, special health problems that might complicate use of the drug, and the conditions for storing the drug. Check to see if the names of the drug's active ingredients and the name and address of the manufacturer or distributor are listed. If all this information is not on the label, do not buy the product. If all the information *is* on the label, make certain you understand it *before* you buy the product. If you have questions, ask your pharmacist or doctor. You should know when a product can be used safely and effectively to treat a specific condition.

Note: It is not mandatory that manufacturers list concentrations of ingredients for some products; however, we feel that you deserve to know what's going into your body when you take an over-the-counter medication. Only when the manufacturer supplies a complete listing of the concentrations of the active ingredients in a product can you make a true price comparison. We believe such a listing is advisable for every over-the-counter remedy.

• *Treat only the symptoms you have.* If you have acid indigestion, choose a product that's pure antacid, not a combination antacid-analgesic or antacid-antiflatulent. If your nose is stuffy, take a pure decongestant, not a decongestant combined with an analgesic. Don't take drugs you don't need. A corollary to this rule of thumb is "choose drugs with a single action." If you have a fever and a stuffy nose, buy two different drug products: aspirin to reduce the fever and a decongestant to relieve the stuffiness. Once the fever goes down, you can stop taking the aspirin while you continue to take the decongestant as long as your nose is stuffy.

• *Follow the directions* for use of the drug. Remember that OTC drugs can be ineffective—and perhaps deadly—if they are misused.

- *Evaluate how you are responding to the drug.* Pay attention to your daily weight, temperature, and overall well-being.
- *Watch for side effects.* Be familiar with the side effects that could be caused by the drugs you are taking.
- *Store drugs properly.* The active ingredients in a drug may lose their effectiveness if the drug is not stored properly. And *always* keep drugs out of the reach of children.
- *Know when to see your doctor.* Call your doctor if you are not responding to the OTC medication, if you develop troublesome side effects, or if you accidentally take too much medication.
- *Learn about the specific dangers of self-treatment.* Become aware of possible side effects, allergies, and drug interactions. Be aware, too, that using OTC drugs may mask symptoms of serious disease, thus delaying necessary treatment or leading to an incorrect diagnosis of your condition.

CONSUMER GUIDE® Ratings

To help you choose the safest and most effective nonprescription drug product to treat your minor illnesses, the editors of CONSUMER GUIDE® have rated the products profiled in this book. The ratings fall into five categories: "Preferred," "Acceptable," "Fair," "Unacceptable," and "Not Evaluated."

A product receiving a "Preferred" rating is considered one of the best available over the counter for treatment of a specified condition. The ingredients in "Preferred" products have been proven effective and safe for the majority of users. They cause minimal adverse effects when taken as directed. "Preferred" products are generally single-ingredient or single-action drugs; these are generally more economical than combination products meant to relieve a number of different symptoms.

Products rated "Acceptable" are also effective. However, their ingredients may not be as effective as those in the "Preferred" category, or, in addition to the top-rated ingredient, they may include other, less effective and unnecessary ingredients.

Products rated "Fair" are safe to use and have no serious drawbacks such as potential toxicity, nor are they grossly overpriced. However, neither are they as effective as products in the "Preferred" or "Acceptable" categories.

A rating of "Unacceptable," on the other hand, indicates a serious problem with the product. For example, an ingredient may have no proven effectiveness in treating the specified condition. A product may also be rated "Unacceptable" because it has an "everything but the kitchen sink" formulation; a cough remedy, for example, that includes a suppressant, an expectorant, a decongestant, and an antihistamine is rated "Unacceptable." In some cases, products rated "Unacceptable" contain ingredients that are potentially toxic.

The final category, "Not Evaluated," applies only to those products for which the manufacturer has failed to supply sufficient information on which to base an evaluation.

Dosage

The most obvious mistake a consumer can make is to take too much of a drug. Some people think that if they take two tablets instead of the recommended one, they will get well twice as fast; or that if they take a teaspoonful every two hours instead of one every four hours as recommended, their symptoms will go away sooner.

A slight overdose of an OTC drug, however, may produce toxic effects. For example, twice the recommended dose of OTC sleeping-aid tablets may produce severe drowsiness. Some laxatives may actually cause constipation if they are taken more than once or twice a week. Be careful of the amount of drug you take each time and of how often you take your medication. The rate at which your body can eliminate drugs is fixed. If you ingest more of a drug than your body can handle, the concentration of the drug in your body can build to a dangerous level, and that can occur whether you ingest that amount all at once or by taking the drug more frequently than recommended.

Indications

Suppose you have an upset stomach. You take an OTC drug that contains two active ingredients, one to relieve your upset stomach and aspirin for a headache. If you don't have a headache, you don't need the aspirin. And you are taking the wrong product for your problem. You are taking more medication and spending more money than necessary.

There are hundreds of thousands of OTC drugs on the market. To choose the right one for your health problem, read the label carefully, especially the indications for using the product. The indications specify those conditions that can be relieved by taking the drug. If the indications do not match your self-diagnosis or your symptoms—if the item isn't intended to do what you want—don't buy the product. Indications tell you when you can use the product safely and effectively.

Side Effects

Any drug—even aspirin—can cause side effects. Aspirin can upset the stomach. Antihistamines make some people drowsy. Some ointments cause itching, and some liniments burn the skin. Decongestants make some people nervous and raise the blood pressure of others.

Most OTC drugs are safe for most people. Still, side effects may occur. They are more likely to occur when you take a product that contains several active ingredients, when you take several drugs at the same time, or when you take large quantities of one drug for a long period of time. To avoid side effects:

• *Choose products that have only one or two active ingredients—no more.*

- *Take the smallest amount of the drug* that you can for the shortest possible time.
- *Keep to a minimum the number of different OTC drugs that you take,* and don't take any OTC medication without your doctor's knowledge while also taking prescription drugs.
- *Don't ignore side effects.* Discontinue use of the OTC drug and call your doctor immediately whenever worrisome side effects occur.

Drug Interactions

An OTC drug can interact with any other OTC or prescription drug you take. Most drug interactions are not serious. However, you should be aware of the ones that can be. Aspirin, for example, may intensify the effects of anticoagulant, or blood-thinning, drugs. Occasionally, a decongestant may interact with a tranquilizer to raise blood pressure to dangerously high levels. Antacids and iron supplements may prevent the absorption of tetracycline antibiotics used to treat an infection.

The possibility of an interaction should be kept in mind whenever you use drugs. Keep track of the OTC and prescription drugs you take and cross-check their labels to see whether they interact.

When you get a prescription filled, ask your pharmacist if there is any OTC drug you should avoid using. When you purchase an unfamiliar over-the-counter drug, study its label to find out what other drugs you should refrain from using. (For specific drug interactions, see the individual drugs in the drug profile section. If you have any questions, ask your pharmacist.)

Misdiagnosing and Masking Symptoms

Suppose your doctor has prescribed medication for your high blood pressure. The medication makes your nose stuffy, so you begin taking decongestant tablets. One of the results of taking the decongestant tablets is an increase in your blood pressure. When your doctor discovers the increase, he concludes that the medication he has prescribed is not helping, and he decides to increase the dosage or to prescribe a different drug. He will be overtreating your high blood pressure.

Or suppose you have been taking aspirin, but fail to mention it to your doctor. The aspirin relieves some of the symptoms of arthritis, and because the symptoms are hidden, your doctor misdiagnoses your condition.

OTC drugs can hide symptoms or cause a reaction that misleads your doctor. Furthermore, you can be misled by your own symptoms. Let's say, for example, you have an upset stomach. You think you have heartburn and decide to treat it with a product like Maalox antacid. However, an upset stomach is also a symptom of peptic ulcer. By taking the antacid, you are masking the symptoms of the ulcer.

One way to guard against this problem is to take OTC medications judiciously. If you find that you are taking an OTC drug on a regular basis for more than a few days, you probably should see your doctor to make sure that the drug is not masking the symptoms of a more serious disease.

How Your Pharmacist Can Help

Few of us know enough about drugs, cars, or houses to make intelligent choices on our own. Most of us try to find an expert in the field who will help us make a good choice. When it comes to OTC drugs, that expert is a pharmacist.

But don't choose the first pharmacist you see in the first drugstore you find. Many drugstores are self-service, and you may get no more advice from the pharmacist than you would from a checker in a supermarket. You should shop around for a pharmacy and a pharmacist. Choose a pharmacy, no matter how large or small, in which you feel comfortable talking to the pharmacist. Select one that has a counter or special area where you can talk with the pharmacist privately, and try to choose a pharmacist with whom you feel comfortable.

Your pharmacist should be able not only to give you advice but also to save you money, for example, by recommending generic drugs instead of brand-name items. Popular OTC drugs have brand names such as Anacin, Dristan, and Contac. Only one manufacturer can use a given brand name. For example, only Glenbrook Laboratories can produce Bayer aspirin tablets. Any drug manufacturer can, however, produce and sell generic drugs.

Almost all drugstores carry a line of generic OTC drugs. Rexall, Revco, Walgreen, and other major pharmacy chains have their own lines of products that are comparable to brand-name drugs but usually cost less. For most people in most circumstances, generic OTC drugs will be just as effective as brand-name products. And your pharmacist is in the position to know whether a generic drug is right for you. The decision depends on the specific drug involved, your health problem or condition, and the amount of money you can save.

Another way your pharmacist can save you money is by substituting one type of drug for another. Suppose you have a headache and want to take Anacin analgesic tablets. Anacin analgesic tablets are mostly aspirin, plus some caffeine. Aspirin is not the generic equivalent of Anacin analgesic tablets. But if you take aspirin instead of Anacin analgesic tablets, you will probably get just as good an effect and will pay less money for it. Because the two products are not comparable, the pharmacist is not making a generic substitution. He is making a therapeutic substitution, or choosing a different kind of drug that can do the job every bit as well as a more expensive product.

Buying, Storing, and Using Drugs

In a prescription for medication, your doctor tells your pharmacist how many tablets or capsules or how much liquid medication to give you. When you buy nonprescription medications, you must decide how much you need. You might think that choosing between a 200-tablet bottle and a 12-tablet tin merely depends on how much money you have. But the amount of a drug to buy depends on other factors, too.

The first is the kind of drug you will be taking and how long you expect to take it. For instance, a cold lasts about a week; when buying cold remedies, buy enough for five to seven days. An ulcer can continue for months, and you may want to purchase enough antacid to last 60 or 90 days.

The second is convenience. If you live far away from a store or pharmacy and must make several trips to replenish your supply of an OTC drug, you may be wise to buy a large amount of medication. A good rule of thumb is to buy enough medication to be economical but not so much that you may have to throw some away. Convenience gives way to caution, however. If you have small children, you may not want to keep large quantities of drugs on hand.

The third factor is your response to drugs. If you have been plagued with annoying side effects or allergic reactions to some OTC or prescription drugs, be sure to buy small quantities of any new drug until you are sure it agrees with you. You may have to pay more per dose when you buy only a small amount of the product, but you won't be paying for a supply of medication you may not be able to take.

The last factor to consider is the drug's expiration date. All OTC drugs have expiration dates on their labels. An expiration date indicates the time beyond which the OTC product may no longer be totally effective. It usually is based on the time at which 5 percent of the drug will have been destroyed or converted.

A drug may be effective after its expiration date has elapsed, but you cannot be sure and should not take chances. Do not buy a product if the expiration date is near or has already passed. Do not buy large quantities of drugs if you may not be able to take them before the expiration date.

Storing OTC Medications

Drugs can lose potency if they are not protected from light, heat, and moisture. Therefore, you should know and follow some basic rules for storing medications to keep them fresh and active.

Most OTC products can be stored safely out of direct sunlight and at room temperature—or between 59° and 86° F. Although many drugs are dispensed in colored containers to protect them from light, they still should be kept out of direct sunlight.

Drugs that should be kept at room temperature should *not* be refrigerated. Some liquid medications will thicken as they become cold and will not pour from the bottle. To be sure you're storing your drugs at the proper temperature, check their labels. And be sure to keep *all* drugs away from excessive heat. One of the worst places to keep any medical product is in the glove compartment of your car in the summertime. The temperature inside the glove compartment may reach 160° F or more, and such intense heat may completely destroy the active ingredients in an drug in a very short time.

Another problem to guard against when storing drugs is moisture. The slightest amount of moisture can destroy some tablets. Avoid, for example, purchasing tablets of aspirin or other pain relievers that come in small tins or flat plastic boxes. These containers do not close tightly and will allow moisture to enter. Finally, tightly close all liquid drug containers to prevent evaporation.

Almost everyone keeps OTC and prescription drugs in one place—usually the bathroom medicine cabinet. But the medicine cabinet is one of the worst places to keep drugs. Changes in temperature and humidity in the bathroom can adversely affect the stability of many drug products. And children can easily climb onto the bathroom sink and reach the items that have been stored above it. If you have small children, make sure all drugs are locked up. You can get an inexpensive lock for a cabinet or closet at your local hardware store. And remember to use it.

The Well-Stocked Medicine Cabinet

Your medicine cabinet probably has over-the-counter and current prescription drugs, assorted first-aid "odds and ends," cosmetics, toiletries, disinfectants, and the like. It probably has some items that don't belong there—unused prescription medications, outdated OTC drugs, and empty bottles.

Now is a good time to take stock of your medicine cabinet, to remove anything that is not intended to treat sickness—perfumes, aftershave lotions, and household cleaning products—and to separate drugs for external use from those for internal use.

The ideal home medicine cabinet should contain the drugs you use frequently plus those you might need in an emergency. You, of course, know what you use frequently. For what you might need in a hurry, see the accompanying table.

The Home Medicine Cabinet

Medication	To Treat
antinauseant	nausea, vomiting
antihistamine	colds and allergy
decongestant	colds and allergy
cough syrup	coughs of colds
aspirin, acetaminophen	pain and fever
activated charcoal	poisoning
ipecac syrup	poisoning
rubbing alcohol	skin irritations
anti-infective cream	minor cuts
topical anesthetic	burns, insect bites, etc.
hydrogen peroxide	minor cuts
petroleum jelly	skin irritations
epsom salts	swollen tissues (sprained ankle, etc.)

Supplies

adhesive tape ($\frac{1}{2}$ " wide)
sterile bandages ($2'' \times 2''$, $3'' \times 3''$, and $4'' \times 4''$)
cotton-tipped swabs
gauze bandage rolls (1" wide and 4" wide)
adhesive bandages (assorted sizes)
elastic bandage (3" wide)
scissors
tweezers
thermometers (oral and rectal)
wooden tongue depressors
flashlight
stethoscope
sphygmomanometer
first aid manual
insect sting kit (if someone in family is allergic to insect stings)
ice bag
heating pad

The ideal home medicine cabinet deliberately leaves out drugs that should be picked up when you need them rather than stocked in advance. Many health problems progress slowly enough for you to purchase an OTC drug before the symptoms get too bad: for example, constipation, athlete's foot, diaper rash, poison ivy, nasal congestion, and fever blisters. The ideal home medicine cabinet also contains a sphygmomanometer (used to measure blood pressure) and a stethoscope.

Your medicine cabinet should have an emergency first-aid section. It should contain a supply of adhesive bandage strips, gauze rolls and gauze pads, cotton swabs, a bottle of rubbing alcohol, a tube of anti-infective cream, a topical anesthetic, activated charcoal, and ipecac syrup. Additionally, you should have a small pair of scissors, a pair of tweezers, and wooden tongue depressors (which you may buy from most drug stores). We also recommend that you buy and study a first-aid manual. This will help you in time of emergency, and should answer most of your questions about common first-aid measures.

The Right Way To Use OTC Products

Once you've decided to treat your minor ailments with over-the-counter drugs, you must learn how to use them. There is a correct way to use drugs: a correct way to take tablets, capsules, and liquids, and to use powders, creams, ointments, or aerosol sprays. If you use your drugs correctly, you will get their full benefit. But if you don't, you may actually lengthen your illness and waste money as well.

Tablets and capsules. Some people have trouble swallowing tablets or capsules. If you're one of them, try swallowing a mouthful of water, or at least wet your mouth, before taking the tablet or capsule. Then, place the tablet or capsule on the back of the tongue, and take a drink of water. You can also empty the contents of the capsule or crush the tablet into a spoon, and add a little applesauce, soup, or even chocolate syrup. Be careful to check with your pharmacist first, however. Some tablets and capsules must be swallowed whole, and your pharmacist can tell you which ones they are.

Another alternative is to buy chewable tablets or a liquid form of the drug. Liquids and chewable tablets, however, usually cost more than regular tablets or capsules, and liquids are not as easy to carry with you.

Liquids. Clear liquids are called solutions. The proper way to take a solution is to measure out a dose of the medication and swallow it. But you must be sure to measure accurately. Some drug labels call for a tablespoon, and others, a teaspoon. Read the label to be certain. Since many household spoons vary in size, you may want to ask your pharmacist for a special measuring spoon to help you avoid errors.

Liquids that are not clear, or those that contain particles that settle in the bottom of the bottle are called mixtures, emulsions, or suspensions. They must be shaken before use. If you don't shake them well each time, the active drug ingredient in these liquids may remain at the bottom of the bottle. When you pour off a dose from the top of the liquid you get little active ingredient. Then, as the volume of liquid in the bottle becomes smaller, you'll pour off doses that contain more and more of the active ingredient. The greater concentration of the active ingredient in each dose may cause poisoning. So, be sure to shake the bottle before taking a dose of a cloudy liquid medication.

It is sometimes difficult to administer liquid medications to a young child. Your pharmacist can supply you with a dropper or an oral syringe if this is the case at your house. Droppers are most often used with infants or very young children.

Hold the child on your lap; then fill the dropper or syringe with the right amount of the medication. Before filling a syringe, pour some medication into a clean container. Remove the cap from the tip of the syringe, and push the plunger on the syringe all the way in. Place the tip in the medicine you've poured out. Pull back on the syringe until the correct amount of medication according to the calibrations has been drawn up.

If the child will "open wide," release the medicine slowly into the side of the child's mouth. Don't squirt the medicine into the back of the child's mouth; you may cause him to choke and gag. If the child refuses to open his mouth, use one of your arms to restrain his arms and place your other hand around his face so that you can pull his chin down with your thumb. Then squeeze the medicine into the side of his mouth.

After use, a syringe should be washed and dried. You can return a dropper to its bottle without washing it first. If you do wash it, make sure it's dry before you return it to the bottle.

Ointments and creams. Most creams and ointments should be applied to the skin as thinly as possible. Squeeze a small amount of the medication onto the affected area, and gently massage it into the skin until it is gone. Use your fingers unless you are treating an infection which is easily transmitted by physical contact (such as impetigo), in which case you should use a cotton-tipped swab. If your skin is very dry, immerse the affected area in water or moisten it with a damp, clean cloth before applying the cream or ointment. Blot the skin dry. Then, apply the ointment as directed. You should feel no greasiness or wetness after applying a cream. However, your skin may feel slightly greasy or slippery after applying an ointment.

Creams are preferable to ointments in most situations. Creams are greaseless and do not stain clothing. They are best for use on the scalp or other hairy areas of the body. Ointments, however, are favored for people with extremely dry skin. Ointments keep skin soft for a long period of time.

Aerosol sprays. For use on tender or hairy parts of the body, pressurized aerosol sprays are more effective than creams or ointments. But aerosols usually cost more than other forms of the same medication.

Before using an aerosol, shake the can. Then, hold it upright about four to six inches away from your skin, press the nozzle for a few seconds, and release.

Do not spray an aerosol near the face or eyes. If it enters the eyes or the nose, the spray can cause long-lasting pain. It may even damage the eyes. If you must apply medication from a pressurized aerosol can to your face, spray it onto your hand and pat it onto the affected area.

Aerosol sprays feel cold when they are applied. If you find this feeling uncomfortable, ask your pharmacist if the medication is available in another form.

Wet soaks. Wet soaks, either hot or cold, are used to relieve itching due to rashes such as poison ivy. Cold soaks relieve pain and reduce inflammation of minor burns. The procedure consists of applying a clean cloth that has been soaked in water or some solution to the affected area of the skin. If a hot soak is desired, warm the solution above body temperature before immersing the cloth, but use your hand to check that the temperature is not too hot. When applying the cloth, take care to protect clothing and furniture from drips.

Resoak the cloth about every 30 minutes if the soak is to be continuous; leave it on for a total of two to three hours. A hot soak should be renewed whenever it cools, or you can keep the soak at the right temperature by using a hot water bottle or a wet-proof heating pad.

Eyedrops. Before administering eyedrops, wash your hands, lie or sit down, and tilt your head back. Then, pull the lower eyelid down to form a pouch.

To insert eyedrops, hold the dropper as close to the eyelid as possible without touching it. Squeeze out the recommended number of drops into the pouch. Do not place eyedrops directly onto the eyeball; you will probably blink and wash away the medication. After inserting the eyedrops, close your eye and keep it closed for a few moments. When you open your eye, your vision may be blurred for a minute or two. Replace the dropper in the bottle without washing or wiping it.

Nose drops and sprays. Gently blow your nose, if possible, before administering nose drops or a nasal spray. To insert nose drops, tilt your head back and place the prescribed number of drops in the nose without touching it with the dropper. Afterward, keep your head tilted for a few moments and sniff gently several times.

When using a nasal spray, do not tilt your head back. Insert the sprayer into a nostril, but try to avoid touching the lining of the nose. Squeeze the sprayer and sniff at the same time. Keep squeezing the sprayer until you have withdrawn it from your nose so mucus and bacteria cannot be drawn into the sprayer. After spraying the prescribed number of times in one or both nostrils, sniff several times.

Ideally, nose drops and sprays should not be used for more than two or three days. Do not use nose drops or spray from the same container after a week; bacteria from the nose can easily enter the container and contaminate the solution. If you must use medication for more than a week, purchase a new container. Do not allow another person to use your nose drops or spray. Always purchase a separate bottle or spray for each person.

Inhalers. To use a nasal inhaler, insert the cylinder into a nostril and sniff; remove the cylinder. Wait three or four minutes. Then, gently blow your nose. Repeat once or twice if necessary.

Most oral inhalers must be assembled before use. The mouthpiece must be lifted off the top of the bottle and fitted to a nozzle. Usually, you hold the bottle upside down to use it. Insert the mouthpiece into your mouth, and close your teeth and lips around it. Exhale through your nose to empty your lungs of air, and then breathe in deeply while squeezing the bottom of the bottle. Take the inhaler apart after you use it, and wash it with water before storing it.

Rectal suppositories. To insert a suppository, lie on your side and push it, pointed end first, as far as you can into the rectum without discomfort. If, at first, you feel like defecating, lie still until the feeling goes away. If insertion causes pain or is difficult, try coating the suppository with a thin layer of petroleum jelly or mineral oil.

If a suppository is wrapped in aluminum foil, remove the foil. In hot weather, a suppository may be too soft to handle properly. A suppository that has softened may be placed inside the refrigerator or in a glass of cool water for a few minutes. Unless your fingernails are extremely long and sharp, you need not wear rubber finger cots or disposable rubber gloves when inserting a suppository.

Vaginal ointments or creams. Most vaginal creams or ointments include explicit directions for their use. The directions usually amplify these basic steps: First, screw the applicator onto the top of the tube. Be sure the plunger is pushed all the way down before you screw the applicator onto the tube. Squeeze the tube from the bottom until the applicator plunger has been pushed out as far as it will go. Lie on your back with your knees drawn up. Keep the applicator horizontal or pointed downward slightly, and push it into the vagina as far as it will comfortably go. Press the plunger down to empty the medication into the vagina. After the plunger has been withdrawn, wash it in warm, soapy water, rinse it thoroughly, and allow it to dry completely. Once it is dry, return the plunger to its package.

Choosing the OTC Remedy for Your Ailment

Acne Preparations

Common acne is an inflammatory disease of the skin characterized by overactivity of the oil-secreting glands. The excess oil (or sebum) tends to clog the pores. While the exact cause is unknown, acne is thought to be genetically related. Acne is more common in males, although it does occur in females. It first appears, ordinarily, at the time of the increase in sex hormones during puberty. Acne may continue through the fourth or fifth decade of life although it usually ends by the late teens or early twenties.

Several factors seem to be associated with the course of the disease, including the ingestion of certain drugs (oral contraceptives in particular), diet, physical trauma, climate, the menstrual cycle, and emotional stress.

Inflamed, severe, or resistant cases of acne should be treated by a doctor. Mild cases can be self-treated. OTC acne preparations are helpful in that they open blocked skin pores. Most OTC drugs include chemicals (such as sulfur, resorcinol, salicylic acid, or benzoyl peroxide) that remove the plug from the pore and promote the sloughing of the skin as well. Because products with these ingredients cause some irritation, they should not be used too often or applied too vigorously. If irritation is severe, use of the product should be discontinued. The most effective products, those containing benzoyl peroxide, may increase your sensitivity to the sun. Use them carefully if you expect to be in the sun or to use a sunlamp.

Home treatment should also include washing the affected area two or three times a day with soap and lots of water. More frequent washing usually does not eliminate excess oil and, in fact, may cause drying of the skin. Washing with a medicated soap is no more effective than washing with regular soap. The medication is rinsed off when you rinse your face. Picking at or pinching lesions may cause deep-pitted permanent scar formation.

Someone with acne should avoid greasy cleansing creams and cosmetics, should shampoo at least once or twice a week, and should remove any blackheads with a comedo extractor.

The use of a soft complexion brush or an abrasive cleanser may be beneficial if not done to excess, but should be avoided if lesions are inflamed. Either should be used gently. Those with especially sensitive, fair, or dark skin should talk to a doctor before using one of these abrasive products. A doctor should also be consulted about the use of a sunlamp or ultraviolet lamp.

Recommendations on OTC Acne Preparations

The most effective ingredient in over-the-counter acne remedies is benzoyl peroxide. We recommend products containing benzoyl peroxide as the single active ingredient. Among our profiled drugs, such products include Clearasil; Dry and Clear (lotion, cream); Oxy-5; Oxy-10; Stri-Dex B.P.; and Topex.

Profiled acne preparations: Acne-Aid; Clearasil; Clearasil Pore Deep Cleanser; Dry and Clear (liquid cleanser; lotion, cream); Fostex; Fostril; Ionax Foam; Ionax Scrub; Komed; Microsyn; Oxy-5, Oxy-10; Oxy-Scrub; pHisoAc; pHisoDerm; Stri-Dex; Stri-Dex B.P.; Sulforcin; Topex; Vanoxide

Antacids (for relief of indigestion and heartburn)

Antacids are alkaline substances that combine with excessive stomach acid and neutralize it. They are commonly used in the self-treatment of indigestion and heartburn, and they are a mainstay in the treatment of peptic ulcer disease. Hundreds of antacids are available in different forms—tablets, liquids, lozenges, gums, powders, and pills—and Americans spend hundreds of millions of dollars on them every year. Most of these products contain one or more of only four ingredients: sodium bicarbonate, calcium carbonate, magnesium salts, and aluminum salts.

Sodium bicarbonate. Also known as baking soda and contained in products such as Alka-Seltzer antacid tablets, sodium bicarbonate is the most powerful and the most dangerous of the antacid chemicals. If excess sodium bicarbonate is absorbed into the bloodstream, it can interfere with heart or kidney function. Its action is short, and it must be taken more often than other antacid chemicals. Baking soda or a sodium bicarbonate-containing antacid can be taken safely for no more than two or three consecutive days without consulting a doctor.

Calcium carbonate. Calcium carbonate-containing products are quick-acting and potent, and they generate few side effects. The most severe side effect is "acid rebound." After one or two weeks of constant acid neutralization by calcium carbonate, the stomach responds by secreting more acid, causing more discomfort.

Magnesium salts. Magnesium salts products are not as potent as those with calcium carbonate, but they are effective. Their major drawback is their laxative effect. Antacids with magnesium salts can cause severe diarrhea if full doses are used regularly for more than one to two weeks. These antacids can also cause drowsiness or kidney problems in certain people. Anyone with kidney disease should talk to a doctor before taking any OTC product containing magnesium.

Aluminum salts. Aluminum salts are the least potent of all the antacid chemicals. Nevertheless, they have side effects. One side effect is constipation. To relieve constipation, drink plenty of water throughout the day or take a stool softener. Some products, like Gelusil II or Maalox antacids, contain both magnesium and aluminum salts. The laxative effect of the magnesium is balanced by the constipating effect of the aluminum. The use of antacids containing only magnesium or aluminum salts is not recommended; it is preferable to use products containing both. However, note that magaldrate, a mixture of aluminum and magnesium hydroxides, although a less potent antacid than other forms combining these two ingredients, still has the potential to produce the same side effects.

Other ingredients. Many antacid products (Mylanta and Di-Gel tablets, for example) contain the antiflatulent simethicone, a drug that reduces gas in the gastrointestinal tract. Such products—a combination antacid with antiflatulent—have been found to be safe and effective by the Food and Drug Administration's advisory review panel on antacids. However, it is generally advisable to purchase just an antacid or antiflatulent rather than a combination product. Avoid taking simethicone except when needed to reduce excess gas.

Some antacid products also contain a pain killer (or an analgesic), usually aspirin or acetaminophen. Aspirin causes stomach upset in many people, and its use in products intended for the treatment of indigestion has been termed irrational by the FDA. If you have both an upset stomach and a headache (a common combination of symptoms caused by overindulgence in alcohol), a combination antacid-analgesic may be useful. However, if you are treating only gastrointestinal symptoms, look for a product that is pure antacid.

Indigestion and heartburn are common disorders, and occasional occurrences can be safely and effectively treated with OTC antacids. If discomfort is severe, doses of the antacid may need to be taken as frequently as every hour or two. Pain relief will usually be felt within a few minutes of taking an antacid. If, however, your distress is not relieved by an antacid, or if you experience symptoms of indigestion and heartburn frequently, you should seek medical diagnosis.

Recommendations on OTC Antacids

We recommend Gaviscon (liquid), Kolantyl, Maalox, Maalox #1, and Maalox #2 antacids. These products contain only magnesium and aluminum salts.

Liquid antacids are far superior to tablets or wafers. Antacids neutralize stomach acid best when they have been ground into small particles, and antacid particles in liquids are much smaller than those in tablets or wafers. Tablets or wafers, however, may be more convenient to use during the day.

If you occasionally suffer from intestinal gas pains and cramping, you could try a product containing simethicone (Mylicon or Mylicon-80 antiflatulents). Simethicone makes it easier to eliminate gas by belching or passing flatus.

Profiled antacids: Alka-Seltzer; Amphojel; Gaviscon (liquid); Gaviscon (tablet), Gaviscon II; Kolantyl; Maalox, Maalox #1, Maalox #2; Riopan; Rolaids; Tums

Profiled antacids and antiflatulents: Di-Gel; Gelusil, Gelusil II; Gelusil-M; Maalox Plus; Mylanta, Mylanta II; Riopan Plus

Profiled antiflatulents: Mylicon, Mylicon-80

Antacids

Product/ Dosage Form(s)	sodium bicarbonate (mg)	calcium carbonate (mg)	magnesium salts (mg)	aluminum salts (mg)	simethicone (mg)	sodium (mg)	other (mg)
Alka-Seltzer effervescent tablet	1008					276	citric acid, 800; potassium bicarbonate, 300
Amphojel suspension (per tsp)				320			
tablet				300, 600		NA	
Di-Gel liquid (per tsp)			87	282	25	8.5	
tablet			85		25	10.6	aluminum hydroxide-magnesium carbonate codried gel, 282
Gaviscon liquid (per Tbsp)			411	95		NA	
tablet	70		20	80		1.8	alginic acid, 200
Gaviscon II chewable tablet	140		40	160		NA	alginic acid, 400

Note: The symbol "<" means "less than"; "NA" means "information not available."

22

Antacids *(cont'd)*

Product/ Dosage Form(s)	sodium bicarbonate (mg)	calcium carbonate (mg)	magnesium salts (mg)	aluminum salts (mg)	simethicone (mg)	sodium (mg)	other (mg)
Gelusil liquid (per tsp)			200	200	25	0.9	
tablet			200	200	25	1.6	
Gelusil II liquid (per tsp)			400	400	30	1.3	
tablet			400	400	30	2.7	
Gelusil-M liquid (per tsp)			200	300	25	1.0	
tablet			200	300	25	3.0	
Kolantyl gel (per tsp)			150	150		2.2	
tablet			185	300		<15	
wafer			170	180		NA	
Maalox suspension (per tsp)			200	225		2.5	
Maalox #1 tablet			200	200		0.8	
Maalox #2 tablet			400	400		1.8	
Maalox Plus liquid (per tsp)			200	225	25	2.5	
tablet			200	200	25	1.4	
Mylanta suspension (per tsp), tablet			200	200	20	<0.7	
Mylanta II suspension (per tsp), tablet			400	400	30	<1.4	
Mylicon chewable tablet, drop (per 0.6 ml)					40	NA	

Note: The symbol "<" means "less than"; "NA" means "information not available."

Antacids *(cont'd)*

Product/ Dosage Form(s)	sodium bicarbonate (mg)	calcium carbonate (mg)	magnesium salts (mg)	aluminum salts (mg)	simethicone (mg)	sodium (mg)	other (mg)
Mylicon-80 chewable tablet					80	NA	
Riopan suspension (per tsp), tablet						0.3	magaldrate, 480
Riopan Plus liquid (per tsp)					20	<0.7	magaldrate, 400
chewable tablet					20	<0.7	magaldrate, 480
Rolaids tablet						53	dihydroxy-aluminum sodium carbonate, 334
Tums tablet		500				NA	

Note: The symbol "<" means "less than"; "NA" means "information not available."

Appetite Suppressants

A wide variety of OTC items aim to depress the appetite and make it easier for a dieter to restrict caloric intake. Products containing phenylpropanolamine hydrochloride (Super Odrinex tablets, for example) can reduce the appetite for a short period of time, but their effect wears off after a week or two of continuous use. It is recommended that such a product be taken from Monday through Friday with weekends "off," or for periods of up to two weeks with one-week intervals between. Despite advertising claims to the contrary, these products may cause side effects such as nervousness, high blood pressure, or palpitations, and it is recommended that they not be taken by people with diabetes mellitus, hypertension, or heart or thyroid disease.

Many OTC diet aids contain caffeine in addition to phenylpropanolamine. Caffeine has a mild diuretic effect—it increases the flow of urine, promoting water loss. This water loss does not contribute to permanent weight loss, and the caffeine content is likely to worsen side effects such as nervousness. If you choose to use a dieting aid that contains phenylpropanolamine, look for one without caffeine.

Some appetite suppressants provide vitamins. Not everyone who diets needs to take vitamins. If you want to take vitamins, buy them separately so that you can be sure of getting the dosages you want. You will also save money.

Over-the-counter diuretics (drugs that increase the flow of urine) are sometimes used as diet aids. Any weight lost by such a method is only a temporary water loss. Furthermore, these products can disturb the entire acid balance system of the body.

Recommendations on OTC Appetite Suppressants

No drug can take the place of limiting the amount of food consumed each day. A successful weight-loss program involves a nutritionally balanced diet that will help the dieter learn sound eating habits. Remember, you should consult your doctor before starting any diet.

Profiled appetite suppressants: Appedrine; Ayds; Control; Dex-A-Diet II; Dexatrim; Dietac (capsule, tablet, liquid, maximum strength capsule); Prolamine; P.V.M.; Super Odrinex

Asthma Remedies

From 2 to 4 percent of American children under age 12 have asthma. Most of them will grow out of it. But the rest will periodically experience a feeling of tightness in the chest, followed by difficulty in breathing. Then they will begin wheezing and coughing, due to narrowing of the air-carrying tubes in the lungs and excessive production of mucus.

An asthma attack may last for less than an hour, or more than one or two days. To prevent an attack, asthmatics try to avoid whatever triggers it. Some must try to keep away from pollen; others must try to avoid dust, stress, fatigue, or breathing cold air. Many must refrain from taking certain drugs, especially aspirin.

People who have been told by their doctors that they have asthma often take OTC drugs either to prevent an attack or to relieve it once it has begun. OTC products that act to prevent an asthma attack must be taken by mouth as tablets, capsules, or liquids. Those that help relieve an attack must be inhaled. No OTC asthma remedy should ever be used without your doctor's knowledge and approval.

Tablets, capsules, liquids. Over-the-counter medications that prevent attacks of asthma are called bronchodilators because they open up the air passages (called bronchioles) in the lungs. The most effective OTC bronchodilators contain theophylline. Products containing ephedrine are the next best choice.

Theophylline and ephedrine are effective, but they also cause some uncomfortable side effects, namely jitteriness and insomnia. Products containing theophylline or ephedrine must be taken as directed. For effective prevention of asthma attacks, the amount of the drug in the patient's blood must be constant. Skipping a dose or two may lower the levels of the drug in the blood and decrease protection against an attack. Theophylline-containing products also often upset the stomach. To reduce the stomach upset they cause, take them with food or milk.

Some bronchodilators contain antihistamines or expectorants. Antihistamines, such as pyrilamine maleate, are included because the body's release of the chemical histamine is believed to cause an asthma attack. However, an antihistamine often merely intensifies the problems. Antihistamines dry the tissues and thicken the mucus in the lungs, and the thicker mucus is harder to remove from the lungs. Therefore, do not take an asthma reliever that has an antihistamine.

Also, avoid taking an asthma reliever that has the expectorant guaifenesin. Such products stimulate secretions in the lungs to dilute mucus and aid in coughing it up. The only problem is that these products do not contain enough guaifenesin to do any good. At least 200 mg of guaifenesin is needed, but OTC products have only 100 mg. If you try to double the dose of guaifenesin by taking two tablets instead of one, you will take too much of the other ingredients in the product. When you want to get an expectorant action along with antiasthmatic action, take Robitussin expectorant cough remedy (refer to the product profile for more information on this preparation) and an OTC asthma reliever that does not have an expectorant. In addition, make sure that you drink eight to ten glasses of water a day. Use of a humidifier or vaporizer will also be helpful in thinning mucus secretion.

Regardless of its type, do not take an OTC asthma reliever if you are also taking prescription drugs for asthma. Many antiasthmatic prescription drugs have some of the same ingredients as the OTC products. Taking both at the same time could result in an overdose.

Oral inhalers. OTC products that relieve asthma attacks contain epinephrine. To work effectively, epinephrine must be inhaled directly into the lungs. And to release epinephrine directly into the lungs, you must use the inhaler properly.

First, hold the container upside down and put it into your mouth. Close your lips and teeth around the mouthpiece, but keep your tongue away from it. Exhale through your nose as forcefully as you can. Inhale slowly while pressing down on the container. Then, hold your breath for a few seconds and exhale. Repeat only if the label directs you to, and call your doctor if the attack continues for more than 20 minutes.

Pay strict attention to the label's directions, and use the inhaler only as often as directed. If you use it too often, you may become tolerant to the medication; that is, you may feel no effect after several weeks and, therefore, will increase the dose. But increased doses may bring on side effects, such as nervousness, insomnia, and pounding in the chest, or palpitations.

Wash the inhaler each day with warm water, and do not carry it in your pocket unless it is wrapped in paper or cloth. Dirt particles from your pocket may plug the holes of the inhaler.

Recommendations on OTC Asthma Remedies

Treatment of asthma requires a doctor's evaluation. If your doctor approves, we recommend that you use Bronkaid Mist asthma remedy, which contains epinephrine, for mild asthma attacks. Epinephrine is rapidly effective and useful for acute attacks of asthma. Used as an inhaler and in the recommended doses, it causes minimal side effects. We do not recommend that asthma be treated without a doctor's assistance.

Profiled asthma remedies: Bronitin; Bronkaid; Bronkaid Mist; Primatene M; Primatene P; Tedral

Athlete's Foot and Jock Itch Remedies

Athlete's foot, a form of ringworm, is the most common type of fungal infection in the United States. Up to 70 percent of the population will have athlete's foot at some time in their lives. Adults are the most likely candidates; in fact, some doctors feel that a child under 12 suspected of having athlete's foot should be taken to a doctor to confirm the diagnosis.

Wearing tight shoes and close-fitting socks is likely to irritate and weaken the skin of the feet, making them more susceptible to the fungus, which then attacks the weakened area. Athlete's foot easily spreads in gyms and locker rooms, and it may produce severe itching and pain.

Similar to athlete's foot is jock itch; or ringworm of the groin. More common in men, the fungal infection may cause severe itching in the groin and adjoining areas, such as the legs, abdomen, and buttocks.

Other forms of ringworm affect the scalp, nails, and upper torso. These forms of ringworm respond best to prescription medication taken orally, although for ringworm of the upper body, a doctor may also prescribe the use of an OTC product on the lesions themselves.

A variety of OTC medications are sold to treat athlete's foot and jock itch. Products containing tolnaftate (for example, Tinactin athlete's foot remedy) are the most effective therapy for athlete's foot or jock itch. Tolnaftate is safe; toxic reactions are rare and mild, and it is available as a cream, solution, powder, and aerosol powder.

When the skin of the affected area is thick, a keratolytic agent may be applied first to soften the skin so that tolnaftate can penetrate more easily. Keratolytics, like salicylic acid, are agents that soften and peel off the outer layer of the skin, and are sometimes included in athlete's foot remedies. Keratolytics must be used long enough to allow the skin on the affected area to become softened, which may take weeks or months, and in the process, the skin may become irritated from the keratolytic.

For years, undecylenic acid was the most widely used ingredient in antifungal preparations. If a tolnaftate-containing preparation is not available or, for some reason, does not work for you, choose one that has undecylenic acid (for example, Desenex ointment).

When using an OTC drug to treat athlete's foot or jock itch, choose the ointment or cream form, which keeps the active ingredient in the drug close to the skin longer than a liquid. If you do use a liquid, allow it to air-dry completely. CONSUMER GUIDE® magazine does not recommend using an aerosol spray. Aerosol sprays are expensive, and they evaporate and wash away quickly.

Between applications of a cream, ointment, or liquid, sprinkle a powder into your socks and shoes to counteract athlete's foot, or into your underwear to treat jock itch. Athlete's foot and jock itch may take months to resolve completely, but if you do not see improvement within three to four weeks, consult your doctor; you may have an infection caused by something other than a fungus.

Like other fungal infections, athlete's foot and jock itch are difficult to treat. The feet and the groin are moist, a factor conducive to fungal infections. To help keep the affected area dry, athlete's foot sufferers should switch to wearing sandals, if possible, and those with jock itch should switch to loose-fitting undershorts.

If you have athlete's foot, be sure to use a separate towel and bathmat, and do not walk barefooted through the house to avoid spreading it to other members of your family.

Recommendations on OTC Athlete's Foot and Jock Itch Remedies

Tolnaftate is the most effective treatment for athlete's foot. Recommended brands that contain tolnaftate include Aftate and Tinactin athlete's foot remedies.

Traditionally, sulfur and salicylic acid ointments were used for topical fungal infections. If you choose one of these ointments, use your pharmacy's generic brand. Undecylenic acid is an extremely effective medication that has generally replaced sulfur and salicylic acid combinations. Among the preparations containing undecylenic acid, we prefer Desenex products.

Profiled athlete's foot remedies: Enzactin

Profiled athlete's foot and jock itch remedies: Aftate; Cruex; Desenex; NP-27; Tinactin

Burn Remedies

(See "Sunscreens" for information on protecting yourself from sunburn.)

The skin can be burned by flames, hot objects, rays from the sun, or by electrical, radioactive, or chemical agents. Common chemical burns are caused by strong acid or alkali substances and by gas such as mustard gas or lewisite (an arsenic-containing gas). Regardless of the cause, burns can result in severe damage. Someone severely burned may go into shock and lose consciousness. There may be severe pain, fright, or anxiety. In addition, whenever the skin is broken, bacteria and other infective organisms may enter to cause internal infections.

Burns are classified into three types. A first-degree burn damages the outer layer of skin, causing a sensation of increased warmth, tenderness, and pain. Redness and mild swelling occur. Most sunburn can be classified as first-degree burns.

A second-degree burn involves the outer layer of skin and the layer immediately beneath it. Second-degree burns blister and are more painful than first-degree burns because nerve endings are affected.

A third-degree burn destroys all layers of skin and damages deeper tissues. Because the nerve endings are destroyed, a third-degree burn is painless once the initial damage is done. The skin may appear charred or white and lifeless. Someone with a third-degree burn usually goes into shock as evidenced by lowered blood pressure, weak pulse, pale face, cold perspiration, increased respiration, restlessness, and confusion. The extremities feel cold and clammy.

First-degree burns usually heal within two weeks without complications or scarring. Home remedies are sufficient for first-degree burns. Cold water soaks or milk compresses will relieve the pain and reduce swelling by reducing heat. With any burn, the skin and underlying tissues are damaged because of heat. If heat can be reduced, permanent damage to the tissue can be minimized. Prompt application of cold water (but not ice water) to a burned area helps keep the skin temperature down and, at the same time, reduces pain. Cold water also may prevent inflammation and swelling.

To apply cold water, you can immerse the burned area in a tub of cold water, or cover it with a clean towel or sheet that has been soaked in cold water. Add more water as needed to keep the temperature down, but do not add ice water. Ice water may further damage the area.

In addition, take aspirin or acetaminophen to reduce pain. A first-aid aerosol, cream, or ointment containing a local anesthetic may also be used to reduce pain. OTC preparations containing anesthetics, such as lidocaine, butamben picrate, diperodon hydrochloride, and tetracaine, may provide at least partial relief.

Other ingredients found in over-the-counter burn remedies include local anesthetics such as phenol and antibacterials such as benzethonium chloride and benzalkonium chloride. The antibacterial agents may help prevent secondary infection. A topically applied antihistamine or steroid may also be used. But a 20-percent concentration of the anesthetic benzocaine (as in Americaine anesthetic aerosol or ointment) provides the best relief.

When applying an anesthetic ointment or cream, place a small amount on the burned area and rub it in gently. Do not reapply more often than indicated on the label. Because a burned area is painful, you may prefer using an aerosol. If you do use an aerosol, be sure to follow directions.

Used on minor burns, OTC anesthetics have few side effects because little drug is absorbed into the bloodstream. Products containing benzocaine may produce a rash in some people with a fair complexion and blond hair. And products that have a high concentration of alcohol may further irritate the skin.

Second- or third-degree burns should be treated by a doctor. No cream or ointment should be applied to the burn area until after the doctor's examination because it will have to be removed before proper therapy can be performed.

Recommendations on OTC Burn Remedies

Americaine local anesthetic is recommended to relieve the pain of a first-degree burn. It contains 20 percent benzocaine.

Profiled local anesthetics and burn remedies: Americaine; Nupercainal

Profiled antiseptics and burn remedies: Medi-Quik; Noxzema; Solarcaine

Profiled antihistamine cream: Benadryl

Profiled topical steroids: Cortaid; Dermolate

Canker Sore and Fever Blister Remedies

Canker sores. Canker sores occur on the mucous lining of the lips, cheeks, tongue, or gums, usually around areas already irritated. For example, they may arise where lips or cheeks have been bitten repeatedly or where improperly fitted dentures have been rubbing against the gums. They may also appear after eating certain foods, including chocolate, tomatoes, walnuts, melons, vinegar, spices, or citrus fruits. Their cause is not always clear; some cases appear to be psychosomatic.

Canker sores produce a burning or tingling sensation that may be extremely painful. Sometimes pain precedes the appearance of the canker sore by as much as a day. Usually only a few canker sores appear at one time, although there may be as many as 60 present. Canker sores last for about 10 to 14 days, and they tend to recur. They usually heal without scarring.

Fever blisters. Fever blisters, or cold sores, occur on the lips, on and around the nostrils, and in the mouth, and they are caused by the herpes simplex virus. They can be painful and irritating, and usually accompany a fever. Bad breath, loss of appetite, increased flow of saliva, and pain or a tingling sensation are frequent forerunners of fever blisters. These symptoms may occur as much as two days before the sore appears. Fever blisters rarely last more than ten days.

Cold sores accompanied by other symptoms—an extremely sore throat, fever, joint pain, or palpitations—can indicate more serious disease and require diagnosis by a doctor.

OTC drugs for canker sores and fever blisters have the same objective: to relieve pain. Some OTC products for canker sores include tannic acid, benzoin, camphor and/or menthol, or benzocaine. CONSUMER GUIDE® magazine recommends products containing carbamide peroxide. Carbamide peroxide releases oxygen in the mouth. The oxygen acts as an antiseptic to clean the area around the canker sore and promote healing.

Lactinex diarrhea remedy has been suggested as a remedy for canker sores. However, Lactinex has not yet proved to be effective, and the extra cost of this product over the cost of other, more medically sound drugs is not warranted. If you've found Lactinex to work for you, try eating yogurt or drinking buttermilk instead. They are essentially the same, but cheaper and more tasty.

Recommendations on OTC Canker Sore and Fever Blister Remedies

Gly-Oxide, which contains carbamide peroxide, is more effective than those products containing other ingredients.

Profiled canker sore and fever blister remedies: Blistex; Gly-Oxide

Cold and Allergy Remedies

A cold is a set of symptoms brought on by an infecting organism. An allergy is the body's abnormal reaction to substances such as pollen, dust, smoke, ragweed, grass, grains, drugs, or certain foods. Although these disorders have different causes, the symptoms they present and the treatments used for them are similar.

Cold symptoms usually affect the respiratory tract: a runny or stuffy nose, a sore throat, coughing, and sneezing. Headache and feverishness are also common complaints. These symptoms are self-limiting; most colds run their course in five to seven days.

Allergic symptoms vary widely, but they are generally caused by the release of histamine in response to contact with an allergen. The release of histamine leads to the dilation of small blood vessels and the contraction of smooth muscle. If the irritant is inhaled, swelling in the throat may lead to difficulty in breathing—wheezing and coughing. Although some allergy sufferers do complain of headaches, pain and fever are not among the symptoms usually caused by allergy. If the allergy is seasonal (those caused by pollen, for example), the symptoms generally occur at the same time every year. A perennial allergy (to house dust or pet dander, for example) is likely to cause symptoms year round, although they may be exacerbated by prolonged contact with the allergen.

Dozens of other diseases affect the head and chest and have symptoms similar to those of colds and allergies. They include tonsillitis, sinusitis, laryngitis, tracheitis, and pharyngitis. Cold symptoms may also stem from a severe infection such as pneumonia. Consequently, if home treatment and OTC remedies don't bring relief of symptoms in two or three days, or if your pharmacist suggests it, see your doctor; you may have a much more serious disorder. Also, call your doctor whenever any of your symptoms becomes more severe than usual: If, for example, your throat is so sore that mild lozenges do not ease the pain, if a fever lasts more than 24 to 36 hours, or if a rash doesn't disappear when the fever breaks. Otherwise, you can do the doctoring yourself.

OTC Treatment

No drug can cure a viral illness like the common cold, and there is no foolproof method to make someone "unallergic." Treatment, therefore, is directed toward alleviating the symptoms caused by these disorders. The drugs most commonly used in OTC cold and allergy remedies are the decongestants and the antihistamines.

Decongestants. The nose becomes stuffy or congested when blood vessels enlarge and begin to exude fluid. The enlarged blood vessels take up more space in the nose so less air enters with each breath. The fluid that leaks out of the blood vessels collects in the tissues of the nose.

Sympathomimetic amines, decongestants, reverse congestion by constricting the minute blood vessels located within the nasal mucosa. This results in decreased vessel permeability with a reduction in fluid production and, subsequently, larger breathing passages, improving both nasal and sinus drainage. In addition, decongestants are thought to open the passage from the ear to the upper respiratory tract and thereby allow air pressure to equalize between the outside environment and the inner ear, thus relieving earache somewhat. Decongestants can be taken orally (tablets) or topically (sprays, drops, and inhalers).

Decongestant tablets shrink the blood vessels in other parts of the body as well as in the nose and thereby raise the blood pressure. They should be used prudently by those with heart disease, diabetes, or thyroid malfunction.

Nasal sprays cost more than drops, but they are better for most people. Sprays deliver medicine in a fine mist that penetrates far back into the nose. Sprays are easy to administer to children over age six, but drops are preferred for younger children who have smaller nostrils.

After using a spray or drops for several days, the nose may become more congested. These products work by constricting the blood vessels, and their repeated use fatigues the muscles that cause the blood vessels to constrict. The fatigued muscles relax completely, making the nose more congested than it was before the product was used. Increased congestion may lead to the use of even more spray or drops and even more congestion—thus, the term "rebound congestion." Some sprays and drops contain long-acting ingredients (oxymetazoline and xylometazoline) with decongestant action that may last up to 12 hours. Because these products need to be used only about twice a day, they are somewhat less likely to cause rebound congestion than products that must be used more often.

Nasal sprays and drops can inhibit the movement of the cilia that line the nose and lungs. If the cilia do not move properly, foreign particles may enter and infect the lungs. To avoid these effects, the use of a nasal spray or drops should be limited to three or four days at a time, or decongestant tablets should be substituted. Decongestant tablets do not have a rebound effect nor do they interfere with the cilia.

Nasal inhalers work only when there is some airflow in the nose. Consequently, inhalers are effective only for mild congestion. Make sure the container is capped tightly between uses, so the decongestant does not evaporate. Inhaler decongestants may irritate the nose, produce rebound congestion, and damage the cilia.

Antihistamines. Because the symptoms of an allergy are caused by histamine, the most effective drugs to relieve them contain an antihistamine. For best results, an antihistamine must be taken when the first symptom appears. Antihistamines are not very effective once allergy symptoms have become prominent; that is, when histamine has already been released. And they are generally ineffective in treating most cold symptoms, although they may alleviate a stuffy nose, tearing, and sneezing.

Some antihistamines cause drowsiness or sedation, but others do not. If a product containing one antihistamine makes you drowsy, take another product containing a different antihistamine. Or use an antihistamine that makes you drowsy at night, but another one that doesn't make you drowsy during the day. If you're giving antihistamines to a child, note that they may have the opposite side effect on children under 12. If your child complains of jitteriness or insomnia, you should stop administering the antihistamine and consult your pharmacist about substituting another medication.

Multiple-Ingredient Products. Most OTC cold products have multiple ingredients. Analgesics (usually aspirin or acetaminophen) and stimulants (often caffeine) are often included along with the decongestant and antihistamine ingredients. Not surprisingly, a multiplicity of different drug actions is likely to produce a multiplicity of adverse effects. In addition, there is a danger of double dosing with these products. For example, if someone were taking Comtrex cold remedy for a stuffy nose and also decided to take acetaminophen for achiness, the person would be receiving a double dose of acetaminophen.

The use of certain ingredients in cold products is controversial. For example, stimulants such as caffeine have no proven benefit in treating a cold or allergy. Presumably, the caffeine is included to counteract the drowsiness caused by an antihistamine. However, there is no proof that caffeine in the doses present in these medications will counteract antihistamine-induced drowsiness. If the product you use makes you drowsy, try one containing a different antihistamine.

Treating Your Cold

It has frequently been said that if you treat a cold it will go away in a week, whereas if you allow it to run its course, it usually takes seven days. Generally, the intent of treatment is to make those seven days more comfortable.

Most of the discomfort associated with a cold involves the nose, and an estimated 20 percent of all illnesses involving the nose are the result of insufficient moisture in the air. Thus, adding moisture to the air with a humidifier can bring much relief.

Someone with a cold need stay in bed only if the cold is especially severe and a high fever is present. Otherwise, taking it easy and avoiding overexertion usually suffices. In addition, a light liquid diet should be followed, and at least eight to ten glasses of water a day should be consumed. If you take OTC remedies, choose single-ingredient products aimed at treating the specific symptoms you have.

Treating Your Allergy

If you think you have an allergy, consult your doctor to verify the diagnosis. Ideally, you will be able to identify and avoid the irritating substance. Even if this is impossible, you can still usually relieve your symptoms with nonprescription medication.

OTC treatment of choice for an allergy is a product that's pure antihistamine. Because an allergy often causes nasal congestion or a runny nose, decongestants may be helpful. But OTC Drugs that contain both an antihistamine and a decongestant should not be used unless relief of your symptoms requires both ingredients. If your allergy causes only itchy eyes, you should use only an antihistamine. If it causes both itching and a runny nose, you can take a product with both an antihistamine and a decongestant. Better yet, buy the decongestant and the antihistamine separately. That way you can treat specific symptoms as they

occur—you won't be locked into taking unnecessary medication.
Topical decongestants (nasal sprays, drops, and inhalers) should be used very cautiously to treat a runny nose caused by an allergy. Remember, allergic symptoms may last for weeks—or months—and topical decongestants may cause rebound congestion after as little as three or four days.

Aspirin or acetaminophen is contained in some allergy medications. Although some hay fever sufferers do complain of headaches, pain and fever are not among the symptoms usually caused by an allergy, and regular use of analgesics to treat an allergy is not necessary.

Recommendations on OTC Cold and Allergy Remedies

When you have a cold, treat only the symptoms you have. If you feel feverish and achy, take an analgesic, aspirin or acetaminophen. Either will make you more comfortable.

For a stuffy nose, Sudafed cold remedy is recommended.

Decongestants in the form of a nasal spray or drops can be used for only two to three days effectively. Recommended brands include Afrin and Duration.

If you're treating an allergy, try an OTC antihistamine. OTC antihistamines are as effective as prescription products, and we recommend the least expensive form of the antihistamine chlorpheniramine maleate that your pharmacy carries. Chlorpheniramine-containing products are the most likely to be effective without causing excessive drowsiness. A decongestant may also be useful. If you need a decongestant, we recommend Sudafed cold remedy.

To treat a cough, see "Cough Remedies."

Profiled cold remedies: Bayer Children's; Comtrex; Coryban-D Decongestant; CoTylenol Children's; CoTylenol (liquid; tablet); 4-Way; Neo-Synephrine Compound Decongestant; Ornex; St. Joseph Children's; Sudafed; Sudafed Plus; Viro-Med (liquid; tablet); Vicks DayCare

Profiled allergy remedies: Allerest; A.R.M.; chlorpheniramine maleate; Chlor-Trimeton; Dimetane; Teldrin

Profiled cold and allergy remedies: Alka-Seltzer Plus; Bayer Decongestant; Chlor-Trimeton; Congespirin Children's; Contac; Contac Jr. Children's; Coricidin; Coricidin 'D' Decongestant; Demazin; Dristan; Dristan AF; Dristan Timed-Release; Novahistine; Ornade 2 for Children; Sinarest; Sine-Off; Sine-Off Extra Strength; Sinutab; Sinutab-II; Triaminicin

Profiled nasal decongestants (topical): Afrin; Allerest; Benzedrex; Coricidin; Dristan (inhaler; spray); Duration; Neo-Synephrine Intranasal; NTZ; Privine; Sine-Off Once-A-Day; Sinex; Sinex Long-Acting; Sinutab Long-Lasting; Vicks Inhaler

Cold and Allergy Remedies

Product/ Dosage Form(s)	aspirin (mg)	acetaminophen (mg)	dextromethorphan hydrobromide (mg)	phenylpropanolamine hydrochloride (mg)	phenylephrine hydrochloride (mg)	pseudoephedrine (mg)	alcohol (%)
	Analgesics				**Decongestants**		
Alka-Seltzer Plus effervescent tablet	324			24.08			
Allerest chewable tablet				9.4			
tablet				18.7			
timed-release capsule				50			
A.R.M. tablet				37.5			
Bayer Children's chewable tablet	81			3.125			
Bayer Decongestant tablet	325			12.5			
Chlor-Trimeton timed-release tablet							
Chlor-Trimeton (decongestant) tablet						60	
long-acting tablet						120	
Comtrex capsule, tablet		325	10	12.5			
liquid (per fluid oz)		649.2	19.8	25.2			20
Congespirin Children's chewable tablet	81				1.25		
Contac timed-release capsule				75			

Antihistamines						
chlorpheniramine maleate (mg)	brompheniramine maleate (mg)	phenyltoloxamine citrate (mg)	thenyldiamine hydrochloride (mg)		other (mg)	Product/ Dosage Form(s)
2						**Alka-Seltzer Plus** effervescent tablet
1						**Allerest** chewable tablet
2						tablet
4						timed-release capsule
4						**A.R.M.** tablet
						Bayer Children's chewable tablet
2						**Bayer Decongestant** tablet
8						**Chlor-Trimeton** timed-release tablet
4						**Chlor-Trimeton (decongestant)** tablet
8						long-acting tablet
1						**Comtrex** capsule, tablet
2						liquid (per fluid oz)
						Congespirin Children's chewable tablet
8						**Contac** timed-release capsule

Cold and Allergy Remedies *(cont'd)*

Product/Dosage Form(s)	Analgesics			Decongestants			
	aspirin (mg)	acetaminophen (mg)	dextromethorphan hydrobromide (mg)	phenylpropanolamine hydrochloride (mg)	phenylephrine hydrochloride (mg)	pseudoephedrine (mg)	alcohol (%)
Contac Jr. Children's liquid (per tsp)		162.5	5	9.375			10
Coricidin tablet	325						
Coricidin 'D' Decongestant tablet	325			12.5			
Coryban-D Decongestant capsule				25			
CoTylenol tablet		325				30	
liquid (per 2 Tbsp)		650	20			60	7.5
CoTylenol Children's liquid (per tsp)		120				7.5	7
Demazin repeat action tablet					20		
Dimetane liquid (per tsp)							
tablet							
Dristan tablet		325			5		
Dristan AF tablet		325			5		
Dristan Timed-Release capsule					20		
4-Way tablet	324			12.5			
Neo-Synephrine Compound tablet		150			5		

| | Antihistamines | | | | | |
chlorpheniramine maleate (mg)	brompheniramine maleate (mg)	phenyltoloxamine citrate (mg)	thenyldiamine hydrochloride (mg)	other (mg)	Product/ Dosage Form(s)
					Contac Jr. Children's liquid (per tsp)
2					**Coricidin** tablet
2					**Coricidin 'D' Decongestant** tablet
2				caffeine, 30	**Coryban-D Decongestant** capsule
2					**CoTylenol** tablet
4					liquid (per 2 Tbsp)
0.5					**CoTylenol Children's** liquid (per tsp)
4					**Demazin** repeat action tablet
	2				**Dimetane** liquid (per tsp)
	4				tablet
2				caffeine, 16.2	**Dristan** tablet
2				caffeine, 16.2	**Dristan AF** tablet
4					**Dristan Timed-Release** capsule
2					**4-Way** tablet
			7.5	caffeine, 15	**Neo-Synephrine Compound** tablet

Cold and Allergy Remedies *(cont'd)*

Product/ Dosage Form(s)	Analgesics			Decongestants			
	aspirin (mg)	acetaminophen (mg)	dextromethorphan hydrobromide (mg)	phenylpropanolamine hydrochloride (mg)	phenylephrine hydrochloride (mg)	pseudoephedrine (mg)	alcohol (%)
Novahistine liquid (per tsp)				18.7			5
tablet				18.7			
Ornade 2 for Children liquid (per tsp)				12.5			5
Ornex capsule		325		18			
St. Joseph Children's chewable tablet	81			3.125			
Sinarest tablet		325		18.7			
extra-strength tablet		500		18.7			
Sine-Off tablet	325			18.75			
Sine-Off extra-strength tablet		500		18.75			
Sinutab tablet		325		25			
extra-strength tablet		500		25			
extra-strength capsule		500		18.75			
Sinutab II tablet		325		25			
Sudafed liquid (per tsp.)						30	
tablet						30; 60	
Sudafed Plus liquid (per tsp)						30	
tablet						60	

chlorpheniramine maleate (mg)	brompheniramine maleate (mg)	phenyltoloxamine citrate (mg)	thenyldiamine hydrochloride (mg)	other (mg)	Product/ Dosage Form(s)
2					**Novahistine** liquid (per tsp)
2					tablet
2					**Ornade 2 for Children** liquid (per tsp)
					Ornex capsule
					St. Joseph Children's chewable tablet
2					**Sinarest** tablet
2					extra-strength tablet
2					**Sine-Off** tablet
2					**Sine-Off** extra-strength tablet
		22			**Sinutab** tablet
		22			extra-strength tablet
2					extra-strength capsule
					Sinutab II tablet
					Sudafed liquid (per tsp.)
					tablet
2					**Sudafed Plus** liquid (per tsp)
4					tablet

Cold and Allergy Remedies (cont'd) Product/ Dosage Form(s)	Analgesics			Decongestants			
	aspirin (mg)	acetaminophen (mg)	dextromethorphan hydrobromide (mg)	phenylpropanolamine hydrochloride (mg)	phenylephrine hydrochloride (mg)	pseudoephedrine (mg)	alcohol (%)
Teldrin timed-release capsule							
Triaminicin tablet	450			25			
Vicks DayCare liquid (per 2 Tbsp)		650	20	25			10
Viro-Med liquid (per 2 Tbsp)		600	20			30	16.63
tablet	324		7.5			15	

Corn and Callus Removers

Corns. A corn is a mass of tightly packed, dead skin cells that occurs at a point of constant pressure on the toes or between them. Corns on the toes may be white, gray, yellow, or dark red; corns between the toes (soft corns) absorb moisture and are white, gray, or yellow spongy sores.

Corns are usually caused by pressure due to poorly fitting shoes, irregularities in shoes or stockings, or walking on hard surfaces. The pressure enlarges capillary blood vessels and reddens the skin. Then, as dead skin cells accumulate, the skin in one small area thickens and becomes swollen. At first, the thickened area may cause no pain, but as a corn grows larger, pain increases due to the compression of underlying nerves.

Calluses. Like a corn, a callus is a mass of dead skin cells. Unlike a corn, a callus appears on the ball of the foot or around the heel, and it is due to prolonged friction, irritation, or constant pressure.

Severe corns and calluses should be seen by a podiatrist (foot doctor), but a mild case can be treated with OTC pads, cushions, or medication. Pads or cushions insulate the corn or callus and help alleviate the pain. Medication helps loosen the corn or callus so it can be removed. Most OTC products for corns and calluses contain keratolytics, such as salicylic acid, which soften the skin and cause the cells of the outer layer of the skin to slough off.

Corns and calluses may take a week or more to remove, and the medication must be applied as directed each day. When using a

| Antihistamines | | | | | |
chlorpheniramine maleate (mg)	brompheniramine maleate (mg)	phenyltoloxamine citrate (mg)	thenyldiamine hydrochloride (mg)	other (mg)	Product/ Dosage Form(s)
8; 12					Teldrin timed-release capsule
2				caffeine, 30	Triaminicin tablet
					Vicks Day Care liquid (per 2 Tbsp)
				sodium citrate, 500	Viro-Med liquid (per 2 Tbsp)
1				guaifenesin, 50	tablet

product to remove a corn or a callus, be sure to keep it away from the skin that surrounds the affected area. Place tape around the corn or callus, and then apply medication in the center. Or cover the surrounding tissue with petroleum jelly or some other protective ointment before applying the medication.

Corn and callus removers generally are contraindicated only for those people who are allergic to them. However, people who have diabetes or impaired circulation should never take care of corns and calluses themselves.

Corn and callus removers should not be applied to broken skin and should be discontinued if a rash develops. Products of this type are intended for use on a temporary basis until the cause of the problem has been corrected.

Keep the container of liquid corn or callus remover tightly closed between applications. The liquid is highly volatile and will evaporate in the air. Also, keep these containers out of the reach of children; the ingredients in these products are highly toxic.

To help prevent corns and calluses, use an ointment such as petroleum jelly that will lubricate the area and keep it soft. The best way to avoid corns and calluses is to get shoes and socks that fit well and have no irregularities that rub against the toes.

Recommendations on Corn and Callus Removers

Choose Freezone liquid corn and callus remover. It contains salicylic acid, a mild keratolytic, and will remove corns and calluses. However, to avoid the development of corns and calluses, you must determine and correct the cause.

Profiled corn and callus removers: Dr. Scholl's Corn/Callus Salve; Dr. Scholl's "2" Drop; Dr. Scholl's Waterproof Corn Pads; Freezone

Cough Remedies

Coughing is a reflex that can be brought on by many factors. It may be associated with influenza, tuberculosis, or pneumonia. Or it may be the result of inhaling an irritating substance. The very act of coughing may elicit more coughing. When you cough, air moves rapidly across tissues in the throat. The air irritates the throat and can provoke more coughing.

Coughing serves to expel foreign substances (irritants as well as bacterial and viral germs) and secretions that enter your lungs. Therefore, it should never be totally suppressed. But you may want to control it so it does not waken you during the night or spread germs to other people.

People who are over age 65, those with heart disease or excessively high blood pressure, and those who are in otherwise poor health should control coughing as much as possible. Harsh coughing over excessively long periods of time can further weaken diseased heart muscle and can reduce the body's ability to ward off illness.

Coughing can be either productive or nonproductive. Productive coughing usually can be traced to a bacterial infection in the lungs. When infecting bacteria attack the lungs, lung tissue produces large amounts of secretions in defense. As more and more secretions accumulate, the lungs must try to remove them, and the result is coughing that brings up fluid.

Nonproductive coughing does not bring up fluid. It occurs when sinuses drain into the throat, when smoke, dust, or pollen enters the lungs. It may be touched off by drinking fluids that are too hot, or by eating foods that are highly spiced. And it can be controlled by a cough suppressant, or antitussive.

Cough suppressants. The most widely used cough suppressant is codeine, which works directly on that part of the brain that controls coughing. In doses present in nonprescription cough remedies, codeine has a mild sedative effect on the nervous system. This effect is so mild, in fact, that most people do not notice it. Codeine also has a drying effect, which will relieve a runny nose but may complicate an illness such as asthma. People who have a cold and want to suppress a nonproductive cough can use OTC medications containing codeine. But those who have lung disease should not, unless directed otherwise by their doctors.

Codeine is available in many states without a prescription. At doses present in OTC cough medicines, codeine is safe and does not lead to narcotic addiction unless it is taken in large amounts for a long period of time. When taken as directed, codeine-

44

containing cough medicine causes few problems.

An alternative to codeine is dextromethorphan hydrobromide. Dextromethorphan works in the same way and is just as effective as codeine, but it is not a narcotic. It does not cause sedation nor affect breathing as codeine does. And it is safe to use; nausea and vomiting are its only side effects.

Expectorants. Expectorants stimulate the production of fluid in the lungs so secretions can be coughed up more easily. The way they work is somewhat similar to the way the mouth salivates. When you salivate, the glands at the back of the mouth and under the tongue produce more fluid than usual. Expectorants are intended to stimulate the lungs to produce more fluid.

The most commonly recommended OTC expectorant in the United States is guaifenesin. However, there is no definite proof that it works. Some studies show that people who use guaifenesin are able to cough up secretions more easily than those who do not; but other studies report contrary results. Consequently, the FDA advisory panel on OTC cough, cold, allergy, bronchodilator, and antiasthmatic products has been unable to classify guaifenesin as being effective. If you or your pharmacist thinks you need an expectorant, you could try guaifenesin. Guaifenesin is safe. It causes no side effects other than nausea or vomiting in some people, and future studies may show it to be effective.

Other ingredients. Some cough remedies also include decongestants, antihistamines, or other ingredients not directly related to treatment of a cough. Remember that the more ingredients a product has, the greater its potential for producing side effects, and causing drug interactions and other problems. Treat the symptoms you have with products with a single effective ingredient.

Remember, too, that coughing can result from insufficient moisture in the air. The respiratory passages become dry and irritated, and coughing develops. This occurs especially in the winter months when the humidity is lowest. The use of a humidifier or vaporizer to add moisture to the air may provide greater relief than any drug, but do not use one of the volatile oils or products in the vaporizer. They do nothing other than impart a pleasant odor to the room. Also, remember that the most effective expectorant is water. If you are coughing, drink eight to ten glasses of water a day.

Recommendations on OTC Cough Remedies

For a codeine-containing cough syrup, we recommend Cheracol. For dextromethorphan, choose Benylin DM, Pertussin 8-Hour Cough Formula, or Silence Is Golden. Among products containing guaifenesin, we prefer 2/G or Robitussin cough remedies.

(See page 48 for the list of nonprescription cough remedies profiled in this publication.)

Cough Remedies

Product/ Dosage Form(s)	dextromethorphan hydrobromide (mg)	codeine phosphate (mg)	guaifenesin (mg)	phenylpropanolamine hydrochloride (mg)	phenylephrine hydrochloride (mg)	pseudoephedrine hydro... (mg)
Benylin DM liquid (per tsp)	10					
Cheracol liquid (per tsp)		10	100			
Cheracol D liquid (per tsp)	10		100			
Chlor-Trimeton Expectorant liquid (per tsp)			50	10		
Coricidin liquid (per tsp)	10		100	12.5		
Coryban-D liquid (per tsp)	7.5		50		5	
Dimacol capsule	15		100			30
liquid (per tsp)	15		100			30
Formula 44 Cough Control Discs lozenge	5					
Formula 44-D liquid (per tsp)	10		50	12.5		
Hold lozenge	7.5					
children's lozenge	3.75			6.25		
Novahistine DMX liquid (per tsp)	10		100			30
Novahistine Expectorant liquid (per tsp)		10	100	18.75		
NyQuil liquid (per 2 Tbsp)	15					
Ornacol capsule	30			25		
liquid (per tsp)	15			12.5		

Note: The symbol "≦" means "less than or equal to."

	Antihistamines					
chlorpheniramine maleate (mg)	pyrilamine maleate (mg)	pheniramine maleate (mg)	pheniramine maleate (mg)	alcohol (%)	other (mg)	Product/Dosage Form(s)
			5			**Benylin DM** liquid (per tsp)
			3			**Cheracol** liquid (per tsp)
			3			**Cheracol D** liquid (per tsp)
2			≦1		ammonium chloride, 100; sodium citrate, 50	**Chlor-Trimeton expectorant** liquid (per tsp)
			<0.5			**Coricidin** liquid (per tsp)
			15		acetamino-phen, 120	**Coryban-D** liquid (per tsp)
						Dimacol capsule
			4.75			liquid (per tsp)
					benzocaine, 1.25; men-thol; ane-thole; pep-permint oil	**Formula 44 Cough Control Discs** lozenge
			10			**Formula 44-D** liquid (per tsp)
					benzocaine, 3.75	**Hold** lozenge
						children's lozenge
			10			**Novahistine DMX** liquid (per tsp)
			7.5			**Novahistine Expectorant** liquid (per tsp)
			25		ephedrine sulfate, 8; doxylamine succinate, 75; acetamin-ophen, 600	**NyQuil** liquid (per 2 Tbsp)
						Ornacol capsule
			8			liquid (per tsp)

47

Product/ Dosage Form(s)	dextromethorphan hydrobromide (mg)	codeine phosphate (mg)	guaifenesin (mg)	phenylpropanolamine hydrochloride (mg)	phenylephrine hydrochloride (mg)	pseudoephedrine hydrochloride (mg)
Pediaquil liquid (per tsp)			50		2.5	
Pertussin 8-Hour Cough Formula liquid (per 4 tsp)	30.5					
Robitussin liquid (per tsp)			100			
Robitussin A-C liquid (per tsp)		10	100			
Robitussin-DM liquid (per tsp)	15		100			
Robitussin-DM Cough Calmers lozenge	7.5		50			
Robitussin-PE liquid (per tsp)			100			30
Silence Is Golden liquid (per tsp)	10					
Triaminic Expectorant liquid (per tsp)			100	12.5		
Triaminic Expectorant with Codeine liquid (per tsp)		10	100	12.5		
Trind liquid (per tsp)			50		2.5	
Trind-DM liquid (per tsp)	7.5		50		2.5	
2/G liquid (per tsp)			100			
2/G-DM liquid (per tsp)	15		100			
Vicks liquid (per tsp)	10.5		75			

Profiled cough remedies: Benylin DM; Cheracol; Cheracol D; Chlor-Trimeton Expectorant; Coricidin; Coryban-D; Dimacol; Formula 44 Cough Control Discs; Formula 44-D; Hold; Novahistine DMX; Novahistine Expectorant; NyQuil; Ornacol Capsules, Ornacol Liquid; Pediaquil; Pertussin 8-Hour Cough Formula; Robitussin; Robitussin A-C; Robitussin-DM; Robitussin-DM Cough Calmers; Robitussin-PE; Silence Is Golden; Triaminic Ex-

	Antihistamines					
chlorpheniramine maleate (mg)	pyrilamine maleate (mg)	pheniramine maleate (mg)	alcohol (%)	other (mg)	Product/Dosage Form(s)	
			5		**Pediaquil** liquid (per tsp)	
			9.5		**Pertussin 8-Hour Cough Formula** liquid (per tsp)	
			3.5		**Robitussin** liquid (per tsp)	
			3.5		**Robitussin A-C** liquid (per tsp)	
			1.4		**Robitussin-DM** liquid (per tsp)	
					Robitussin-DM Cough Calmers lozenge	
			1.4		**Robitussin-PE** liquid (per tsp)	
				honey flavor	**Silence Is Golden** liquid (per tsp)	
			5		**Triaminic Expectorant** liquid (per tsp)	
6.25	6.25		5		**Triaminic Expectorant with Codeine** liquid (per tsp)	
			15	acetamino-phen, 120	**Trind** liquid (per tsp)	
			15	acetamino-phen, 120	**Trind-DM** liquid (per tsp)	
			3.5		**2/G** liquid (per tsp)	
			5		**2/G-DM** liquid (per tsp)	
			5	sodium citrate, 600	**Vicks** liquid (per tsp)	

pectorant; Triaminic Expectorant with Codeine; Trind; Trind-DM; 2/G; 2/G-DM; Vicks

Diarrhea Remedies

Diarrhea is usually an attempt by the body to rid itself of some ir-ritating or toxic substance. Acute diarrhea never lasts more than diarrhea may be of toxic, infectious, or dietary origin. It could be the result of some acute illness or a response to emotional stress.

If diarrhea lasts more than three days, it is considered chronic diarrhea. Because it is usually the result of multiple causes, it is difficult to diagnose and treat. It may be a symptom of a serious organic disease such as cancer of the colon or rectum, chronic ulcerative colitis, amebic colitis, tuberculous enteritis, sprue, or a host of other causes. Chronic diarrhea requires medical help.

Several hundred OTC products are currently available to treat diarrhea. OTC antidiarrheal ingredients include adsorbents, paregoric, bacterial cultures, and anticholinergics.

Adsorbents. Kaolin, bismuth subgallate, pectin, activated charcoal, alumina gel, and attapulgite coat the walls of the stomach and intestine and absorb irritating materials by attracting irritants and keeping them from being absorbed into the bloodstream. Their effectiveness as antidiarrheal drugs is questionable.

Paregoric. Paregoric, a preparation of powdered opium, is used in some nonprescription diarrhea remedies. Paregoric slows the contraction of the intestines to reduce the number of bowel movements. Pure paregoric requires a prescription, but it is preferable to the OTC antidiarrheals combining paregoric with other ingredients. Only low doses of paregoric are available in OTC products such as Parepectolin diarrhea remedy. Contrary to popular belief, these low doses will not lead to abuse nor produce serious side effects.

Anticholinergics. Atropine sulfate, hyoscyamine sulfate, homatropine methylbromide, and hyoscine hydrobromide reduce the movement of the intestine. However, to be effective, anticholinergics must be taken in high doses, and no OTC antidiarrheal product contains enough. The anticholinergics can also cause annoying side effects such as dry mouth, blurred vision, and palpitations.

Bacterial cultures. Live bacteria, such as those in yogurt, supposedly restore bowel movement to normal. While many people swear by these products, little scientific evidence proves that they work. The same effect may be achieved by drinking milk or buttermilk or eating yogurt—and at less cost.

Recommendations on OTC Diarrhea Remedies

The best treatment for acute diarrhea is to rest and drink plenty of fluids. Heavy foods and rough vegetables should be avoided. Medical help should be sought if diarrhea persists for more than three days and/or the stool contains blood, pus, or mucus.

For those who insist on taking an antidiarrheal preparation, a combination of kaolin and pectin (for example, Kaopectate and Kaopectate Concentrate diarrhea remedies), is recommended. A product that combines these ingredients with paregoric (e.g., Parepectolin) is also acceptable. Such products are the most economical and the safest. OTC products containing an anticholinergic should be avoided.

Profiled diarrhea remedies: Donnagel; Donnagel-PG; Kaopectate, Kaopectate Concentrate; Lactinex; Parepectolin; Pepto-Bismol

Eyedrops

Use caution when treating your own eye conditions. Red, watery, tender eyes may accompany a cold or an allergy or may result from eyestrain or exposure to noxious or irritating substances in the air. But, red, watery, tender eyes may also be the result of a bacterial or viral infection or a serious eye disease.

For most eye conditions, treatment should not continue for more than one or two days without consulting a doctor, especially if you have blurred vision or pain. Eyes are precious; don't take chances with your vision. OTC eyedrops are appropriate if you want to wash a foreign object from the eye, as long as it is not embedded, or to ease irritation from an allergy or a sty. Use an OTC artificial tear solution to lubricate dry eyes.

Some eyedrops contain a decongestant ingredient, such as phenylephrine, naphazoline, or tetrahydrozoline. Decongestants shrink tiny blood vessels in the eye to reduce redness due to minor eye irritation, but overuse can increase redness. Use of eyedrops for more than one or two days at a time may make the eyes excessively dry and more itchy. OTC products containing decongestants may also worsen glaucoma.

A solution of boric acid has been used an as eyewash and antiseptic by many people for many years. However, a boric acid solution has not been proven effective as an eyewash. Preparing a solution yourself from boric acid crystals or powder and using it as an eyewash can be dangerous. The solution will not be sterile, and any undissolved crystals may scratch the eye. Because boric acid itself is toxic when swallowed, keeping it around the house seems hardly worth the risk.

Before using any eyedrops, make sure the expiration date has not lapsed. If there is no expiration date, discard the bottle.

Recommendations on OTC Eyedrops

Isopto Plain eyedrops is meant to be used to lubricate the eyes; it is not medicated. It is the treatment of choice for mild irritations.

Profiled decongestant eyedrops: Allerest; Isopto-Frin; Murine Plus; Ocusol; Visine

Profiled eyedrops: Isopto Plain; Murine

First-Aid Products

First-aid products are used to prevent infection from cuts and abrasions, or to treat the skin disease impetigo. First-aid products can be loosely divided into two types: the antiseptics, used to clean and disinfect a wound; and the antibiotics, used to prevent or treat infections. Applying either type of first-aid product to a minor cut or abrasion is usually not necessary. Washing with soap and water most likely will prevent infection.

If you choose to use OTC first-aid products, first use a clean cloth or sterile gauze pad to wash the cut or abrasion with hydrogen peroxide or a mild soap. Rinse well and pat dry with a second clean cloth or sterile gauze pad. Apply a thin layer of the medication. If applying an ointment, carefully rub it in with a cotton-tipped swab or a sterile gauze pad (which should be discarded after use). Choose iodine or an antibiotic ointment to apply to a minor wound. Either will effectively prevent infection and will cause few side effects, although the antibiotic neomycin can, on occasion, cause skin irritation. Do not choose an ointment that contains neomycin if you are especially sensitive or allergic to medication.

Impetigo is an infection of the top layer of the skin caused by bacteria. It is easily transmitted from one person to another by contact with the skin or with clothing or towels that the infected individual has touched.

Impetigo sores continually drain and form scabs on the face, arms, and legs. Occasionally, the sores produce vesicles, or sacs, that are filled with amber-colored fluid. Vesicles usually burst in a few hours, and the fluid dries to a honey-colored crust that can easily be picked off.

Nonprescription antibiotic ointments can be used to treat impetigo. These ointments contain the antibiotics polymyxin, neomycin, or bacitracin, or a combination of any two of them. Products containing polymyxin are effective on impetigo as long as they also contain bacitracin or neomycin. Polymyxin has no effect on two kinds of bacteria that frequently cause impetigo, and it usually is included to kill bacteria that neomycin and bacitracin cannot.

If impetigo has not markedly improved within four to five days, see your doctor. The infection can spread to other parts of the body through the bloodstream. In fact, no first-aid product should be used for more than four or five days or on large areas of the body. Nor should they be applied to a bleeding wound or when fever is present, and diabetics and persons with impaired circulation should avoid using them.

Recommendations on OTC First-Aid Products

Remember, unless deep, cuts generally do not need to be treated with an antiseptic. If you do choose to use one of the first-aid products, we recommend using hydrogen peroxide to aid in washing the wound, and then using iodine tincture or an antibiotic ointment to prevent infection. The antibiotic ointments Baciguent, Mycitracin, Neo-Polycin, Neosporin, and Polysporin can be used to treat the skin infection impetigo.

Profiled first-aid products: Baciguent; Bactine; hydrogen peroxide; iodine tincture; Mercurochrome; Merthiolate (thimerosal) tincture; Mycitracin; Neo-Polycin; Neosporin; Polysporin

Hemorrhoidal Preparations

Hemorrhoids (piles) often occur during pregnancy and among the obese, and are sometimes attributed to chronic constipation or straining at the stool. They are one of the most common disorders of the gastrointestinal tract.

Hemorrhoids are enlarged veins near the anus. The veins dilate and swell, causing severe inflammation. The inflammation can then lead to more swelling, which causes intense itching and discomfort. External hemorrhoids arise on the outer (skin) surface of the anus, whereas internal hemorrhoids develop in the rectal canal. Internal hemorrhoids may visibly protrude from the anus. Only a doctor can determine how extensive internal hemorrhoids are.

Most hemorrhoids can be helped with OTC products. The most effective OTC hemmorhoidal preparations contain hydrocortisone, a steroid. Until recently, these products were available only by prescription, but now you can purchase hydrocortisone over the counter in strengths up to 0.5%. Hydrocortisone is a hormone produced in the body by the adrenal gland. It is valuable in the treatment of inflammatory, allergic, and rheumatoid disorders, but if used for more than ten days, it can cause serious adverse effects. It can mask symptoms of infection and interfere with the body's immune processes. When using hydrocortisone to treat hemorrhoids, be sure to follow directions carefully and do not apply more frequently than directed.

The next most effective ingredient in OTC hemorrhoidal preparations is benzocaine, a local anesthetic. Local anesthetics relieve pain and itching, although they do nothing to relieve the underlying condition. Products containing benzocaine or other local anesthetics (such as tetracaine, phenacaine hydrochloride, pramoxine hydrochloride, and dibucaine) should not be used for longer than several days at a time. They may induce further irritation and increased itching.

OTC cream and ointment products are preferable to OTC suppositories. Suppositories normally are inserted past the site of pain or irritation and, therefore, do not provide effective pain relief.

Sitting in a tub of warm water for 20 to 30 minutes or applying hot wet packs several times daily may help soothe irritated hemorrhoids. During an intense flare-up, taking a stool softener will reduce pain on defecation. Someone with hemorrhoids should avoid rough and irritating foods and should lose weight if obese. Hemorrhoids that develop during pregnancy will probably disappear following delivery. For severe hemorrhoids, the doctor may advise surgery.

Any hemorrhoids that do not improve within several days, or that are bleeding profusely, should be seen by a doctor.

Recommendations on OTC Hemorrhoidal Preparations

Cortef Acetate and Dermolate anal-itch products contain hydrocortisone and are effective, but should not be used for any extended period of time without a doctor's approval.

Profiled hemorrhoidal preparations: Americaine; Anusol; Gentz Wipes; Hazel-Balm; Lanacane; Nupercainal; Preparation H; Tucks; Vaseline Hemorr-Aid; Wyanoid

Profiled anal-itch products: Cortef Acetate; Dermolate

Laxatives

Constipation in its true sense refers to abnormally difficult or infrequent passage of stools. Constipation is a symptom, not a disease. Bowel movements are motivated primarily by the nature of foods eaten, the time of day, and the proximity of and familiarity with a particular toilet, as well as by psychological factors. It is not absolutely necessary to have a bowel movement every day. Normal frequency may vary from three bowel movements per day to three per week.

In healthy individuals, the colon should be conditioned to expel feces in response to normal stimulation. Having a bowel movement at the same time every day is quite beneficial, although not necessary for good health. For many people, this time occurs in the early morning, about 30 to 60 minutes after breakfast, when the ingestion of food on an empty stomach activates and increases intestinal peristalsis. During the night, residue from the previous day's meals has moved to the rectal area and is ready to be eliminated. This is also the reason many laxatives and cathartics work best if they are taken at night before bedtime. Their action is then ready for the morning.

To prevent constipation, modify the diet to include adequate fiber, drink at least eight to ten glasses of water each day, exercise, and develop good bathroom habits—your body's own reflexes are your best guide. Laxatives should be used only when absolutely necessary; their prolonged use can impair normal bowel function. The use of laxatives to treat abdominal pain, vomiting, and other serious digestive tract symptoms can lead to life-threatening situations.

The basic types of laxatives include the stimulants, salines, bulk-forming, and lubricant or stool-softening agents. The terms laxative and cathartic are interchangeable in that all agents lead to the same result—that of facilitating bowel movements. Laxatives are usually thought of as agents that produce a mild passage of stools, while cathartics are more forceful, producing a watery and sometimes explosive bowel movement.

Stimulant laxatives increase the movement of the intestines. Saline laxatives increase moisture in the intestine. Bulk-forming agents add fiber, and lubricants and stool-softeners add oil to lubricate or reduce the hardness of the material within the intestine.

Individual products within any category of laxatives (stimulant, saline, bulk-forming, or lubricant and stool softener) do not vary much. Some may be stronger than others, but this problem can be solved by adjusting the dosage. Some may cause more cramping than others, but, in this case, a switch to another product will probably solve the problem.

Stimulant laxatives. Stimulants lead all other laxatives in sales; yet they are the least desirable. They irritate the walls of the intestines, and after prolonged use (one to two months), they may cause intense cramping, diarrhea, and fluid depletion. People who take stimulants repeatedly may come to depend on them to have a bowel movement, or they may develop ulcerative colitis or a nutritional disease. If a stimulant laxative must be taken, products such as Dulcolax tablets, Dorbane tablets, or Modane tablets should be chosen. These products have mild agents such as bisacodyl, casanthranol, or danthron. These mild agents produce less cramping than do stronger agents such as cascara sagrada and aloe.

When bisacodyl tablets are taken, the individual must be advised not to crush or chew them nor to take them with antacids or milk in order not to destroy the enteric coating of the tablets. If the enteric coating is destroyed, the bisacodyl will be prematurely released to irritate the esophagus and stomach, possibly causing intense cramping.

Lubricants and stool softeners. In the past, people have used vegetable, mineral, or other oils as laxatives. Some of these oils—including mineral oil—are absorbed into the body and produce serious side effects. Repeated or prolonged use (one to two months) of mineral oil may lead to pneumonia, or it may retard the body's absorption of vitamins A, D, and K.

While some people swear that "light" mineral oil is better than regular mineral oil, it has not been shown to provide any better laxative effect. Light mineral oil is usually more expensive than heavy (or regular) mineral oil and can cause rectal leakage, which may stain undergarments.

Stool softeners have been used to prevent constipation or to treat long-term constipation. Stool-softening agents may take two to three days to produce any effect. But after that, their action is continuous. Liquid stool softeners can be mixed with milk, cola drinks, or fruit juices to disguise the taste of the stool softener. Mixing will not decrease the laxative effect. Capsules are more agreeable and less expensive.

Bulk-forming laxatives. Most bulk-forming laxatives have fibers from seeds or other parts of plants that cannot be digested or absorbed by the body but do, however, have a high affinity for water.

Laxatives

	Stimulant	Stool Softener/ Lubricant	Bulk-Forming	Saline
Carter's Little Pills	X			
Colace		X		
Correctol	X	X		
Dorbane	X			
Dorbantyl, Dorbantyl Forte	X	X		
Doxidan	X	X		
Dulcolax	X			
Ex-Lax	X			
Fleet Enema				X
Fletcher's Castoria	X			
Haley's M-O				X
Metamucil			X	
Modane, Modane Mild	X			
Modane Bulk			X	
Nature's Remedy	X			
Neoloid	X			
Nujol		X		
Peri-Colace	X	X		
Phillips' Milk of Magnesia				X
Senokot	X			
Serutan			X	
Surfak		X		

When they come in contact with water in the intestine, they swell, thus increasing the bulk of material in the intestine. They also produce a gel that lubricates the bowel.

Bulk-forming laxatives do not irritate the intestine as the stimulants do, and they cause less urgency than the saline laxatives do. For these reasons, they are the best choice for controlling long-term constipation. There is one precaution, however, about their use. Bulk-forming laxatives must be completely mixed with water before swallowing. If they are swallowed dry, they may swell in the throat and cause choking.

Saline laxatives. Chemicals in saline laxatives dissolve in water, but do not easily pass through the intestine into the bloodstream. When these products are taken with a full glass of water, the water stays in the intestine and lubricates the bowel. Because saline laxatives attract water molecules, they must be taken with at least one full glass of water to avoid pulling water out of the body into the intestine. Saline laxatives usually act within 30 to 60 minutes and produce a watery and somewhat explosive bowel movement. Therefore, they must be taken only at a convenient time.

Recommendations on OTC Laxatives

To prevent constipation, be sure your diet includes adequate fiber, drink at least eight to ten glasses of water each day, exercise, and develop good bathroom habits. Laxatives should be used only when absolutely necessary. Consult your pharmacist about choosing a laxative to counteract the constipating effects of drugs such as the antacids, antispasmodics, iron medications, narcotics, phenothiazines, and tricyclic antidepressants.

Our treatment of choice for constipation not induced by drugs is a bulk-forming laxative, such as Serutan, Metamucil, or Modane Bulk. These laxatives are safe and cause few side effects.

Profiled laxatives: Carter's Little Pills; Colace; Correctol; Dorbane; Dorbantyl, Dorbantyl Forte; Doxidan; Dulcolax; Ex-Lax; Fleet Enema; Fletcher's Castoria; Haley's M-O; Metamucil; Modane, Modane Mild; Modane Bulk; Nature's Remedy; Neoloid; Nujol; Peri-Colace; Phillips' Milk of Magnesia; Senokot; Serutan; Surfak

Muscular Pain Remedies

Muscular aches and pains may follow strenuous exercise or long periods of immobility (for example, sitting or standing for long periods of time). Unusual use of your muscles—your first ski run of the winter, a once-a-year baseball game—is likely to leave you sore and achy. Exposure to damp, cold air has also caused sore, stiff muscles.

Ordinarily, muscular aches and pains go away in a few days. But, sometimes, pain persists. Persistent pain in a joint may be due to arthritis or dislocation of the joint. A recurring backache may be due to a torn muscle or a kidney infection. If muscular aches and pains last more than a week or recur frequently, or if the pain is accompanied by blood in the urine, nausea, or extreme tiredness, see your doctor for treatment. Otherwise, treat yourself.

Most OTC products to treat muscular aches and pains are basically the same. These products, called external analgesics, relieve soreness due to overexertion, cold weather, or arthritis by increasing the flow of blood to the muscle, thereby producing warmth.

Although these products can be quite complex, they usually

contain methyl salicylate (or wintergreen oil), turpentine oil, camphor, or other substances that generate heat. Products containing methyl salicylate or other salicylates can be rubbed in well. But those that include any one of the other ingredients may cause blistering or a rash when rubbed in vigorously. Because rubbing a sore muscle provides some relief from pain, CONSUMER GUIDE® magazine recommends muscular pain remedies that contain a salicylate.

But do not buy pure oil of wintergreen. It is highly toxic; as little as a teaspoonful can kill a child. Because wintergreen oil smells pleasant, children are attracted to it. Therefore, if you have any pure wintergreen oil around the house, get rid of it by flushing it down the toilet, then rinse and discard the bottle. Also, keep products which contain methyl salicylate out of the reach of children.

When buying a muscular pain remedy, choose a cream or ointment. Creams and ointments take time to spread over and rub into the skin. And the continued rubbing brings pain relief. Also, creams and ointments stay on the skin longer than do liquids and lotions.

Before applying a muscular pain remedy cream or ointment, soak the sore muscle in hot water for about 15 or 20 minutes. Frequently, a soak is all that is needed to alleviate even the most annoying muscle pains. Application of heat, moist or dry, is also beneficial.

After applying a muscular pain remedy, wash your hands thoroughly with soap and water. Small traces of the analgesic left on the hands may cause severe stinging if they come in contact with the eyes, nose, ears, or lips.

Recommendations on OTC Muscular Pain Remedies

If you want to use an OTC muscular pain remedy, choose a product that contains a salicylate, but not capsicum, camphor, or turpentine oil. Such products include Ben-Gay, Aspercreme, Icy Hot Balm, Icy Hot Rub, and Mentholatum Deep Heating (lotion) muscular pain remedies. Products containing salicylates can be rubbed vigorously into the skin without causing irritation. The vigorous rubbing will help relieve pain.

Profiled muscular pain remedies: Absorbine Jr.; Aspercreme; Benalg; Ben-Gay; Deep-Down; Heet; Icy Hot Balm; Icy Hot Rub; Infra-Rub; Mentholatum Deep Heating; Vicks Vaporub

Nutritional Supplements

Vitamins and minerals may be used to prevent, or to treat, a nutritional deficiency. The problem is knowing whether you are preventing or treating a *true* deficiency.

Vitamin E, for example, has been touted as a cure for a large number of ailments, but so far it has been impossible to demonstrate the effects of a deficiency. Perhaps testing methods are not sophisticated enough, or vitamin E is present in so many foods, that people cannot help but get enough. Just as no one knows exactly how vitamin E works, no one knows exactly how much of it represents an overdose.

Researchers do know that too much of vitamins A, D, and K can cause severe side effects. And, because vitamin dosages are not limited by law unless drug claims are made by the manufacturer, it is possible to purchase and consume these vitamins in high dosages. Since vitamins E, A, D, and K tend to accumulate in the body, CONSUMER GUIDE® magazine warns against taking large doses of any of them.

The B vitamins and vitamin C do not accumulate in the body as the other vitamins do, and definite deficiencies of these vitamins have been shown. Usually, a deficiency does not involve only one member of the group of B vitamins. Therefore, a B-complex vitamin supplement is preferred over supplements of individual B vitamins. Also, there is some evidence that large amounts of some vitamins may lower blood levels of other vitamins. In other words, some tests show that by taking one vitamin you may increase the need for another.

Vitamin C supplements are taken to treat scurvy, a deficiency of vitamin C. Taking large doses of vitamin C to prevent a cold is still controversial, however. If you do decide to take vitamin C to prevent or treat a cold, be sure to drink eight to ten glasses of water a day to help prevent kidney stone formation, the only serious adverse effect now associated with use of vitamin C.

Of all the minerals available without a prescription, iron is by far the most toxic, particularly to children. Taking small doses of iron, such as those found in multiple vitamin-mineral combination products, to prevent iron-deficiency anemia is acceptable, especially for women during the menstrual years, or for others who, for one reason or another, readily lose iron. However, it is easy to take too much iron. Be careful when taking iron supplements. Remember, the quantity of iron in a single dose of most multiple vitamin-mineral combination products is sufficient. And keep iron supplements away from children.

Iron tablets may upset the stomach. To lessen the upset, take them with food. They also discolor the stools. This effect is normal and should not alarm you.

Deficiencies of other minerals, such as calcium, manganese, and zinc, are rare because these minerals are found in so many foods. Few people need supplements of these minerals. The small quantities that are found in multiple vitamin-mineral products are unlikely to produce any serious side effects.

Recommendations on OTC Nutritional Supplements

The best way to prevent a vitamin or mineral deficiency is to eat a balanced diet. But multiple vitamin-mineral products are appropriate for some people: those who, for example, have a vitamin or mineral deficiency, women who need more vitamins and minerals to meet the increased demands of pregnancy and breast-feeding, children who need extra vitamins and minerals for proper growth, and, finally, those who, because of illness, must compensate for decreased intake or poor absorption of certain vitamins and minerals. If you think you need extra vitamins, consult your doctor to see if a true deficiency exists. Taking large doses of certain vitamins can cause severe side effects.

Profiled nutritional supplements: Allbee with C; Femiron; Femiron (Iron only); Feosol; Fergon; Fer-In-Sol; ferrous gluconate; ferrous sulfate; Geritol (liquid; tablet); Multicebrin; Myadec; One-A-Day; One-A-Day Plus Iron; One-A-Day Plus Minerals; Poly-Vi-Sol; Stresscaps; Stresstabs 600; Thera-Combex H-P; Theragran; Theragran-M; Unicap M; Unicap Multivitamin; Unicap T; vitamin A (retinol); vitamin B_1 (thiamine); vitamin B_2 (riboflavin); vitamin B_3 (nicotinic acid); vitamin B_5 (pantothenic acid); vitamin B_6 (pyridoxine); vitamin B_{12} (cyanocobalamin); vitamin C (ascorbic acid); vitamin D (calciferol); vitamin E (tocopherol)

Pain Relievers

For relief of mild headache, toothache, and other minor pains, over-the-counter pain remedies are usually sufficient. Most OTC pain remedies (or analgesics) are primarily aspirin or acetaminophen; some have added ingredients—commonly caffeine, antihistamines, or antacids. Anacin analgesic, for example, combines aspirin with caffeine, which has no proven pain-relieving properties; Excedrin analgesic combines aspirin with salicylamide, a very small amount of acetaminophen, and caffeine. No test has shown that a combination of ingredients is more effective than an equivalent dose of plain aspirin or acetaminophen, and these combination products are almost always a great deal more expensive.

Until recently, phenacetin was commonly included in some OTC analgesics. Because phenacetin has been found to cause kidney damage and blood disorders, the FDA is removing it from over-the-counter products. However, some products with phenacetin may still be available at home or in stores. We recommend that you check the label on any analgesic before you take it. If it contains phenacetin, discard it by flushing it down the toilet.

Each of the major OTC analgesics, aspirin and acetaminophen, has its certain advantages and disadvantages. Aspirin effectively reduces pain, fever, and inflammation. On the debit side, aspirin causes stomach irritation (which may lead to internal bleeding) in some people, it retards blood clotting and affects blood formation in several ways, and people who have asthma are often hypersensitive to it. Acetaminophen does not provide anti-inflammatory effects, making it less useful than aspirin for treating arthritic pain.

However, acetaminophen is less likely to upset the stomach and affect blood clotting than is aspirin. Therefore, while aspirin is more likely to relieve pain associated with redness or swelling, if you have a combination headache and an upset stomach, acetaminophen may be a better choice for you.

Aspirin cannot be taken by everyone. People with allergies or asthma should avoid taking aspirin, unless they are sure that they will not react to it. People with diabetes or gout should use aspirin carefully, and those with peptic ulcers or blood-clotting diseases should not take it at all.

Pain Relievers

Product/Dosage Form(s)	aspirin (mg)	acetaminophen (mg)	caffeine (mg)	alcohol (%)	other (mg)
Alka-Seltzer effervescent tablet	324				sodium bicarbonate, 1904; citric acid, 1000
Anacin tablet, capsule	400		32		
Anacin, Maximum Strength tablet	500		32		
Anacin-3 tablet		500	32		
Arthritis Pain Formula tablet	486				dried aluminum hydroxide gel, 20; magnesium hydroxide, 60
Arthritis Strength Bufferin tablet	486				aluminum glycinate, 72.9; magnesium carbonate, 145.8
Ascriptin tablet	325				magnesium-aluminum hydroxide, 150
Ascriptin A/D tablet	325				magnesium-aluminum hydroxide, 300
Bayer Aspirin tablet	325				
Bayer Children's Chewable Aspirin chewable tablet	81				

Pain Relievers *(cont'd)*

Product/ Dosage Form(s)	aspirin (mg)	acetaminophen (mg)	caffeine (mg)	alcohol (%)	other (mg)
Bayer Timed-Release Aspirin timed-release tablet	650				
Bromo-Seltzer granules (per capful)		325			sodium bicarbonate, 2800; citric acid, 2200
Bufferin tablet	324				aluminum glycinate, 48.6; magnesium carbonate, 97.2
extra-strength tablet, capsule	486				aluminum glycinate, 48.6; magnesium carbonate, 97.2
Datril tablet		325			
Doan's Pills tablet			32		magnesium salicylate, 325
Ecotrin enteric-coated tablet	325				
Empirin tablet	325				
Excedrin tablet, capsule	250	250	65		
Excedrin P.M. tablet		500			pyrilamine maleate, 25
Liquiprin liquid (per dropper)		120			
Measurin timed-release tablet	650				
Percogesic tablet		325			phenyltoloxamine citrate, 30
Sine-Aid tablet		325			phenylpropanolamine hydrochloride, 25

Product/ Dosage Form(s)	aspirin (mg)	acetaminophen (mg)	caffeine (mg)	alcohol (%)	other (mg)
Tempra					
drop (per dropper)		60		10	
syrup (per tsp)		120		10	
Tylenol					
chewable tablet		80			
drop (per dropper)		60			
elixir (per tsp)		120			
tablet, capsule		325			
Tylenol Extra Strength					
capsule, tablet		500			
liquid (per Tbsp)		500		8.5	
Vanquish					
caplet	227	194	33		dried aluminum hydroxide gel, 25; magnesium hydroxide, 50

Recommendations on OTC Analgesics

The most economical, safe, and effective drugs to be used in treating pain (and fever as well) are plain aspirin and acetaminophen. Choose a moderately priced product; bargain-priced drug items may not be absorbed at the same rate, and they may be less effective than other brands.

Buffered products contain aspirin plus antacids. However, no substantial difference in effectiveness between buffered and non-buffered products has been shown. Buffered products may produce less gastric upset in some people. Likewise, enteric-coated products are formulated with a special coating so that they dissolve in the intestines rather than the stomach, thus preventing stomach upset. Among the enteric-coated aspirin products, we recommend Ecotrin, although we suggest that you try acetaminophen or a buffered product first if aspirin upsets your stomach.

Profiled analgesics: acetaminophen; Alka-Seltzer; Anacin; Anacin, Maximum Strength; Anacin-3; Arthritis Pain Formula; Arthritis Strength Bufferin; Ascriptin, Ascriptin A/D; aspirin; Bayer Aspirin; Bayer Children's Chewable Aspirin; Bayer Timed-Release

Aspirin; Bromo-Seltzer; Bufferin; Datril; Doan's Pills; Ecotrin; Empirin; Excedrin; Excedrin P.M.; Liquiprin; Measurin; Percogesic; Sine-Aid; Tempra; Tylenol; Tylenol Extra Strength; Vanquish

Poison Ivy/Poison Oak Remedies

The plant family called Rhus has caused an enormous amount of summer time misery, for it is this family that includes poison ivy and poison oak. These plants contain the chemical urushiol. If someone who is sensitive to this chemical comes in contact with it, it causes severe itching, blistering, and watering. Sensitivity to poison ivy or poison oak usually produces a reaction only on the skin, but if fumes from burning the plants are inhaled, the respiratory tract may be affected. About 70 percent of the American population is susceptible.

Everyone should be guided by the old saying, "leaves three, let them be," because the triple-leaf growth habit of these plants is their most distinguishing feature. However, many people aren't able to recognize the plants in all seasons and locales. Depending on the habitat, poison ivy, for example, can be a trailing vine or a free-standing bush ten feet tall. The leaves may be thick and glossy or broad and dull, and they change color during the year. They're purplish in the spring, green in the summer, and yellow, red, or orange in the fall.

If the plant is recognized only after contact has been made, a shower should be taken immediately to abate the reaction. Someone who has been exposed should take care to wash completely with soap and shampoo, to scrub under the nails, and to dry thoroughly after the shower.

Any clothing, sports equipment, or garden tools that could have been contaminated must be washed. If the family dog was romping through a patch of poison ivy or poison oak, it should be bathed, and the bather should be sure to wash his hands, arms, and under his nails afterward.

Most rashes due to poison ivy or poison oak go away without treatment in one or two weeks. The following treatment will reduce discomfort somewhat: Wash the hands and the affected area in hot, soapy water. Rinse well, and dry. Using a clean, wooden tongue depressor, or other blunt object—such as a butter knife—gently scrape across the skin until the tops of the blisters are loose. Allow the fluid to escape from the blisters so it will not interfere with medication, and pat the area dry. Then, apply an OTC product that contains calamine or zinc oxide.

Calamine and zinc oxide protect underlying tissue and dry the affected area. However, they are messy and will leave a crust on the skin after they have dried. Therefore, many people do not want to use them during the day. An alternative to calamine or zinc oxide is a solution of rubbing alcohol and water (half-and-half). It will sting for a minute, but it will relieve the itching. Witch hazel (used full strength) can be used in place of rubbing alcohol. If itching is still intense, soak in a tub of hot water for 15 to 20 minutes. Avoid scratching. Scratching may lead to infection and skin damage.

Topical OTC products for poison ivy or poison oak that contain either an anesthetic or an antihistamine are not recommended. Either ingredient can cause further irritation (pain, itching, and rash) in susceptible people. Anesthetics in OTC products include benzocaine, diperodon hydrochloride, dibucaine, tetracaine hydrochloride, cyclomethycaine, and pramoxine hydrochloride. Of these, benzocaine is the best for the relief of itching. However, at least a 5 percent concentration of benzocaine is needed, and a 20 percent concentration is even better. We know of no OTC poison ivy/poison oak remedy that contains more than 10 percent benzocaine.

Antihistamines are included in these products to help relieve itching, but only one antihistamine—diphenhydramine hydrochloride—actually offers any significant relief. And, it may cause further irritation in some people. The topical steroids now available over the counter will help relieve inflammation. However, several days of therapy are necessary before this effect occurs.

Avoid any product that contains zirconium oxide (or zirconia). After one or two weeks of use, it has been shown to cause severe skin irritation in some people.

For severe cases of poison ivy or poison oak or any case that seems to affect the breathing, see a doctor. He may prescribe a strong glucocorticoid steroid product.

Recommendations on OTC Poison Ivy/Poison Oak Remedies

Your pharmacy's generic brands of calamine lotion and rubbing alcohol are recommended for relief of itching.

Profiled poison ivy/poison oak remedies: Caladryl; calamine lotion; Ivy Dry Cream; Rhulicream; Rhulihist; Ziradryl

Profiled topical steroids: Cortaid; Dermolate

Profiled rash remedy: zinc oxide

Sleep Aids

Insomnia is extremely common—up to 50 per cent of Americans suffer from it at least occasionally—and may stem from a number of causes. Excitement, anxiety, stress, or more serious psychological problems may keep someone from falling asleep. Environmental factors like a hot or stuffy room, an uncomfortable bed, noise, or unusual quiet may make it difficult for some people to fall asleep; so may indigestion, lack of exercise, the ingestion of mild stimulants (tea, coffee, or cola) before going to bed, or other minor problems such as itching, shortness of breath, palpitations, or pain. Temporary insomnia occurs at the onset of many illnesses. Many people who experience occasional insomnia turn to OTC sleep aids for relief, but these are not effective.

The products that are available over the counter contain antihistamines, such as pyrilamine maleate, which may cause side effects such as palpitations, blurred vision, dizziness, and dryness of the mouth and throat. The elderly are more likely than other people to suffer side effects from the use of these drugs and should not take them without first consulting a doctor.

Recommendations on OTC Sleep Aids

OTC sleep aids are generally no more effective than plain aspirin, and they may cause unpleasant side effects. If a minor ache or pain is keeping you awake, take aspirin or acetaminophen. Otherwise, try to identify and correct the cause of your sleeplessness.

Profiled sleep aids: Compoz; Nervine; Nytol; Sleep-Eze; Sominex; Unisom Nighttime

Stimulants

OTC stimulants contain caffeine as the active ingredient in dosages ranging from 100 to 200 mg. One cup of brewed coffee contains 100 to 150 mg caffeine. In high doses, caffeine can evoke uncomfortable side effects; rapid heartbeat, palpitations, jitteriness or nervousness, and insomnia. It also increases urination and may, over a period of time, enhance the risk of developing a peptic ulcer.

Recommendations on OTC Stimulants

We do not recommend the use of OTC stimulants. OTC stimulants can cause uncomfortable side effects. If you feel you need a stimulant, you might try drinking a cup of coffee, tea, or a cola beverage. You should also look for the underlying cause of your tiredness—insufficient sleep or exercise or inadequate diet, for example—and try to correct it.

Profiled stimulants: No Doz; Vivarin

Sunscreens

(See "Burn Remedies" for information on treating a sunburn.)

Sunburns are caused by overexposure to ultraviolet (UV) light. Ultraviolet light damages the skin much as flames or hot liquid would; it penetrates the skin and affects its content of melanin, a dark pigment. The severity of a sunburn is affected by several factors: the person's complexion (the more melanin present, the less the chance of burning), the time of day and length of exposure (10 am to 2 pm is the most dangerous time), and the latitude at

Sunscreens

If you:	the recommended product is one providing:	having an SPF range of:	which:
tan readily; burn minimally	Minimal Protection	2- 4	offers least protection from burning, but permits tanning
tan gradually; burn moderately	Moderate Protection	4- 6	offers moderate protection from burning, but permits some tanning
tan minimally; burn easily	Extra Protection	6- 8	offers extra protection from burning, but permits limited tanning
never tan; always burn	Maximal Protection or	8-15	offers maximal protection from burning, and permits little or no tanning
	Ultra Protection	15 +	offers the most protection from burning, and permits no tanning

which the exposure took place (the "sunbelt" is worse than northern areas). Certain drugs cause increased sensitivity to the sun—Declomycin antibiotic and certain diuretics, for example.

Needless to say, it is far better to prevent a sunburn than to treat it after it occurs. Many doctors believe that two or three aspirin tablets taken one to two hours before exposure to the sun will help prevent sunburn and hasten its healing should it occur. Nonprescription sunscreens are another way to prevent sunburn.

Basically, sunscreens are agents that physically or chemically block the penetration of ultraviolet light into the skin. Sunscreens are rated according to their Sun Protective Factor (SPF). The SPF indicates how much more sun exposure you can withstand before burning when using a particular product. If you use a product with an SPF of 15, you can stay in the sun 15 times longer than you could without the sunscreen. With a product rated SPF 2, you can stay in the sun twice as long before contracting a burn.

Manufacturers have been encouraged to include SPF values on the labels of sunscreens, and the products have also been categorized as offering minimal, moderate, extra, maximal, or ultra sun protection.

Recommendations on OTC Sunscreens

Choose a sunscreen according to how well you tan and the circumstances to which you will be exposed. See accompanying table for guidelines on choosing the sunscreen appropriate for you.

Profiled sunscreens: Eclipse Partial Suntan, Eclipse Lip and Face Protectant, Eclipse Total, Eclipse Original; Noskote; Presun 15, Presun 8, Presun 8 Creamy, Presun 4, Presun Lip Protection; RVP, RVPlus, RVPaba; Sundown Sunblock Ultra Protection, Sundown Maximal Protection, Sundown Extra Protection, Sundown Moderate Protection

Urine Tests

Urine contains the products of metabolism of the body's cells and is the most extensively studied body fluid. It is a valuable means for diagnosing several diseases. OTC urine-testing products are easy to use and are inexpensive. You can get in minutes the same information that may take a laboratory several days to get, but you must learn how to use them properly.

First, completely wash, rinse, and dry the urine collection container. Or, use a disposable paper cup. Unless otherwise directed, collect the urine immediately before testing. Sometimes, a urine sample must be taken in the early morning or at some other specific time. Usually, testing immediately follows collection. If the urine sample must be kept for more than a few minutes, put it in the refrigerator and indicate the time the sample was taken on a piece of tape placed on the container. Then, before you do the actual test, allow the urine to sit at room temperature for a few minutes. The following are among the most commonly used urine tests.

Testing for glucose. One of the most common urine tests is a test for sugar, or glucose. It can be used to detect the presence of diabetes, or it can be used by diabetics to determine if they have been using too little insulin.

These tests may be of two types: dip-and-read tests or tablet tests. A dip-and-read product is dipped into a urine sample, kept there for a specific length of time, withdrawn, and read by comparing its color against a color chart.

The tablet test products include test tubes and tablets. A tablet is added to the urine sample in the test tube. As soon as the testing period is up, the color of the sample in the test tube is "read" by comparing it to a color chart.

Dip-and-read tests rely on enzyme action and are susceptible to damage from exposure to heat or humidity. These products must be stored in a cool, dry place (not in the refrigerator). Tablet tests should also be stored in a cool, dry place. Cotton should not be placed in the bottle. The tablets are toxic if swallowed; keep them out of the reach of children. Dip-and-read products that have turned brown, or tablets with black spots should be discarded.

Testing for ketones. Dip-and-read products and tablets also test for ketones, chemicals that are released into the urine when the body is burning fat. The presence of ketones in the urine may be due to diabetes. See a doctor whenever a ketone test is positive.

Testing for protein. Protein is normally present in the blood but not in the urine. The presence of protein in the urine indicates kidney disease. Tests for protein are of the dip-and-read type. Because residue on the inside of the urine collection container may influence test results, the container should be washed with a strong soap—not a detergent—rinsed well, and allowed to dry completely. If a urine sample has been refrigerated, allow it to warm before testing. Discard the sample if it appears cloudy after it has warmed. To detect cloudiness, hold the container against a black background and shine a light on it.

Pregnancy tests. To conduct a pregnancy test, the test material is added to a urine sample in a special glass tube. The tube is allowed to stand undisturbed for two hours. A brown ring in the bottom of the tube indicates pregnancy. If these tests are performed nine days or more after the first missed menstrual period and the results are positive (i.e., pregnancy is indicated), they are 97 percent accurate. If, however, the results are negative, there is still a 25 percent chance that the woman is pregnant (i.e., the result is false negative). The chance of having false negative results is greater the earlier the test is done. Therefore, negative results indicate the need for a second test.

A woman considering the use of one of these tests may want to consult her gynecologist or obstetrician. Most doctors will want to confirm the test's results if they are positive—meaning that the woman will probably end up paying for two tests no matter what the result.

Recommendations on OTC Urine Tests

Profiled urine tests for glucose: Clinistix Strips; Clinitest; Tes-Tape

Profiled urine tests for ketones: Acetest Reagent Tablets; Ketostix Strips

Profiled urine tests for pregnancy: Answer; Daisy 2; e.p.t.; Predictor

Drug Profiles

On the following pages you'll find profiles for more than four hundred nonprescription drugs. By studying these drug profiles, you can learn what to expect from your medication, when to be concerned about possible side effects or drug interactions, and how to take the drug to achieve its maximum benefit. Each profile includes the following information:

Product Name. The product name appears in bold letters centered over each profile. The first letter of a trade name (such as Visine, Allerest) is always capitalized, unless the manufacturer has decided upon a special treatment of the word (pHisoDerm, for example). Products sold generically (without a trade name) are denoted by lower-case initial letters, unless they appear at the beginning of a sentence. The product's drug classification (for example, "cold remedy," "eyedrops") is listed after its name.

It is common for a manufacturer to change the name of a product, or to remove or add certain ingredients to the product without changing the name. Thus, the ingredients in an item that you purchase may be different from those indicated in the profile.

Manufacturer. The name of the drug's manufacturer is specified. Because generics are produced and sold by many different companies, no specific manufacturer is listed for them.

Dosage Form/Ingredients. This category lists the dosage forms (tablet, capsule, liquid, suppository, etc.) and formulations in which the product is available. All available information on the formulation is listed; this generally includes the names of the active chemical components and the amount of each that is included in each dosage form. Generic items are generally single-ingredient (pure aspirin, for example) and are often available in many different dosage forms and strengths. Those most commonly available are listed.

Use. This category includes the most important and most common clinical uses for each profiled drug.

Side Effects. Possible side effects are listed here. Most of these side effects, if they occur, disappear in a day or two. Do not expect to experience these side effects, but if they occur and are particularly annoying, do not hesitate to seek the advice of your doctor or pharmacist. You may be advised to try an alternative drug.

Warnings. This category lists those people who should be using the profiled product cautiously. For example, a close monitor is usually necessary when people with liver or kidney disease use drugs. Most drugs should not be used by pregnant women, nursing mothers, and newborn or premature infants. Diabetics and people with impaired circulation should be careful about using many kinds of drugs. This category will also alert you if a drug is potentially toxic, if it may interact with other drugs you could be taking, if bothersome side effects may occur, and about any other dangers that could be associated with use of the drug.

Comments. Under the heading "Comments" you will find information on how to use the drug for the best effect: whether to take it at mealtimes or with food or milk, for example. Any special instructions about administering the drug will also be found in "Comments." Other information included could concern price of the drug, other products with similar action, limits on the drug's effectiveness, and comments on the dosage forms. Never be reluctant to ask your doctor or pharmacist for further information.

Ratings. The editors of CONSUMER GUIDE® have rated the products profiled in this book according to the information available about the contents and properties of each. The ratings fall into five categories: "Preferred," "Acceptable," "Fair," "Unacceptable," and "Not Evaluated." "Preferred" products are considered the best available over the counter for the treatment of a specific condition; generally, they contain ingredients that have been proven safe and effective, and they do not contain unnecessary extras. They are not overpriced. The ingredients in "Acceptable" products are also effective, but they may be less effective than those in "Preferred" products, or an "Acceptable" product may contain additional, unnecessary ingredients. "Fair" products are safe to use, but their ingredients may be less effective than those in "Preferred" or "Acceptable" categories. An "Unacceptable" product may contain ingredients that have not been proven effective or that are potentially toxic. The formulation of an "Unacceptable" product may include ingredients with many different actions, thereby increasing the product's potential for causing adverse effects and drug interactions. The final category, "Not Evaluated," applies only to those products for which the manufacturer has failed to supply sufficient information on which to base an evaluation.

Absorbine Jr. muscular pain remedy

Manufacturer: W. F. Young, Inc.

Dosage Form/Ingredients: Lotion: unspecified quantities of acetone, chloroxylenol, menthol, thymol, wormwood oil

Use: Used externally to temporarily relieve pain in muscles and other areas

Side Effects: Allergic reactions (rash, itching, soreness); local irritation

Warnings: This product is for external use only. • Do not use it on broken or irritated skin, or on large areas of the body; keep it away from the eyes. • If the pain in muscles or other areas persists, call your doctor. • While you are using this product, avoid exposure to direct sunlight, heat lamp, or sun lamp. • Discontinue use and consult your pharmacist if irritation (rash, itching, or swelling) or pain occurs. • Before using this product on a child under 12 years of age, consult your doctor. • Children might be attracted to the smell of this product; it should be stored safely out of their reach. • If a child swallows some of this product, call your doctor immediately. • Do not rub this product into the skin.

Not Evaluated: The manufacturer fails to provide sufficient information about this product on which to base an evaluation.

acetaminophen analgesic

Manufacturer: Various
Dosage Forms: Capsule, Chewable tablet, Liquid, Suppository, Tablet: various concentrations
Use: For the relief of pain of headache, toothache, sprains, muscular aches, menstruation; for relief of discomforts and fever following immunizations or of colds or "flu"; for temporary relief of minor aches and pains of arthritis and rheumatism
Side Effects: When taken in overdose: blood disorders; rash
Warnings: This product should not be taken by persons with certain blood disorders or with heart, lung, liver or kidney disease without a doctor's approval. • When taken in overdose, this product is more toxic than aspirin. The dosage instructions listed on the package should be followed carefully; toxicity may occur in adults or children with repeated doses.
Comments: Acetaminophen does not relieve inflammation, so if pain is caused by swelling or inflammation, it should not be used. Try aspirin instead.
Preferred: Generic acetaminophen is recommended highly; it effectively relieves pain without causing the stomach upset associated with aspirin. Choose a moderately priced product.

Acetest Reagent Tablets urine test for ketones

Manufacturer: Ames Division, Miles Laboratories
Product Form: Tablet
Use: To test urine for ketones
Warnings: Keep these tablets out of the reach of children; they are toxic if swallowed.
Comments: Be certain to remind your doctor and pharmacist of any OTC item or prescription drug you are taking. It may affect this test. • Test only freshly collected urine. • Keep the container tightly closed and store in a dry place out of the sun. Do not refrigerate. • Compare the color to the color chart at the exact time indicated on the label. • This product can also be used to test blood samples for the presence of ketones. • Do not use these tablets if they have changed color.
Preferred: This test is effective for the specified purpose and offers good value for the money.

Acne-Aid acne preparation

Manufacturer: Stiefel Laboratories, Inc.
Dosage Forms/Ingredients: Cream: chloroxylenol, 0.375%; resorcinol, 1.25%; sulfur, 2.5%. Lotion: alcohol, 10%; sulfur, 10%
Use: Treatment of acne
Side Effects: Allergy; local irritation
Warnings: Do not get this product in or near the eyes. • If the condition worsens or if skin irritation develops, stop using this product and consult your physician.

Comments: Wash area gently with warm water and pat dry before applying this product.

Fair: Products containing more effective ingredients are available.

Afrin nasal decongestant

Manufacturer: Schering Corporation

Dosage Forms/Ingredients: Drop, Nasal spray (content per 1 ml): oxymetazoline hydrochloride, 0.05%; phenylmercuric acetate, 0.02 mg. Pediatric drop: oxymetazoline hydrochloride, 0.025%. Mentholated drop: oxymetazoline hydrochloride, 0.05%; phenylmercuric acetate, 0.02 mg; unspecified quantities of menthol, camphor, and eucalyptol

Use: For temporary relief of nasal congestion due to colds, sinusitis, hay fever, or other upper respiratory allergies

Side Effects: Blurred vision; burning, dryness of nasal mucosa; increased nasal congestion or discharge; sneezing, and/or stinging; dizziness; drowsiness; headache; insomnia; nervousness; palpitations; slight increase in blood pressure; stimulation

Warnings: This product should not be used by persons who have glaucoma (certain types). • It should be used with special caution by persons who have diabetes, advanced hardening of the arteries, heart disease, high blood pressure, or thyroid disease. If you have any of these conditions, consult your doctor before using this product. • This product interacts with monoamine oxidase inhibitors, thyroid preparations, and tricyclic antidepressants. If you are currently taking any drugs of these types, check with your doctor before taking this product. If you are unsure of the type or contents of your medications, ask your doctor or pharmacist.

Comments: To avoid side effects such as burning, sneezing, or stinging, and a "rebound" increase in nasal congestion and discharge, do not exceed the recommended dose, and do not use this product for more than three or four continuous days. • This product should not be used by more than one person; sharing the dispenser may spread infection. • This product works best when it is used correctly. Refer to the instructions for the use of nasal sprays and drops in the chapter on "Buying, Storing, and Using Drugs." • The long-acting ingredient in this product has a decongestant action that may last up to 12 hours. Because it needs to be administered only twice a day, this product is less likely to cause "rebound" congestion than nasal products containing different ingredients. • The mentholated version of this product contains aromatic substances that add no therapeutic value. • The spray form of this product, although slightly more expensive than the drop, is preferred for adult use. The spray penetrates far back into the nose, covering the nasal area more completely, and is more convenient to use. The drop is preferable for administration to children.

Preferred: We recommend the use of a product containing oxymetazoline hydrochloride because it requries less frequent use and is therefore less likely to cause "rebound" congestion.

Aftate athlete's foot and jock itch remedy

Manufacturer: Plough, Inc.

Dosage Forms/Ingredients: Aerosol liquid: tolnaftate, 1%; alcohol, 36%. Aerosol powder: tolnaftate, 1%; alcohol, 14 %. Gel, Powder: tolnaftate, 1%. Pump spray liquid: tolnaftate, 1%; alcohol, 83%

Use: For the prevention and treatment of athlete's foot and jock itch

Side Effects: Allergy; local irritation

Warnings: Diabetics and other persons with impaired circulation should not use this product without first consulting a physician. • Do not apply this product to mucous membranes. • If your condition worsens, or if irritation occurs, stop using this product and consult your pharmacist. • When using the aerosol form of this product, be careful not to inhale any of the powder. • Check with your doctor before using this product on a child. Some doctors believe that children under the age of 12 do not get athlete's foot, and that a rash appearing between a child's toes may be dermatitis or some other condition that this product would not relieve.

Comments: Some lesions take months to heal, so it is important not to stop treatment too soon. • If foot lesions are consistently a problem, check the fit of your shoes. • Wash your hands thoroughly after applying this product. • The gel and liquid forms of this product are preferable to the powders for effectiveness; the best action of the powders may be in drying the infected area. The aerosol sprays may be more expensive than the other forms of this product; check prices before paying for convenience you do not need.

Preferred: *This product contains tolnaftate, which is the treatment of choice for athlete's foot and other fungal skin infections. Tolnaftate products were formerly sold only with a doctor's prescription, but are now available OTC.*

Alka-Seltzer
analgesic and antacid

Manufacturer: Miles Laboratories, Inc.

Dosage Form/Ingredients: Effervescent tablet: aspirin, 324 mg; sodium bicarbonate, 1904 mg; citric acid, 1000 mg

Use: Relief of upset stomach, heartburn, or acid indigestion accompanied by headache or body aches and pains

Side Effects: Dizziness; mental confusion; nausea and vomiting; ringing in the ears; slight blood loss; sweating

Warnings: Persons with asthma, hay fever, or other allergies should be extremely careful about using this product. The product may interfere with the treatment of gout. This product may cause an increased bleeding tendency and should not be taken by persons with a history of bleeding, peptic ulcer, or stomach bleeding. If you have any of these conditions, consult your doctor or pharmacist before using this medication. • Do not use this product if you are on a low-salt diet. • Do not use this product if you are consuming alcohol, or taking methotrexate, oral anticoagulants, oral antidiabetics, probenecid, steroids, and/or sulfinpyrazone; if you are unsure of the type or contents of your medications, ask your doctor or pharmacist. • The dosage instructions listed on the package should be followed carefully; toxicity may occur in adults or children with repeated doses.

Comments: These tablets must be completely dissolved in water before swallowing; three ounces of water per tablet is sufficient. • You can save money by taking aspirin instead of this product. Because it is taken in solution, this product does reach the bloodstream in less time and will give faster pain relief than plain aspirin. However, if you take your regular dose of aspirin, and follow it with a cup of hot water, the aspirin will reach your bloodstream almost as quickly as would this product.

Fair: *This is an overpriced version of aspirin. The added ingredients do not justify the product's cost.*

Alka-Seltzer antacid

Manufacturer: Miles Laboratories, Inc.

Dosage Form/Ingredients: Effervescent tablet: citric acid, 800 mg; potassium bicarbonate, 300 mg; sodium bicarbonate, 1008 mg; sodium, 276 mg

Use: For relief of acid indigestion, heartburn, and/or sour stomach

Side Effects: Bloating; gas; gastric fullness

Warnings: Persons with heart or kidney disease, those on a salt-free diet, or those drinking large quantities of milk should not use this product. • Do not take this product within two hours of a dose of a tetracycline antibiotic. • Consult your physician or pharmacist before taking this product if you are already taking iron, a vitamin-mineral product, chlorpromazine, phenytoin, digoxin, quinidine, or warfarin, or if you are unsure of the type and contents of the medications you are taking. • Never self-medicate with this product if your symptoms occur regularly (two or three or more times a month). Consult your doctor if the symptoms are worse than usual, if you have chest pains or feel "tightness" in the chest, or if you are sweating or short of breath. In fact, we do not recommend self-treatment for severe attacks of heartburn, indigestion, or stomach upset in any circumstances. If you do decide that your symptoms are mild enough to warrant self-medication, remember that this product is safe and effective only when used on an occasional basis. Repeated use over several weeks may result in "rebound acidity," which causes increased acid production and makes your symptoms worse instead of better.

Comments: This product must be dissolved in water before use. • For best results, take this product one hour after meals or at bedtime, unless directed otherwise by your doctor or pharmacist.

Unacceptable: *We consider this product to be an overpriced version of sodium bicarbonate. Sodium bicarbonate is the most powerful and dangerous of the antacid chemicals; this product contains an extremely high amount of this ingredient.*

Alka-Seltzer Plus cold and allergy remedy

Manufacturer: Miles Laboratories, Inc.

Dosage Form/Ingredients: Effervescent tablet: phenylpropanolamine bitartrate, 24.08 mg; chlorpheniramine maleate, 2 mg; aspirin, 324 mg

Use: For relief of symptoms of colds, "flu," sinus congestion, and hay fever and other upper respiratory allergies

Side Effects: Anxiety; blurred vision; chest pain; confusion; constipation; difficult and painful urination; dizziness; drowsiness; dry mouth; headache; increased blood pressure; insomnia; loss of appetite; mild stimulation; nausea; nervousness; palpitations; rash; reduced sweating; ringing in the ears; slight blood loss; tension; tremor; vomiting

Warnings: This product should be used with special caution by the elderly or debilitated, those on sodium-restricted diets, and by those persons who have asthma, diabetes, an enlarged prostate, glaucoma (certain types), heart disease, high blood pressure, kidney disease, liver disease, obstructed bladder, obstructed intestine, peptic ulcer, bleeding or stomach bleeding, gout, or thyroid disease. If you have any of these conditions, consult your doctor before taking this product. It should not be used by pregnant or nursing women, or be given to newborn or premature infants. • This product may cause drowsiness. Do not take it if you must drive, operate heavy machinery, or perform other tasks requiring mental alertness. To prevent oversedation, avoid the use of alcohol or other drugs that have sedative properties. • This product interacts with alcohol, ammonium chloride, guanethidine, methotrexate, monoamine oxidase inhibitors, oral anticoagulants, oral antidiabetics, probenecid, sedative drugs, steroids, sulfinpyrazone, tricyclic antidepressants, and vitamin C. If you are currently taking any drugs of these types, check with your doctor before taking this product. If you are unsure of the type or contents of your medications, ask your doctor or pharmacist. • Because this product reduces sweating, avoid excessive work or exercise in hot weather. • The dosage instructions listed on the package should be followed carefully; toxicity may occur in adults or children with repeated doses.

Comments: Many other conditions (some serious) mimic the common cold. If symptoms persist beyond one week, or if they occur regularly without regard to season, consult your doctor. • The effectiveness of this product may diminish after being taken for seven to ten days; consult your pharmacist about substituting a different product if this product begins to lose its effectiveness for you. • Chew gum or suck on ice chips or a piece of hard candy to reduce mouth dryness. • Do not swallow these tablets whole; they must be completely dissolved in water. Use approximately three ounces of water per tablet. Drink the medication only after the fizzing is done.

Acceptable: We prefer single-ingredient products rather than combination analgesic-antihistamine-decongestant products like this one.

Allbee with C nutritional supplement

Manufacturer: A. H. Robins Company

Dosage Form/Ingredients: Capsule: ascorbic acid, 300 mg; thiamine, 15 mg; riboflavin, 10.2 mg; niacin, 50 mg; pyridoxine hydrochloride, 5 mg; pantothenic acid, 10 mg

Use: To supplement diet

Side Effects: None

Warnings: This product contains vitamin B_6 (pyridoxine) in an amount great enough that it may interact with levodopa (L-dopa). If you are currently taking L-dopa, check with your doctor before taking this product. • If two or more capsules are taken daily, this product may interfere with the results of urine tests. If your urine is being tested, inform your doctor and/or pharmacist that you are taking this product.

Comments: Dietary deficiencies of vitamins are uncommon in the United States. Most people who have vitamin deficiencies should be under a doctor's care, and they should not be self-medicating with OTC vitamin products. • If you choose to take supplemental vitamins, choose a generic product to save money. Ask your pharmacist for assistance.

Acceptable: If you choose to take a vitamin supplement, this is an acceptable product.

Allerest allergy remedy

Manufacturer: Pharmacraft, Div. of Pfizer Pharmaceuticals

Dosage Forms/Ingredients: Chewable tablet: phenylpropanolamine hydrochloride, 9.4 mg; chlorpheniramine maleate, 1 mg. Tablet: phenylpropanolamine hydrochloride, 18.7 mg; chlorpheniramine maleate, 2 mg. Timed-release capsule: phenylpropanolamine hydrochloride, 50 mg; chlorpheniramine maleate, 4 mg

Use: For relief of symptoms of hay fever, allergies, sinusitis, and nasal congestion

Side Effects: Anxiety; blurred vision; chest pain; confusion; constipation; dry mouth; difficult and painful urination; dizziness; drowsiness;

headache; increased blood pressure; insomnia; loss of appetite; mild stimulation; nausea; nervousness; palpitations; rash; reduced sweating; tension; tremor; vomiting

Warnings: This product should be used with special caution by the elderly or debilitated, and by persons who have asthma, diabetes, enlarged prostate, glaucoma (certain types), heart disease, high blood pressure, kidney disease, liver disease, obstructed bladder, obstructed intestine, peptic ulcer, or thyroid disease. If you have any of these conditions, consult your doctor before taking this product. • It should not be used by pregnant or nursing women, or be given to newborn or premature infants. • This product may cause drowsiness. Do not take it if you must drive, operate heavy machinery, or perform other tasks requiring mental alertness. To prevent oversedation, avoid the use of alcohol or other drugs that have sedative properties. • This product interacts with alcohol, guanethidine, monoamine oxidase inhibitors, sedative drugs, and tricyclic antidepressants. If you are currently taking any drugs of these types, check with your doctor before taking this product. If you are unsure of the type or contents of your medications, ask your doctor or pharmacist. • Because this product reduces sweating, avoid excessive work or exercise in hot weather. • The capsule form of this product has sustained action; never increase the recommended dose or take it more frequently than directed. A serious overdose could result.

Comments: Many other conditions (some serious) mimic the common cold. If symptoms persist beyond one week, or if they occur regularly without regard to season, consult your doctor. • The effectiveness of this product may diminish after being taken for seven to ten days; consult your pharmacist about substituting a product with another antihistamine if this product begins to lose its effectiveness for you. • Chew gum or suck on ice chips or a piece of hard candy to reduce mouth dryness. • The chewable form of this product is intended for use by children. • The timed-release version should be taken every eight hours. It should not be crushed or chewed. It must be swallowed whole.

Acceptable: We prefer single-ingredient products rather than combination antihistamine-decongestant products like this one.

Allerest decongestant eyedrops

Manufacturer: Pharmacraft Division, Pennwalt Corporation

Dosage Form/Ingredients: Drop: benzalkonium chloride, .01%; edetate disodium, .01%; naphazoline chloride, 0.012%; unspecified quantity of methylcellulose

Use: For relief of minor eye irritation and redness

Side Effects: Allergic reactions (rash, itching, soreness); local irritation; momentary blurred vision

Warnings: Do not use this product if you have glaucoma. • Do not use this product for more than two consecutive days without checking with your doctor. • Keep this product out of the reach of children. If swallowed, this drug is likely to cause overstimulation in children. Call your doctor immediately if this product is accidentally swallowed. • Do not touch the dropper or bottle top to the eye or other tissue because contamination of the solution will result. • Use this product only for minor eye irritations. • The use of more than one eye product at a time may cause severe irritation to the eye.

Comments: This product works best when used correctly. Refer to the instructions on eye products in "Buying, Storing, and Using Drugs."

Acceptable: This product offers a satisfactory treatment for the relief of minor eye irritation.

Allerest nasal decongestant

Manufacturer: Pharmacraft Division, Pennwalt Corporation

Dosage Form/Ingredient: Nasal spray: phenylephrine hydrochloride, 0.5%

Use: For temporary relief of nasal congestion due to colds, sinusitis, hay fever, or other upper respiratory allergies

Side Effects: Blurred vision; burning; dryness of nasal mucosa; increased nasal congestion or discharge; sneezing, and/or stinging; dizziness; drowsiness; headache; insomnia; nervousness; palpitations; slight increase in blood pressure; stimulation

Warnings: This product should not be used by persons who have glaucoma (certain types). • It should be used with special caution by persons who have diabetes, advanced hardening of the arteries, heart disease, high blood pressure, or thyroid disease. If you have any of these conditions, consult your doctor before using this product. • This product interacts with monoamine oxidase inhibitors, thyroid preparations, and tricyclic antidepressants. If you are currently taking any drugs of these types, check with your doctor before taking this product. If you are unsure of the type or contents of your medications, ask your doctor or pharmacist.

Comments: To avoid side effects such as burning, sneezing, or stinging, and a "rebound" increase in nasal congestion and discharge, do not exceed the recommended dose, and do not use this product for more than three or four continuous days. • This product should not be used by more than one person; sharing the dispenser may spread infection. • This product works best when it is used correctly. Refer to the instructions for the use of nasal decongestants in the chapter on "Buying, Storing, and Using Drugs." • Many nasal drops or sprays on the market contain oxymetazoline hydrochloride. This drug has a duration of action of about 12 hours, and because it needs to be used less often, it is less likely to cause "rebound" nasal congestion during use. Therefore, we recommend a product containing oxymetazoline hydrochloride over this product, which does not contain the ingredient.

Acceptable: Although we prefer a product containing oxymetazoline hydrochloride, this product also offers an effective formula for treating the conditions specified.

Americaine
hemorrhoidal preparation

Manufacturer: American Critical Care

Dosage Forms/Ingredients: Ointment: benzocaine, 20%; benzethonium chloride, 0.1%; polyethylene glycol base. Suppository: benzocaine, 10%; benzethonium chloride, 0.1%; zinc oxide, 10.7%

Use: For relief of pain, burning, and itching of hemorrhoids and other irritated anorectal tissue

Side Effects: Irritation

Warnings: Sensitization (continued itching and redness) may occur with long-term and repeated use. • Certain ingredients in this product may cause an allergic reaction; do not use for longer than seven days at a time unless your doctor has advised you otherwise. • The suppository is not recommended for external hemorrhoids or bleeding internal hemorrhoids. Use the ointment form. Use caution when inserting applicator. • Never self-medicate for hemorrhoids if pain is continuous or throbbing, if bleeding or itching is excessive, or if you feel a large pressure within the rectum. • Discontinue use if irritation (pain, itching, or swelling) or rash occurs; consult your pharmacist.

Comments: Hemorrhoidal (pile) preparations relieve itching, reduce pain and inflammation, and check bleeding, but they do not heal, dry up, or give lasting relief from hemorrhoids. • Hemorrhoidal suppositories work best when they are used correctly. Refer to the instructions for their use in the chapter "Buying, Storing, and Using Drugs."

Acceptable: The benzocaine in this product will help relieve hemorrhoidal discomfort.

Americaine local anesthetic

Manufacturer: American Critical Care, Div. A/H Lambert Co.

Dosage Forms/Ingredients: Aerosol: benzocaine, 20%; water-dispersible base. Ointment: benzethonium chloride, 0.1%; benzocaine, 20%; water soluble PEG base

Use: For temporary relief of pain of sunburn and other minor burns, poison ivy, insect bites, and chapping

Side Effects: Local irritation; allergic rash; stinging

Warnings: Do not use this product on broken skin or on large areas of the body because it is possible that a toxic amount of medication may be absorbed. • Discontinue use if irritation (rash, itching, or swelling) or pain appears. Consult your physician. • The fluid in burn blisters helps healing of underlying tissue. Blisters should not be broken. If you have blisters that are extremely large or painful, contact your doctor. • The aerosol spray is flammable; do not use it while you are smoking or near a fire. Avoid inhalation and keep away from eyes. • Contact your doctor or pharmacist if this product does not bring relief within three or four days.

Comments: To relieve burn pain, take aspirin and cool the burned area. • If itching is intolerable, we recommend the use of a "wet soak" once daily. See the chapter "Buying, Storing, and Using Drugs" for directions. • Remember that ointments that are put on serious (second- or third-degree) burns will have to be taken off before definitive treatment can be given. Consult your doctor or pharmacist if you have any questions concerning the use of this product.

Preferred: This product contains an effective local anesthetic, benzocaine, in a high enough concentration to relieve the pain of sunburn and other minor burns.

Amphojel antacid

Manufacturer: Wyeth Laboratories

Dosage Forms/Ingredient: Suspension (content per teaspoon): aluminum hydroxide, 320 mg. Tablet: aluminum hydroxide, 300 mg, 600 mg

Use: For relief of acid indigestion, heartburn, and/or sour stomach; to treat excess phosphate levels in the blood

Side Effects: Constipation

Warnings: Long-term (several weeks) use of this product may lead to intestinal obstruction and dehydration. Phosphate depletion may occur, leading to weakness, loss of appetite, and eventually bone pain. Phosphate depletion may be prevented by drinking at least one glass of milk a day. • Do not take this product within two hours of a dose of a tetracycline antibiotic. • Consult your physician or pharmacist before taking this product if you are already taking iron, a vitamin-mineral product, chlorpromazine, phenytoin, digoxin, quinidine, or warfarin, or if you are

unsure of the type and contents of the medications you are taking. •
Never self-medicate with this product if your symptoms occur regularly
(two or three or more times a month). Consult your doctor if the symptoms
are worse than usual, if you have chest pains or feel "tightness" in the
chest, or if you are sweating or short of breath. In fact, we do not recommend self-treatment for severe attacks of heartburn, indigestion, or
stomach upset in any circumstances. If you do decide that your symptoms are mild enough to warrant self-medication, limit treatment to two
weeks. If symptoms persist, consult your doctor.

Comments: To prevent constipation, drink at least eight glasses of
water a day. If constipation persists, consult your doctor or pharmacist. •
This product must be taken exactly as directed on the label, unless your
doctor has instructed you otherwise. Never skip a dose just because you
feel better. If you grow tired of the taste, ask your pharmacist to suggest a
different product. • The suspension form of this product is superior to the
tablet form and should be used unless you have been specifically
directed to use the tablet.

*Fair: We prefer antacid products combining aluminum and magnesium; a
product containing only aluminum is more likely to cause constipation.*

Anacin analgesic

Manufacturer: Whitehall Laboratories

Dosage Forms/Ingredients: Tablet, Capsule: aspirin, 400 mg; caffeine,
32 mg

Use: For the relief of pain of headache, toothache, sprains, muscular
aches, nerve inflammation, menstruation; for the relief of discomforts
and fevers of colds; for the temporary relief of minor aches and pains of
arthritis and rheumatism

Side Effects: Dizziness; mental confusion; mild stimulation; nausea
and vomiting; ringing in the ears; slight blood loss; sweating

Warnings: Persons with asthma, hay fever, or other allergies should be
extremely careful about using this product. This product may interfere
with the treatment of gout. This product may cause an increased bleeding
tendency and should not be taken by persons with a history of bleeding,
peptic ulcer, or stomach bleeding. If you have any of these conditions,
consult your doctor or pharmacist before using this medication. • Do not
use this product if you are consuming alcohol, or taking methotrexate,
oral anticoagulants, oral antidiabetics, probenecid, steroids, and/or
sulfinpyrazone; if you are unsure of the type or contents of your medications, ask your doctor or pharmacist. • The dosage instructions listed on
the package should be followed carefully; toxicity may occur in adults or
children with repeated doses.

Comments: You can save money by taking plain aspirin and a cup of
coffee or tea instead of this product; there is no evidence that combinations of ingredients are more effective than similar doses of a single-
ingredient product. • This product contains extra aspirin per tablet, but
you can get about the same amount of aspirin in three regular aspirin
tablets as you would in two of these. • The caffeine in this product may
have a slight stimulant effect, but has no pain-relieving value.

*Unacceptable: Since it has not been proven that caffeine has any pain-
relieving value, the caffeine in this product appears to be unnecessary.
We consider the product overpriced.*

80

Anacin, Maximum Strength analgesic

Manufacturer: Whitehall Laboratories
Dosage Form/Ingredients: Tablet: aspirin, 500 mg; caffeine, 32 mg
Use: For the relief of pain of headache, toothache, sprains, muscular aches, nerve inflammation, menstruation; for the relief of discomforts and fever of colds; for the temporary relief of minor aches and pains of arthritis and rheumatism
Side Effects: Dizziness; mental confusion; mild stimulation; nausea and vomiting; ringing in the ears; slight blood loss; sweating
Warnings: Persons with asthma, hay fever, or other allergies should be extremely careful about using this product. This product may interfere with the treatment of gout. This product may cause an increased bleeding tendency and should not be taken by persons with a history of bleeding, peptic ulcer, or stomach bleeding. If you have any of these conditions, consult your doctor or pharmacist before using this medication. • Do not use this product if you are consuming alcohol, or taking methotrexate, oral anticoagulants, oral antidiabetics, probenecid, steroids, and/or sulfinpyrazone; if you are unsure of the type or contents of your medications, ask your doctor or pharmacist. • The dosage instructions listed on the package should be followed carefully; toxicity may occur in adults or children with repeated doses.
Comments: You can save money by taking plain aspirin and a cup of coffee or tea instead of this product; there is no evidence that combinations of ingredients are more effective than similar doses of a single-ingredient product. • This product contains extra aspirin per tablet, but you can get about the same amount of aspirin in three regular aspirin tablets as you would in two of these. • The caffeine in this product may have a slight stimulant effect, but has no pain-relieving value.

Unacceptable: Since it has not been proven that caffeine has any pain-relieving value, the caffeine in this product appears to be unnecessary. We consider the product overpriced.

Anacin-3 analgesic

Manufacturer: Whitehall Laboratories
Dosage Form/Ingredients: Tablet: acetaminophen, 500 mg; caffeine, 32 mg
Use: For the relief of pain of headache, toothache, sinusitis, muscular aches and strains, menstruation, colds or "flu"; for the temporary relief of minor arthritis pain and the reduction of fever
Side Effects: When taken in overdose: blood disorders; rash; mild stimulation
Warnings: This product should not be taken by persons with certain blood disorders or with heart, lung, liver, or kidney disease without a doctor's approval. • When taken in overdose, acetaminophen is more toxic than aspirin. The dosage instructions listed on the package should be followed carefully; toxicity may occur in adults or children with repeated doses.
Comments: You can save money by taking plain acetaminophen instead of this product; there is no evidence that combinations of ingredients are more effective than similar doses of a single-ingredient product. • The caffeine this product may have a slight stimulant effect, but has no pain-relieving value. • Acetaminophen does not relieve inflammation, so if pain is caused by swelling or inflammation, it should not be used. Aspirin is better.

Unacceptable: Since it has not been proven that caffeine has any pain-relieving value, the caffeine in this product appears to be unnecessary. We consider the product overpriced.

Answer urine test for pregnancy

Manufacturer: Diagnostic Testing, Inc.
Product Form: Test tube and testing materials
Use: To test urine for determination of pregnancy
Comments: Use only a urine sample that has been freshly collected in the morning. • For accurate results, follow package directions carefully. The test tube must be left undisturbed and unvibrated for two hours, and must be kept away from heat and direct sunlight. Read the results between two and four hours after starting the test. If a brown ring forms in the bottom of the test tube, you should assume that you are pregnant. Consult your doctor. • Test results may be interfered with if the urine contains a large quantity of protein, or if the patient is taking medication. • This test is highly accurate, except if it is performed earlier than nine days after the date on which the first missed menstrual period would have begun.

Acceptable: Pregnancy test kits are convenient, but may not be economical. A negative result often requires retesting; a positive result indicates that you should see a doctor who will probably want to confirm the results. Either way you are likely to pay for two tests.

Anusol hemorrhoidal preparation

Manufacturer: Parke-Davis
Dosage Forms/Ingredients: Suppository: benzyl benzoate, 1.2%; bismuth resorcin compound, 1.75%; bismuth subgallate, 2.25%; Peruvian balsam, 1.8%; zinc oxide, 11%; vegetable oil base. Ointment: benzyl benzoate, 1.2%; Peruvian balsam, 1.8%; pramoxine hydrochloride, 1%, zinc oxide, 11%
Use: Relief of pain, itching, and burning of hemorrhoids and other irritated anorectal tissue
Side Effects: Irritation
Warnings: Sensitization (continued itching and redness) may occur with long-term and repeated use. • Certain ingredients in this product may cause an allergic reaction; do not use for longer than seven days at a time unless your doctor has advised you otherwise. • The suppository is not recommended for external hemorrhoids or bleeding internal hemorrhoids. Use the ointment form. Use caution when inserting applicator. • Never self-medicate for hemorrhoids if pain is continuous or throbbing, if bleeding or itching is excessive, or if you feel a large pressure within the rectum. • Discontinue use if irritation (pain, itching, or swelling) or rash occurs; consult your pharmacist.
Comments: Hemorrhoidal (pile) preparations relieve itching, reduce pain and inflammation, and check bleeding, but they do not heal, dry up, or give lasting relief from hemorrhoids. • Hemorrhoidal suppositories work best when they are used correctly. Refer to the instructions for their use in the chapter "Buying, Storing, and Using Drugs."
Fair: Better-formulated products are available.

Appedrine appetite suppressant

Manufacturer: Thompson Medical Company, Inc.

Dosage Form/Ingredients: Tablet: phenylpropanolamine hydrochloride, 25 mg; caffeine, 100 mg; vitamin A, 1667 IU; vitamin D, 133 IU; vitamin E, 10 IU; vitamin B_1, 0.5 mg; vitamin B_2, 0.6 mg; vitamin B_3, 6.7 mg; vitamin B_5, 3.3 mg; vitamin B_6, 0.7 mg; vitamin B_{12}, 2 mcg; vitamin C, 20 mg; folic acid, 0.13 mg; unspecified quantity of sodium carboxymethylcellulose

Use: As an aid in dietary control

Side Effects: Blurred vision; diarrhea; nausea; dizziness; drowsiness; headache; increase in blood pressure, blood sugar, heart rate, and thyroid activity; insomnia; nervousness; palpitations. In larger than the recommended dose: irregular heartbeat; nasal dryness; upset stomach

Warnings: Persons with heart disease, high blood pressure, diabetes, kidney or thyroid disease; children under 16 years of age; and pregnant or nursing women should not use this product. Consult your doctor for recommendations. • This product interacts with alcohol, guanethidine, monoamine oxidase inhibitors, sedative drugs, and tricyclic antidepressants. If you are currently taking any of these drugs, or if you are unsure of the type or contents of your medications, consult your doctor or pharmacist before taking this product. • Avoid taking this drug while using a decongestant. • Avoid continuous use for longer than three months. • Discontinue use if you experience rapid pulse, dizziness, or palpitations.

Comments: During the first week of therapy with this product, expect increased frequency of urination. • Many medical authorities believe that the ingredient phenylpropanolamine does not help in weight-loss programs. However, the FDA Review Panel has reported that it is effective. • If you want to use this product, remember that you become tolerant to any beneficial effects after a couple of weeks. After each two weeks of use, stop for one week, then resume use. • The primary value in a product of this nature is in following the caloric reduction plan that goes with it. • If you want to take vitamins, buy them separately from your appetite suppressant so that you can be sure of getting the dosages you want.

Unacceptable: We recommend that specific health needs be treated singly. If you need vitamins, buy them separately from your appetite suppressant.

A.R.M. allergy remedy

Manufacturer: Menley & James Laboratories

Dosage Form/Ingredients: Tablet: chlorpheniramine maleate, 4 mg; phenylpropanolamine hydrochloride, 37.5 mg

Use: For relief of symptoms of hay fever, allergies, sinusitis, and nasal congestion

Side Effects: Anxiety; blurred vision; chest pain; confusion; constipation; dry mouth; difficult and painful urination; dizziness; drowsiness; headache; increased blood pressure; insomnia; loss of appetite; mild stimulation; nausea; nervousness; palpitations; rash; reduced sweating; tension; tremor; vomiting

Warnings: This product should be used with special caution by the elderly or debilitated, and by persons who have asthma, diabetes, an enlarged prostate, glaucoma (certain types), heart disease, high blood pressure, kidney disease, liver disease, obstructed bladder, obstructed intestine, peptic ulcer, or thyroid disease. If you have any of these conditions, consult your doctor before taking this product. • It should not be used by pregnant or nursing women, or be given to newborn or premature infants. • This product may cause drowsiness. Do not take it if you must drive, operate heavy machinery, or perform other tasks requiring mental alertness. To prevent oversedation, avoid the use of alcohol or other drugs that have sedative properties. • This product interacts with alcohol, guanethidine, monoamine oxidase inhibitors, sedative drugs, and tricyclic antidepressants. If you are currently taking any drugs of these types, check with your doctor before taking this product. If you are unsure of the type or contents of your medications, ask your doctor or pharmacist. • Because this product reduces sweating, avoid excessive work or exercise in hot weather.

Comments: Many other conditions (some serious) mimic the common cold. If symptoms persist beyond one week, or if they occur regularly without regard to season, consult your doctor. • The effectiveness of this product may diminish after being taken for seven to ten days; consult your pharmacist about substituting a product with another antihistamine if this product begins to lose its effectiveness for you. • Chew gum or suck on ice chips or a piece of hard candy to reduce mouth dryness.

Acceptable: We prefer single-ingredient products rather than combination antihistamine-decongestant products like this one.

Arthritis Pain Formula analgesic

Manufacturer: Whitehall Laboratories

Dosage Form/Ingredients: Tablet: micronized aspirin, 486 mg; dried aluminum hydroxide gel, 20 mg; magnesium hydroxide, 60 mg

Use: For the relief of pain of headache, temporary relief of minor arthritic pain, discomforts and fever of colds and "flu," menstrual cramps, muscle aches and pains, toothache, inflammation, fever

Side Effects: Dizziness; mental confusion; nausea and vomiting; ringing in the ears; slight blood loss; sweating

Warnings: Persons with kidney disease, asthma, hay fever, or other allergies should be extremely careful about using this product. The product may interfere with the treatment of gout. This product may cause an increased bleeding tendency and should not be taken by persons with a history of bleeding, peptic ulcer, or stomach bleeding. If you have any of these conditions, consult your doctor or pharmacist before using this medication. • Do not use this product if you are consuming alcohol, or taking methotrexate, oral anticoagulants, oral antidiabetics, probenecid, steroids, and/or sulfinpyrazone; if you are unsure of the type or contents of your medications, ask your doctor or pharmacist. • The dosage instructions listed on the package should be followed carefully; toxicity may occur in adults or children with repeated doses.

Comments: Magnesium interacts with tetracycline antibiotics. There may not be enough magnesium in this product to cause any problem, but if you are taking a tetracycline antibiotic in addition to this product, separate the dosages by at least two hours. • Pain-relief tablets, such as this product, that contain salts of magnesium or aluminum are known as buffered tablets. Such products dissolve faster than unbuffered products, but there is no evidence that they relieve pain faster or better than those products that do not contain buffers. Buffered tablets may be less likely to cause gastric upset in some people. • This product contains extra aspirin per tablet, but you can get about the same amount of aspirin in three regular aspirin tablets as you would in two of these.

Acceptable: This is a buffered product. Although buffered aspirin may produce less gastric upset in some people, there is no proof that it relieves pain faster than a nonbuffered product.

Arthritis Strength Bufferin analgesic

Manufacturer: Bristol-Myers Products

Dosage Form/Ingredients: Tablet: aspirin, 486 mg; aluminum glycinate, 72.9 mg; magnesium carbonate, 145.8 mg

Use: For the relief of pain of headache, temporary relief of minor arthritic pain, discomforts and fever of colds and "flu," menstrual cramps, muscle aches and pains, toothache, inflammation, fever

Side Effects: Dizziness; mental confusion; nausea and vomiting; ringing in the ears; slight blood loss; sweating

Warnings: Persons with kidney disease, asthma, hay fever, or other allergies should be extremely careful about using this product. The product may interfere with the treatment of gout. This product may cause an increased bleeding tendency and should not be taken by persons with a history of bleeding, peptic ulcer, or stomach bleeding. If you have any of these conditions, consult your doctor or pharmacist before using this medication. • Do not use this product if you are consuming alcohol, or taking methotrexate, oral anticoagulants, oral antidiabetics, probenecid, steroids, and/or sulfinpyrazone; if you are unsure of the type or contents of your medications, ask your doctor or pharmacist. • The dosage instructions listed on the package should be followed carefully; toxicity may occur in adults or children with repeated doses.

Comments: Magnesium interacts with tetracycline antibiotics. There may not be enough magnesium in this product to cause any problem, but if you are taking a tetracycline antibiotic in addition to this product, separate the dosages by at least two hours. • Pain-relief tablets, such as this product, that contain salts of magnesium or aluminum are known as buffered tablets. Such products dissolve faster than unbuffered products, but there is no evidence that they relieve pain faster or better than those products that do not contain buffers. Buffered tablets may be less likely to cause gastric upset in some people. • This product contains extra aspirin per tablet, but you can get about the same amount of aspirin in three regular aspirin tablets as you would in two of these.

Acceptable: This is a buffered product. Although buffered aspirin may produce less gastric upset in some people, there is no proof that it relieves pain faster than a nonbuffered product.

Ascriptin A/D analgesic

Manufacturer: William H. Rorer, Inc.

Dosage Form/Ingredients: Tablet: aspirin, 325 mg; magnesium-aluminum hydroxide, 300 mg

Use: For the relief of pain of headache, temporary relief of minor arthritic pain, discomforts and fever of colds and "flu," menstrual cramps, muscle aches and pains, toothache, inflammation, fever

Side Effects: Dizziness; mental confusion; nausea and vomiting; ringing in the ears; slight blood loss; sweating

Warnings: Persons with kidney disease, asthma, hay fever, or other allergies should be extremely careful about using this product. The product may interfere with the treatment of gout. This product may cause an increased bleeding tendency and should not be taken by persons with a history of bleeding, peptic ulcer, or stomach bleeding. If you have any of these conditions, consult your doctor or pharmacist before using this medication. • Do not use this product if you are consuming alcohol, or taking methotrexate, oral anticoagulants, oral antidiabetics, probenecid, steroids, and/or sulfinpyrazone; if you are unsure of the type or contents of your medications, ask your doctor or pharmacist. • The dosage instructions listed on the package should be followed carefully; toxicity may occur in adults or children with repeated doses.

Comments: Magnesium interacts with tetracycline antibiotics. There may not be enough magnesium in this product to cause any problem, but if you are taking a tetracycline antibiotic in addition to this product, separate the dosages by at least two hours. • Pain-relief tablets, such as this product, that contain salts of magnesium or aluminum are known as buffered tablets. Such products dissolve faster than unbuffered products, but there is no evidence that they relieve pain faster or better than those products that do not contain buffers. Buffered tablets may be less likely to cause gastric upset in some people.

Acceptable: This is a buffered product. Although buffered aspirin may produce less gastric upset in some people, there is no proof that it relieves pain faster than a nonbuffered product.

Ascriptin analgesic

Manufacturer: William H. Rorer, Inc.

Dosage Form/Ingredients: Tablet: aspirin, 325 mg; magnesium-aluminum hydroxide, 150 mg

Use: For the relief of pain of headache, temporary relief of minor arthritic pain, discomforts and fever of colds and "flu," menstrual cramps, muscle aches and pains, toothache, inflammation, fever

Side Effects: Dizziness, mental confusion; nausea and vomiting; ringing in the ears; slight blood loss; sweating

Warnings: Persons with kidney disease, asthma, hay fever, or other allergies should be extremely careful about using this product. The product may interfere with the treatment of gout. This product may cause an increased bleeding tendency and should not be taken by persons with a history of bleeding, peptic ulcer, or stomach bleeding. If you have any of these conditions, consult your doctor or pharmacist before using this medication. • Do not use this product if you are consuming alcohol, or taking methotrexate, oral anticoagulants, oral antidiabetics, probenecid, steroids, and/or sulfinpyrazone; if you are unsure of the type or contents of your medications, ask your doctor or pharmacist. • The dosage instructions listed on the package should be followed carefully; toxicity may occur in adults or children with repeated doses.

Comments: Magnesium interacts with tetracycline antibiotics. There may not be enough magnesium in this product to cause any problem, but if you are taking a tetracycline antibiotic in addition to this product, separate the dosages by at least two hours. • Pain-relief tablets, such as this product, that contain salts of magnesium or aluminum are known as buffered tablets. Such products dissolve faster than unbuffered products, but there is no evidence that they relieve pain faster or better than those products that do not contain buffers. Buffered tablets may be less likely to cause gastric upset in some people.

Acceptable: This is a buffered product. Although buffered aspirin may produce less gastric upset in some people, there is no proof that it relieves pain faster than a nonbuffered product.

Aspercreme muscular pain remedy

Manufacturer: Thompson Medical Company, Inc.

Dosage Form/Ingredient: Lotion: triethanolamine salicylate, 10%

Use: Used externally to temporarily relieve pain in muscles and other areas.

Side Effects: Allergic reactions (rash, itching, soreness); local irritation; local numbness; peeling of skin

Warnings: This product is for external use only. • Do not use it on broken or irritated skin, or on large areas of the body; keep it away from the eyes. • If the pain in muscles or other areas persists, call your doctor. • While you are using this product, avoid exposure to direct sunlight, heat lamp, or sun lamp. • Discontinue use and consult your pharmacist if irritation (rash, itching, or swelling) or pain occurs. • Before using this product on a child under 12 years of age, consult your doctor. • Children might be attracted to the smell of this product; it should be stored safely out of their reach. • If a child swallows some of this product, call your doctor immediately.

Comments: Be sure to rub this product vigorously into the skin.

Preferred: *The salicylate in this product provides an effective treatment for the temporary relief of muscle pain.*

aspirin analgesic

Manufacturer: Various

Dosage Form: Tablet: 325 mg (usually)

Use: For the relief of pain of headache, temporary relief of minor arthritic pain, discomforts and fever of colds and "flu," menstrual cramps, muscle aches and pains, toothache, inflammation, fever

Side Effects: Dizziness; mental confusion; nausea and vomiting; ringing in the ears; slight blood loss; sweating

Warnings: Persons with kidney disease, asthma, hay fever, or other allergies should be extremely careful about using this product. The product may interfere with the treatment of gout. This product may cause an increased bleeding tendency and should not be taken by persons with a history of bleeding, peptic ulcer, or stomach bleeding. If you have any of these conditions, consult your doctor or pharmacist before using this medication. • Do not use this product if you are consuming alcohol, or taking methotrexate, oral anticoagulants, oral antidiabetics, probenecid, steroids, and/or sulfinpyrazone; if you are unsure of the type or contents of your medications, ask your doctor or pharmacist. • The dosage instructions listed on the package should be followed carefully; toxicity may occur in adults or children with repeated doses.

Preferred: *Aspirin is the treatment of choice for most minor pains.*

Ayds appetite suppressant

Manufacturer: Purex Corporation

Dosage Form/Ingredient: Drops (per 12 drops): phenylpropanolamine hydrochloride, 25 mg

Use: As an aid in dietary control

Side Effects: Blurred vision; diarrhea; nausea; dizziness; drowsiness; headache; increase in blood pressure, blood sugar, heart rate, and thyroid activity; insomnia; nervousness; palpitations. In larger than the recommended dose: irregular heartbeat; nasal dryness; upset stomach

Warnings: Persons with heart disease, high blood pressure, diabetes, kidney or thyroid disease; children under 16 years of age; and pregnant or nursing women should not use this product. Consult your doctor for recommendations. • This product interacts with alcohol, guanethidine, monoamine oxidase inhibitors, sedative drugs, and tricyclic antidepressants. If you are currently taking any of these drugs, or if you are unsure of the type or contents of your medications, consult your doctor or pharmacist. • Avoid taking this drug while using a decongestant. • Avoid continuous use for longer than three months. • Discontinue use if you experience rapid pulse, dizziness, or palpitations.

Comments: During the first week of therapy with this product, expect increased frequency of urination. • Many medical authorities believe that the ingredient phenylpropanolamine does not help in weight-loss programs. However, the FDA Review Panel has reported that it is effective. • If you want to use this product, remember that you become tolerant to any beneficial effects after a couple of weeks. After each two weeks of use, stop for one week, then resume use. • The primary value in a product of this nature is in following the caloric reduction plan that goes with it.

Acceptable: This product is preferable to other available dietary aids because it uses a single effective ingredient.

Baciguent first-aid product

Manufacturer: The Upjohn Co.

Dosage Form/Ingredient: Ointment (content per gram): bacitracin, 500 units

Use: To prevent infection from cuts and abrasions; to treat impetigo

Side Effects: Allergic reaction (rash, itching, soreness); local irritation

Warnings: Diabetics and persons with impaired circulation should not use this product. • If the condition seems to get worse while using this product, call your doctor at once. • If the infection does not clear in four or five days, consult your doctor or pharmacist.

Comments: Apply this product at least three times daily to maintain effectiveness. • If using this product to treat impetigo, apply it with a cotton-tipped applicator. Do not touch the cotton part with your fingers after applying the medication. Wash your hands thoroughly after applying medication to impetigo sores.

Preferred: This product is effective for the uses specified.

Bactine first-aid product

Manufacturer: Miles Laboratories, Inc.

Dosage Forms/Ingredients: Aerosol spray, Liquid spray: alcohol, 3.17%; benzalkonium chloride, 0.13%

Use: To disinfect minor burns, cuts, and scrapes on skin

Side Effects: Allergy; local irritation

Warnings: Do not use this product on animal bites or puncture wounds. • Do not use it on large areas of the body, or for more than ten consecutive days. • Do not inhale the aerosol spray.

Acceptable: This product is effective for the use specified.

Banalg muscular pain remedy

Manufacturer: O'Neal, Jones and Feldman

Dosage Form/Ingredients: Lotion: unspecified quantities of menthol, methyl salicylate, camphor, and eucalyptus oil

Use: Used externally to temporarily relieve pain in muscles and other areas

Side Effects: Allergic reactions (rash, itching, soreness); local irritation; local numbness

Warnings: This product is for external use only. • Do not use it on broken or irritated skin, or on large areas of the body; keep it away from the eyes. • If the pain in muscles or other areas persists, call your doctor. • While you are using this product, avoid exposure to direct sunlight, heat lamp, or sun lamp. • Discontinue use and consult your pharmacist if irritation (rash, itching, or swelling) or pain occurs. • Before using this product on a child under 12 years of age, consult your doctor. • Children might be attracted to the smell of this product; it should be stored safely out of their reach. • If a child swallows some of this product, call your doctor immediately. • Do not rub this product into the skin.

Not Evaluated: The manufacturer fails to provide sufficient information about this product on which to base an evaluation.

Bayer Aspirin analgesic

Manufacturer: Glenbrook Laboratories
Dosage Form/Ingredient: Tablet: aspirin, 325 mg
Use: For the relief of pain of headache, temporary relief of minor arthritic pain, discomforts and fever of colds and "flu," menstrual cramps, muscle aches and pains, toothache, inflammation, fever
Side Effects: Dizziness; mental confusion; nausea and vomiting; ringing in the ears; slight blood loss; sweating
Warnings: Persons with kidney disease, asthma, hay fever, or other allergies should be extremely careful about using this product. The product may interfere with the treatment of gout. This product may cause an increased bleeding tendency and should not be taken by persons with a history of bleeding, peptic ulcer, or stomach bleeding. If you have any of these conditions, consult your doctor or pharmacist before using this medication. • Do not use this product if you are consuming alcohol, or taking methotrexate, oral anticoagulants, oral antidiabetics, probenecid, steroids, and/or sulfinpyrazone; if you are unsure of the type or contents of your medications, ask your doctor or pharmacist. • The dosage instructions listed on the package should be followed carefully; toxicity may occur in adults or children with repeated doses.
Comments: Generic substitutes for this product are available and may save you money. Ask your pharmacist for assistance.
Preferred: Aspirin is the treatment of choice for most minor pains.

Bayer Children's Chewable Aspirin analgesic

Manufacturer: Glenbrook Laboratories
Dosage Form/Ingredient: Chewable tablet: aspirin, 81 mg
Use: For the relief of pain of headache, toothache, sprains, muscular aches; for the relief of discomforts and fevers of colds or "flu," or following immunizations; for the temporary relief of minor pains of arthritis and rheumatism
Side Effects: Dizziness; mental confusion; nausea and vomiting; ringing in the ears; slight blood loss; sweating
Warnings: Persons with kidney disease, asthma, hay fever, or other allergies should be extremely careful about using this product. The product may interfere with the treatment of gout. This product may cause an increased bleeding tendency and should not be taken by persons with a history of bleeding, peptic ulcer, or stomach bleeding. If you or your child have any of these conditions, consult your doctor or pharmacist before using this medication. • This product should not be taken at the same

time as alcohol, methotrexate, oral anticoagulants, oral antidiabetics, probenecid, steroids, or sulfinpyrazone; if you are unsure of the type or contents of your or your child's medications, ask your doctor or pharmacist. • The dosage instructions listed on the package should be followed carefully; toxicity may occur in adults or children with repeated doses. • Chewable tablets are very appealing to children. Keep them out of children's reach between doses.

Comments: These tablets should be chewed, not swallowed whole. • Generic substitutes for this product are available and may save you money. Ask your pharmacist for assistance.

Preferred: This product provides pure aspirin, the treatment of choice for most minor pains, in a convenient dosage form.

Bayer Children's cold remedy

Manufacturer: Glenbrook Laboratories

Dosage Form/Ingredients: Chewable tablet: phenylpropanolamine hydrochloride, 3.125 mg; aspirin, 81 mg

Use: To reduce fever, relieve nasal congestion and minor aches and pains due to colds and "flu"

Side Effects: Blurred vision; dizziness; drowsiness or stimulation; dry mouth; headache; insomnia; nervousness; nausea; palpitations; ringing in the ears; slight blood loss; slight increase in blood pressure; vomiting

Warnings: This product should be used with special caution by persons who have diabetes, heart disease, high blood pressure, peptic ulcer, bleeding or stomach bleeding, gout, asthma, or thyroid disease. If your child has any of these conditions, consult your doctor before administering this product. • This product should not be given to newborn or premature infants or taken by pregnant or nursing women. • This product interacts with alcohol, ammonium chloride, guanethidine, methotrexate, monoamine oxidase inhibitors, oral anticoagulants, oral antidiabetics, probenecid, sedative drugs, steroids, sulfinpyrazone, tricyclic antidepressants, and vitamin C. If your child is currently taking any drugs of these types, check with your doctor before administering this product. If you are unsure of the type or contents of your child's medications, ask your doctor or pharmacist. • The dosage instructions listed on the package should be followed carefully; toxicity may occur in adults or children with repeated doses. • Be sure to keep the tablets out of the reach of your children between doses.

Comments: Many other conditions (some serious) mimic the common cold. If symptoms persist beyond one week, or if they occur regularly without regard to season, consult your doctor. • The effectiveness of this product may diminish after being taken regularly for seven to ten days; consult your pharmacist about substituting another medication if this product begins to lose its effectiveness for your child. • Generic versions of this product are available and may save you money. Consult your pharmacist. • Have your child chew gum or suck on ice chips to reduce mouth dryness.

Acceptable: We prefer single-ingredient products rather than analgesic-decongestant combination products like this one.

Bayer Decongestant cold and allergy remedy

Manufacturer: Glenbrook Laboratories

Dosage Form/Ingredients: Tablet: phenylpropanolamine hydrochloride, 12.5 mg; chlorpheniramine maleate, 2 mg; aspirin, 325 mg

Use: To relieve nasal congestion, fever, aches, pains, and general discomfort due to colds or upper respiratory allergies

Side Effects: Anxiety; blurred vision; chest pain; confusion; constipation; difficult and painful urination; dizziness; drowsiness; dry mouth; headache; increased blood pressure; insomnia; loss of appetite; mild stimulation; nausea; nervousness; palpitations; rash; reduced sweating; ringing in the ears; slight blood loss; tension; tremor; vomiting

Warnings: This product should be used with special caution by the elderly or debilitated, and by persons who have asthma, diabetes, enlarged prostate, kidney disease, liver disease, obstructed bladder, obstructed intestine, peptic ulcer, bleeding or stomach bleeding, gout, or thyroid disease. If you have any of these conditions, consult your doctor before taking this product. • It should not be used by pregnant or nursing women, or be given to newborn or premature infants. • This product may cause drowsiness. Do not take it if you must drive, operate heavy machinery, or perform other tasks requiring mental alertness. To prevent oversedation, avoid the use of alcohol or other drugs that have sedative properties. • This product interacts with alcohol, ammonium chloride, guanethidine, methotrexate, monoamine oxidase inhibitors, oral anticoagulants, oral antidiabetics, probenecid, sedative drugs, steroids, sulfinpyrazone, tricyclic antidepressants, and vitamin C. If you are currently taking any drugs of these types, check with your doctor before taking this product. If you are unsure of the type of contents of your medications, ask your doctor or pharmacist. • Because this product reduces sweating, avoid excessive work or exercise in hot weather. • The dosage instructions listed on the package should be followed carefully; toxicity may occur in adults or children with repeated doses.

Comments: Many other conditions (some serious) mimic the common cold. If symptoms persist beyond one week or if they occur regularly without regard to season, consult your doctor. • The effectiveness of this product may diminish after being taken for seven to ten days; consult your pharmacist about substituting another product if this one begins to lose its effectiveness for you. • Chew gum or suck on ice chips or a piece of hard candy to reduce mouth dryness.

Acceptable: We prefer single-ingredient products rather than combination analgesic-antihistamine-decongestant products like this one.

Bayer Timed-Release Aspirin analgesic

Manufacturer: Glenbrook Laboratories

Dosage Form/Ingredient: Timed-release tablet: aspirin, 650 mg

Use: For the relief of pain of headache, temporary relief of minor arthritic pain, discomforts and fever of colds and "flu," menstrual cramps, muscle aches and pains, toothache, inflammation, fever

Side Effects: Dizziness; mental confusion; nausea and vomiting; ringing in the ears; slight blood loss; sweating

Warnings: Persons with asthma, hay fever, or other allergies should be extremely careful about using this product. The product may interfere with the treatment of gout. This product may cause an increased bleeding tendency and should not be taken by persons with a history of bleeding, peptic ulcer, or stomach bleeding. If you have any of these conditions, consult your doctor or pharmacist before using this medication. • Do not use this product if you are consuming alcohol, or taking methotrexate, oral anticoagulants, oral antidiabetics, probenecid, steroids, and/or sulfinpyrazone; if you are unsure of the type or contents of your medications, ask your doctor or pharmacist. • The dosage instructions listed on the package should be followed carefully; toxicity may occur in adults or children with repeated doses.

Comments: This product should not be crushed or chewed; it must be swallowed whole. • Generic substitutes for this product are available and may save you money. Ask your pharmacist for assistance.

Fair: This is an overpriced version of aspirin. The sustained release formulation does not justify the product's cost.

Benadryl antihistamine cream

Manufacturer: Parke-Davis Company

Dosage Form/Ingredients: Cream: diphenhydramine hydrochloride, 2%; water-soluble base

Use: For temporary relief of itching due to eczema, hives, poison ivy, insect bites, and other skin irritations

Side Effects: Allergic rash; local irritation; stinging

Warnings: Do not use this product on broken skin or on large areas of the body because it is possible that a toxic amount of medication may be absorbed. • Discontinue use if irritation (rash, itching, or swelling) or pain appears. Consult your physician. • Do not use this product in or near the eyes or on mucous membranes. • Contact your doctor or pharmacist if this product does not bring relief within three or four days.

Comments: If itching is intolerable, we recommend the use of a "wet soak" once daily. See the chapter "Buying, Storing, and Using Drugs" for directions. • Consult your doctor or pharmacist if you have any questions concerning the use of this product.

Acceptable: This product is effective for the uses specified, but it has a high potential for causing irritation.

Ben-Gay muscular pain remedy

Manufacturer: Leeming/Pacquin, Division of Pfizer Inc.

Dosage Forms/Ingredients: Lotion: menthol, 7%; methyl salicylate, 15%. Ointment: menthol, 16%; methyl salicylate 18.3%. Greaseless ointment: menthol, 10%; methyl salicylate, 15%

Use: Used externally to temporarily relieve pain in muscles and other areas

Side Effects: Allergic reactions (rash, itching, soreness); local irritation; local numbness

Warnings: This product is for external use only. • Do not use it on broken or irritated skin, or on large areas of the body; keep it away from the eyes. • If the pain in muscles or other areas persists, call your doctor. • While you are using this product, avoid exposure to direct sunlight, heat lamp, or sun lamp. • Discontinue use and consult your pharmacist if irritation (rash, itching, or swelling) or pain occurs. • Before using this product on a child under 12 years of age, consult your doctor. • Children might be attracted to the smell of this product; it should be stored safely out of their reach. • If a child swallows some of this product, call your doctor immediately.

Comments: Be sure to rub this product vigorously into the skin.

Preferred: The methyl salicylate in this product provides an effective treatment for the temporary relief of muscle pain.

Benylin DM cough remedy

Manufacturer: Parke-Davis
Dosage Form/Ingredients: Liquid (content per teaspoon): dextromethorphan hydrobromide, 10 mg; alcohol, 5%
Use: For temporary relief of coughs due to colds or minor throat and bronchial irritation
Side Effects: Drowsiness; nausea; vomiting
Warnings: Do not give this product to children under six years of age. • If your cough persists, or is accompanied by high fever, consult your doctor promptly. • This product interacts with monoamine oxidase inhibitors. If you are currently taking any drugs of this type, check with your doctor before taking this product. If you are unsure of the type or contents of your medications, ask your doctor or pharmacist. • Do not use this product to treat chronic coughs, such as those from smoking or asthma. • Do not use this product to treat productive (hacking) coughs that produce phlegm.

Preferred: Dextromethorphan hydrobromide has been proven effective as a cough suppressant.

Benzedrex nasal decongestant

Manufacturer: Menley & James Laboratories
Dosage Form/Ingredients: Inhaler: prophylhexedrine, 250 mg; menthol, 12.5 mg; unspecified quantity of aromatics
Use: For temporary relief of nasal congestion due to colds, sinusitis, hay fever, or other upper respiratory allergies
Side Effects: Blurred vision; burning, dryness of nasal mucosa; increased nasal congestion or discharge; sneezing, and/or stinging; dizziness; drowsiness; headache; insomnia; nervousness; palpitations; slight increase in blood pressure; stimulation
Warnings: This product should not be used by persons who have glaucoma (certain types). • It should be used with special caution by persons who have diabetes, advanced hardening of the arteries, heart disease, high blood pressure, or thyroid disease. If you have any of these conditions, consult your doctor before using this product. • This product interacts with monoamine oxidase inhibitors, thyroid preparations, and tricyclic antidepressants. If you are currently taking any drugs of these types, check with your doctor before taking this product. If you are unsure of the type or contents of your medications, ask your doctor or pharmacist.
Comments: To avoid side effects such as burning, sneezing, or stinging, and a "rebound" increase in nasal congestion and discharge, do not exceed the recommended dose, and do not use this product for more than three or four continuous days. • This product should not be used by more than one person; sharing the dispenser may spread infection. • This product works best when it is used correctly. Refer to the instructions for the use of nasal inhalers in the chapter on "Buying, Storing, and Using Drugs." • Many nasal drops or sprays on the market contain oxymetazoline hydrochloride. This drug has a duration of action of about 12 hours, and because it needs to be used less often, it is less likely to cause "rebound" nasal congestion during use. Therefore, we recommend a product containing oxymetazoline hydrochloride rather than this product, which does not contain the ingredient.
Fair: Products containing better ingredients are available.

Blistex canker sore and fever blister remedy

Manufacturer: Blistex, Inc.

Dosage Form/Ingredients: Ointment: camphor, 1%; phenol, 0.4%; unspecified quantities of mineral oil, lanolin petrolatum, paraffin, peppermint oil, ammonium carbonate, ammonia, beeswax, polyglyceryl-3 diiosostearate (PEG laurate), sodium borate, and alcohol

Use: For local treatment of minor oral inflammations such as canker sores and fever blisters

Side Effects: Allergic reactions (rash, itching, soreness); local irritation

Warnings: Discontinue use if irritation (pain, swelling, or itching) or rash appears. Consult your pharmacist.

Comments: If you have an oral ulcer that does not heal within three weeks, see your doctor or dentist. • Aspirin will also relieve the pain of oral ulcers. Swallow the tablets as you normally do; do not allow them to dissolve in your mouth.

Acceptable: Although generally we prefer a product containing carbamide peroxide for the treatment of minor oral inflammation, this product also contains good ingredients.

Bromo-Seltzer analgesic

Manufacturer: Warner-Lambert Company

Dosage Form/Ingredients: Granules (content per capful): acetaminophen, 325 mg; sodium bicarbonate, 2800 mg; citric acid, 2200 mg

Use: For the relief of upset stomach, acid indigestion, or heartburn, accompanied by headache or body aches and pains

Side Effects: Bloating; gas; gastric fullness. Only when overdose is taken or in hypersensitive persons: Abdominal cramping; blood disorders; liver disease (jaundice); nausea and vomiting; rash

Warnings: Do not use this product if you are on a low-salt diet. • Persons with heart, lung, liver, or kidney disease, certain blood disorders, and those drinking large quantities of milk should not use this product. • Do not take this product within two hours of a dose of a tetracycline antibiotic. • Consult your physician or pharmacist before taking this product if you are already taking iron, a vitamin-mineral product, chlorpromazine, phenytoin, digoxin, or quinidine, or if you are unsure of the type and contents of the medications you are taking. • Never self-medicate with this product if your symptoms occur regularly (two or three or more times a month). Consult your doctor if the symptoms are worse than usual, if you have chest pains or feel "tightness" in the chest, or if you are sweating or short of breath. In fact, we do not recommend self-treatment for severe attacks of heartburn, indigestion, or stomach upset in any circumstances. If you do decide that your symptoms are mild enough to warrant self-medication, remember that this product is safe and effective only when used on an occasional basis. Repeated use may result in "rebound acidity," which causes increased acid production and makes your symptoms worse instead of better.

Comments: The granules must be dissolved in water before being swallowed. When taken as directed, this product rarely causes side effects, and any that occur are usually mild. • You can save money by taking plain acetaminophen instead of this product; there is no evidence that the ingredients in this product that make it fizz make it more effective than similar doses of a non-fizzy product. • This product has recently been reformulated, but it is still marketed in the same way. •

Acetaminophen does not relieve inflammation, so if pain is caused by swelling or inflammation, it should not be used. Aspirin is better.

Fair: This is an overpriced version of acetaminophen. The added ingredients do not justify the product's cost.

Bronitin asthma remedy

Manufacturer: Whitehall Laboratories

Dosage Form/Ingredients: Tablet: ephedrine hydrochloride, 24 mg; guaifenesin, 100 mg; pyrilamine maleate, 16.6 mg; theophylline, 120 mg

Use: For control of bronchial asthma

Side Effects: Anxiety; blurred vision; chest pain; confusion; constipation; dizziness; drowsiness; dry mouth and respiratory passages; increased blood pressure; increased frequency of urination; insomnia; loss of appetite; nausea; nervousness; palpitations; rash; reduced sweating; restlessness; tension; tremors; urinary retention; vomiting. Children may react with primary symptoms of excitement: convulsions; flushed skin; nervousness; tremors; twitching of muscles; and uncoordinated movements

Warnings: Overdose may result in convulsions, coma, and cardiovascular collapse. • While taking this product, avoid the use of sedative drugs or alcohol, guanethidine, monoamine oxidase inhibitors, or tricyclic antidepressants. If you are taking any medication of these types, or if you are unsure of the type of medication you are taking, consult your doctor or pharmacist. • Persons with persistent coughs, high blood pressure, diabetes, or heart or thyroid disease should consult a doctor before using this product. • Repeated use of this product may cause nausea and vomiting, depressed reflexes, and breathing difficulties in people with kidney disease. • Asthma is too serious a condition to be routinely self-treated. Asthmatics should be under a doctor's care. Be sure to tell your doctor that you are taking this or any other OTC asthma remedy. • Because this product reduces sweating, avoid excessive work or exercise in hot weather. • This product may cause drowsiness. Do not take it if you must drive, operate heavy machinery, or perform other tasks requiring mental alertness.

Comments: The effectiveness of this product may diminish after being taken regularly for seven to ten days. Consult your pharmacist about substituting another product containing a different active ingredient if this product begins to lose its effectiveness for you. • Chew gum or suck on ice chips or a piece of hard candy to reduce mouth dryness. • If you require an expectorant, you need more moisture in your environment. Drink eight to ten glasses of water each day. The use of a vaporizer or humidifier may also be beneficial.

Unacceptable: This product contains both an antihistamine and an expectorant. We do not recommend that you take an asthma reliever which contains either of these ingredients.

Bronkaid asthma remedy

Manufacturer: Winthrop Laboratories

Dosage Form/Ingredients: Tablet: ephedrine sulfate, 24 mg; guaifenesin, 100 mg; theophylline anhydrous, 100 mg

Use: For control of bronchial asthma

Side Effects: Anxiety; blurred vision; chest pain; confusion; constipation; dizziness; drowsiness; dry mouth and respiratory passages; increased blood pressure; increased frequency of urination; insomnia; loss of appetite; nausea; nervousness; palpitations; rash; reduced sweating; restlessness; tension; tremors; urinary retention; vomiting. Children may react with primary symptoms of excitement: convulsions; flushed skin; nervousness; tremors; twitching of muscles; and uncoordinated movements

Warnings: Overdose may result in convulsions, coma, and cardiovascular collapse. • While taking this product, avoid the use of sedative drugs or alcohol, guanethidine, monoamine oxidase inhibitors, or tricyclic antidepressants. If you are taking any medication of these types, or if you are unsure of the type of medication you are taking, consult your doctor or pharmacist. • Persons with persistent coughs, high blood pressure, diabetes, or heart or thyroid disease should consult a doctor before using this product. • Repeated use of this product may cause nausea and vomiting, depressed reflexes, and breathing difficulties in people with kidney disease. • Asthma is too serious a condition to be routinely self-treated. Asthmatics should be under a doctor's care. Be sure to tell your doctor that you are taking this, or any other OTC asthma remedy. • Because this product reduces sweating, avoid excessive work or exercise in hot weather.

Comments: The effectiveness of this product may diminish after being taken regularly for seven to ten days. Consult your pharmacist about substituting another product containing a different active ingredient if this product begins to lose its effectiveness for you. • Chew gum or suck on ice chips or a piece of hard candy to reduce mouth dryness. • If you require an expectorant, you need more moisture in your environment. Drink eight to ten glasses of water each day. The use of a vaporizer or humidifier may also be beneficial. • If fever is present, consult your doctor.

Fair: *This product contains guaifenesin, which is an expectorant. We do not recommend the use of asthma remedies which contain an expectorant.*

Bronkaid Mist asthma remedy

Manufacturer: Winthrop Laboratories

Dosage Form/Ingredients: Oral inhalant: alcohol, 34%; ascorbic acid, 0.07%; epinephrine USP, 0.5%; hydrochloric acid and nitric acid buffers

Use: For temporary relief of severe attacks of bronchial asthma

Side Effects: Anxiety; bronchial irritation; chest pain; dizziness; dry mouth; headache; increase in blood pressure; insomnia; loss of appetite; nausea; nervousness; palpitations; restlessness; sweating; tension; tremors; vomiting

Warnings: Persons with high blood pressure, diabetes, or heart or thyroid disease should use this product with caution. Consult your doctor or pharmacist if you have any questions regarding use of this product. • Asthma is too serious a condition to be routinely self-treated. Asthmatics should be under a doctor's care. Be sure to tell your doctor that you are taking this, or any other OTC asthma remedy.

Comments: Use this product only as directed. Side effects are rare when directions are followed. • Relief of symptoms should occur within five to ten minutes. • Do not use more than once every three to four hours except on advice of your doctor. • After using this product, rinse or gargle with water or mouthwash to help avoid a "dry throat" feeling. • Do not use this product if it is discolored.

Preferred: *The epinephrine provides effective relief of an asthma attack.*

Bufferin analgesic

Manufacturer: Bristol-Myers Products

Dosage Forms/Ingredients: Tablet: aspirin, 324 mg; aluminum glycinate, 48.6 mg; magnesium carbonate, 97.2 mg. Extra-strength tablet and capsule: aspirin, 486 mg; aluminum glycinate, 48.6 mg; magnesium carbonate, 97.2 mg

Use: For the relief of pain of headache, temporary relief of minor arthritic pain. For the discomforts and fever of colds and "flu," menstrual cramps, muscle aches and pains, toothache, inflammation, fever

Side Effects: Dizziness; mental confusion; nausea and vomiting; ringing in the ears; slight blood loss; sweating

Warnings: Persons with kidney disease, asthma, hay fever, or other allergies should be extremely careful about using this product. The product may interfere with the treatment of gout. This product may cause an increased bleeding tendency and should not be taken by persons with a history of bleeding, peptic ulcer, or stomach bleeding. If you have any of these conditions, consult your doctor or pharmacist before using this medication. • Do not use this product if you are consuming alcohol, or taking methotrexate, oral anticoagulants, oral antidiabetics, probenecid, steroids, and/or sulfinpyrazone; if you are unsure of the type or contents of your medications, ask your doctor or pharmacist. • The dosage instructions listed on the package should be followed carefully; toxicity may occur in adults or children with repeated doses.

Comments: Magnesium interacts with tetracycline antibiotics. There may not be enough magnesium in this product to cause any problem, but if you are taking a tetracycline antibiotic in addition to this product, separate the dosages by at least two hours. • Pain-relief tablets, such as this product, that contain salts of magnesium or aluminum are known as buffered tablets. Such products dissolve faster than unbuffered products, but there is no evidence that they relieve pain faster or better than those products that do not contain buffers. Buffered tablets may be less likely to cause gastric upset in some people.

Acceptable: This is a buffered product. Although buffered aspirin may produce less gastric upset in some people, there is no proof that it relieves pain faster than a nonbuffered product.

Caladryl poison ivy/poison oak remedy

Manufacturer: Parke-Davis

Dosage Forms/Ingredients: Cream: camphor, 0.1%; diphenhydramine hydrochloride, 1%; unspecified quantity of calamine. Lotion: alcohol, 2%; camphor, 0.1%; diphenhydramine hydrochloride, 1%; unspecified quantity of calamine

Use: For relief of itching of poison ivy or oak, insect bites, mild sunburn, or other minor skin irritations

Side Effects: Allergic reactions (rash, itching, soreness); local irritation

Warnings: Do not apply this product to extensive or raw, oozing areas of the skin, or use for a prolonged time, except as directed by a physician. • Do not use near the eyes, on mucous membranes, on genitalia, or on infected areas. • Discontinue use and consult your pharmacist if irritation (pain, itching, or swelling) or rash occurs. • Avoid scratching, which may cause irritation and secondary infection.

Comments: Before applying the medication, soak the area in warm water or apply wet towels for five to ten minutes; dry gently by patting with a soft towel and then apply medication. • If itching is intolerable and this product does not relieve it sufficiently, we recommend the use of a "wet soak." In fact, a wet soak may work well enough that you do not need to use this product. See "Buying, Storing, and Using Drugs."

Fair: This product costs more than calamine lotion (which is equally effective), and it is more likely to cause irritation due to the antihistamine content.

calamine lotion poison ivy/poison oak remedy

Manufacturer: Various

Dosage Form/Ingredients: Lotion: calamine, 8%; zinc oxide, 8%; unspecified quantities of glycerin and bentonite magma in calcium hydroxide solution

Use: For relief of itching of poison ivy and oak, insect bites, mild sunburn, and other minor skin irritations

Side Effects: None when used topically. If swallowed: abdominal pains; nausea; numbness of extremities; vomiting

Warnings: Do not apply this product to extensive or raw, oozing areas of the skin, or use for a prolonged time, except as directed by a physician. • Do not use near the eyes, on mucous membranes, on genitalia, or on infected areas. • Discontinue use and consult your pharmacist if irritation (pain, itching, or swelling) or rash occurs. • Avoid scratching, which may cause irritation and secondary infection.

Comments: Shake the lotion thoroughly before each use. As this product dries, a thin, pink-colored crust remains on the skin, which may be objectionable to some people. • If severe itching is a problem, purchase this product with 0.5 to 1% phenol (carbolic acid) added. (Or, ask your pharmacist to add the phenol to your calamine lotion.) The phenol will help relieve itching, but note that it may cause burning, rash, or skin irritation.

Preferred: This product effectively relieves itching caused by poison ivy or poison oak.

Carter's Little Pills laxative

Manufacturer: Carter Products

Dosage Form/Ingredient: Tablet: bisacodyl, 5 mg

Use: For relief of constipation

Side Effects: Allergic reactions; excess loss of fluid; griping (cramps); mucus in feces; rectal burning

Warnings: Persons with a high fever (100° F or more), black or tarry stools, nausea, vomiting, abdominal pain; pregnant women; and children under the age of three should not use this product unless directed to do so by a doctor. • Do not use this product when constipation is caused by megacolon or other diseases of the intestine, or hypothyroidism. • Excessive use (daily for a month or more) of these products may cause diarrhea, vomiting, and loss of certain blood electrolytes. • Do not crush or chew this product, and do not take this product within an hour of taking an antacid or drinking milk. Severe abdominal cramping will result. • Never self-medicate with this product if constipation lasts longer than two weeks or if the medication does not produce a laxative effect within a week. • Limit use to seven days unless directed otherwise by a doctor since this product may cause laxative-dependence (addiction) if used for a longer time.

Comments: Evacuation may occur within six to twelve hours.

Acceptable: We prefer bulk-forming laxatives; however, this is an effective stimulant laxative.

Cheracol cough remedy

Manufacturer: The Upjohn Company

Dosage Form/Ingredients: Liquid (content per teaspoon): codeine phosphate, 10 mg; guaifenesin, 100 mg; alcohol, 3%

Use: For temporary relief of cough due to colds or "flu"; to convert a dry, nonproductive cough to a productive, phlegm-producing cough

Side Effects: Constipation; nausea; slight drying of respiratory passages; vomiting

Warnings: Do not give this product to children under two years of age unless directed to do so by your doctor. • This product should be used with caution by persons who have asthma or other respiratory diseases. If you have such a condition, consult your doctor before taking this product. • Because this product contains codeine, it has the potential for abuse and must be used with caution. It usually should not be taken for more than seven to ten days. Tolerance may develop quickly, but do not increase the dose without consulting your doctor. • This product interacts with alcohol, guanethidine, monoamine oxidase inhibitors, sedative drugs, and tricyclic antidepressants. If you are currently taking any drugs of these types, check with your doctor before taking this product. If you are unsure of the type or contents of your medications, ask your doctor or pharmacist. • If your cough persists, or is accompanied by high fever, consult your doctor promptly. • Do not use this product to treat chronic coughs, such as those from smoking or asthma. • Do not use this product to treat productive (hacking) coughs that produce phlegm.

Comments: If you require an expectorant, you need more moisture in your environment. Drink eight to ten glasses of water daily. The use of a vaporizer or humidifier may also be beneficial. • Over-the-counter sale of this product may not be permitted in some states.

Preferred: The codeine in this product has been proven effective as a cough suppressant.

Cheracol D cough remedy

Manufacturer: The Upjohn Company

Dosage Form/Ingredients: Liquid (content per teaspoon): dextromethorphan hydrobromide, 10 mg; guaifenesin, 100 mg; alcohol, 3%

Use: For temporary relief of cough due to colds or "flu"; to convert a dry, nonproductive cough to a productive, phlegm-producing cough

Side Effects: Drowsiness; nausea; vomiting

Warnings: Do not give this product to children under six years without consulting a doctor. • This product interacts with monoamine oxidase inhibitors. If you are currently taking any drugs of this type, check with your doctor before taking this product. If you are unsure of the type or contents of your medications, ask your doctor or pharmacist. • Do not use this product to treat chronic coughs, as from smoking or asthma, or to treat productive (hacking) coughs that produce phlegm. • If your cough persists, or is accompanied by a high fever, consult your doctor promptly.

Comments: If you require an expectorant, you need more moisture in your environment; drink eight to ten glasses of water daily. The use of a humidifier or vaporizor may also be beneficial.

Acceptable: Dextromethorphan hydrobromide is an effective cough suppressant. Although guaifenesin has not been proven effective, it is safe to use and future studies may prove its effectiveness.

chlorpheniramine maleate allergy remedy

Manufacturer: Various

Dosage Forms: Tablet, Time-release tablet, Time-release capsule, Syrup: various concentrations

Use: For relief of symptoms of hay fever and other upper respiratory allergies

Side Effects: Anxiety; blurred vision; chest pain; confusion; constipation; dry mouth; difficult and painful urination; dizziness; drowsiness; headache; increased blood pressure; insomnia; loss of appetite; mild stimulation; nausea; nervousness; palpitations; rash; reduced sweating; tension; tremor; vomiting

Warnings: This product should be used with special caution by the elderly or debilitated, and by persons who have asthma, diabetes, an enlarged prostate, glaucoma (certain types), heart disease, high blood pressure, kidney disease, liver disease, obstructed bladder, obstructed intestine, peptic ulcer, or thyroid disease. If you have any of these conditions, consult your doctor before taking this product. • It should not be used by pregnant or nursing women, or be given to newborn or premature infants. • This product may cause drowsiness. Do not take it if you must drive, operate heavy machinery, or perform other tasks requiring mental alertness. To prevent oversedation, avoid the use of alcohol or other drugs that have sedative properties. • This product interacts with alcohol, guanethidine, monoamine oxidase inhibitors, sedative drugs, and tricyclic antidepressants. If you are currently taking any drugs of these types, check with your doctor before taking this product. If you are unsure of the type or contents of your medications, ask your doctor or pharmacist. • Because this product reduces sweating, avoid excessive work or exercise in hot weather.

Comments: The effectiveness of this product may diminish after being taken for seven to ten days; consult your pharmacist about substituting another antihistamine if this product begins to lose its effectiveness for you. • Chew gum or suck on ice chips or a piece of hard candy to reduce mouth dryness.

Preferred: *Chlorpheniramine maleate is probably the most effective antihistamine, and it is inexpensive. It is our treatment of choice for the symptoms of upper respiratory allergies.*

Chlor-Trimeton allergy remedy

Manufacturer: Schering Laboratories

Dosage Form/Ingredient: Timed-release tablet: chlorpheniramine maleate, 8 mg

Use: For relief of symptoms of hay fever and other upper respiratory allergies

Side Effects: Anxiety; blurred vision; chest pain; confusion; constipation; difficult and painful urination; dizziness; drowsiness; dry mouth; headache; increased blood pressure; insomnia; loss of appetite; mild stimulation; nausea; nervousness; palpitations; rash; reduced sweating; tension; tremor; vomiting

Warnings: This product should be used with special caution by the elderly or debilitated, and by persons who have asthma, diabetes, an enlarged prostate, glaucoma (certain types), heart disease, high blood pressure, kidney disease, liver disease, obstructed bladder, obstructed intestine, peptic ulcer, or thyroid disease. If you have any of these conditions, consult your doctor before taking this product. It should not be used by pregnant or nursing women, or be given to newborn or premature infants. • This product may cause drowsiness. Do not take it if you must drive, operate heavy machinery, or perform other tasks requiring mental alertness. To prevent oversedation, avoid the use of alcohol or other drugs that have sedative properties. • This product interacts with alcohol, guanethidine, monoamine oxidase inhibitors, sedative drugs, and tricyclic antidepressants. If you are currently taking any drugs of these types, check with your doctor before taking this product. If you are unsure of the type or contents of your medications, ask your doctor or pharmacist. • Because this product reduces sweating, avoid excessive work or exercise in hot weather. • This product has sustained action; never increase the recommended dose or take it more frequently than directed. A serious overdose could result.

Comments: The effectiveness of this product may diminish after being taken regularly for seven to ten days; consult your pharmacist about substituting another product containing a different antihistamine if this product begins to lose its effectiveness for you. • This product should not be crushed or chewed. It must be swallowed whole. • Chew gum or suck on ice chips or a piece of hard candy to reduce mouth dryness. • Products equivalent to this one are available and vary widely in cost. Check prices; you may save money by comparison shopping.

Preferred: *Chlorpheniramine maleate is probably the most effective antihistamine, and it is inexpensive. It is our treatment of choice for the symptoms of upper respiratory allergies.*

Chlor-Trimeton cold and allergy remedy

Manufacturer: Schering Corporation

Dosage Forms/Ingredients: Tablet: chlorpheniramine maleate, 4 mg; pseudoephedrine sulfate, 60 mg. Long-acting tablet: chlorpheniramine maleate, 8 mg; pseudoephedrine sulfate, 120 mg

Use: Temporary relief of nasal congestion due to colds and upper respiratory allergies

Side Effects: Anxiety; blurred vision; chest pain; confusion; constipation; dry mouth; difficult and painful urination; dizziness; drowsiness; headache; increased blood pressure; insomnia; loss of appetite; mild stimulation; nausea; nervousness; palpitations; rash; reduced sweating; tension; tremor; vomiting

Warnings: This product should be used with special caution by the elderly or debilitated, and by persons who have asthma, diabetes, enlarged prostate, glaucoma (certain types) heart disease, high blood pressure, kidney disease, liver disease, obstructed bladder, obstructed intestine, peptic ulcer, or thyroid disease. If you have any of these conditions, consult your doctor before taking this product. It should not be used by pregnant or nursing women, or be given to newborn or premature infants. • This product may cause drowsiness. Do not take it if you must drive, operate heavy machinery, or perform other tasks requiring mental alertness. To prevent oversedation, avoid the use of alcohol or other drugs that have sedative properties. • This product interacts with alcohol, guanethidine, monoamine oxidase inhibitors, sedative drugs, and tricyclic antidepressants. If you are currently taking any drugs of these types, check with your doctor before taking this product. If you are unsure of the type or contents of your medications, ask your doctor or pharmacist. • Because this product reduces sweating, avoid excessive work or exercise in hot weather. • One form of this product is long lasting; never increase the recommended dose or take it more frequently than directed. A serious overdose could result.

Comments: Many other conditions (some serious) mimic the common cold. If symptoms persist beyond one week, or if they occur regularly without regard to season, consult your doctor. • The effectiveness of this product may diminish after being taken for seven to ten days; consult your pharmacist about substituting a product with another antihistamine if this product begins to lose its effectiveness for you. • Chew gum or suck on ice chips or a piece of hard candy to reduce mouth dryness. • The long-acting version of this product should be taken every eight hours. It should not be crushed or chewed. It must be swallowed whole.

Acceptable: *We prefer single-ingredient products rather than combination antihistamine-decongestant products like this one.*

Chlor-Trimeton Expectorant cough remedy

Manufacturer: Schering Corporation

Dosage Form/Ingredients: Liquid (content per teaspoon): chlorpheniramine maleate, 2 mg; phenylephrine hydrochloride, 10 mg; ammonium chloride, 100 mg; sodium citrate, 50 mg; guaifenesin, 50 mg; alcohol, 1% or less

Use: For temporary relief of cough, nasal congestion, and other symptoms of colds or "flu"; to convert a dry, nonproductive cough to a productive, phlegm-producing cough

Side Effects: Anxiety; blurred vision; chest pain; confusion; constipation; difficult and painful urination; dizziness; drowsiness; headache; increased blood pressure; insomnia; loss of appetite; mild stimulation; nausea; nervousness; palpitations; rash; reduced sweating; tension; tremor; vomiting

Warnings: This product should not be given to newborns or premature infants, or taken by pregnant women. • This product should be used with special caution by children under two years of age, the elderly or debilitated, and by persons who have asthma, diabetes, an enlarged prostate, glaucoma (certain types), heart disease, high blood pressure, kidney disease, obstructed bladder, obstructed intestine, peptic ulcer, or thyroid disease. In these situations, consult your doctor before taking this product. • This product may cause drowsiness. Do not take it if you must drive, operate heavy machinery, or perform other tasks requiring mental alertness. To prevent oversedation, avoid the use of alcohol or other drugs that have sedative properties. • This product interacts with alcohol, guanethidine, monoamine oxidase inhibitors, sedative drugs, and tricyclic antidepressants. If you are currently taking any drugs of these types, check with your doctor before taking this product. If you are unsure of the type or contents of your medications, ask your doctor or pharmacist. • Because this product reduces sweating, avoid excessive work or exercise in hot weather. • If your cough persists, or is accompanied by high fever, consult your doctor promptly. • Do not use this product to treat chronic coughs, such as those from smoking or asthma. Do not use this product to treat productive (hacking) coughs that produce phlegm.

Comments: Many other conditions (some serious) mimic the common cold. If symptoms persist beyond one week, or if they occur regularly without regard to season, consult your doctor. • If you require an expectorant, you need more moisture in your environment. Drink eight to ten glasses of water daily. The use of a vaporizer or humidifier may also be beneficial. • Chew gum or suck on ice chips or a piece of hard candy to reduce mouth dryness. • The effectiveness of this product may diminish after being taken regularly for seven to ten days; consult your pharmacist about substituting another product containing a different active ingredient if this product begins to lose its effectiveness.

Unacceptable: The combination of ingredients in this product—a suppressant, two expectorants, an antihistamine, and a decongestant—is illogical for the treatment of a cough.

Clearasil acne preparation

Manufacturer: Vicks Toiletry Products Division, Richardson-Merrell, Inc.
Dosage Forms/Ingredient: Lotion: benzoyl peroxide, 5%. Cream: benzoyl peroxide, 10%
Use: Treatment of acne
Side Effects: Allergy, local irritation
Warnings: Do not get this product in or near the eyes. • Persons having a known sensitivity to benzoyl peroxide should not use this product. • While using this product, do not use harsh, abrasive cleansers. • If excessive redness or peeling occurs, reduce the frequency of this product's use. • Avoid exposure to heat lamps and sunlamps, as well as prolonged exposure to sunlight, when using this product. • This product may be especially active on fair-skinned people. • If the condition worsens or if skin irritation develops, stop using this product and consult your physician.
Comments: Wash the affected area gently in warm water and pat dry before applying this product. • There may be a slight transitory stinging or burning sensation on initial application of this product. • This product may damage certain fabrics including rayon. • This product comes in tinted and vanishing formulas.
Preferred: Benzoyl peroxide has been shown to be the most effective ingredient in acne preparations.

Clearasil Pore Deep Cleanser acne preparation

Manufacturer: Vicks Toiletry Products Division, Richardson-Merrell, Inc.
Dosage Form/Ingredients: Liquid cleanser: alcohol, 43%; salicylic acid, 0.3%; allantoin, 0.1%
Use: Treatment of acne
Side Effects: Allergy; local irritation
Warnings: Do not get this product in or near the eyes. • If the condition worsens or if skin irritation develops, stop using this product and consult your physician.
Comments: This product is to be used instead of soap. Apply to face with cotton and massage into skin for one to two minutes; do not rinse.
Fair: Products containing more effective ingredients are available.

Clinistix Strips urine test for glucose

Manufacturer: Ames Division, Miles Laboratories
Product Form: Dip-and-read strip
Use: To test urine for glucose
Comments: Do not use this product if the strip has turned brown. • Be certain to remind your doctor and pharmacist of any over-the-counter item or prescription drug you are taking. It may affect this test. • Test only freshly collected urine. • Keep the container tightly closed and store in a dry place out of the sun. Do not refrigerate. • Do not keep the stick im-

mersed in urine longer than the directions state. • Compare the color quickly to the chart on the package. Read the color in a bright light. • Before reading the color, tap the stick on the side of the container to remove excess fluid.

Preferred: *This test is effective for the specified purpose, and offers good value for the money.*

Clinitest urine test for glucose

Manufacturer: Ames Division, Miles Laboratories
Product Form: Tablet
Use: To test urine for glucose
Warnings: These tablets cause severe toxicity and possible death if they are swallowed. Keep them out of the reach of children. • Do not hold them in your hand for longer than a few seconds and wash your hands after the test is completed.
Comments: We recommend that you use this product if your urine glucose is 4% or more. • Be certain to remind your doctor and pharmacist of any over-the-counter item or prescription drug you are taking. It may affect this test. • Test only freshly collected urine. • Keep the container tightly closed and store in a dry place out of the sun. Do not refrigerate. • Compare the color to the color chart at the exact time indicated on the label. • If the test produces an orange color that quickly fades to brown, call your doctor. • Use only the test tubes that are supplied by the manufacturer. • Do not use these tablets if they have changed color. • If you use this product only occasionally (once or twice a week), buy the small package of foil-wrapped tablets to ensure freshness.

Preferred: *This test is effective for the specified purpose, and offers good value for the money.*

Colace laxative

Manufacturer: Mead Johnson Co., Pharmaceutical Division
Dosage Forms/Ingredient: Capsule: docusate sodium, 50 mg, 100 mg. Liquid (content per teaspoon): docusate sodium, 10 mg. Syrup (content per teaspoon): docusate sodium, 20 mg
Use: For relief of constipation; as a stool softener
Side Effects: Transitory cramping pains; nausea; rash
Warnings: Persons with high fever (100° F or more), black or tarry stools, nausea, vomiting, abdominal pain; children under age three; and pregnant women should not use this product unless directed by a doctor. • Do not use this product when constipation is caused by megacolon or other diseases of the intestine, or hypothyroidism. • Excessive use (daily for a month or more) of this product may cause diarrhea, vomiting, and loss of certain blood electrolytes. • This product is referred to as a stool softener and is recommended for relief of constipation when the stool is hard and dry. Do not take another product containing a stool softener at the same time as you are taking this product. • Never self-medicate with this product if constipation lasts longer than two weeks, or if the medication does not produce a laxative effect within a week. • Limit use to seven days unless directed otherwise by your doctor; this product may cause laxative-dependence (addiction) if used for a longer period.
Comments: Take the liquid form of this product in one-half glass of milk or fruit juice to help mask the taste. • Evacuation may occur within 72 hours. • Although an exact generic equivalent of this item may not be

available, very similar products are. Ask your pharmacist if you can save money by purchasing another item.

Acceptable: *This product is an acceptable stool softener laxative.*

Compoz sleep aid

Manufacturer: Jeffrey Martin, Inc.
Dosage Form/Ingredient: Tablet: pyrilamine maleate, 25 mg
Use: To induce drowsiness and assist in falling asleep
Side Effects: Blurred vision; confusion; constipation; difficult urination; dizziness; drowsiness; dry mouth and respiratory passages; headache; insomnia; low blood pressure; nausea; nervousness; palpitations; rash; restlessness; vomiting. Children may react with primary symptoms of excitement: convulsions; flushed skin; nervousness; tremors; twitching of muscles; uncoordinated movements
Warnings: Persons with asthma, diabetes, glaucoma (certain types), heart disease, high blood pressure, kidney disease, liver disease, thyroid disorders, certain types of peptic ulcer, enlarged prostate, obstructed bladder, or obstructed intestine; pregnant and nursing women; children under 12 years of age; and elderly or debilitated persons should not take this medication. • This product may interact with other drugs. If you are currently taking any medication, do not use this product without first consulting your doctor. • This product also interacts with alcohol, so avoid alcohol or other central nervous system sedatives while you are using it. • Since its purpose is to make you sleepy, do not use it while driving, operating heavy machinery, or performing other tasks that require you to be mentally alert. • Tolerance to this product may develop; do not increase the recommended dose unless your doctor recommends you to do so. • Insomnia may be a symptom of serious illness. Seek your doctor's advice if your sleeplessness continues, and do not take this product for more than two weeks without consulting your doctor.
Comments: This product may cause dryness of the mouth. To reduce this feeling, chew gum or suck on ice chips or a piece of hard candy. • There is probably no need to purchase this drug. You would be better advised to try to find and correct the cause of your insomnia. A glass of warm milk and a soak in a hot tub may work just as well as this product. • Many OTC sleep aids are very similar. If you wish to use one, look for a generic equivalent at a cheaper price. Ask your pharmacist for assistance.

Unacceptable: *We consider that OTC sleep aids should not be taken without the advice of a doctor.*

Comtrex cold remedy

Manufacturer: Bristol-Myers Products
Dosage Forms/Ingredients: Capsule, Tablet: acetaminophen, 325 mg; phenylpropanolamine hydrochloride, 12.5 mg; chlorpheniramine maleate, 1 mg; dextromethorphan hydrobromide, 10 mg. Liquid (content per one fluid ounce): acetaminophen, 649.2 mg; phenylpropanolamine hydrochloride, 25.2 mg; chlorpheniramine maleate, 2 mg; dextromethorphan hydrobromide, 19.8 mg; alcohol, 20%
Use: For relief of nasal congestion, cough, fever, aches, pains, and general discomfort due to colds
Side Effects: Anxiety; blurred vision; chest pain; confusion; constipation; dry mouth; difficult and painful urination; dizziness; drowsiness;

headache; increased blood pressure; insomnia; loss of appetite; mild stimulation; nausea; nervousness; palpitations; rash; reduced sweating; tension; tremor; vomiting. In overdose: Blood disorders; rash

Warnings: This product should be used with special caution by the elderly or debilitated, and by persons who have asthma, diabetes, enlarged prostate, glaucoma (certain types), heart disease, high blood pressure, kidney disease, liver disease, lung disease, certain blood disorders, obstructed bladder, obstructed intestine, peptic ulcer, or thyroid disease. If you have any of these conditions, consult your doctor before taking this product. It should not be used by pregnant or nursing women, or be given to newborn or premature infants. • This product may cause drowsiness. Do not take it if you must drive, operate heavy machinery, or perform other tasks requiring mental alertness. To prevent oversedation, avoid the use of alcohol or other drugs that have sedative properties. • This product interacts with alcohol, guanethidine, monoamine oxidase inhibitors, sedative drugs, and tricyclic antidepressants. If you are currently taking any drugs of these types, check with your doctor before taking this product. If you are unsure of the type or contents of your medications, ask your doctor or pharmacist. • Because this product reduces sweating, avoid excessive work or exercise in hot weather. • If your cough persists or is accompanied by high fever, consult your doctor promptly. • When taken in overdose, acetaminophen is more toxic than aspirin. Follow dosage instructions carefully.

Comments: Many other conditions (some serious) mimic the common cold. If symptoms persist beyond one week, or if they occur regularly without regard to season, consult your doctor. • The effectiveness of this product may diminish after being taken regularly for seven to ten days; consult your pharmacist about substituting another medication if this product begins to lose its effectiveness for you. • Chew gum or suck on ice chips or a piece of hard candy to relieve mouth dryness.

Unacceptable: This product contains an analgesic, an antihistamine, a decongestant, and a cough suppressant. We believe you should treat your symptoms individually rather than with multiple-ingredient products like this.

Congespirin Children's cold and allergy remedy

Manufacturer: Bristol-Myers Products

Dosage Form/Ingredients: Chewable tablet: aspirin, 81 mg; phenylephrine hydrochloride, 1.25 mg

Use: To reduce fever, relieve nasal congestion and minor aches and pains due to colds, "flu," or upper respiratory allergies

Side Effects: Dizziness; mental confusion; mild to moderate stimulation; nausea and vomiting; ringing in the ears; slight blood loss; sweating

Warnings: This product should be used with special caution by persons who have diabetes, heart disease, high blood pressure, peptic ulcer, bleeding or stomach bleeding, gout, asthma, or thyroid disease. If your child has any of these conditions, consult your doctor before administering this product. • This product should not be given to newborn or premature infants or taken by pregnant or nursing women. • This product interacts with alcohol, ammonium chloride, guanethidine, methotrexate, monoamine oxidase inhibitors, oral anticoagulants, oral antidiabetics, probenecid, sedative drugs, steroids, sulfinpyrazone, tricyclic antidepressants, and vitamin C. If your child is currently taking any drugs of these types, check with your doctor before administering this product. If you are unsure of the type or contents of your child's medications, ask your doctor or pharmacist. • The dosage instructions listed on the package should be followed carefully; toxicity may occur in adults or children with repeated doses. • Be sure to keep the tablets out of the reach of your children between doses.

Comments: Many other conditions (some serious) mimic the common cold. If symptoms persist beyond one week, or if they occur regularly without regard to season, consult your doctor. • The effectiveness of this product may diminish after being taken regularly for seven to ten days; consult your pharmacist about substituting another medication if this product begins to lose its effectiveness for your child. • Generic versions of this product are available and may save you money. Consult your pharmacist. • Have your child chew gum or suck on ice chips to reduce mouth dryness.

Acceptable: We prefer single-ingredient products rather than analgesic-decongestant combination products like this one.

Contac cold and allergy remedy

Manufacturer: Menley & James Laboratories

Dosage Form/Ingredients: Time-release capsule: phenylpropanolamine hydrochloride, 75 mg; chlorpheniramine maleate, 8 mg

Use: For relief of nasal congestion due to colds and upper respiratory allergies

Side Effects: Anxiety, blurred vision; chest pain; confusion; constipation; dry mouth; difficult and painful urination; dizziness; drowsiness; headache; increased blood pressure; insomnia; loss of appetite; mild stimulation; nausea; nervousness; palpitations; rash; reduced sweating; tension; tremor; vomiting

Warnings: This product should be used with special caution by the elderly or debilitated, and by persons who have asthma, diabetes, enlarged prostate, glaucoma (certain types), heart disease, high blood pressure, kidney disease, liver disease, obstructed bladder, obstructed intestine, peptic ulcer, or thyroid disease. If you have any of these conditions, consult your doctor before taking this product. It should not be used by pregnant or nursing women, or be given to newborn or premature infants. • This product may cause drowsiness. Do not take it if you must drive, operate heavy machinery, or perform other tasks requiring mental alertness. To prevent oversedation, avoid the use of alcohol or other drugs that have sedative properties. • This product interacts with alcohol, guanethidine, monoamine oxidase inhibitors, sedative drugs, and tricyclic antidepressants. If you are currently taking any drugs of these types, check with your doctor before taking this product. If you are unsure of the type or contents of your medications, ask your doctor or pharmacist. • Because this product reduces sweating, avoid excessive work or exercise in hot weather. • This product has sustained action; never increase the recommended dose or take it more frequently than directed. A serious overdose could result.

Comments: Many other conditions (some serious) mimic the common cold. If symptoms persist beyond one week, or if they occur regularly without regard to season, consult your doctor. • The effectiveness of this product may diminish after being taken for seven to ten days; consult your pharmacist about substituting a different product if this product begins to lose its effectiveness for you. • This product should not be crushed or chewed. It must be swallowed whole. • Chew gum or suck on ice chips or a piece of hard candy to reduce mouth dryness.

Acceptable: We prefer single-ingredient products rather than combination antihistamine-decongestant products like this one.

Contac Jr.
Children's cold and allergy remedy

Manufacturer: Menley & James Laboratories

Dosage Form/Ingredients: Liquid (content per teaspoon): phenylpropanolamine hydrochloride, 9.375 mg; acetaminophen, 162.5 mg; dextromethorphan hydrobromide, 5 mg; alcohol, 10%

Use: For relief of nasal congestion, fever, coughing, aches, pains, and general discomfort due to colds, "flu" or upper respiratory allergies

Side Effects: Mild to moderate stimulation; nausea; vomiting; drowsiness; dry mouth. In overdose: Blood disorders, rash

Warnings: This product should be used with special caution by persons who have diabetes, heart disease, lung disease, liver or kidney disease, certain blood disorders, high blood pressure, or thyroid disease. If your child has any of these conditions, consult your doctor before using this product. • This product interacts with alcohol, guanethidine, monoamine oxidase inhibitors, sedative drugs, and tricyclic antidepressants. If your child is currently taking any drugs of these types, check with your doctor before giving this product to your child. If you are unsure of the type or contents of your child's medications, ask your doctor or pharmacist. • This product should not be given to newborn or premature infants, or taken by pregnant or nursing women. • When taken in overdose, acetaminophen is more toxic than aspirin. Follow dosage instructions carefully. • This product may cause drowsiness. Do not take it if you must drive, operate heavy machinery, or perform other tasks requiring mental alertness. To prevent oversedation, avoid the use of alcohol or other drugs that have sedative properties. • If your child's cough persists or is accompanied by high fever, consult your doctor promptly.

Comments: Many other conditions (some serious) mimic the common cold. If symptoms persist beyond one week, or if they occur regularly without regard to season, consult your doctor. • The effectiveness of this product may diminish after being taken regularly for seven to ten days; consult your pharmacist about substituting another medication if this product begins to lose its effectiveness for your child. • Have your child suck on ice chips or chew gum to reduce mouth dryness.

Acceptable: We prefer single-ingredient products rather than combination analgesic-decongestant-cough suppressant products like this one.

Control
appetite suppressant

Manufacturer: Thompson Medical Company, Inc.

Dosage Forms/Ingredient: Capsule: phenylpropanolamine hydrochloride, 75 mg. Drops (per 4 drops): phenylpropanolamine hydrochloride, 25 mg

Use: As an aid in dietary control

Side Effects: Blurred vision; diarrhea; nausea; dizziness; drowsiness; headache; increase in blood pressure, blood sugar, heart rate, and thyroid activity; insomnia; nervousness; palpitations. In larger than the recommended dose: Irregular heartbeat; nasal dryness; upset stomach

Warnings: Persons with heart disease, high blood pressure, diabetes, kidney or thyroid disease; children under 16 years of age; and pregnant or nursing women should not use this product. Consult your doctor for recommendations. • This product interacts with alcohol, guanethidine, monoamine oxidase inhibitors, sedative drugs, and tricyclic anti-depressants. If you are currently taking any of these drugs, or if you are unsure of the type or contents of your medications, consult your doctor or pharmacist before taking this product. • Avoid taking this drug while using a decongestant. • Avoid continuous use for longer than three months. • Discontinue use if you experience rapid pulse, dizziness, or palpitations.

Comments: During the first week of therapy with this product, expect increased frequency of urination. • Many medical authorities believe that the ingredient phenylpropanolamine does not help in weight loss programs. However, the FDA Review Panel has reported that it is effective. • If you want to use this product, remember that you become tolerant to any beneficial effects after a couple of weeks. After each two weeks of use, stop for one week, then resume use. • The primary value in a product of this nature is in following the caloric reduction plan that goes with it. • The capsule form of this product has sustained action. To avoid sleep disturbance, do not take it less than 12 hours before bedtime.

Acceptable: This product is preferable to other available dietary aids because it uses a single effective ingredient.

Coricidin
cold and allergy remedy

Manufacturer: Schering Corporation
Dosage Form/Ingredients: Tablet: chlorpheniramine maleate, 2 mg; aspirin, 325 mg
Use: For relief of cold and allergy symptoms
Side Effects: Anxiety; blurred vision; chest pain; confusion; constipation; difficult and painful urination; dizziness; drowsiness; dry mouth; headache; increased blood pressure; insomnia; loss of appetite; mild stimulation; nausea; nervousness; palpitations; rash; reduced sweating; ringing in the ears; slight blood loss; tension; tremor; vomiting
Warnings: This product should be used with special caution by the elderly or debilitated, and by persons who have asthma, diabetes, enlarged prostate, glaucoma (certain types), heart disease, high blood pressure, kidney disease, liver disease, obstructed bladder, obstructed intestine, peptic ulcer, bleeding or stomach bleeding, gout, or thyroid disease. If you have any of these conditions, consult your doctor before taking this product. • It should not be used by pregnant or nursing women, or be given to newborn or premature infants. • This product may cause drowsiness. Do not take it if you must drive, operate heavy machinery, or perform other tasks requiring mental alertness. To prevent oversedation, avoid the use of alcohol or other drugs that have sedative properties. • This product interacts with alcohol, ammonium chloride, guanethidine, methotrexate, monoamine oxidase inhibitors, oral anticoagulants, oral antidiabetics, probenecid, sedative drugs, steroids, sulfinpyrazone, tricyclic antidepressants, and vitamin C. If you are currently taking any drugs of these types, check with your doctor before taking this product. If you are unsure of the type or contents of your medications, ask your doctor or pharmacist. • Because this product reduces sweating, avoid excessive work or exercise in hot weather. • The dosage instructions listed on the package should be followed carefully; toxicity may occur in adults or children with repeated doses.
Comments: Many other conditions (some serious) mimic the common cold. If symptoms persist beyond one week, or if they occur regularly

without regard to season, consult your doctor. • The effectiveness of this product may diminish after being taken for seven to ten days; consult your pharmacist about substituting a product with another antihistamine if this product begins to lose its effectiveness for you. • Chew gum or suck on ice chips or a piece of hard candy to reduce mouth dryness.

Acceptable: We prefer single-ingredient products rather than combination analgesic-antihistamine products like this one.

Coricidin cough remedy

Manufacturer: Schering Corporation

Dosage Form/Ingredients: Liquid (content per teaspoon): dextromethorphan hydrobromide, 10 mg; phenylpropanolamine hydrochloride, 12.5 mg; guaifenesin, 100 mg; alcohol, less than 0.5%

Use: For temporary relief of cough and nasal congestion due to colds or "flu"; to convert a dry, nonproductive cough to a productive, phlegm-producing cough

Side Effects: Drowsiness; mild stimulation; blurred vision; flushing; palpitations; nervousness; dizziness; insomnia; nausea; vomiting

Warnings: This product should be used with special caution by children under two years of age, and by persons who have diabetes, heart disease, high blood pressure, or thyroid disease. In these situations, consult your doctor before taking this product. • This product interacts with guanethidine and monoamine oxidase inhibitors. If you are currently taking any drugs of these types, check with your doctor before taking this product. If you are unsure of the type or contents of your medications, ask your doctor or pharmacist. • If your cough persists, or is accompanied by high fever, consult your doctor promptly. • Do not use this product to treat chronic coughs, such as those from smoking or asthma. • Do not use this product to treat productive (hacking) coughs that produce phlegm.

Comments: If you require an expectorant, you need more moisture in your environment. Drink eight to ten glasses of water daily. The use of a vaporizer or humidifier may also be beneficial. • Many other conditions (some serious) mimic the common cold. If symptoms persist beyond one week or if they occur regularly without regard to season, consult your doctor.

Fair: This product contains a decongestant, an ingredient not directly related to treatment of a cough. Products containing more appropriate ingredients are available.

Coricidin 'D' Decongestant cold and allergy remedy

Manufacturer: Schering Corporation

Dosage Form/Ingredients: Tablet: chlorpheniramine maleate, 2 mg; phenylpropanolamine hydrochloride, 12.5 mg; aspirin, 325 mg

Use: To relieve nasal congestion, fever, aches, pains, and general discomfort due to colds or upper respiratory allergies

Side Effects: Anxiety; blurred vision; chest pain; confusion; constipation; difficult and painful urination; dizziness; drowsiness; dry mouth; headache; increased blood pressure; insomnia; loss of appetite; mild stimulation; nausea; nervousness; palpitations; rash; reduced sweating; ringing in the ears; slight blood loss; tension; tremor; vomiting

Warnings: This product should be used with special caution by the elderly or debilitated, and by persons who have asthma, diabetes, enlarged prostate, glaucoma (certain types), heart disease, high blood pressure, kidney disease, liver disease, obstructed bladder, obstructed intestine, peptic ulcer, bleeding or stomach bleeding, gout, or thyroid disease. If you have any of these conditions, consult your doctor before taking this product. • It should not be used by pregnant or nursing women, or be given to newborn or premature infants. • This product may cause drowsiness. Do not take it if you must drive, operate heavy machinery, or perform other tasks requiring mental alertness. To prevent oversedation, avoid the use of alcohol or other drugs that have sedative properties. • This product interacts with alcohol, ammonium chloride, guanethidine, methotrexate, monoamine oxidase inhibitors, oral anticoagulants, oral antidiabetics, probenecid, sedative drugs, steroids, sulfinpyrazone, tricyclic antidepressants, and vitamin C. If you are currently taking any drugs of these types, check with your doctor before taking this product. If you are unsure of the type or contents of your medications, ask your doctor or pharmacist. • Because this product reduces sweating, avoid excessive work or exercise in hot weather. • The dosage instructions listed on the package should be followed carefully; toxicity may occur in adults or children with repeated doses.

Comments: Many other conditions (some serious) mimic the common cold. If symptoms persist beyond one week or if they occur regularly without regard to season, consult your doctor. • The effectiveness of this product may diminish after being taken for seven to ten days; consult your pharmacist about substituting another product if this one begins to lose its effectiveness for you. • Chew gum or suck on ice chips or a piece of hard candy to reduce mouth dryness.

Acceptable: We prefer single-ingredient products rather than combination analgesic-antihistamine-decongestant products like this one.

Coricidin nasal decongestant

Manufacturer: Schering Corporation

Dosage Form/Ingredient: Nasal spray: phenylephrine hydrochloride, 0.5%

Use: For temporary relief of nasal congestion due to colds, sinusitis, hay fever, or other upper respiratory allergies

Side Effects: Blurred vision; burning, dryness of nasal mucosa; increased nasal congestion or discharge; sneezing, and/or stinging; dizziness; drowsiness; headache; insomnia; nervousness; palpitations; slight increase in blood pressure; stimulation

Warnings: This product should not be used by persons who have glaucoma (certain types). • It should be used with special caution by persons who have diabetes, advanced hardening of the arteries, heart disease, high blood pressure, or thyroid disease. If you have any of these conditions, consult your doctor before using this product. • This product interacts with monoamine oxidase inhibitors, thyroid preparations, and tricyclic antidepressants. If you are currently taking any drugs of these types, check with your doctor before taking this product. If you are unsure of the type or contents of your medications, ask your doctor or pharmacist.

Comments: To avoid side effects such as burning, sneezing, or stinging, and a "rebound" increase in nasal congestion and discharge, do not exceed the recommended dose, and do not use this product for more than three or four continuous days. • This product should not be used by more than one person; sharing the dispenser may spread infection. • This product works best when it is used correctly. Refer to the instructions for the use of nasal sprays in the chapter on "Buying, Storing, and Using Drugs."

- Many nasal drops or sprays on the market contain oxymetazoline hydrochloride. This drug has a duration of action of about 12 hours, and because it needs to be used less often, it is less likely to cause "rebound" nasal congestion during use. Therefore, we recommend a product containing oxymetazoline hydrochloride over this product, which does not contain the ingredient.

Acceptable: Although we prefer a product containing oxymetazoline hydrochloride, this product also offers an effective formula for treating the conditions specified.

Correctol laxative

Manufacturer: Plough, Inc.

Dosage Form/Ingredients: Tablet: docusate sodium, 100 mg; yellow phenolphthalein, 64.8 mg

Use: For relief of constipation; as a stool softener

Side Effects: Excess loss of fluid; griping (cramps); mucus in feces; pink to purple rash with blistering

Warnings: Persons with a high fever (100° F or more), black or tarry stools, nausea, vomiting, abdominal pain; pregnant women; and children under the age of three should not use this product unless directed to do so by a doctor. • Do not use this product when constipation is caused by megacolon or other diseases of the intestine, or hypothyroidism. • Excessive use (daily for a month or more) of these products may cause diarrhea, vomiting, and loss of certain blood electrolytes. • Persons with a sensitivity to phenolphthalein should not use this product. • Never self-medicate with this product if constipation lasts longer than two weeks, or if the medication does not produce a laxative effect within a week. • Limit use to seven days unless directed otherwise by a doctor since this product may cause laxative-dependence (addiction) if used for a longer time. • An ingredient in this product is referred to as a stool softener. This product is recommended for relief of constipation only when the stool is hard and dry. Do not take another product containing mineral oil at the same time as you are taking this product.

Comments: This product may discolor the urine. • Evacuation may occur within six to twelve hours. • Although an exact generic equivalent of this item may not be available, very similar products are. Ask your pharmacist if you can save money by purchasing another item.

Acceptable: This product is an acceptable combination stimulant-stool softener laxative.

Cortaid topical steroid

Manufacturer: The Upjohn Company

Dosage Forms/Ingredient: Cream, Lotion, Ointment: hydrocortisone acetate, 0.5%

Use: For temporary relief of skin inflammation, irritation, itching, and rashes associated with such conditions as dermatitis, eczema, or poison ivy

Side Effects: Burning sensation; dryness; irritation; itching; rash; secondary infections

Warnings: Do not use this product if you have a disease that severely impairs blood circulation, or if you have a bacterial or viral infection. • This product is for external use only. • Avoid contact with the eyes. • Do not use this product for prolonged periods of time, and do not use it more frequently than directed on the label. If the condition does not improve after three days, discontinue use and consult your doctor or pharmacist. • If irritation (pain, itching, swelling, or rash) occurs, discontinue use. Consult your pharmacist. • Do not use on children under two years of age without consulting a physician.

Comments: While the label states that this product relieves itching, this action may take a couple of days to achieve. Use this product as directed; meanwhile, apply rubbing alcohol or witch hazel diluted with an equal amount of water to the area to relieve itching. Or, if the itching is intolerable, we recommend the use of a wet soak at least once a day along with regular use of this product. See "Buying, Storing, and Using Drugs" for directions. • If the affected area is extremely dry or is scaling, the skin may be moistened before applying the medication by soaking in water or by applying water with a clean cloth. The ointment form is preferred for use on dry skin. • Until recently, hydrocortisone-containing products required a prescription for purchase. They are now sold OTC in strengths of up to 0.5%. • There are generic equivalents to this product on the market. Consult your pharmacist for the best buy.

Preferred: *Hydrocortisone-containing products are preferred for relief of inflammatory rashes.*

Cortef Acetate anal-itch ointment

Manufacturer: The Upjohn Company

Dosage Form/Ingredient: Ointment: hydrocortisone acetate, 0.5%

Use: For temporary relief of burning, minor pain, skin inflammation, and itching around the rectum associated with hemorrhoids

Side Effects: Burning sensation; dryness; irritation; itching, rash; secondary infections

Warnings: Do not use this product in the presence of diseases that severely impair blood circulation, or in the presence of a bacterial or viral infection. • Use externally only, and avoid contact with the eyes. • Do not use this product if hemorrhoids are bleeding. • Do not use more frequently than indicated on the label. Discontinue use if irritation (pain, itching, or swelling) or rash appears, or if the condition does not improve in two or three days; consult your doctor or pharmacist. • Consult a doctor for use on children under two years of age.

Comments: If the affected area is extremely dry or is scaling, you may moisten the skin before applying the medication by soaking in water or applying water with a clean cloth. • While the label states that this product relieves itching, this action may take a couple of days to achieve. Use the product as directed; meanwhile, apply rubbing alcohol or witch hazel diluted half-and-half with water to the area between applications of the medication. If the itching is intolerable, we recommend the use of a "wet soak" at least once a day, along with use of this product. • There are generic equivalents of this product on the market. Ask your pharmacist for advice on the best buy. • Until recently, products containing hydrocortisone were available only by prescription. The drug may now be included in OTC products in strengths up to 0.5%.

Preferred: *The hydrocortisone in this product is an effective treatment for the relief of hemorrhoidal discomfort.*

Coryban-D cough remedy

Manufacturer: Pfipharmecs, Div. of Pfizer Pharmaceuticals

Dosage Form/Ingredients: Liquid (content per teaspoon): dextromethorphan hydrobromide, 7.5 mg; guaifenesin, 50 mg; phenylephrine hydro-chloride, 5 mg; acetaminophen, 120 mg; alcohol, 15%

Use: For temporary relief of cough, nasal congestion, fever, aches, and pains due to colds or "flu"; to convert a dry, nonproductive cough to a productive, phlegm-producing cough

Side Effects: Drowsiness; mild stimulation; nausea; vomiting; blurred vision; palpitations; flushing; nervousness; dizziness; insomnia. In over-dose: Blood disorders; rash

Warnings: This product should not be given to children under six years of age, and should be used with special caution by persons who have diabetes, heart disease, lung disease, liver or kidney disease, certain blood disorders, high blood pressure, or thyroid disease. If you have any of these conditions, consult your doctor before taking this product. • This product interacts with guanethidine and monoamine oxidase inhibitors. If you are currently taking any drugs of these types, check with your doctor before taking this product. If you are unsure of the type or contents of your medications, ask your doctor or pharmacist. • Pregnant women should not take this product, and it should not be given to newborn or premature infants. • When taken in overdose, acetaminophen is more toxic than aspirin. Follow dosage instructions carefully. • If your cough persists, or is accompanied by high fever, consult your doctor promptly. • Do not use this product to treat chronic coughs such as those from smok-ing or asthma, or to treat productive (hacking) coughs that produce phlegm.

Comments: If you require an expectorant, you need more moisture in your environment; drink eight to ten glasses of water daily. The use of a vaporizer or humidifier may also be beneficial. • The effectiveness of this product may diminish after it has been taken regularly for seven to ten days; consult your pharmacist about substituting another product. • Many other conditions (some serious) mimic the common cold. If symp-toms persist beyond one week, or if they occur regularly without regard to season, consult your doctor.

Unacceptable: *The combination of ingredients in this product—including an analgesic and a decongestant—is illogical for treatment of a cough.*

Coryban-D Decongestant cold remedy

Manufacturer: Pfipharmecs, Div. of Pfizer Pharmaceuticals

Dosage Form/Ingredients: Capsule: caffeine, 30 mg; chlorpheniramine maleate, 2 mg; phenylpropanolamine hydrochloride, 25 mg

Use: For relief of nasal congestion due to colds

Side Effects: Anxiety; blurred vision; chest pain; confusion; constipa-tion; dry mouth; difficult and painful urination; dizziness; drowsiness; headache; increased blood pressure; insomnia; loss of appetite; mild stimulation; nausea; nervousness; palpitations; rash; reduced sweating; tension; tremor; vomiting

Warnings: This product should be used with special caution by the elderly or debilitated, and by persons who have asthma, diabetes, en-larged prostate, glaucoma (certain types), heart disease, high blood pressure, kidney disease, liver disease, obstructed bladder, obstructed intestine, peptic ulcer, or thyroid disease. if you have any of these condi-tions, consult your doctor before taking this product. It should not be used by pregnant or nursing women, or be given to newborn or premature infants. • This product may cause drowsiness. Do not take it if you must drive, operate heavy machinery, or perform other tasks requiring mental alertness. To prevent oversedation, avoid the use of alcohol or other drugs that have sedative properties. • This product interacts with alcohol, guanethidine, monoamine oxidase inhibitors, sedative drugs, and tricyclic antidepressants. If you are currently taking any drugs of these types, check with your doctor before taking this product. If you are unsure of the type or contents of your medications, ask your doctor or pharmacist. • Because this product reduces sweating, avoid excessive work or exercise in hot weather.

Comments: Many other conditions (some serious) mimic the common cold. If symptoms persist beyond one week, or if they occur regularly without regard to season, consult your doctor. • The effectiveness of this product may diminish after being taken for seven to ten days; consult your pharmacist about substituting a product with another antihistamine if this product begins to lose its effectiveness for you. • Chew gum or suck on ice chips or a piece of hard candy to reduce mouth dryness.

Unacceptable: *The caffeine included in this product has no value in treatment of the condition specified.*

CoTylenol Children's cold remedy

Manufacturer: McNeil Consumer Products Company

Dosage Form/Ingredients: Liquid (content per teaspoon) pseudoephedrine hydrochloride, 7.5 mg; chlorpheniramine maleate, 0.5 mg; acetaminophen, 120 mg; alcohol, 7%

Use: For relief of nasal congestion, fever, aches, pains, and general discomfort due to colds

Side Effects: Anxiety; blurred vision; chest pain; confusion; constipation; dry mouth; difficult and painful urination; dizziness; drowsiness; headache; increased blood pressure; insomnia; loss of appetite; mild stimulation; nausea; nervousness; palpitations; rash; reduced sweating; tension; tremor; vomiting. In overdose: Blood disorders; rash

Warnings: This product should be used with special caution by the elderly or debilitated, and by persons who have asthma, diabetes, enlarged prostate, glaucoma (certain types), heart disease, high blood pressure, kidney disease, liver disease, obstructed bladder, obstructed intestine, lung disease, certain blood disorders, peptic ulcer, or thyroid disease. If your child has any of these conditions, consult your doctor before using this product. • It should not be used by pregnant or nursing women, or be given to newborn or premature infants. • This product may cause drowsiness and affect mental alertness. To prevent oversedation, avoid giving your child other drugs that have sedative properties. • This product interacts with alcohol, guanethidine, monoamine oxidase inhibitors, sedative drugs, and tricyclic antidepressants. If your child is currently taking any drugs of these types, check with your doctor before administering this product. If you are unsure of the type or contents of your child's medications, ask your doctor or pharmacist. • Because this product reduces sweating, the child should avoid excessive play or exercise in hot weather. • When taken in overdose, acetaminophen is more toxic than aspirin. Follow dosage instructions carefully.

Comments: Many other conditions (some serious) mimic the common cold. If symptoms persist beyond one week, or if they occur regularly without regard to season, consult your doctor. • The effectiveness of this product may diminish after being taken regularly for seven to ten days; consult your pharmacist about substituting another medication if this product begins to lose its effectiveness for your child. • Have your child chew gum or suck on ice chips or a piece of hard candy to relieve mouth dryness.

Acceptable: We prefer single-ingredient products rather than combination analgesic-decongestant-antihistamine products like this one.

CoTylenol cold remedy (liquid)

Manufacturer: McNeil Consumer Products Company

Dosage Form/Ingredients: Liquid (content per two tablespoons): acetaminophen, 650 mg; chlorpheniramine maleate, 4 mg; pseudoephedrine hydrochloride, 60 mg; dextromethorphan hydrobromide, 20 mg; alcohol, 7.5%

Use: For relief of nasal congestion, cough, fever, aches, pains, and general discomfort due to colds

Side Effects: Anxiety; blurred vision; chest pain; confusion; constipation; dry mouth; difficult and painful urination; dizziness; drowsiness; headache; increased blood pressure; insomnia; loss of appetite; mild stimulation; nausea; nervousness; palpitations; rash; reduced sweating; tension; tremor; vomiting. In overdose: Blood disorders; rash

Warnings: This product should be used with special caution by the elderly or debilitated, and by persons who have asthma, diabetes, enlarged prostate, glaucoma (certain types), heart disease, high blood pressure, kidney disease, liver disease, obstructed bladder, obstructed intestine, lung disease, certain blood disorders, peptic ulcer, or thyroid disease. If you have any of these conditions, consult your doctor before taking this product. It should not be used by pregnant or nursing women, or be given to newborn or premature infants. • This product may cause drowsiness. Do not take it if you must drive, operate heavy machinery or perform other tasks requiring mental alertness. To prevent oversedation, avoid the use of alcohol or other drugs that have sedative properties. • This product interacts with alcohol, guanethidine, monoamine oxidase inhibitors, sedative drugs, and tricyclic antidepressants. If you are currently taking any drugs of these types, check with your doctor before taking this product. If you are unsure of the type or contents of your medications, ask your doctor or pharmacist. • Because this product reduces sweating, avoid excessive work or exercise in hot weather. • If your cough persists or is accompanied by high fever, consult your doctor promptly. • When taken in overdose, acetaminophen is more toxic than aspirin. Follow dosage instructions carefully.

Comments: Many other conditions (some serious) mimic the common cold. If symptoms persist beyond one week, or if they occur regularly without regard to season, consult your doctor. • The effectiveness of this product may diminish after being taken regularly for seven to ten days; consult your pharmacist about substituting another medication if this product begins to lose its effectiveness for you. • Chew gum or suck on ice chips or a piece of hard candy to relieve dryness of the mouth.

Unacceptable: This product contains an analgesic, an antihistamine, a decongestant, and a cough suppressant. We believe you should treat your symptoms individually rather than with multiple-ingredient products like this.

CoTylenol cold remedy (tablet)

Manufacturer: McNeil Consumer Products Company

Dosage Form/Ingredients: Tablet: acetaminophen, 325 mg; chlorpheniramine maleate, 2 mg; pseudoephedrine hydrochloride, 30 mg

Use: For relief of nasal congestion, fever, aches, pains, and general discomfort due to colds

Side Effects: Anxiety; blurred vision; chest pain; confusion; constipation; dry mouth; difficult and painful urination; dizziness; drowsiness; headache; increased blood pressure; insomnia; loss of appetite; mild stimulation; nausea; nervousness; palpitations; rash; reduced sweating; tension; tremor; vomiting. In overdose: Blood disorders; rash

Warnings: This product should be used with special caution by the elderly or debilitated, and by persons who have asthma, diabetes, enlarged prostate, glaucoma (certain types), heart disease, high blood pressure, certain blood disorders, kidney disease, liver disease, obstructed bladder, obstructed intestine, lung disease, peptic ulcer, or thyroid disease. If you have any of these conditions, consult your doctor before taking this product. It should not be used by pregnant or nursing women, or be given to newborn or premature infants. • This product may cause drowsiness. Do not take it if you must drive, operate heavy machinery, or perform other tasks requiring mental alertness. To prevent oversedation, avoid the use of alcohol or other drugs that have sedative properties. • This product interacts with alcohol, guanethidine, monoamine oxidase inhibitors, sedative drugs, and tricyclic antidepressants. If you are currently taking any drugs of these types, check with your doctor before taking this product. If you are unsure of the type or contents of your medications, ask your doctor or pharmacist. • Because this product reduces sweating, avoid excessive work or exercise in hot weather. • When taken in overdose, acetaminophen is more toxic than aspirin. Follow dosage instructions carefully.

Comments: Many other conditions (some serious) mimic the common cold. If symptoms persist beyond one week, or if they occur regularly without regard to season, consult your doctor. • The effectiveness of this product may diminish after being taken regularly for seven to ten days; consult your pharmacist about substituting another medication if this product begins to lose its effectiveness for you. • Chew gum or suck on ice chips or a piece of hard candy to relieve mouth dryness.

Acceptable: We prefer single-ingredient products rather than combination analgesic-decongestant-antihistamine products like this one.

Cruex athlete's foot and jock itch remedy

Manufacturer: Pharmacraft Division, Pennwalt Corporation

Dosage Forms/Ingredients: Cream: zinc undecylenate, 20%; parachlorometaxylenol, 3%. Powder, Aerosol powder: calcium undecylenate, 10%

Use: For the prevention and treatment of athlete's foot and jock itch

Side Effects: Allergy; local irritation

Warnings: Diabetics and other persons with impaired circulation should not use this product without first consulting a physician. • Do not apply this product to mucous membranes, scraped areas, or to large areas of skin. • If your condition worsens, or if irritation occurs, stop using this product and consult your pharmacist. • When using the aerosol form of this product, be careful not to inhale any of the powder. • Check with your doctor before using this product on a child. Some doctors believe that children under 12 do not get athlete's foot, and a rash appearing between the toes of such an individual may be dermatitis or some other condition that this product would not treat.

Comments: Some lesions take months to heal, so it is important not to stop treatment too soon. • If foot lesions are consistently a problem, check the fit of your shoes. • Wash your hands thoroughly after applying this product. • The cream form of this product is more effective than the powders; the best action of the powders may be in drying the infected area. • The aerosol powder may be more expensive than the other forms of this product; check prices before paying for convenience you do not need.

Acceptable: *Although we prefer a tolnaftate product, this product contains zinc undecylenate, which is also a satisfactory treatment for athlete's foot.*

Daisy 2 urine test for pregnancy

Manufacturer: Bio-Dynamics Home Healthcare, Inc.
Product Form: Test tube and testing materials
Use: To test urine for determination of pregnancy
Comments: Use only a urine sample that has been freshly collected in the morning. • For accurate results, follow package directions carefully. The test tube must be left undisturbed and unvibrated for one hour, and must be kept away from heat and direct sunlight. • Read the results exactly one hour after starting the test. If a brown ring forms in the bottom of the test tube, you should assume that you are pregnant. Consult your doctor. • Test results may be interfered with if the urine contains a large quantity of protein, or if the patient is taking medication. • This test is highly accurate, unless it is performed earlier than nine days after the date on which the first missed menstrual period would have begun. • This kit contains supplies for two urine tests so that you can verify your first results.

Acceptable: *Pregnancy test kits are convenient, but may not be economical. A positive result indicates that you should see a doctor, and your doctor will probably do a pregnancy test to confirm the result. You are likely to pay for two tests.*

Datril analgesic

Manufacturer: Bristol-Myers Products
Dosage Form/Ingredient: Tablet: acetaminophen, 325 mg
Use: For the relief of pain of headache, toothache, sprains, muscular aches, menstruation; for the relief of discomforts and fever following immunizations or of colds or "flu"; for the temporary relief of minor aches and pains of arthritis and rheumatism
Side Effects: When taken in overdose: Blood disorders; rash
Warnings: This product should not be taken by those persons with certain blood disorders; or with heart, lung, liver, or kidney disease. • When taken in overdose, this product is more toxic than aspirin. The dosage instructions listed on the package should be followed carefully; toxicity may occur in adults or children with repeated doses.
Comments: Acetaminophen does not relieve inflammation, so if pain is caused by swelling or inflammation, it should not be used. Aspirin is better. • Generic substitutes for this product are available and may save you money. Ask your pharmacist for assistance.

Preferred: *We recommend this product because it contains a single effective ingredient.*

Deep-Down muscular pain remedy

Manufacturer: The J. B. Williams Company, Inc.

Dosage Form/Ingredients: Ointment: camphor, 0.5%; menthol, 5%; methyl nicotinate, 0.7%; methyl salicylate, 15%

Use: Used externally to temporarily relieve pain in muscles and other areas

Side Effects: Allergic reactions (rash, itching, soreness); local irritation; local numbness

Warnings: This product is for external use only. • Do not use it on broken or irritated skin, or on large areas of the body; keep it away from the eyes. • If the pain in muscles or other areas persists, call your doctor. • While you are using this product, avoid exposure to direct sunlight, heat lamp, or sun lamp. • Discontinue use and consult your pharmacist if irritation (rash, itching, or swelling) or pain occurs. • Before using this product on a child under 12 years of age, consult your doctor. • Children might be attracted to the smell of this product; it should be stored safely out of their reach. • If a child swallows some of this product, call your doctor immediately. • Do not rub this product into the skin.

Acceptable: We prefer a product that does not contain camphor.

Demazin cold and allergy remedy

Manufacturer: Schering Corporation

Dosage Form/Ingredients: Sustained-action tablet: phenylephrine hydrochloride, 20 mg; chorpheniramine maleate, 4 mg

Use: For relief of nasal congestion due to colds and upper respiratory allergies

Side Effects: Anxiety; blurred vision; chest pain; confusion; constipation; dry mouth; difficult and painful urination; dizziness; drowsiness; headache; increased blood pressure; insomnia; loss of appetite; mild stimulation; nausea; nervousness; palpitations; rash; reduced sweating; tension; tremor; vomiting

Warnings: This product should be used with special caution by the elderly or debilitated, and by persons who have asthma, diabetes, an enlarged prostate, glaucoma (certain types), heart disease, high blood pressure, kidney disease, liver disease, obstructed bladder, obstructed intestine, peptic ulcer, or thyroid disease. If you have any of these conditions, consult your doctor before taking this product. It should not be used by pregnant or nursing women, or be given to newborn or premature infants. • This product may cause drowsiness. Do not take it if you must drive, operate heavy machinery, or perform other tasks requiring mental alertness. To prevent oversedation, avoid the use of alcohol or other drugs that have sedative properties. • This product interacts with alcohol, guanethidine, monoamine oxidase inhibitors, sedative drugs, and tricyclic antidepressants. If you are currently taking any drugs of these types, check with your doctor before taking this product. If you are unsure of the type or contents of your medications, ask your doctor or pharmacist. • Because this product reduces sweating, avoid excessive work or exercise in hot weather. • This product has sustained action; never increase the recommended dose or take it more frequently than directed. A serious overdose could result.

Comments: Many other conditions (some serious) mimic the common cold. If symptoms persist beyond one week, or if they occur regularly without regard to season, consult your doctor. • The effectiveness of this product may diminish after being taken for seven to ten days; consult your pharmacist about substituting a different product if this product begins to lose its effectiveness for you. • Chew gum or suck on ice chips or a piece of hard candy to reduce mouth dryness. • This product should not be crushed or chewed. It must be swallowed whole.

Acceptable: We prefer single-ingredient products rather than combination antihistamine-decongestant products like this one.

Dermolate anal-itch ointment

Manufacturer: Schering Corporation
Dosage Form/Ingredient: Ointment: hydrocortisone, 0.5%
Use: For temporary relief of burning, minor pain, skin inflammation, and itching around the rectum associated with hemorrhoids
Side Effects: Burning sensation; dryness; irritation; itching; rash; secondary infections
Warnings: Do not use this product in the presence of diseases that severely impair blood circulation, or in the presence of a bacterial or viral infection. • Use externally only, and avoid contact with the eyes. • Do not use this product if hemorrhoids are bleeding. • Do not use more frequently than indicated on the label. Discontinue use if irritation (pain, itching, or swelling) or rash appears, or if the condition does not improve in two or three days; consult your doctor or pharmacist. • Consult a doctor for use on children under two years of age.
Comments: If the affected area is extremely dry or is scaling, you may moisten the skin before applying the medication by soaking in water or applying water with a clean cloth. • While the label states that this product relieves itching, this action may take a couple of days to achieve. Use the product as directed; meanwhile, apply rubbing alcohol or witch hazel diluted half-and-half with water to the area between applications of the medication. If the itching is intolerable, we recommend the use of a "wet soak" at least once a day, along with use of this product. There are generic equivalents of this product on the market. Ask your pharmacist for advice on the best buy. • Until recently, products containing hydrocortisone were available only by prescription. The drug may now be included in OTC products in strengths up to 0.5%. • This product comes packaged in an oversize box, which may be deceiving; there is no applicator included with the ointment.

Preferred: The hydrocortisone in this product is an effective treatment for the relief of hemorrhoidal discomfort.

Dermolate topical steroid

Manufacturer: Schering Corporation
Dosage Forms/Ingredients: Cream, Lotion: hydrocortisone, 0.5%; Spray: alcohol, 24%; hydrocortisone, 0.5%
Use: For temporary relief of skin inflammation, irritation, itching, and rashes associated with such conditions as dermatitis, eczema, or poison ivy
Side Effects: Burning sensation; dryness; irritation; itching; rash; secondary infections
Warnings: Do not use this product if you have a disease that severely impairs blood circulation, or if you have a bacterial or viral infection. • This product is for external use only. • Avoid contact with the eyes. • Do not use this product for prolonged periods of time, and do not use it more frequently than directed on the label. If the condition does not improve

after three days, discontinue use and consult your doctor or pharmacist. • If irritation (pain, itching, swelling, or rash) occurs, discontinue use. Consult your pharmacist. • Do not use on children under two years of age without consulting a physician.

Comments: While the label states that this product relieves itching, this action may take a couple of days to achieve. Use this product as directed; meanwhile, apply rubbing alcohol or witch hazel diluted with an equal amount of water to the area to relieve itching. Or, if the itching is intolerable, we recommend the use of a wet soak at least once a day along with regular use of this product. See "Buying, Storing, and Using Drugs" for directions. • If the affected area is extremely dry or is scaling, the skin may be moistened before applying the medication by soaking in water or by applying water with a clean cloth. • Until recently, hydrocortisone-containing products required a prescription for purchase. They are now sold OTC in strengths of up to 0.5%. • There are generic equivalents to this product on the market. Consult your pharmacist for the best buy.

Preferred: *Hydrocortisone-containing products are preferred for relief of inflammatory rashes.*

Desenex athlete's foot and jock itch remedy

Manufacturer: Pharmacraft Division, Pennwalt Corporation

Dosage Forms/Ingredients: Ointment: undecylenic acid, 5%; zinc undecylenate, 20%. Powder, Aerosol powder: undecylenic acid, 2%; zinc undecylenate, 20%. Soap: undecylenic acid, 2%. Solution: undecylenic acid, 10%; isopropyl alcohol, 47%

Use: For the treatment of athlete's foot and jock itch

Side Effects: Allergy; local irritation

Warnings: Diabetics and other persons with impaired circulation should not use this product without first consulting a physician. • Do not apply this product to mucous membranes, scraped skin, or to large areas of skin. • If your condition worsens, or if irritation occurs, stop using this product and consult your pharmacist. When using the aerosol form of this product, be careful not to inhale any of the powder. • Check with your doctor before using this product on a child. Some doctors believe that children under 12 do not get athlete's foot, and a rash appearing between the toes of such an individual may be dermatitis or some other condition that this product would not treat.

Comments: Some lesions take months to heal, so it is important not to stop treatment too soon. • If foot lesions are consistently a problem, check the fit of your shoes. • Wash your hands thoroughly after applying this product. • The ointment and solution forms of this product are preferable to the powders and soap for effectiveness; the best action of the powders may be in drying the infected area. Use the soap frequently for best results, unless directed otherwise by your doctor. • The aerosol powder may be more expensive than the other forms of this product; check prices before paying for convenience you do not need.

Acceptable: *Although we prefer a tolnaftate product, this product contains undecylenic acid, which is also a satisfactory treatment for athlete's foot.*

Dex-A-Diet II appetite suppressant

Manufacturer: O'Connor Products Company

Dosage Form/Ingredients: Capsule: phenylpropanolamine hydrochloride, 75 mg; caffeine, 200 mg

Use: As an aid in dietary control

Side Effects: Blurred vision; diarrhea; nausea; dizziness; drowsiness; headache; increase in blood pressure, blood sugar, heart rate, and thyroid activity; insomnia; nervousness; palpitations. In larger than the recommended dose: Irregular heartbeat; nasal dryness; upset stomach

Warnings: Persons with heart disease, high blood pressure, diabetes, kidney or thyroid disease; children under 16 years of age; and pregnant or nursing women should not use this product. Consult your doctor for recommendations. • This product interacts with alcohol, guanethidine, monoamine oxidase inhibitors, sedative drugs, and tricyclic antidepressants. If you are currently taking any of these drugs, or if you are unsure of the type or contents of your medications, consult your doctor or pharmacist before taking this product. • Avoid taking this drug while using a decongestant. • Avoid continuous use for longer than three months. • Discontinue use if you experience rapid pulse, dizziness, or palpitations.

Comments: During the first week of therapy with this product, expect increased frequency of urination. • Many medical authorities believe that the ingredient phenylpropanolamine does not help in weight-loss programs. However, the FDA Review Panel has reported that it is effective. • If you want to use this product, remember that you become tolerant to any beneficial effects after a couple of weeks. After each two weeks of use, stop for one week, then resume use. • The primary value in a product of this nature is in following the caloric reduction plan that goes with it. • This is a sustained release product. To avoid sleep disturbances, do not take it less than 12 hours before bedtime.

Fair: *This product contains caffeine, which does not contribute to permanent weight loss and may worsen side effects such as nervousness.*

Dexatrim appetite suppressant

Manufacturer: Thompson Medical Company, Inc.

Dosage Forms/Ingredients: Capsule: phenylpropanolamine hydrochloride, 50 mg; caffeine, 200 mg. Extra strength capsule: phenylpropanolamine 75 mg; caffeine, 200 mg

Use: As an aid in dietary control

Side Effects: Blurred vision; diarrhea; nausea; dizziness; drowsiness; headache; increase in blood pressure, blood sugar, heart rate, and thyroid activity; insomnia; nervousness; palpitations. In larger than the recommended dose: Irregular heartbeat; nasal dryness; upset stomach

Warnings: Persons with heart disease, high blood pressure, diabetes, kidney or thyroid disease; children under 16 years of age; and pregnant or nursing women should not use this product. Consult your doctor for recommendations. • This product interacts with alcohol, guanethidine, monoamine oxidase inhibitors, sedative drugs, and tricyclic antidepressants. If you are currently taking any of these drugs, or if you are unsure of the type or contents of your medications, consult your doctor or pharmacist before taking this product. • Avoid taking this drug while using a decongestant. • Avoid continuous use for longer than three months. • Discontinue use if you experience rapid pulse, dizziness, or palpitations.

Comments: During the first week of therapy with this product, expect increased frequency of urination. • Many medical authorities believe that the ingredient phenylpropanolamine does not help in weight-loss programs. However, the FDA Review Panel has reported that it is effective. •

If you want to use this product, remember that you become tolerant to any beneficial effects after a couple of weeks. After each two weeks of use, stop for one week, then resume use. • The primary value in a product of this nature is in following the caloric reduction plan that goes with it. • This is a sustained release product. To avoid sleep disturbances, do not take it less than 12 hours before bedtime.

Fair: This product contains caffeine, which does not contribute to permanent weight loss and may worsen side effects such as nervousness.

Dietac appetite suppressant (capsule)

Manufacturer: Menley and James Laboratories
Dosage Form/Ingredients: Capsule: phenylpropanolamine hydrochloride, 50 mg; caffeine, 200 mg
Use: As an aid in dietary control
Side Effects: Blurred vision; diarrhea; nausea; dizziness; drowsiness; headache; increase in blood pressure, blood sugar, heart rate, and thyroid activity; insomnia; nervousness; palpitations. In larger than the recommended dose: Irregular heartbeat; nasal dryness; upset stomach
Warnings: Persons with heart disease, high blood pressure, diabetes, kidney or thyroid disease; children under 16 years of age; and pregnant or nursing women should not use this product. Consult your doctor for recommendations. • This product interacts with alcohol, guanethidine, monoamine oxidase inhibitors, sedative drugs, and tricyclic antidepressants. If you are currently taking any of these drugs, or if you are unsure of the type or contents of your medications, consult your doctor or pharmacist before taking this product. • Avoid taking this drug while using a decongestant. • Avoid continuous use for longer than three months. • Discontinue use if you experience rapid pulse, dizziness, or palpitations.
Comments: During the first week of therapy with this product, expect increased frequency of urination. • Many medical authorities believe that the ingredient phenylpropanolamine does not help in weight-loss programs. However, the FDA Review Panel has reported that it is effective. • If you want to use this product, remember that you become tolerant to any beneficial effects after a couple of weeks. After each two weeks of use, stop for one week, then resume use. • The primary value in a product of this nature is in following the caloric reduction plan that goes with it. • This product has sustained action. To avoid sleep disturbance, do not take it less than 12 hours before bedtime.

Fair: This product contains caffeine, which does not contribute to permanent weight loss and may worsen side effects such as nervousness.

Dietac appetite suppressant
(tablet, liquid, maximum strength capsule)

Manufacturer: Menley and James Laboratories
Dosage Forms/Ingredient: Tablet, Liquid (content per 5 drops): phenylpropanolamine hydrochloride, 25 mg. Maximum strength capsule: phenylpropanolamine hydrochloride, 37.5 mg or 75 mg
Use: As an aid in dietary control
Side Effects: Blurred vision; diarrhea; nausea; dizziness; drowsiness; headache; increase in blood pressure, blood sugar, heart rate, and thyroid activity; insomnia; nervousness; palpitations. In larger than the recommended dose: Irregular heartbeat; nasal dryness; upset stomach
Warnings: Persons with heart disease, high blood pressure, diabetes, kidney or thyroid disease; children under 16 years of age; and pregnant or

nursing women should not use this product. Consult your doctor for recommendations. • This product interacts with alcohol, guanethidine, monoamine oxidase inhibitors, sedative drugs, and tricyclic anti-depressants. If you are currently taking any of these drugs, or if you are unsure of the type or contents of your medications, consult your doctor or pharmacist before taking this product. • Avoid taking this drug while using a decongestant. • Avoid continuous use for longer than three months. • Discontinue use if you experience rapid pulse, dizziness, or palpitations.

Comments: During the first week of therapy with this product, expect increased frequency of urination. • Many medical authorities believe that the ingredient phenylpropanolamine does not help in weight-loss programs. However, the FDA Review Panel has reported that it is effective. • If you want to use this product, remember that you become tolerant to any beneficial effects after a couple of weeks. After each two weeks of use, stop for one week, then resume use. • The primary value in a product of this nature is in following the caloric reduction plan that goes with it. • The 75 mg maximum strength capsule form of this product has sustained action. To avoid sleep disturbance, do not take it less than 12 hours before bedtime.

Acceptable: This product is preferable to other available dietary aids because it uses a single effective ingredient.

Di-Gel antacid and antiflatulent

Manufacturer: Plough, Inc.

Dosage Forms/Ingredients: Liquid (content per teaspoon): aluminum hydroxide, 282 mg; magnesium hydroxide, 87 mg; simethicone, 25 mg; sodium, 8.5 mg. Tablet: aluminum hydroxide-magnesium carbonate codried gel, 282 mg; magnesium hydroxide, 85 mg; simethicone, 25 mg; sodium, 10.6 mg

Use: For relief of acid indigestion, heartburn, and/or sour stomach when accompanied by painful gas symptoms

Side Effects: Constipation; diarrhea; dizziness; mouth irritation; nausea; rash; abdominal discomfort; vomiting

Warnings: Persons with kidney disease or those on a salt-free diet should not use this product. In persons with kidney disease, repeated (daily) use of this product may cause nausea, vomiting, depressed reflexes, or breathing difficulties. • Long-term (several weeks) use of this product may lead to intestinal obstruction and dehydration. Phosphate depletion may occur, leading to weakness, loss of appetite, and eventually bone pain. Phosphate depletion may be prevented by drinking at least one glass of milk a day. • Do not take this product within two hours of a dose of a tetracycline antibiotic. • Consult your physician or pharmacist before taking this product if you are already taking iron, a vitamin-mineral product, chlorpromazine, phenytoin, digoxin, quinidine, or warfarin, or if you are unsure of the type and contents of the medications you are taking. • Never self-medicate with this product if your symptoms occur regularly (two or three or more times a month). Consult your doctor if the symptoms are worse than usual, if you have chest pains or feel "tightness" in the chest, or if you are sweating or short of breath. In fact, we do not recommend self-treatment for severe attacks of heartburn, indigestion, or stomach upset in any circumstances. If you do decide that your symptoms are mild enough to warrant self-medication, limit treatment to two weeks. If symptoms persist, consult your doctor.

Comments: To prevent constipation, drink at least eight glasses of

water a day. If constipation persists, consult your doctor or pharmacist. •
This product must be taken exactly as directed on the label, unless your
doctor has instructed you otherwise. Never skip a dose just because you
feel better. If you grow tired of the taste, ask your pharmacist to suggest a
different product. • The liquid form of this product is superior to the tablet
form and should be used unless you have been specifically directed to
use the tablet. • Exact generic equivalents of this product may not be
available. However, your pharmacist may be able to suggest a similar
product that can save you money. • Simethicone is included to relieve
bloating and gas formation; this ingredient makes it easier for you to
eliminate gas by belching and passing flatus. If you do not suffer from
bloating and gas pains, use a product without simethicone. You will probably save money.

*Acceptable: Generally, we consider it preferable to treat acid indigestion
and flatulence (gas) separately rather than with a combination product.*

Dimacol cough remedy

Manufacturer: A. H. Robins Company
Dosage Forms/Ingredients: Capsule: guaifenesin, 100 mg; pseudoephedrine hydrochloride, 30 mg; dextromethorphan hydrobromide, 15 mg.
Liquid (content per teaspoon): guaifenesin, 100 mg; pseudoephedrine hydrochloride, 30 mg; dextromethorphan hydrobromide, 15 mg; alcohol,
4.75%
Use: For temporary relief of cough and nasal congestion due to colds
or "flu"; to convert a dry, nonproductive cough to a productive, phlegm-
producing cough
Side Effects: Drowsiness; mild stimulation; nausea; vomiting; blurred
vision; palpitations; flushing; nervousness; dizziness; insomnia
Warnings: This product should be used with special caution by children
under two years of age, and by persons who have diabetes, heart disease,
high blood pressure, or thyroid disease. In these situations, consult your
doctor before taking this product. • This product interacts with
guanethidine and monoamine oxidase inhibitors. If you are currently taking any drugs of these types, check with your doctor before taking this
product. If you are unsure of the type or contents of your medications,
ask your doctor or pharmacist. • If your cough persists, or is accompanied by high fever, consult your doctor promptly. • Do not use this product to treat chronic coughs, such as from smoking or asthma. • Do not
use this product to treat productive (hacking) coughs that produce
phlegm.
Comments: If you require an expectorant, you need more moisture in
your environment. Drink eight to ten glasses of water daily. The use of a
vaporizer or humidifier may also be beneficial. • Many other conditons
(some serious) mimic the common cold. If symptoms persist beyond one
week or if they occur regularly without regard to season, consult your
doctor.

*Fair: This product contains a decongestant, an ingredient not directly
related to treatment of a cough. Products containing more appropriate ingredients are available.*

Dimetane allergy remedy

Manufacturer: A. H. Robins Company
Dosage Forms/Ingredients: Liquid (content per teaspoon): brompheniramine maleate, 2 mg. Tablet: brompheniramine maleate, 4 mg

Use: For temporary relief of symptoms of hay fever and upper respiratory allergy; treatment of mild inflammatory skin conditions

Side Effects: Blurred vision; confusion; constipation; diarrhea; difficult urination; dizziness; drowsiness; dry mouth; headache; insomnia; nasal congestion; nausea; nervousness; palpitations; rash; rash from exposure to sunlight; reduced sweating; restlessness; severe abdominal cramping; sore throat; vomiting

Warnings: This product should be used with special caution by persons who have asthma, diabetes, enlarged prostate, glaucoma (certain types), heart disease, high blood pressure, kidney disease, liver disease, obstructed bladder, obstructed intestine, peptic ulcer, or thyroid disease. If you have any of these conditions, consult your doctor before taking this product. • It should not be used by pregnant or nursing women, or be given to newborn or premature infants. • The elderly should use this product with special caution; they are more likely to suffer side effects to the medication than are other people. • Children taking this product may become restless and excited; if this occurs, consult your doctor. • This product may cause drowsiness. Do not take it if you must drive, operate heavy machinery, or perform other tasks requiring mental alertness. To prevent oversedation, avoid the use of alcohol or other drugs that have sedative properties. • This product interacts with alcohol, guanethidine, monoamine oxidase inhibitors, sedative drugs, and tricyclic anti-depressants. If you are currently taking any drugs of these types, check with your doctor before taking this product. If you are unsure of the type or contents of your medications, ask your doctor or pharmacist. • Because this product reduces sweating, avoid excessive work or exercise in hot weather.

Comments: The effectiveness of this product may diminish after being taken for seven to ten days; consult your pharmacist about substituting another antihistamine if this product begins to lose its effectiveness for you. • Chew gum or suck on ice chips or a piece of hard candy to reduce mouth dryness.

Acceptable: *We prefer the antihistamine chlorpheniramine maleate; however this product is also effective.*

Doan's Pills analgesic

Manufacturer: Purex Corporation

Dosage Form/Ingredients: Tablet: caffeine, 32 mg; magnesium salicylate, 325 mg

Use: For temporary relief from pain of backache

Side Effects: Minor nausea

Warnings: Persons with asthma, hay fever, or other allergies should be extremely careful about using this product. This product may interfere with the treatment of gout. It may cause an increased bleeding tendency and should not be taken by persons with a history of bleeding, peptic ulcer, or stomach bleeding. If you have any of the conditions described above, consult your doctor or pharmacist before using this product. • Do not use this product if you are consuming alcohol, or taking methotrexate, oral anticoagulants, oral antidiabetics, probenecid, steroids, or sulfinpyrazone; if you are unsure of the type or contents of your medications, ask your doctor or pharmacist. • The dosage instructions listed on the package should be followed carefully; toxicity may occur in adults or children with repeated doses. Salicylates are involved in more poisonings in children under age five than any other group of drugs.

Comments: Caffeine has no proven pain-relieving value; the caffeine in this product may have a slight stimulating effect. You could get the same effect by taking an aspirin tablet with a cup of coffee or tea, and by doing so you would save money.

Unacceptable: The caffeine in this product has no proven pain-relieving value.

Dr. Scholl's Corn/Callus Salve corn and callus remover

Manufacturer: Scholl, Inc.

Dosage Form/Ingredient: Ointment: unspecified quantity of salicylic acid

Use: For removal of corns and calluses

Warnings: Do not use this product if you have diabetes or poor circulation. • Do not apply if the corn or callus is infected. • This product is extremely corrosive, and its overuse can cause the death of surrounding skin. Follow the directions on the package carefully and exactly. Cover the surrounding skin with tape or petroleum jelly before use. • Do not stop treatment too soon; some lesions take months to heal. • If the condition worsens, stop using the product and call your pharmacist.

Comments: After applying this product, wash your hands thoroughly. • Remember to check the fit of your shoes. Well-fitting footwear helps prevent corns and calluses.

Not Evaluated: We cannot evaluate this product because the manufacturer fails to supply sufficient information about its ingredients.

Dr. Scholl's "2" Drop corn and callus remover

Manufacturer: Scholl, Inc.

Dosage Form/Ingredients: Liquid (content per ounce): alcohol, 15%; ether, 9.63 gm; unspecified quantity of salicylic acid

Use: For removal of corns and calluses

Side Effects: Allergy; local irritation

Warnings: Do not use this product if you have diabetes or poor circulation. • Do not apply if the corn or callus is infected. • This product is extremely corrosive, and its overuse can cause the death of surrounding skin. Follow the directions on the package carefully and exactly. Cover the surrounding skin with tape or petroleum jelly before use. When applying between the toes, hold them apart until the product is dry. • This product is flammable; do not use around an open flame. • This product creates a film over the area as it is applied. Do not be alarmed, and do not remove the film. • Do not stop treatment too soon; some lesions take months to heal. • If the condition worsens, stop using the product and call your pharmacist.

Comments: After applying this product, wash your hands thoroughly. • Remember to check the fit of your shoes. Well-fitting footwear helps prevent corns and calluses. • Keep the bottle tightly capped between uses.

Not Evaluated: We cannot evaluate this product because the manufacturer fails to supply sufficient information about its ingredients.

Dr. Scholl's Waterproof Corn Pads
corn and callus remover

Manufacturer: Scholl, Inc.

Dosage Form/Ingredient: Medicated disc: unspecified quantity of salicylic acid

Use: To relieve pressure, soften corn, and allow its removal

Side Effects: Allergy; local irritation

Warnings: Do not use this product if you have diabetes or poor circulation. • Do not apply if the corn or callus is infected. • This product is extremely corrosive, and its overuse can cause the death of surrounding skin. Follow the directions on the package carefully and exactly. Cover the surrounding skin with tape or petroleum jelly before use. • Do not stop treatment too soon; some lesions take months to heal. • If the condition worsens, stop using the product and call your pharmacist.

Comments: After applying this product, wash your hands thoroughly. • Remember to check the fit of your shoes. Well-fitting footwear helps prevent corns and calluses.

Not Evaluated: *We cannot evaluate this product because the manufacturer fails to supply sufficient information about its ingredients.*

Donnagel diarrhea remedy

Manufacturer: A. H. Robins Company

Dosage Form/Ingredients: Suspension (content per 2 tablespoons): atropine sulfate, 0.0194 mg; hyoscine hydrobromide, 0.0065 mg; hyoscyamine sulfate, 0.1037 mg; kaolin, 6 gm; pectin, 142.8 mg

Use: For the treatment of common diarrhea

Side Effects: Blurred vision; coughing and sore throat; difficult urination; drowsiness; dry mouth; fever; headache; nervousness; palpitations; warm skin; weakness

Warnings: Persons with glaucoma, myasthenia gravis, and certain types of heart, liver, or kidney disease should not use this product. • If you are taking any other drugs, do not take this product until you have first checked with your doctor or pharmacist. • This product should not be used without first consulting a doctor by a person who is under age three or over age 60, has a history of asthma, heart disease, peptic ulcer, or is pregnant. • Discontinue use if blurring of vision, rapid pulse, or dizziness occurs. • Do not use frequently or for prolonged periods and do not exceed the recommended dosage. • If eye pain occurs, discontinue use and see your doctor immediately. • Decrease dosage if the product makes your mouth dry. • Diarrhea should stop in two or three days. If it persists longer, or recurs frequently or in the presence of a high fever, call your doctor. • Since this product reduces sweating, avoid excessive work or exercise in hot weather.

Comments: Donnagel requires a lower dose than many other antidiarrheals. Be sure to read the label carefully. • Be sure to drink at least eight glasses of water each day while taking this product. • This product may cause dryness of the mouth. To reduce this feeling, chew gum or suck on ice chips or a piece of hard candy.

Unacceptable: *We do not recommend the use of diarrhea remedies that, like this one, contain anticholinergics.*

Donnagel-PG diarrhea remedy

Manufacturer: A. H. Robins Company

Dosage Form/Ingredients: Suspension (content per 2 tablespoons): alcohol, 5%; atropine sulfate, 0.0194 mg; hyoscine hydrobromide, 0.0065 mg; hyoscyamine sulfate, 0.1037 mg; kaolin, 6 gm; pectin, 142.8 mg; powdered opium, 24 mg

Use: For the treatment of common diarrhea

Side Effects: Blurred vision; coughing and sore throat; difficult urination; dizziness; drowsiness; dry mouth; faintness; fever, flushing of face; headache; loss of appetite; mental confusion; nervousness; palpitations; sedation; skin rash; warm skin; weakness

Warnings: Persons with glaucoma, myasthenia gravis, and certain types of heart, liver, or kidney disease should not use this product. • If you are taking any other drugs, do not take this product until you have first checked with your doctor or pharmacist. • This product should not be used without first consulting a doctor by a person who is under age three or over age 60, has a history of asthma, heart disease, peptic ulcer, or is pregnant. • Discontinue use if blurring of vision, rapid pulse, or dizziness occurs. • Do not use frequently or for prolonged periods, and do not exceed the recommended dosage. • If eye pain occurs, discontinue use and see your doctor immediately. • Decrease dosage if the product makes your mouth dry. • Diarrhea should stop in two or three days. If it persists longer, or recurs frequently or in the presence of a high fever, call your doctor. • Avoid excessive use of alcohol, tranquilizers, or any drug that sedates the nervous system. • Since this product reduces sweating, avoid excessive work or exercise in hot weather.

Comments: This product contains a narcotic, but when used as directed, you need not worry about addiction to it. Be sure to drink at least eight glasses of water each day while taking this product. • This product may cause dryness of the mouth. To reduce this feeling, chew gum or suck on ice chips or a piece of hard candy. • Over-the-counter sale of this product may not be permitted in some states.

Unacceptable: *We do not recommend the use of diarrhea remedies that, like this one, contain anticholinergics.*

Dorbane laxative

Manufacturer: Riker Laboratories, Inc.

Dosage Form/Ingredient: Tablet: danthron, 75 mg

Use: For relief of constipation

Side Effects: Excess loss of fluid; griping (cramps); mucus in feces

Warnings: Persons with a high fever (100° F or more), black or tarry stools, nausea, vomiting, abdominal pain; pregnant women; and children under the age of three should not use this product unless directed to do so by a doctor. • Do not use this product when constipation is caused by megacolon or other diseases of the intestine, or hypothyroidism. • Excessive use (daily for a month or more) of these products may cause diarrhea, vomiting, and loss of certain blood electrolytes. • Never self-medicate with this product if constipation lasts longer than two weeks, or if the medication does not produce a laxative effect within a week. • Limit use to seven days unless directed otherwise by a doctor since this product may cause laxative-dependence (addiction) if used for a longer time.

Comments: Evacuation may occur within six to twelve hours. • This product may discolor the urine.

Acceptable: *We prefer bulk-forming laxatives; however, this product is also effective.*

Dorbantyl, Dorbantyl Forte laxatives

Manufacturer: Riker Laboratories, Inc.

Dosage Forms/Ingredients: Dorbantyl: Capsule: danthron, 25 mg;

docusate sodium, 50 mg. Dorbantyl Forte: Capsule: danthron, 50 mg; docusate sodium, 100 mg

Use: For relief of constipation; as a stool softener

Side Effects: Excess loss of fluid; griping (cramps); mucus in feces

Warnings: Persons with a high fever (100° F or more), black or tarry stools, nausea, vomiting, abdominal pain; pregnant women; and children under the age of three should not use these products unless directed to do so by a doctor. • Do not use these products when constipation is caused by megacolon or other diseases of the intestine, or hypothyroidism. • Excessive use (daily for a month or more) of these products may cause diarrhea, vomiting, and loss of certain blood electrolytes. • Never self-medicate with these products if constipation lasts longer than two weeks, or if the medication does not produce a laxative effect within a week. • Limit use to seven days unless directed otherwise by a doctor since these products may cause laxative-dependence (addiction) if used for a longer time. • An ingredient in these products is referred to as a stool softener. These products are recommended for relief of constipation only when the stool is hard and dry. Do not take another product containing mineral oil at the same time as you are taking one of these products.

Comments: These products may discolor the urine. • Evacuation may occur within six to twelve hours. • Although exact generic equivalents of these items may not be available, very similar products are. Ask your pharmacist if you can save money by purchasing another item.

Acceptable: This product is an acceptable combination stimulant-stool softener laxative.

Doxidan laxative

Manufacturer: Hoechst-Roussel Pharmaceuticals Inc.

Dosage Form/Ingredients: Capsule: danthron, 50 mg; docusate calcium, 60 mg

Use: For relief of constipation; as a stool softener

Side Effects: Excess loss of fluid; griping (cramps); mucus in feces

Warnings: Persons with a high fever (100° F or more), black or tarry stools, nausea, vomiting, abdominal pain; pregnant women; and children under the age of three should not use this product unless directed to do so by a doctor. • Do not use this product when constipation is caused by megacolon or other diseases of the intestine, or hypothyroidism. • Excessive use (daily for a month or more) of these products may cause diarrhea, vomiting, and loss of certain blood electrolytes. • Never self-medicate with this product if constipation lasts longer than two weeks, or if the medication does not produce a laxative effect within a week. • Limit use to seven days unless directed otherwise by a doctor since this product may cause laxative-dependence (addiction) if used for a longer time. • An ingredient in this product is referred to as a stool softener. This product is recommended for relief of constipation only when the stool is hard and dry. Do not take another product containing mineral oil at the same time as you are taking this product.

Comments: This product may discolor the urine. • Evacuation may occur within six to twelve hours. • Although an exact generic equivalent of this item may not be available, very similar products are. Ask your pharmacist if you can save money by purchasing another item.

Acceptable: This product is an acceptable combination stimulant-stool softener laxative.

Dristan-AF cold and allergy remedy

Manufacturer: Whitehall Laboratories

Dosage Form/Ingredients: Tablet: phenylephrine hydrochloride, 5 mg; chlorpheniramine maleate, 2 mg; acetaminophen, 325 mg; caffeine, 16.2 mg

Use: For relief of nasal congestion, fever, aches, pains, and general discomfort due to colds and upper respiratory allergies

Side Effects: Anxiety; blurred vision; chest pain; confusion; constipation; dry mouth; difficult and painful urination; dizziness; drowsiness; headache; increased blood pressure; insomnia; loss of appetite; mild stimulation; nausea; nervousness; palpitations; rash; reduced sweating; tension; tremor; vomiting. In overdose: Blood disorders; rash

Warnings: This product should be used with special caution by the elderly or debilitated, and by persons who have asthma, diabetes, enlarged prostate, glaucoma (certain types), heart disease, high blood pressure, kidney disease, liver disease, obstructed bladder, obstructed intestine, lung disease, certain blood disorders, peptic ulcer, or thyroid disease. If you have any of these conditions, consult your doctor before taking this product. It should not be used by pregnant or nursing women, or be given to newborn or premature infants. • This product may cause drowsiness. Do not take it if you must drive, operate heavy machinery, or perform other tasks requiring mental alertness. To prevent oversedation, avoid the use of alcohol or other drugs that have sedative properties. • This product interacts with alcohol, guanethidine, monoamine oxidase inhibitors, sedative drugs, and tricyclic antidepressants. If you are currently taking any drugs of these types, check with your doctor before taking this product. If you are unsure of the type or contents of your medications, ask your doctor or pharmacist. • Because this product reduces sweating, avoid excessive work or exercise in hot weather. • When taken in overdose, acetaminophen is more toxic than aspirin. Follow dosage instructions carefully.

Comments: Many other conditions (some serious) mimic the common cold. If symptoms persist beyond one week, or if they occur regularly without regard to season, consult your doctor. • The effectiveness of this product may diminish after being taken regularly for seven to ten days; consult your pharmacist about substituting another medication if this product begins to lose its effectiveness for you. • Chew gum or suck on ice chips or a piece of hard candy to relieve mouth dryness.

Unacceptable: The caffeine included in this product has no value in treatment of the conditions specified.

Dristan cold and allergy remedy

Manufacturer: Whitehall Laboratories

Dosage Form/Ingredients: Tablet: phenylephrine hydrochloride, 5 mg; chlorpheniramine maleate, 2 mg; aspirin, 325 mg; caffeine, 16.2 mg

Use: To relieve nasal congestion, fever, aches, pains, and general discomfort due to colds or upper respiratory allergies

Side Effects: Anxiety; blurred vision; chest pain; confusion; constipation; difficult and painful urination; dizziness; drowsiness; dry mouth; headache; increased blood pressure; insomnia; loss of appetite; mild stimulation; nausea; nervousness; palpitations; rash; reduced sweating; ringing in the ears; slight blood loss; tension; tremor; vomiting

Warnings: This product should be used with special caution by the elderly or debilitated, and by persons who have asthma, diabetes, enlarged prostate, glaucoma (certain types), heart disease, high blood pressure, kidney disease, liver disease, obstructed bladder, obstructed intestine, peptic ulcer, bleeding or stomach bleeding, gout, or thyroid disease. If you have any of these conditions, consult your doctor before taking this product. It should not be used by pregnant or nursing women, or be given to newborn or premature infants. • This product may cause drowsiness. Do not take it if you must drive, operate heavy machinery, or perform other tasks requiring mental alertness. To prevent oversedation, avoid the use of alcohol or other drugs that have sedative properties. • This product interacts with alcohol, ammonium chloride, guanethidine, methotrexate, monoamine oxidase inhibitors, oral anticoagulants, oral antidiabetics, probenecid, sedative drugs, steroids, sulfinpyrazone, tricyclic antidepressants, and vitamin C. If you are currently taking any drugs of these types, check with your doctor before taking this product. If you are unsure of the type or contents of your medications, ask your doctor or pharmacist. • Because this product reduces sweating, avoid excessive work or exercise in hot weather. • The dosage instructions listed on the package should be followed carefully; toxicity may occur in adults or children with repeated doses.

Comments: Many other conditions (some serious) mimic the common cold. If symptoms persist beyond one week or if they occur regularly without regard to season, consult your doctor. • The effectiveness of this product may diminish after being taken for seven to ten days; consult your pharmacist about substituting another product if this one begins to lose its effectiveness for you. • Chew gum or suck on ice chips or a piece of hard candy to reduce mouth dryness.

Unacceptable: The caffeine included in this product has no value in treatment of the conditions specified.

Dristan nasal decongestant (inhaler)

Manufacturer: Whitehall Laboratories

Dosage Form/Ingredients: Inhaler: propylhexedrine, 250 mg; unspecified quantities of menthol, methyl salicylate, and eucalyptol

Use: For temporary relief of nasal congestion due to colds, sinusitis, hay fever, or other upper respiratory allergies

Side Effects: Blurred vision; burning, dryness of nasal mucosa; increased nasal congestion or discharge; sneezing, and/or stinging; dizziness; drowsiness; headache; insomnia; nervousness; palpitations; slight increase in blood pressure; stimulation

Warnings: This product should not be used by persons who have glaucoma (certain types). • It should be used with special caution by persons who have diabetes, advanced hardening of the arteries, heart disease, high blood pressure, or thyroid disease. If you have any of these conditions, consult your doctor before using this product. • This product interacts with monoamine oxidase inhibitors, thyroid preparations, and tricyclic antidepressants. If you are currently taking any drugs of these types, check with your doctor before taking this product. If you are unsure of the type or contents of your medications, ask your doctor or pharmacist.

Comments: To avoid side effects such as burning, sneezing, or stinging, and a "rebound" increase in nasal congestion and discharge, do not exceed the recommended dose, and do not use this product for more than three or four continuous days. • This product should not be used by more than one person; sharing the dispenser may spread infection. • This product works best when it is used correctly. Refer to the instructions for the use of nasal inhalers in the chapter on "Buying, Storing, and Using

Drugs." • Many topical decongestants on the market contain oxymetazoline hydrochloride. This drug has a duration of action of about 12 hours, and because it needs to be used less often, it is less likely to cause "rebound" nasal congestion during use. Therefore, we recommend a product containing oxymetazoline hydrochloride rather than this product, which does not contain the ingredient.

Fair: Products containing better ingredients are available.

Dristan nasal decongestant (spray)

Manufacturer: Whitehall Laboratories
Dosage Forms/Ingredients: Nasal spray: phenylephrine hydrochloride, 0.5%; pheniramine maleate, 0.2%; benzalkonium chloride, 1:5000; thimerosal, 0.002%. Mentholated nasal spray: phenylephrine hydrochloride, 0.5%; pheniramine maleate, 0.2%; benzalkonium chloride, 1:5000; thimerosal, 0.002%; unspecified quantities of menthol, camphor, eucalyptol, and methyl salicylate
Use: For temporary relief of nasal congestion due to colds, sinusitis, hay fever, or other upper respiratory allergies
Side Effects: Blurred vision; burning, dryness of nasal mucosa; increased nasal congestion or discharge; sneezing, and/or stinging; dizziness; drowsiness; headache; insomnia; nervousness; palpitations; slight increase in blood pressure; stimulation
Warnings: This product should not be used by persons who have glaucoma (certain types). • It should be used with special caution by persons who have diabetes, advanced hardening of the arteries, heart disease, high blood pressure, or thyroid disease. If you have any of these conditions, consult your doctor before using this product. • This product interacts with monoamine oxidase inhibitors, thyroid preparations, and tricyclic antidepressants. If you are currently taking any drugs of these types, check with your doctor before taking this product. If you are unsure of the type or contents of your medications, ask your doctor or pharmacist.
Comments: To avoid side effects such as burning, sneezing, or stinging, and a "rebound" increase in nasal congestion and discharge, do not exceed the recommended dose, and do not use this product for more than three or four continuous days. • This product should not be used by more than one person; sharing the dispenser may spread infection. • This product works best when it is used correctly. Refer to the instructions for the use of nasal sprays and drops in the chapter on "Buying, Storing, and Using Drugs." • Many nasal drops or sprays on the market contain oxymetazoline hydrochloride. This drug has a duration of action of about 12 hours, and because it needs to be used less often, it is less likely to cause "rebound" nasal congestion during use. Therefore, we recommend a product containing oxymetazoline hydrochloride rather than this product, which does not contain the ingredient. • The mentholated version of this product contains various aromatic substances that add no therapeutic value.

Fair: The antihistamine (pheniramine maleate) in this product is unlikely to be effective for this use.

Dristan Timed-Release cold and allergy remedy

Manufacturer: Whitehall Laboratories
Dosage Form/Ingredients: Timed-release capsule: chlorpheniramine maleate, 4 mg; phenylephrine hydrochloride, 20 mg

Use: For relief of nasal congestion due to colds and upper respiratory allergies

Side Effects: Anxiety; blurred vision; chest pain; confusion; constipation; dry mouth; difficult and painful urination; dizziness; drowsiness; headache; increased blood pressure; insomnia; loss of appetite; mild stimulation; nausea; nervousness; palpitations; rash; reduced sweating; tension; tremor; vomiting

Warnings: This product should be used with special caution by the elderly or debilitated, and by persons who have asthma, diabetes, enlarged prostate, glaucoma (certain types), heart disease, high blood pressure, kidney disease, liver disease, obstructed bladder, obstructed intestine, peptic ulcer, or thyroid disease. If you have any of these conditions, consult your doctor before taking this product. It should not be used by pregnant or nursing women, or be given to newborn or premature infants. • This product may cause drowsiness. Do not take it if you must drive, operate heavy machinery, or perform other tasks requiring mental alertness. To prevent oversedation, avoid the use of alcohol or other drugs that have sedative properties. • This product interacts with alcohol, guanethidine, monoamine oxidase inhibitors, sedative drugs, and tricyclic antidepressants. If you are currently taking any drugs of these types, check with your doctor before taking this product. If you are unsure of the type or contents of your medications, ask your doctor or pharmacist. • Because this product reduces sweating, avoid excessive work or exercise in hot weather. • This product has sustained action; never increase the recommended dose or take it more frequently than directed. A serious overdose could result.

Comments: Many other conditions (some serious) mimic the common cold. If symptoms persist beyond one week, or if they occur regularly without regard to season, consult your doctor. • The effectiveness of this product may diminish after being taken for seven to ten days; consult your pharmacist about substituting a different product if this product begins to lose its effectiveness for you. • Chew gum or suck on ice chips or a piece of hard candy to reduce mouth dryness. • This product should not be crushed or chewed. It must be swallowed whole.

Acceptable: *We prefer single-ingredient products rather than combination antihistamine-decongestant products like this one.*

Dry and Clear acne preparation
(liquid cleanser)

Manufacturer: Whitehall Laboratories

Dosage Form/Ingredients: Liquid cleanser: alcohol, 50%; salicylic acid, 0.5%; benzoic acid, 0.5%; benzethonium chloride, 0.1%

Use: Treatment of acne

Side Effects: Allergy; local irritation

Warnings: Do not get this product in or near the eyes, lips, or mouth. • If skin becomes excessively dry, itchy, or flaky, reduce the frequency of this product's use. • If the condition worsens or if skin irritation develops, stop using this product and consult your physician.

Comments: Even though this product is a cleanser, it is to be used after washing with regular soap and warm water. Apply to skin with cotton; do not rinse.

Fair: *Products containing more effective ingredients are available.*

Dry and Clear acne preparations (lotion, cream)

Manufacturer: Whitehall Laboratories
Dosage Forms/Ingredient: Lotion: benzoyl peroxide, 5%. Cream: benzoyl peroxide, 10%
Use: Treatment of acne
Side Effects: Allergy; local irritation
Warnings: Do not get this product in or near the eyes. • Persons having a known sensitivity to benzoyl peroxide should not use this product. • When using this product, do not use harsh, abrasive cleansers. • If excessive redness or peeling occurs, reduce the frequency of this product's use. • Avoid exposure to heat lamps and sunlamps, as well as prolonged exposure to sunlight, when using this product. • This product may be especially active on fair-skinned people. • If the condition worsens or if skin irritation develops, stop using this product and consult your physician.
Comments: Wash the affected area gently with warm water and pat dry before applying this product. • There may be a slight transitory stinging or burning sensation on initial application of this product. • This product may damage certain fabrics including rayon.

Preferred: Benzoyl peroxide has been shown to be the most effective ingredient in acne preparations.

Dulcolax laxative

Manufacturer: Boehringer Ingelheim Ltd.
Dosage Forms/Ingredient: Suppository: bisacodyl, 10 mg. Tablet: bisacodyl, 5 mg
Use: For relief of constipation
Side Effects: Allergic reactions; excess loss of fluid; griping (cramps); mucus in feces; rectal burning
Warnings: Persons with a high fever (100° F or more), black or tarry stools, nausea, vomiting, abdominal pain; pregnant women; and children under the age of three should not use this product unless directed to do so by a doctor. • Do not use this product when constipation is caused by megacolon or other diseases of the intestine, or hypothyroidism. • Excessive use (daily for a month or more) of these products may cause diarrhea, vomiting, and loss of certain blood electrolytes. • Do not crush or chew the tablet form of this product, and do not take this product within an hour of taking an antacid or drinking milk. Severe abdominal cramping will result. • Never self-medicate with this product if constipation lasts longer than two weeks, or if the medication does not produce a laxative effect within a week. • Limit use to seven days unless directed otherwise by a doctor since this product may cause laxative-dependence (addiction) if used for a longer time. • The suppository may cause a burning sensation within the rectum.
Comments: Evacuation may occur within six to twelve hours.
Acceptable: This product is an acceptable stimulant laxative.

Duration nasal decongestant

Manufacturer: Plough, Inc.
Dosage Forms/Ingredients: Drop, Nasal spray: oxymetazoline hydrochloride, 0.05%; phenylmercuric acetate, 0.002%. Mentholated nasal spray: oxymetazoline hydrochloride, 0.05%; phenylmercuric acetate, 0.002%; unspecified quantities of menthol, camphor, and eucalyptol
Use: For temporary relief of nasal congestion due to colds, sinusitis,

hay fever, or other upper respiratory allergies

Side Effects: Blurred vision; burning, dryness of nasal mucosa; increased nasal congestion or discharge; sneezing, and/or stinging; dizziness; drowsiness; headache; insomnia; nervousness; palpitations; slight increase in blood pressure; stimulation

Warnings: This product should not be used by persons who have glaucoma (certain types). • It should be used with special caution by persons who have diabetes, advanced hardening of the arteries, heart disease, high blood pressure, or thyroid disease. If you have any of these conditions, consult your doctor before using this product. • This product interacts with monoamine oxidase inhibitors, thyroid preparations, and tricyclic antidepressants. If you are currently taking any drugs of these types, check with your doctor before taking this product. If you are unsure of the type or contents of your medications, ask your doctor or pharmacist.

Comments: To avoid side effects such as burning, sneezing, or stinging, and a "rebound" increase in nasal congestion and discharge, do not exceed the recommended dose, and do not use this product for more than three or four continuous days. • This product should not be used by more than one person; sharing the dispenser may spread infection. • This product works best when it is used correctly. Refer to the instructions for the use of nasal sprays and drops in the chapter on "Buying, Storing, and Using Drugs." • The long-acting ingredient in this product has a decongestant action that may last up to 12 hours. Because it needs to be administered only twice a day, this product is less likely to cause "rebound" congestion than nasal products containing different ingredients. • The spray form of this product, although slightly more expensive than the drops, is preferred for adult use. The spray penetrates far back into the nose, covering the nasal area more completely, and is more convenient to use. The drop is preferable for administration to children.

Preferred: *We recommend the use of a product containing oxymetazoline hydrochloride because it requires less frequent use and is therefore less likely to cause "rebound" congestion.*

Eclipse Partial Suntan, Eclipse Lip and Face Protectant, Eclipse Total, Eclipse Original sunscreens

Manufacturer: Herbert Laboratories

Dosage Forms/Ingredients: Eclipse Partial Suntan: Lotion: unspecified quantity of padimate O. Eclipse Lip and Face Protectant: Stick: unspecified quanity of padimate O. Eclipse Total: Lotion: alcohol, 80.9%; unspecified quantities of oxybenzone, padimate O, and glyceryl PABA; alcohol base. Eclipse Original: Lotion: unspecified quantities of padimate O and glyceryl PABA. Gel: alcohol, 55%; unspecified quantities of padimate O and glyceryl PABA

Use: To prevent sunburn, premature aging of the skin, and skin cancer caused by overexposure to sunlight; to protect persons with sun sensitive skin, or those taking photo-sensitizing drugs, against sun toxicity

Side Effects: Occasional irritation; rash

Warnings: Avoid prolonged exposure to the sun, especially if you are sensitive to it. • Do not use this product if you are allergic to benzocaine, procaine, sulfa drugs, thiazide diuretics (water pills or high blood pressure medication), or certain dyes. If you are unaware of the nature of the medications you are taking, ask your doctor or pharmacist. • Do not use this product in or around the eyes. • Discontinue use and consult your pharmacist if irritation (pain, itching, or swelling) or rash appears. •

Follow the directions given on the package, especially regarding frequency of use. Be sure to reapply after swimming or excessive exercise.

Comments: If you are unsure whether this is the proper sunscreen agent for you, refer for clarification to the section on sunscreen products in this book. If you still have questions, ask your pharmacist or doctor. • This product may stain certain types of clothing.

Not Evaluated: The manufacturer fails to provide sufficient information about the formulation of this product on which to base an evaluation.

Ecotrin analgesic

Manufacturer: Menley & James Laboratories
Dosage Form/Ingredient: Enteric-coated tablet: aspirin, 325 mg
Use: For the temporary relief of minor aches and pains of arthritis and rheumatism; protection against gastric upset sometimes caused by regular, uncoated aspirin
Side Effects: Dizziness; mental confusion; nausea and vomiting; ringing in the ears; slight blood loss; sweating
Warnings: Persons with asthma, hay fever, or other allergies should be extremely careful about using this product. The product may interfere with the treatment of gout. This product may cause an increased bleeding tendency and should not be taken by persons with a history of bleeding, peptic ulcer, or stomach bleeding. If you have any of these conditions, consult your doctor or pharmacist before using this medication. • Do not use this product if you are consuming alcohol, or taking methotrexate, oral anticoagulants, oral antidiabetics, probenecid, steroids, and/or sulfinpyrazone; if you are unsure of the type or contents of your medications, ask your doctor or pharmacist. • The dosage instructions listed on the package should be followed carefully; toxicity may occur in adults or children with repeated doses.
Comments: Enteric-coated tablets such as this product are formulated with a coating so that they dissolve in the intestine rather than in the stomach, thus preventing stomach upset. Enteric-coated products do not have a rapid onset for use in relief of headache, but they may be useful for treatment at bedtime of prolonged aches and pains such as arthritis and rheumatism. • Do not take this product with antacids or milk. • The tablets must be swallowed whole.

Preferred: We recommend this product because it contains a single effective active ingredient, and because the dosage form fills a specific need for users in whom aspirin causes gastric disturbance.

Empirin analgesic

Manufacturer: Burroughs Wellcome Co.
Dosage Form/Ingredient: Tablet: aspirin, 325 mg
Use: For the relief of pain of headache, temporary relief of minor arthritic pain, discomforts and fever of colds and "flu," menstrual cramps, muscle aches and pains, toothache, inflammation, fever
Side Effects: Dizziness; mental confusion; nausea and vomiting; ringing in the ears; slight blood loss; sweating
Warnings: Persons with kidney disease, asthma, hay fever, or other allergies should be extremely careful about using this product. The product may interfere with the treatment of gout. This product may cause an increased bleeding tendency and should not be taken by persons with a history of bleeding, peptic ulcer, or stomach bleeding. If you have any of these conditions, consult your doctor or pharmacist before using this

medication. • Do not use this product if you are consuming alcohol, or taking methotrexate, oral anticoagulants, oral antidiabetics, probenecid, steroids, and/or sulfinpyrazone; if you are unsure of the type or contents of your medications, ask your doctor or pharmacist. • The dosage instructions listed on the package should be followed carefully; toxicity may occur in adults or children with repeated doses.

Comments: This product has been reformulated. The current product does not contain phenacetin or caffeine; aspirin is now its only ingredient. You will save money by purchasing generic aspirin instead.

Fair: This is an overpriced version of aspirin.

Enzactin athlete's foot remedy

Manufacturer: Ayerst Laboratories
Dosage Form/Ingredients: Cream: triacetin, 25%
Use: For the treatment of athlete's foot
Side Effects: Allergy; local irritation
Warnings: Diabetics and other persons with impaired circulation should not use this product without first consulting a physician. • Do not apply this product to mucous membranes, scraped skin, or to large areas of skin. • If your condition worsens, or if irritation occurs, stop using this product and consult your pharmacist. • Check with your doctor before using this product on a child. Some doctors believe that children under the age of 12 do not get athlete's foot, and that a rash appearing between a child's toes may be dermatitis or some other condition that this product would not relieve.

Comments: Some lesions take months to heal, so it is important not to stop treatment too soon. • If foot lesions are consistently a problem, check the fit of your shoes. • Wash your hands thoroughly after applying this product. • This product may damage certain fabrics, including rayon.

Fair: Triacetin has not been proven effective in the treatment of athlete's foot.

e.p.t. urine test for pregnancy

Manufacturer: Warner-Lambert Company
Product Form: Test tube and testing materials
Use: To test urine for determination of pregnancy
Comments: Use only a urine sample that has been freshly collected in the morning. • For accurate results, follow package directions carefully. The test tube must be left undisturbed and unvibrated for two hours, and must be kept away from heat and direct sunlight. Read the results two hours after starting the test. If a brown ring forms in the bottom of the test tube, you should assume that you are pregnant. Consult your doctor. • Test results may be interfered with if the urine contains a large quantity of protein, or if the patient is taking medication. • This test is highly accurate, unless it is performed earlier than nine days after the date on which the first missed menstrual period would have begun.

Acceptable: Pregnancy test kits are convenient, but may not be economical. A negative result often requires retesting; a positive result indicates that you should see a doctor. Either way, you are likely to pay for two tests.

Excedrin analgesic

Manufacturer: Bristol-Myers Products

Dosage Forms/Ingredients: Capsule, Tablet: aspirin, 250 mg; acetaminophen, 250 mg; caffeine, 65 mg

Use: Relief of pain of headache, toothache, sprains, muscular aches, nerve inflammation, menstruation; relief of discomforts and fever of colds; temporary relief of minor aches and pains of arthritis and rheumatism

Side Effects: Dizziness; mental confusion; mild to moderate stimulation; nausea and vomiting; ringing in the ears; slight blood loss; sweating. In overdose: Blood disorders; rash

Warnings: Persons with certain blood disorders; or with heart, lung, liver, or kidney disease; asthma; hay fever, or other allergies should be extremely careful about using this product. The product may interfere with the treatment of gout. This product may cause an increased bleeding tendency and should not be taken by persons with a history of bleeding, peptic ulcer, or stomach bleeding. If you have any of these conditions, consult your doctor or pharmacist before using this medication. • Do not use this product if you are consuming alcohol, or taking methotrexate, oral anticoagulants, oral antidiabetics, probenecid, steroids, and/or sulfinpyrazone; if you are unsure of the type or contents of your medications, ask your doctor or pharmacist. • When taken in overdose, this product is more toxic than plain aspirin. The dosage instructions listed on the package should be followed carefully; toxicity may occur in adults or children with repeated doses.

Comments: You can save money by taking plain aspirin or acetaminophen instead of this product; there is no evidence that combinations of ingredients are more effective than similar doses of a single-ingredient product. • The caffeine in this product may have a slight stimulant effect but has no pain-relieving value.

Unacceptable: It has not been proven that caffeine has any pain-relieving value.

Excedrin P.M. analgesic

Manufacturer: Bristol-Myers Products

Dosage Form/Ingredients: Tablet: acetaminophen, 500 mg; pyrilamine maleate, 25 mg

Use: For the relief of pain of headache, bursitis, colds or "flu," sinusitis, muscle aches, menstruation; for temporary relief of toothache and minor arthritic pain; as a sleep aid

Side Effects: Anxiety; hypersensitivity; blurred vision; chest pain; confusion; constipation; difficult and painful urination; dizziness; drowsiness; dry mouth and respiratory passages; headache; insomnia; loss of appetite; nausea; nervousness; palpitations; rash; reduced sweating; restlessness; tremor; tension; vomiting. When taken in overdose: Blood disorders; rash

Warnings: This product should be used with special caution by the elderly or debilitated, and by persons who have asthma, diabetes, enlarged prostate, certain blood disorders, glaucoma (certain types), heart disease, lung disease, high blood pressure, kidney or liver disease, obstructed bladder, obstructed intestine, or peptic ulcer. If you have any of these conditions, consult your doctor before taking this product. • It should not be taken by pregnant women or given to newborn or premature infants. • This product interacts with alcohol, guanethidine, monoamine oxidase inhibitors, sedative drugs, and tricyclic antidepressants. If you are currently taking any drugs of these types, check with your doctor before taking this product. If you are unsure of the type or contents of your medications, ask your doctor or pharmacist. • Because this product reduces sweating, avoid excessive work or exercise in hot weather. • When taken in overdose, this product is more toxic than aspirin. The dosage instructions listed on the package should be followed carefully; toxicity may occur in adults or children with repeated doses. • This product may cause drowsiness. Do not take it if you must drive, operate heavy machinery, or perform other tasks requiring mental alertness. • To prevent oversedation, avoid the use of alcohol or other drugs that have sedative properties.

Comments: Acetaminophen does not relieve inflammation, so if pain is caused by swelling or inflammation, it should not be used. Aspirin is better. • Chew gum or suck on ice chips or a piece of hard candy to reduce mouth dryness. • This product may not work as well after seven to ten days as it did when you began taking it. Consult your pharmacist about using another product if the effectiveness of this medication diminishes.

Fair: There is no proof that a combination of ingredients is more effective than an equivalent dose of aspirin or acetaminophen alone.

Ex-Lax laxative

Manufacturer: Ex-Lax Pharmaceutical Co., Inc.
Dosage Forms/Ingredient: Chocolate tablet, Unflavored pill: yellow phenolphthalein, 90 mg
Use: For relief of constipation
Side Effects: Excess loss of fluid; griping (cramps); mucus in feces; pink to purple rash with blistering (rare)
Warnings: Persons with a high fever (100° F or more), black or tarry stools, nausea, vomiting, abdominal pain; pregnant women; and children under the age of three should not use this product unless directed to do so by a doctor. • Do not use this product when constipation is caused by megacolon or other diseases of the intestine, or hypothyroidism. • Excessive use (daily for a month or more) of this product may cause diarrhea, vomiting, and loss of certain blood electrolytes. • Persons sensitive to phenolphthalein should not use this product. • Never self-medicate with this product if constipation lasts longer than two weeks, or if the medication does not produce a laxative effect within a week. • Limit use to seven days unless directed otherwise by a doctor since this product may cause laxative-dependence (addiction) if used for a longer time.
Comments: This product may discolor the urine and feces. • Evacuation may occur within six to twelve hours. • The chocolate tablet version of this product could be very attractive to children. Never call it candy or leave it within their reach.

Acceptable: We prefer bulk-forming laxatives; however, this product is also effective.

Femiron nutritional supplement

Manufacturer: The J. B. Williams Company, Inc.
Dosage Form/Ingredients: Tablet: iron (from ferrous fumarate), 20 mg; vitamin A, 5000 IU; vitamin D, 400 IU; thiamine, 1.5 mg; riboflavin, 1.7 mg; niacinamide, 20 mg; ascorbic acid, 60 mg; pyridoxine, 2 mg; cyanocobalamin, 6 mcg; calcium pantothenate, 10 mg; folic acid, 0.4 mg; tocopherol acetate, 15 IU

Use: To supplement the diet

Side Effects: Constipation; diarrhea; nausea; stomach pain

Warnings: This product should not be used by persons who have active peptic ulcer or ulcerative colitis. • Alcoholics and persons who have chronic liver or pancreatic disease should use this product with special caution; such persons may have enhanced iron absorption and are therefore more likely than others to experience iron toxicity. • The iron in this product interacts with oral tetracycline antibiotics and reduces the absorption of the antibiotics. If you are currently taking tetracycline, consult your doctor or pharmacist before taking this product. If you are unsure of the type or contents of your medications, ask your doctor or pharmacist. • Accidental iron poisoning is common in children; be sure to keep this product safely out of their reach. • This product contains ingredients that accumulate and are stored in the body. The recommended dose should not be exceeded for long periods (several weeks to months) except by doctor's orders. • If large doses are taken daily, this product may interfere with the results of urine tests. If your urine is being tested, inform your doctor and/or pharmacist that you are taking this product. • Because of its iron content, this product may cause constipation, diarrhea, nausea, or stomach pain. These symptoms usually disappear or become less severe after two to three days. Taking your dose with food or milk may help minimize these side effects. If they persist, ask your pharmacist to recommend another product. • This product contains vitamin B_6 (pyridoxine) in an amount great enough that it may interact with levodopa (L-dopa). If you are currently taking L-dopa, check with your doctor before taking this product.

Comments: Black, tarry stools are a normal consequence of iron therapy. If your stools are not black and tarry, this product may not be working for you. Ask your pharmacist to recommend another product. • Dietary deficiencies of vitamins are uncommon in the United States. Most people who have vitamin deficiencies should be under a doctor's care, and they should not be self-medicating with OTC vitamin products. If you choose to take supplemental vitamins, choose a generic product to save money. Ask your pharmacist for assistance.

Unacceptable: We feel this product is overpriced. consult your pharmacist about choosing another multivitamin and mineral supplement.

Femiron nutritional supplement (iron only)

Manufacturer: The J. B. Williams Company, Inc.

Dosage Form/Ingredients: Tablet: iron (from ferrous fumarate), 20 mg

Use: To supplement the diet

Side Effects: Constipation; diarrhea; nausea; stomach pain

Warnings: This product should not be used by persons who have active peptic ulcer or ulcerative colitis. • Alcoholics and persons who have chronic liver or pancreatic disease should use this product with special caution; such persons may have enhanced iron absorption and are therefore more likely than others to experience iron toxicity. • This product interacts with oral tetracycline antibiotics and reduces the absorption of the antibiotics. If you are currently taking tetracycline, consult your doctor or pharmacist before taking this product. If you are unsure of the type or contents of your medications, ask your doctor or pharmacist. • Accidental iron poisoning is common in children; be sure to keep this product safely out of their reach. • This product may cause constipation, diarrhea, nausea or stomach pain. These symptoms usually disappear or become less severe after two to three days. Taking your dose with food or milk may help minimize these side effects. If they persist, ask your pharmacist to recommend another product.

Comments: Black, tarry stools are a normal consequence of iron therapy. If your stools are not black and tarry, this product may not be working for you. Ask your pharmacist to recommend another product. • Inform your doctor and/or pharmacist that you are taking this product. • Side effects of iron-containing products are proportional to the amount of iron present in the product and not the dosage form or salt form (fumarate, sulphate, or gluconate). We therefore recommend a generic ferrous sulfate product to save money. Ask your pharmacist for assistance.

Unacceptable: This product is overpriced. Consult your pharmacist about generic ferrous sulfate.

Feosol nutritional supplement

Manufacturer: Menley & James Laboratories

Dosage Forms/Ingredients: Liquid (content per teaspoon): iron (from ferrous sulfate), 44 mg; alcohol, 5%. Spansule capsule: iron (from ferrous sulfate), 50 mg. Tablet: iron (from ferrous sulfate), 65 mg

Use: To supplement the diet

Side Effects: Constipation; diarrhea; nausea; stomach pain

Warnings: This product should not be used by persons who have active peptic ulcer or ulcerative colitis. • Alcoholics and persons who have chronic liver or pancreatic disease should use this product with special caution; such persons may have enhanced iron absorption and are therefore more likely than others to experience iron toxicity. • This product interacts with oral tetracycline antibiotics and reduces the absorption of the antibiotics. If you are currently taking tetracycline, consult your doctor or pharmacist before taking this product. If you are unsure of the type or contents of your medications, ask your doctor or pharmacist. • Accidental iron poisoning is common in children; be sure to keep this product safely out of their reach. • This product may cause constipation, diarrhea, nausea or stomach pain. These symptoms usually disappear or become less severe after two to three days. Taking your dose with food or milk may help minimize these side effects. If they persist, ask your pharmacist to recommend another product. The capsule form of this product is less likely than the tablet form to induce stomach upset because it contains less iron per dose.

Comments: Black, tarry stools are a normal consequence of iron therapy. If your stools are not black and tarry, this product may not be working for you. Ask your pharmacist to recommend another product. • Inform your doctor and/or pharmacist that you are taking this product. • Side effects of iron-containing products are proportional to the amount of iron present in the product and not the dosage form or salt form (fumarate, sulphate, or gluconate). We therefore recommend a generic ferrous sulfate product to save money. Ask your pharmacist for assistance.

Acceptable: We prefer generic ferrous sulfate, but this is an acceptable iron supplement.

Fergon nutritional supplement

Manufacturer: Breon Laboratories Inc.

Dosage Forms/Ingredient: Timed-release capsule: iron (from ferrous gluconate), 50 mg. Liquid (content per teaspoon): iron (from ferrous gluconate), 35 mg. Tablet: iron (from ferrous gluconate), 37 mg

Use: To supplement the diet

Side Effects: Constipation; diarrhea; nausea; stomach pain

Warnings: This product should not be used by persons who have active peptic ulcer or ulcerative colitis. • Alcoholics and persons who have chronic liver or pancreatic disease should use this product with special caution; such persons may have enhanced iron absorption and are therefore more likely than others to experience iron toxicity. • This product interacts with oral tetracycline antibiotics and reduces the absorption of the antibiotics. If you are currently taking tetracycline, consult your doctor or pharmacist before taking this product. If you are unsure of the type or contents of your medications, ask your doctor or pharmacist. • Accidental iron poisoning is common in children; be sure to keep this product safely out of their reach. • This product may cause constipation, diarrhea, nausea or stomach pain. These symptoms usually disappear or become less severe after two to three days. Taking your dose with food or milk may help minimize these side effects. If they persist, ask your pharmacist to recommend another product.

Comments: Black, tarry stools are a normal consequence of iron therapy. If your stools are not black and tarry, this product may not be working for you. Ask your pharmacist to recommend another product. • Inform your doctor and/or pharmacist that you are taking this product. • Side effects of iron-containing products are proportional to the amount of iron present in the product and not the dosage form or salt form (fumarate, sulphate, or gluconate). We therefore recommend a generic ferrous sulfate product to save money. Ask your pharmacist for assistance.

Acceptable: We prefer generic ferrous sulfate, but this is an acceptable iron supplement.

Fer-In-Sol nutritional supplement

Manufacturer: Mead Johnson Co., Nutritional Division

Dosage Forms/Ingredients: Capsule: iron (from ferrous sulfate), 60 mg. Drop (content per 0.6 ml): iron (from ferrous sulfate), 15 mg. Liquid (content per teaspoon): iron (from ferrous sulfate), 18 mg

Use: To supplement the diet

Side Effects: Constipation; diarrhea; nausea; stomach pain

Warnings: This product should not be used by persons who have active peptic ulcer or ulcerative colitis. • Alcoholics and persons who have chronic liver or pancreatic disease should use this product with special caution; such persons may have enhanced iron absorption and are therefore more likely than others to experience iron toxicity. • This product interacts with oral tetracycline antibiotics and reduces the absorption of the antibiotics. If you are currently taking tetracycline, consult your doctor or pharmacist before taking this product. If you are unsure of the type or contents of your medications, ask your doctor or pharmacist. • Accidental iron poisoning is common in children; be sure to keep this product safely out of their reach. • This product may cause constipation, diarrhea, nausea or stomach pain. These symptoms usually disappear or become less severe after two to three days. Taking your dose with food or milk may help minimize these side effects. If they persist, ask your pharmacist to recommend another product.

Comments: Black, tarry stools are a normal consequence of iron therapy. If your stools are not black and tarry, this product may not be working for you. Ask your pharmacist to recommend another product. •

Inform your doctor and pharmacist that you are taking this product. •
Side effects of iron-containing products are proportional to the amount of
iron present in the product and not the dosage form or salt form
(fumarate, sulphate, or gluconate). We therefore recommend a generic
ferrous sulfate product to save money. Ask your pharmacist for
assistance.

*Acceptable: We prefer generic ferrous sulfate, but this is an acceptable
iron supplement.*

ferrous gluconate nutritional supplement

Manufacturer: Various
Dosage Forms: Tablet: common strengths are 320 mg (yielding 37 mg of
iron) and 325 mg (yielding 38 mg of iron). Capsule: common strength is
325 mg (yielding 38 mg of iron)
Use: To supplement the diet
Side Effects: Constipation; diarrhea; nausea; stomach pain
Warnings: This product should not be used by persons who have active
peptic ulcer or ulcerative colitis. • Alcoholics and persons who have
chronic liver or pancreatic disease should use this product with special
caution; such persons may have enhanced iron absorption and are therefore more likely than others to experience iron toxicity. • This product
interacts with oral tetracycline antibiotics and reduces the absorption of
the antibiotics. If you are currently taking tetracycline, consult your doctor or pharmacist before taking this product. If you are unsure of the type
or contents of your medications, ask your doctor or pharmacist. • Accidental iron poisoning is common in children; be sure to keep this product safely out of their reach. • This product may cause constipation,
diarrhea, nausea or stomach pain. These symptoms usually disappear or
become less severe after two to three days. Taking your dose with food or
milk may help minimize these side effects. If they persist, ask your pharmacist to recommend another product.
Comments: Black, tarry stools are a normal consequence of iron
therapy. If your stools are not black and tarry, this product may not be
working for you. Ask your pharmacist to recommend another product. •
Inform your doctor and/or pharmacist that you are taking this product. •
Side effects of iron-containing products are proportional to the amount of
iron present in the product and not the dosage form or salt form (fumarate, sulfate, or gluconate). We therefore recommend a generic ferrous
sulfate product to save money. Ask your pharmacist for assistance.

*Acceptable: We prefer generic ferrous sulfate, but this is an acceptable
iron supplement.*

ferrous sulfate nutritional supplement

Manufacturer: Various
Dosage Form: Tablet: common strengths are 195 mg (yielding 39 mg of
iron), 300 mg (yielding 60 mg of iron), and 325 mg (yielding 65 mg of iron)
Use: To supplement the diet
Side Effects: Constipation; diarrhea; nausea; stomach pain
Warnings: This product should not be used by persons who have active
peptic ulcer or ulcerative colitis. • Alcoholics and persons who have
chronic liver or pancreatic disease should use this product with special
caution; such persons may have enhanced iron absorption and are therefore more likely than others to experience iron toxicity. • This product
interacts with oral tetracycline antibiotics and reduces the absorption of
the antibiotics. If you are currently taking tetracycline, consult your doctor or pharmacist before taking this product. If you are unsure of the type

144

or contents of your medications, ask your doctor or pharmacist. • Accidental iron poisoning is common in children; be sure to keep this product safely out of their reach. • This product may cause constipation, diarrhea, nausea or stomach pain. These symptoms usually disappear or become less severe after two to three days. Taking your dose with food or milk may help minimize these side effects. If they persist, ask your pharmacist to recommend another product.

Comments: Black, tarry stools are a normal consequence of iron therapy. If your stools are not black and tarry, this product may not be working for you. Ask your pharmacist to recommend another product. • Inform your doctor and/or pharmacist that you are taking this product. • Side effects of iron-containing products are proportional to the amount of iron present in the product and not the dosage form or salt form (fumarate, sulfate, or gluconate). We therefore recommend a generic ferrous sulfate product to save money. Ask your pharmacist for assistance.

Preferred: *Generic ferrous sulfate is our best buy among iron supplements.*

Fleet Enema laxative

Manufacturer: C. B. Fleet Co., Inc.
Dosage Forms/Ingredients: Adult enema: sodium biphosphate, 19 gm; sodium phosphate, 7 gm. Pediatric enema: sodium biphosphate, 9.5 gm; sodium phosphate, 3.5 gm
Use: For relief of constipation
Side Effects: Excess loss of fluid; griping (cramps); mucus in feces
Warnings: Persons with heart or kidney disease, or those on a salt-free diet should not use this product. • Persons with a high fever (100° F or more), black or tarry stools, nausea, vomiting, abdominal pain; pregnant women; and children under the age of three should not use this product unless directed to do so by a doctor. • Do not use this product when constipation is caused by megacolon or other diseases of the intestine, or hypothyroidism. • Excessive use (daily for a month or more) of these products may cause diarrhea, vomiting, and loss of certain blood electrolytes. • Never self-medicate with this product if constipation lasts longer than two weeks or if the medication does not produce a laxative effect within a week. • Limit use to seven days unless directed otherwise by a doctor since this product may cause laxative-dependence (addiction) if used for a longer time. • Laxatives of this type usually produce an explosive bowel movement within 30 to 60 minutes. Try to take this product at a convenient time.

Acceptable: *This product is an acceptable saline laxative.*

Fletcher's Castoria laxative

Manufacturer: Glenbrook Laboratories
Dosage Form/Ingredient: Liquid: senna, 6.5%
Use: For relief of constipation
Side Effects: Excess loss of fluid; griping (cramps); mucus in feces
Warnings: Persons with a high fever (100° F or more), black or tarry stools, nausea, vomiting, abdominal pain; pregnant women; and children under the age of three should not use this product unless directed to do so by a doctor. • Do not use this product when constipation is caused by megacolon or other diseases of the intestine, or hypothyroidism. • Excessive use (daily for a month or more) of these products may cause diarrhea, vomiting, and loss of certain blood electrolytes. • Never self-medicate with this product if constipation lasts longer than two weeks or if the

medication does not produce a laxative effect within a week. • Limit use to seven days unless directed otherwise by a doctor since this product may cause laxative-dependence (addiction) if used for a longer time.

Comments: This product may discolor the urine. • Evacuation may occur within six to twelve hours.

Acceptable: We prefer bulk-forming laxatives; however, this product is also effective.

Formula 44-D cough remedy

Manufacturer: Vicks Health Care Division, Richardson-Merrell, Inc.

Dosage Form/Ingredients: Liquid (content per teaspoon): dextromethorphan hydrobromide, 10 mg; phenylpropanolamine hydrochloride, 12.5 mg; guaifenesin, 50 mg; alcohol, 10%

Use: For temporary relief of cough and nasal congestion due to colds or "flu"; to convert a dry, nonproductive cough to a productive, phlegm-producing cough

Side Effects: Drowsiness; mild stimulation; nausea; vomiting; blurred vision; palpitations; flushing; nervousness; dizziness; insomnia

Warnings: This product should be used with special caution by children under two years of age, and by persons who have diabetes, heart disease, high blood pressure, or thyroid disease. In these situations, consult your doctor before taking this product. • This product interacts with guanethidine and monoamine oxidase inhibitors. If you are currently taking any drugs of these types, check with your doctor before taking this product. If you are unsure of the type or contents of your medications, ask your doctor or pharmacist. • If your cough persists, or is accompanied by high fever, consult your doctor promptly. • Do not use this product to treat chronic coughs, such as those from smoking or asthma. • Do not use this product to treat productive (hacking) coughs that produce phlegm.

Comments: If you require an expectorant, you need more moisture in your environment. Drink eight to ten glasses of water daily. The use of a vaporizer or humidifier may also be beneficial. • Many other conditions (some serious) mimic the common cold. If symptoms persist beyond one week or if they occur regularly without regard to season, consult your doctor. • The effectiveness of this product may diminish after being taken regularly for seven to ten days; consult your pharmacist about substituting another product.

Fair: This product contains a decongestant, an ingredient not directly related to treatment of a cough. Products containing more appropriate ingredients are available.

Formula 44 Cough
Control Discs cough remedy

Manufacturer: Vicks Health Care Division, Richardson-Merrell, Inc.

Dosage Form/Ingredients: Lozenge: dextromethorphan hydrobromide, 5 mg; benzocaine, 1.25 mg; unspecified quantities of menthol, anethole, and peppermint oil

Use: For temporary relief of cough and throat irritation due to colds or "flu"

Side Effects: Itching; nausea; vomiting; dizziness

Warnings: Do not give this product to children under four years of age. • A sore throat in a child under age six should never be treated without medical supervision. • If your cough persists, or is accompanied by high fever, consult your doctor promptly. • This product interacts with monoamine oxidase inhibitors; if you are currently taking any drugs of this type, check with your doctor before taking this product. If you are unsure of the type or contents of your medications, ask your doctor or pharmacist. • If your cough persists, or is accompanied by high fever, consult your doctor promptly.

Comments: This product may provide greater relief of coughing and it will help soothe a raspy throat better if you lie down while it dissolves in your mouth.

Acceptable: Dextromethorphan hydrobromide is an effective cough suppressant; benzocaine may soothe an irritated throat.

Fostex acne preparation

Manufacturer: Westwood Pharmaceuticals, Inc.
Dosage Forms/Ingredients: Cream, liquid, bar soap: salicylic acid, 2%; sulfur, 2%
Use: Treatment of acne
Side Effects: Allergy; local irritation
Warnings: Do not get this product in or near the eyes. • If the condition worsens or if skin irritation develops, stop using this product and consult your physician.
Comments: When using the cream or liquid form of this product, wash area gently with warm water and pat dry before applying medication. Use the bar soap form of this product instead of regular soap. Apply to wet face and massage into skin for one to two minutes; rinse thoroughly.

Fair: Products containing more effective ingredients are available.

Fostril acne preparation

Manufacturer: Westwood Pharmaceuticals, Inc.
Dosage Form/Ingredients: Lotion: laureth-4, 6%; sulfur, 2%; greaseless base with talc and zinc oxide
Use: Treatment of acne
Side Effects: Allergy; local irritation
Warnings: Do not get this product in or near the eyes. • If the condition worsens or if skin irritation develops, stop using this product and consult your physician.
Comments: Wash area gently with warm water and pat dry before applying this product.

Fair: Products containing more effective ingredients are available.

4-Way cold remedy

Manufacturer: Bristol-Myers Products
Dosage Form/Ingredients: Tablet: aspirin, 324 mg; phenylpropanolamine hydrochloride, 12.5 mg; chlorpheniramine maleate, 2 mg
Use: To relieve nasal congestion, fever, aches, pains, and general discomfort due to colds
Side Effects: Anxiety; blurred vision; chest pain; confusion; constipation; difficult and painful urination; dizziness; drowsiness; dry mouth; headache; increased blood pressure; insomnia; loss of appetite; mild stimulation; nausea; nervousness; palpitations; rash; reduced sweating;

ringing in the ears; slight blood loss; tension; tremor; vomiting

Warnings: This product should be used with special caution by the elderly or debilitated, and by persons who have asthma, diabetes, an enlarged prostate, glaucoma (certain types), heart disease, high blood pressure, kidney disease, liver disease, obstructed bladder, obstructed intestine, peptic ulcer, bleeding or stomach bleeding, gout, or thyroid disease. If you have any of these conditions, consult your doctor before taking this product. • It should not be used by pregnant or nursing women, or be given to newborn or premature infants. • This product may cause drowsiness. Do not take it if you must drive, operate heavy machinery, or perform other tasks requiring mental alertness. To prevent oversedation, avoid the use of alcohol or other drugs that have sedative properties. • This product interacts with alcohol, ammonium chloride, guanethidine, methotrexate, monoamine oxidase inhibitors, oral anticoagulants, oral antidiabetics, probenecid, sedative drugs, steroids, sulfinpyrazone, tricyclic antidepressants, and vitamin C. If you are currently taking any drugs of these types, check with your doctor before taking this product. If you are unsure of the type or contents of your medications, ask your doctor or pharmacist. • Because this product reduces sweating, avoid excessive work or exericse in hot weather. • The dosage instructions listed on the package should be followed carefully; toxicity may occur in adults or children with repeated doses.

Comments: Many other conditions (some serious) mimic the common cold. If symptoms persist beyond one week, or if they occur regularly without regard to season, consult your doctor. • The effectiveness of this product may diminish after being taken for seven to ten days; consult your pharmacist about substituting another product if this one begins to lose its effectiveness for you. • Chew gum or suck on ice chips or a piece of hard candy to reduce mouth dryness.

Acceptable: We prefer single-ingredient products rather than combination analgesic-antihistamine-decongestant products like this one.

Freezone corn and callus remover

Manufacturer: Whitehall Laboratories

Dosage Form/Ingredients: Liquid: salicylic acid, 13.6%; zinc chloride, 2.17%; unspecified quantities of alcohol, castor oil, collodion, and ether

Use: For removal of corns and calluses

Side Effects: Allergy; local irritation

Warnings: Do not use this product if you have diabetes or poor circulation. • Do not apply if the corn or callus is infected. • This product is extremely corrosive, and its overuse can cause the death of surrounding skin. Follow the directions on the package carefully and exactly. Cover the surrounding skin with tape or petroleum jelly before use. When applying between the toes, hold them apart until the product is dry. • This product is flammable; do not use around an open flame. • This product creates a film over the area as it is applied. Do not be alarmed, and do not remove the film. • Do not stop treatment too soon; some lesions take months to heal. • If the condition worsens, stop using the product and call your pharmacist.

Comments: After applying this product, wash your hands thoroughly. • Remember to check the fit of your shoes. Well-fitting footware helps prevent corns and calluses. • Keep the bottle tightly capped between uses.

Acceptable: This product is effective for the use specified.

Gaviscon antacid (liquid)

Manufacturer: Marion Laboratories, Inc.

Dosage Forms/Ingredients: Liquid (content per tablespoon): aluminum hydroxide, 95 mg; magnesium carbonate, 411 mg

Use: For relief of acid indigestion, heartburn, and/or sour stomach

Side Effects: Constipation; diarrhea; dizziness; mouth irritation; nausea; rash; abdominal discomfort; vomiting

Warnings: Persons with kidney disease should not use this product. In persons with kidney disease, repeated (daily) use of this product may cause nausea, vomiting, depressed reflexes, and breathing difficulties. • Long-term (several weeks) use of this product may lead to intestinal obstruction and dehydration. Phosphate depletion may occur, leading to weakness, loss of appetite, and eventually bone pain. Phosphate depletion may be prevented by drinking at least one glass of milk a day. • Do not take this product within two hours of a dose of a tetracycline antibiotic. • Consult your physician or pharmacist before taking this product if you are already taking iron, a vitamin-mineral product, chlorpromazine, phenytoin, digoxin, quinidine, or warfarin, or if you are unsure of the type and contents of the medications you are taking. • Never self-medicate with this product if your symptoms occur regularly (two or three or more times a month). Consult your doctor if the symptoms are worse than usual, if you have chest pains or feel "tightness" in the chest, or if you are sweating or short of breath. In fact, we do not recommend self-treatment for severe attacks of heartburn, indigestion, or stomach upset in any circumstances. If you do decide that your symptoms are mild enough to warrant self-medication, limit therapy to two weeks. If symptoms persist, contact your doctor.

Comments: To prevent constipation, drink at least eight glasses of water a day. If constipation persists, consult your doctor or pharmacist. • This product must be taken exactly as directed on the label, unless your doctor has instructed you otherwise. Never skip a dose just because you feel better. If you grow tired of the taste, ask your pharmacist to suggest a different product.

Preferred: *The liquid form of this antacid contains the most effective antacid ingredients.*

Gaviscon (tablet), Gaviscon II antacids

Manufacturer: Marion Laboratories, Inc.

Dosage Forms/Ingredients: Gaviscon: Tablet: aluminum hydroxide, 80 mg; magnesium trisilicate, 20 mg; alginic acid, 200 mg; sodium bicarbonate, 70 mg; sodium, 1.8 mg. Gaviscon II: Chewable tablet: aluminum hydroxide dried gel, 160 mg; magnesium trisilicate, 40 mg; alginic acid, 400 mg; sodium bicarbonate, 140 mg

Use: For relief of acid indigestion, heartburn, and/or sour stomach

Side Effects: Constipation; diarrhea; dizziness; mouth irritation; nausea; rash; abdominal discomfort; vomiting

Warnings: Persons with kidney disease and those on salt-free diets should not use this product. In persons with kidney disease, repeated (daily) use of this product may cause nausea, vomiting, depressed reflexes, and breathing difficulties. • Long-term (several weeks) use of this product may lead to intestinal obstruction and dehydration. Phosphate depletion may occur, leading to weakness, loss of appetite, and eventually bone pain. Phosphate depletion may be prevented by drinking at least one glass of milk a day. • Do not take this product within two hours of a dose of a tetracycline antibiotic. • Consult your physician or pharmacist before taking this product if you are already taking iron, a vitamin-mineral product, chlorpromazine, phenytoin, digoxin, quinidine, or warfarin, or if you are unsure of the type and contents of the medications you are taking. • Never self-medicate with this product if your symptoms occur regularly (two or three or more times a month). Consult your doctor if the symptoms are worse than usual, if you have chest pains or feel "tightness" in the chest, or if you are sweating or short of breath. In fact, we do not recommend self-treatment for severe attacks of heartburn, indigestion, or stomach upset in any circumstances. If you do decide that your symptoms are mild enough to warrant self-medication, limit treatment to two weeks. If symptoms persist, contact your doctor.

Comments: To prevent constipation, drink at least eight glasses of water a day. If constipation persists, consult your doctor or pharmacist. • This product must be taken exactly as directed on the label, unless your doctor has instructed you otherwise. Never skip a dose just because you feel better. If you grow tired of the taste, ask your pharmacist to suggest a different product.

Fair: Alginic acid has limited effectiveness. Also, these forms of Gaviscon antacid have a high content of sodium, making them unsuitable for persons on a low-sodium diet.

Gelusil, Gelusil II antacids and antiflatulents

Manufacturer: Parke-Davis

Dosage Forms/Ingredients: Gelusil: Liquid (content per teaspoon): aluminum hydroxide, 200 mg; magnesium hydroxide, 200 mg; simethicone, 25 mg; sodium, 0.9 mg. Tablet: aluminum hydroxide, 200 mg; magnesium hydroxide, 200 mg; simethicone, 25 mg; sodium, 1.6 mg. Gelusil II: Liquid (content per teaspoon): aluminim hydroxide, 400 mg; magnesium hydroxide, 400 mg; simethicone, 30 mg; sodium, 1.3 mg. Tablet: aluminum hydroxide, 400 mg; magnesium hydroxide, 400 mg; simethicone, 30 mg; sodium, 2.7 mg.

Use: For relief of acid indigestion, heartburn, and/or sour stomach when accompanied by painful gas symptoms

Side Effects: Constipation; diarrhea; dizziness; mouth irritation; nausea; rash; abdominal discomfort; vomiting

Warnings: Persons with kidney disease should not use these products. In persons with kidney disease, repeated (daily) use of these products may cause nausea, vomiting, depressed reflexes, or breathing difficulties. • Long-term (several weeks) use of these products may lead to intestinal obstruction and dehydration. Phosphate depletion may occur, leading to weakness, loss of appetite, and eventually bone pain. Phosphate depletion may be prevented by drinking at least one glass of milk a day. • Do not take these products within two hours of a dose of a tetracycline antibiotic. • Consult your physician or pharmacist before taking these products if you are already taking iron, a vitamin-mineral product, chlorpromazine, phenytoin, digoxin, quinidine, or warfarin, or if you are unsure of the type and contents of the medications you are taking. • Never self-medicate with these products if your symptoms occur regularly (two or three or more times a month). Consult your doctor if the symptoms are worse than usual, if you have chest pains or feel "tightness" in the chest, or if you are sweating or short of breath. In fact, we do not recommend self-treatment for severe attacks of heartburn, indigestion, or stomach upset in any circumstances. If you do decide that your symptoms are mild enough to warrant self-medication, limit treatment to two weeks. If symptoms persist, consult your doctor.

Comments: To prevent constipation, drink at least eight glasses of water a day. If constipation persists, consult your doctor or pharmacist. • These products must be taken exactly as directed on the label, unless your doctor has instructed you otherwise. Never skip a dose just because you feel better. If you grow tired of the taste, ask your pharmacist to suggest a different product. • The liquid forms of these products are superior to the tablet forms and should be used unless you have been specifically directed to use a tablet. • Exact generic equivalents of these products may not be available. However, your pharmacist may be able to suggest similar products that can save you money. • Simethicone is included to relieve bloating and gas formation; this ingredient makes it easier for you to eliminate gas by belching and passing flatus. If you do not suffer from bloating and gas pains, use a product without simethicone. You will probably save money.

Acceptable: Generally, we consider it preferable to treat acid indigestion and flatulence (gas) separately rather than with a combination product.

Gelusil-M antacid and antiflatulent

Manufacturer: Warner-Chilcott
Dosage Forms/Ingredients: Liquid (content per teaspoon): aluminum hydroxide, 300 mg; magnesium hydroxide, 200 mg; simethicone, 25 mg; sodium, 1.0 mg. Tablet: aluminum hydroxide, 300 mg; magnesium hydroxide, 200 mg; simethicone, 25 mg; sodium, 3.0 mg
Use: For relief of acid indigestion, heartburn, and/or sour stomach when accompanied by painful gas symptoms
Side Effects: Constipation; diarrhea; dizziness; mouth irritation; nausea; rash; abdominal discomfort; vomiting
Warnings: Persons with kidney disease should not use this product. In persons with kidney disease, repeated (daily) use of this product may cause nausea, vomiting, depressed reflexes, or breathing difficulties. • Long-term (several weeks) use of this product may lead to intestinal obstruction and dehydration. Phosphate depletion may occur, leading to weakness, loss of appetite, and eventually bone pain. Phosphate depletion may be prevented by drinking at least one glass of milk a day. • Do not take this product within two hours of a dose of a tetracycline antibiotic. • Consult your physician or pharmacist before taking this product if you are already taking iron, a vitamin-mineral product, chlorpromazine, phenytoin, digoxin, quinidine, or warfarin, or if you are unsure of the type and contents of the medications you are taking. • Never self-medicate with this product if your symptoms occur regularly (two or three or more times a month). Consult your doctor if the symptoms are worse than usual, if you have chest pains or feel "tightness" in the chest, or if you are sweating or short of breath. In fact, we do not recommend self-treatment for severe attacks of heartburn, indigestion, or stomach upset in any circumstances. If you do decide that your symptoms are mild enough to warrant self-medication, limit treatment to two weeks. If symptoms persist, consult your doctor.
Comments: To prevent constipation, drink at least eight glasses of water a day. If constipation persists, consult your doctor or pharmacist. • This product must be taken exactly as directed on the label, unless your doctor has instructed you otherwise. Never skip a dose just because you feel better. If you grow tired of the taste, ask your pharmacist to suggest a different product. • The liquid form of this product is superior to the tablet form and should be used unless you have been specifically directed to

use the tablet. • Exact generic equivalents of this product may not be available. However, your pharmacist may be able to suggest a similar product that can save you money. • Simethicone is included to relieve bloating and gas formation; this ingredient makes it easier for you to eliminate gas by belching and passing flatus. If you do not suffer from bloating and gas pains, use a product without simethicone. You will probably save money.

Acceptable: Generally, we consider it preferable to treat acid indigestion and flatulence (gas) separately rather than with a combination product.

Gentz Wipes hemorrhoidal preparation

Manufacturer: Phillips Roxane Laboratories, Inc.
Dosage Form/Ingredients: Medicated pad: alcloxa, 0.2%; pramoxine hydrochloride, 1%; propylene glycol, 0.1%; witch hazel, 50%
Use: Relief of pain, burning, and itching of hemorrhoids and other irritated anorectal tissue
Side Effects: Irritation
Warnings: Sensitization (continued itching and redness) may occur with long-term and repeated use. • Certain ingredients in this product may cause an allergic reaction; do not use for longer than seven days at a time unless your doctor has advised you otherwise. • Never self-medicate for hemorrhoids if pain is continuous or throbbing, if bleeding or itching is excessive, or if you feel a large pressure within the rectum. • Discontinue use if irritation (pain, itching, or swelling) or rash occurs; consult your pharmacist.
Comments: Hemorrhoidal (pile) preparations relieve itching, reduce pain and inflammation, and check bleeding, but they do not heal, dry up, or give lasting relief from hemorrhoids.

Acceptable: Although generally we prefer a hemorrhoidal discomfort preparation that contains hydrocortisone, this product will also provide some relief.

Geritol nutritional supplement (liquid)

Manufacturer: The J. B. Williams Company, Inc.
Dosage Form/Ingredients: Liquid (content per ounce): iron (from ferric ammonium citrate), 100 mg; thiamine, 5 mg; riboflavin, 5 mg; niacinamide, 100 mg; panthenol, 4 mg; pyridoxine, 1 mg; cyanocobalamin, 1.5 mcg; methionine, 50 mg; choline bitartrate, 100 mg
Use: To supplement the diet
Side Effects: Constipation; diarrhea; nausea; stomach pain
Warnings: This product should not be used by persons who have active peptic ulcer or ulcerative colitis. • Alcoholics and persons who have chronic liver or pancreatic disease should use this product with special caution; such persons may have enhanced iron absorption and are therefore more likely than others to experience iron toxicity. • The iron in this product interacts with oral tetracycline antibiotics and reduces the absorption of the antibiotics. If you are currently taking tetracycline, consult your doctor or pharmacist before taking this product. If you are unsure of the type or contents of your medications, ask your doctor or pharmacist. • Accidental iron poisoning is common in children; be sure to keep this product safely out of their reach. • If large doses are taken, this product may interfere with the results of urine tests. If your urine is being tested, inform your doctor and/or pharmacist that you are taking this product. • Because of its iron content, this product may cause constipation, diarrhea, nausea, or stomach pain. These symptoms usually disap-

pear or become less severe after two to three days. Taking your dose with food or milk may help minimize these side effects. If they persist, ask your pharmacist to recommend another product.

Comments: Black, tarry stools are a normal consequence of iron therapy. If your stools are not black and tarry, this product may not be working for you. Ask your pharmacist to recommend another product. • Dietary deficiencies of vitamins are uncommon in the United States. Most people who have vitamin deficiencies should be under a doctor's care, and they should not be self-medicating with OTC vitamin products. If you choose to take supplemental vitamins, choose a generic product to save money. Ask your pharmacist for assistance. • The need for dietary supplements of methionine and choline bitartrate has not been demonstrated. • This product will taste better chilled, although refrigeration is not required for its stability. • The form of iron in this product is not absorbed into the bloodstream as well as that in other products. If you are taking this product expressly for its iron content, ask your pharmacist to recommend a different supplement product.

Acceptable: If you choose to take a vitamin supplement, this is an acceptable product.

Geritol nutritional supplement (tablet)

Manufacturer: The J. B. Williams Company, Inc.

Dosage Form/Ingredients: Tablet: iron (from ferrous sulfate), 50 mg; thiamine, 5 mg; riboflavin, 5 mg; vitamin C (as sodium ascorbate), 75 mg; niacinamide, 30 mg; calcium pantothenate, 2 mg; pyridoxine, 0.5 mg; cyanocobalamin, 3 mcg

Use: To supplement the diet

Side Effects: Constipation; diarrhea; nausea; stomach pain

Warnings: This product should not be used by persons who have active peptic ulcer or ulcerative colitis. • Alcoholics and persons who have chronic liver or pancreatic disease should use this product with special caution; such persons may have enhanced iron absorption and are therefore more likely than others to experience iron toxicity. • The iron in this product interacts with oral tetracycline antibiotics and reduces the absorption of the antibiotics. If you are currently taking tetracycline, consult your doctor or pharmacist before taking this product. If you are unsure of the type or contents of your medications, ask your doctor or pharmacist. • Accidental iron poisoning is common in children; be sure to keep this product safely out of their reach. • If large doses are taken, this product may interfere with the results of urine tests. If your urine is being tested, inform your doctor and/or pharmacist that you are taking this product. • Because of its iron content, this product may cause constipation, diarrhea, nausea or stomach pain. These symptoms usually disappear or become less severe after two to three days. Taking your dose with food or milk may help minimize these side effects. If they persist, ask your pharmacist to recommend another product.

Comments: Black, tarry stools are a normal consequence of iron therapy. If your stools are not black and tarry, this product may not be working for you. Ask your pharmacist to recommend another product. • Dietary deficiencies of vitamins are uncommon in the United States. Most people who have vitamin deficiencies should be under a doctor's care, and they should not be self-medicating with OTC vitamin products. If you choose to take supplemental vitamins, choose a generic product to save money. Ask your pharmacist for assistance.

Acceptable: If you choose to take a vitamin supplement, this is an acceptable product.

Gly-Oxide canker sore and fever blister remedy

Manufacturer: Marion Laboratories, Inc.

Dosage Form/Ingredients: carbamide peroxide, 10%; unspecified quantities of anhydrous glycerol and flavors

Use: For local treatment of minor oral inflammations such as canker sores and fever blisters.

Side Effects: Allergic reactions (rash, itching, soreness); local irritation

Warnings: Discontinue use if irritation (pain, swelling, or itching) or rash appears. Consult your pharmacist.

Comments: If you have an oral ulcer that does not heal within three weeks, see your doctor or dentist. • Aspirin will also relieve the pain of oral ulcers. Swallow the tablets as you normally do; do not allow them to dissolve in your mouth.

Preferred: *The carbamide peroxide in this product is an effective treatment for minor oral inflammations.*

Haley's M-O laxative

Manufacturer: Winthrop Laboratories

Dosage Form/Ingredients: Emulsion: magnesium hydroxide, 75%; mineral oil, 25%

Use: For relief of constipation

Side Effects: Diarrhea, nausea

Warnings: Persons with high fever (100° F or more), black or tarry stools, nausea, vomiting, abdominal pain; children under age three; and pregnant women should not use this product unless directed by a doctor. • Do not use this product when constipation is caused by megacolon or other diseases of the intestine, or hypothyroidism. • Excessive use (daily for a month or more) of this product may cause diarrhea, vomiting, and loss of certain blood electrolytes. • Repeated (daily) use of this product may cause nausea, vomiting, depressed reflexes, and breathing difficulties in persons with kidney disease. • A type of pneumonia may occur after prolonged (more than two months) and repeated (daily) use. • Mineral oil may interfere with the absorption of vitamins A and D, calcium, and phosphate. If this product leaks through the rectum, the dose should be reduced until this symptom disappears. • Never self-medicate with this product if constipation lasts longer than two weeks or if the medication does not produce a laxative effect within a week. • Limit use to seven days unless directed otherwise by a doctor since this product may cause laxative-dependence (addiction) if used for a longer time.

Comments: Because evacuation may occur within 30 to 60 minutes, this product should be taken at a convenient time; it should not be taken at mealtime. • A glass (eight ounces) of water should be taken with each dose.

Acceptable: *This product is an acceptable saline laxative.*

Hazel-Balm hemorrhoidal preparation

Manufacturer: Arnar-Stone Laboratories, Inc.

Dosage Form/Ingredients: Aerosol: benzethonium chloride, 0.1%; witch hazel, 79.9%; water soluble lanolin derivative, 20%

Use: For relief of pain, burning, and itching of hemorrhoids and other irritated anorectal tissue

Side Effects: Irritation

Warnings: Sensitization (continued itching and redness) may occur with long-term and repeated use. • Certain ingredients in this product may cause an allergic reaction; do not use for longer than seven days at a time unless your doctor has advised you otherwise. • Never self-medicate for hemorrhoids if pain is continuous or throbbing, if bleeding or itching is excessive, or if you feel a large pressure within the rectum. • Discontinue use if irritation (pain, itching, or swelling) or rash occurs; consult your pharmacist.

Comments: Hemorrhoidal (pile) preparations relieve itching, reduce pain and inflammation, and check bleeding, but they do not heal, dry up, or give lasting relief from hemorrhoids.

Acceptable: Although generally we prefer a hemorrhoidal discomfort preparation that contains hydrocortisone, this product will also provide some relief.

Heet muscular pain remedy

Manufacturer: Whitehall Laboratories

Dosage Form/Ingredients: Liniment: alcohol, 70%; camphor, 3.6%; methyl salicylate, 15%; unspecified quantities of capsicum and oleoresin

Use: Used externally to temporarily relieve pain in muscles and other areas

Side Effects: Allergic reactions (rash, itching, soreness); local irritation; local numbness

Warnings: If you have diabetes or impaired circulation, use this product only upon the advice of a physician. • This product is for external use only. • Do not use it on broken or irritated skin, or on large areas of the body; keep it away from the eyes. • If the pain in muscles or other areas persists, call your doctor. • While you are using this product, avoid exposure to direct sunlight, heat lamp, or sun lamp. • Discontinue use and consult your pharmacist if irritation (rash, itching, or swelling) or pain occurs. • Before using this product on a child under 12 years of age, consult your doctor. • Children might be attracted to the smell of this product; it should be stored safely out of their reach. • If a child swallows some of this product, call your doctor immediately. • Do not rub this product into the skin.

Unacceptable: We do not recommend this product's combination of ingredients for the treatment of the conditions specified.

Hold cough remedy

Manufacturer: Beecham Products

Dosage Form/Ingredients: Adult lozenge: benzocaine, 3.75 mg; dextromethorphan hydrobromide, 7.5 mg. Children's lozenge: phenylpropanolamine, 6.25 mg; dextromethorphan hydrobromide, 3.75 mg

Use: For temporary relief of coughs and throat irritation due to colds or "flu"

Side Effects: Nausea; vomiting; itching; drowsiness; blurred vision; palpitations; flushing; nervousness; dizziness; insomnia

Warnings: Do not give this product to children under four years of age. • A sore throat in a child under age six should never be treated without medical supervision. • If your cough persists, or is accompanied by high fever, consult your doctor promptly. • This product interacts with monoamine oxidase inhibitors; if you are currently taking any drugs of this type, check with your doctor before taking this product. If you are unsure of the type or contents of your medications, ask your doctor or pharmacist.

Comments: This product may provide greater relief of coughing and it will help soothe a raspy throat better if you lie down while it dissolves in your mouth.

Acceptable: The adult lozenge contains dextromethorphan hydrobromide, an effective cough suppressant; benzocaine may soothe an irritated throat.

Fair: The children's lozenge contains a decongestant, an ingredient not directly related to treatment of a cough. Products containing more appropriate ingredients are available.

hydrogen peroxide first-aid product

Manufacturer: Various

Dosage Form: Liquid: hydrogen peroxide, 3%

Use: To clean wounds and prevent infection by killing germs; as a mouthwash

Side Effects: None when used topically. If swallowed: mild nausea; feeling of fullness; bloating

Warnings: Do not use this product on abscesses. • Do not apply bandages to the wound until the hydrogen peroxide has stopped bubbling. • Hydrogen peroxide that is intended to bleach the hair must not be used on the skin.

Comments: Store this product in the refrigerator once the container has been opened. Keep the container tightly capped. • The bubbling action of this product indicates that oxygen is being released, removing debris from wounds. If this product does not bubble when placed on an open wound, it is no longer effective and should be replaced. • This product has no activity on unbroken skin.

Preferred: This product is effective for cleaning and disinfecting wounds.

Icy Hot Balm muscular pain remedy

Manufacturer: Searle Consumer Products Division, Searle Pharmaceuticals, Inc.

Dosage Form/Ingredients: Ointment: methyl salicylate, 29%; menthol, 8%

Use: Used externally to temporarily relieve pain in muscles and other areas

Side Effects: Allergic reactions (rash, itching, soreness); local irritation; local numbness

Warnings: This product is for external use only. • Do not use it on broken or irritated skin, or on large areas of the body; keep it away from the eyes. • If the pain in muscles or other areas persists, call your doctor. • While you are using this product, avoid exposure to direct sunlight, heat lamp, or sun lamp. • Discontinue use and consult your pharmacist if irritation (rash, itching, or swelling) or pain occurs. • Before using this product on a child under 12 years of age, consult your doctor. • Children might be attracted to the smell of this product; it should be stored safely out of their reach. • If a child swallows some of this product, call your doctor immediately.

Comments: Be sure to rub this product vigorously into the skin.

Preferred: The methyl salicylate in this product provides an effective treatment for the temporary relief of muscle pain.

Icy Hot Rub muscular pain remedy

Manufacturer: Searle Consumer Products Division, Searle Pharmaceuticals, Inc.

Dosage Form/Ingredients: Cream: methyl salicylate, 12%; menthol, 9%

Use: Used externally to temporarily relieve pain in muscles and other areas

Side Effects: Allergic reactions (rash, itching, soreness); local irritation; local numbness

Warnings: This product is for external use only. • Do not use it on broken or irritated skin, or on large areas of the body; keep it away from the eyes. • If the pain in muscles or other areas persists, call your doctor. • While you are using this product, avoid exposure to direct sunlight, heat lamp, or sun lamp. • Discontinue use and consult your pharmacist if irritation (rash, itching, or swelling) or pain occurs. • Before using this product on a child under 12 years of age, consult your doctor. • Children might be attracted to the smell of this product; it should be stored safely out of their reach. • If a child swallows some of this product, call your doctor immediately.

Comments: Be sure to rub this product vigorously into the skin.

Preferred: *The methyl salicylate in this product provides an effective treatment for the temporary relief of muscle pain.*

Infra-Rub muscular pain remedy

Manufacturer: Whitehall Laboratories

Dosage Form/Ingredients: Cream: unspecified quantities of glycol monosalicylate, histamine dihydrochloride, menthyl nicotinate, capsicum oleoresin

Use: Used externally to temporarily relieve pain in muscles and other areas

Side Effects: Allergic reactions (rash, itching, soreness); local irritation; local numbness

Warnings: If you have diabetes or impaired circulation, use this product only upon the advice of a physician. • This product is for external use only. • Do not use it on broken or irritated skin, or on large areas of the body; keep it away from the eyes. • If the pain in muscles or other areas persists, call your doctor. • While you are using this product, avoid exposure to direct sunlight, heat lamp, or sun lamp. • Discontinue use and consult your pharmacist if irritation (rash, itching, or swelling) or pain occurs. • Before using this product on a child under 12 years of age, consult your doctor. • Children might be attracted to the smell of this product; it should be stored safely out of their reach. • If a child swallows some of this product, call your doctor immediately. • Do not rub this product into the skin.

Unacceptable: *We do not recommend this product's combination of ingredients for the treatment of the conditions specified.*

iodine tincture first-aid product

Manufacturer: Various

Dosage Form/Ingredients: Liquid: iodine, 2%; sodium iodide, 2.4%; unspecified quantity of diluted alcohol

Use: To disinfect minor burns, cuts, and scrapes

Side Effects: Blistering; burning; itching; weeping; stinging. If large doses are swallowed: abdominal cramping; nausea; diarrhea; vomiting;

delirium; fever; shock; thirst or metallic taste in the mouth; death

Warnings: Do not swallow this product. • Keep this product out of the reach of children. • Do not get this product in the eyes or use on mucous membranes.

Comments: Do not use any iodine product stronger than a 2-percent solution. The stronger solutions have no additional benefits, but are more toxic.

Preferred: Used as specified, iodine is a very effective disinfectant.

Ionax Foam acne preparation

Manufacturer: Owen Laboratories

Dosage Form/Ingredients: Aerosol foam: benzalkonium chloride, 0.2%; unspecified quantities of polyoxyethylene ethers and soapless surfactant

Use: Treatment of acne

Side Effects: Allergy; local irritation

Warnings: Do not get this product in or near the eyes. • If the condition worsens or if skin irritation develops, stop using this product and consult your physician.

Comments: Wash area gently with warm water and pat dry before applying this product. • Foam is lemon scented.

Not Evaluated: We cannot evaluate this product because the manufacturer fails to supply sufficient information about its ingredients.

Ionax Scrub acne preparation

Manufacturer: Owen Laboratories

Dosage Form/Ingredients: Abrasive cleansing granules: alcohol, 10%; unspecified quantities of benzalkonium chloride, polyoxyethylene ethers, and polyethylene granules; nonionic/cationic base

Use: Treatment of acne

Side Effects: Allergy; local irritation

Warnings: Do not get this product in or near the eyes. If the condition worsens or if skin irritation develops, consult your physician.

Comments: This product is to be used instead of soap. Apply to wet face and massage into skin for one to two minutes; rinse thoroughly. • Cleanser is lime scented.

Not Evaluated: We cannot evaluate this product because the manufacturer fails to supply sufficient information about its ingredients.

Isopto-Frin decongestant eyedrops

Manufacturer: Alcon Laboratories, Inc.

Dosage Form/Ingredients: Drop: hydroxypropyl methylcellulose, 0.5%; phenylephrine hydrochloride, 0.12%; unspecified quantities of sodium biphosphate, sodium citrate, and sodium phosphate

Use: For relief of minor eye irritation and redness

Side Effects: Allergic reactions (rash, itching, soreness); local irritation; momentary blurred vision

Warnings: Do not use this product if you have glaucoma. • Do not use this product for more than two days without checking with your doctor. • Do not touch the dropper or bottle top to the eye or other tissue because contamination of the solution may result. • The use of more than one eye product at a time may cause severe irritation to the eye.

Comments: This product works best when used correctly. Refer to the instructions for eye products in the chapter "Buying, Storing, and Using Drugs."

Acceptable: This product offers a satisfactory treatment for the relief of minor eye irritation.

Isopto Plain eyedrops

Manufacturer: Alcon Laboratories, Inc.
Dosage Form/Ingredients: Drop: benzalkonium chloride, 0.01%; hydroxypropyl methylcellulose, 0.5%
Use: To lubricate dry eyes
Side Effects: Momentary blurred vision
Warnings: Do not touch the dropper or bottle top to the eye or other tissue because contamination of the solution may result. • The use of more than one eye product at a time may cause severe irritation to the eye.
Comments: This product works best when used correctly. Refer to the instructions for eye products in the chapter "Buying, Storing, and Using Drugs."

Preferred: This product is our lubricant of choice for dry eyes.

Ivy Dry Cream poison ivy/poison oak remedy

Manufacturer: Ivy Corp.
Dosage Form/Ingredients: Cream: tannic acid, 8%; isopropyl alcohol, 7.5%; unspecified quantities of benzocaine, camphor, menthol, methylparaben, propylparaben
Use: For relief of itching and pain due to poison ivy and poison oak
Side Effects: Allergic reactions (rash, itching, soreness); local irritation
Warnings: Do not apply this product to extensive or raw, oozing areas of the skin, or use for a prolonged time, except as directed by a physician. • Do not use near the eyes, on mucous membranes, on genitalia, or on infected areas. Discontinue use and consult your pharmacist if irritation (pain, itching, or swelling) or rash occurs. • Avoid scratching, which may cause irritation and secondary infection.
Comments: Before applying the medication, soak the area in warm water or apply wet towels for five to ten minutes; dry gently by patting with a soft towel and then apply medication. • If itching is intolerable and this product does not relieve it sufficiently, we recommend the use of a "wet soak." In fact, a wet soak may work well enough that you do not need to use this product at all. For more information about how to apply a wet soak, refer to the chapter "Buying, Storing, and Using Drugs."

Fair: Products containing better ingredients are available. The anesthetic in this product may cause further irritation in susceptible people.

Kaopectate, Kaopectate Concentrate diarrhea remedies

Manufacturer: The Upjohn Company
Dosage Form/Ingredients: Kaopectate: Liquid (content per 2 tablespoons): kaolin, 6 gm; pectin, 130 mg. Kaopectate Concentrate: Liquid (content per 2 tablespoons): kaolin, 8.775 gm; pectin, 195 mg
Use: For the treatment of common diarrhea
Side Effects: Constipation after long-term use (seven days to two months)
Warnings: If you are taking other drugs, do not take either of these

products until you have first checked with your doctor or pharmacist. • These products or any other products for diarrhea should not be used to self-medicate without first consulting a doctor if the person is under age three or over age 60, has a history of asthma, heart disease, peptic ulcer, or is pregnant. • Diarrhea should stop in two to three days. If it persists longer, or recurs frequently or in the presence of high fever, call your doctor.

Comments: Be sure to drink at least eight glasses of water each day while taking these products.

Acceptable: The ingredients in these products are safe and may be effective for you.

Ketostix Strips urine test for ketones

Manufacturer: Ames Division, Miles Laboratories
Product Form: Dip-and-read strips
Use: To test urine for ketones
Comments: Do not use this product if the strip has turned brown. • Be certain to remind your doctor and pharmacist of any over-the-counter item or prescription drug you are taking. It may affect this test. • We do not recommend the use of this product to detect ketones in your urine if you are doing so as part of a weight-reduction plan. Consult your doctor first. • Test only freshly collected urine. • Keep the container tightly closed and store in a dry place out of the sun. Do not refrigerate. • Do not keep the stick immersed in urine longer than the directions state. • Compare the color quickly to the chart on the package. Read the color in a bright light. • Before reading the color, tap the stick on the side of the container to remove excess fluid.

Preferred: This test is effective for the purpose specified and offers good value for the money.

Kolantyl antacid

Manufacturer: Merrell-National Laboratories
Dosage Forms/Ingredients: Gel (content per teaspoon): aluminum hydroxide, 150 mg; magnesium hydroxide, 150 mg; sodium, 2.2 mg. Tablet: aluminum hydroxide, 300 mg; magnesium oxide, 185 mg; sodium, <15 mg. Wafer: aluminum hydroxide, 180 mg; magnesium hydroxide, 170 mg
Use: For relief from acid indigestion, heartburn, and/or sour stomach
Side Effects: Constipation, diarrhea; dizziness; mouth irritation; nausea; rash; abdominal discomfort; vomiting
Warnings: Persons with kidney disease should not use this product. In persons with kidney disease, repeated (daily) use of this product may cause nausea, vomiting, depressed reflexes, or breathing difficulties. • Long-term (several weeks) use of this product may lead to intestinal obstruction and dehydration. Phosphate depletion may occur, leading to weakness, loss of appetite, and eventually bone pain. Phosphate depletion may be prevented by drinking at least one glass of milk a day. • Do not take this product within two hours of a dose of a tetracycline antibiotic. • Consult your physician or pharmacist before taking this product if you are already taking iron, a vitamin-mineral product, chlorpromazine, phenytoin, digoxin, quinidine, or warfarin, or if you are unsure of the type and contents of the medications you are taking. • Never self-medicate with this product if your symptoms occur regularly (two or three or more times a month). Consult your doctor if the symptoms are worse than usual, if you have chest pains or feel "tightness" in the chest, or if

you are sweating or short of breath. In fact, we do not recommend self-treatment for severe attacks of heartburn, indigestion, or stomach upset in any circumstances. If you do decide that your symptoms are mild enough to warrant self-medication, limit treatment to two weeks. If symptoms persist, consult your doctor.

Comments: To prevent constipation, drink at least eight glasses of water a day. If constipation persists, consult your doctor or pharmacist. • This product must be taken exactly as directed on the label, unless your doctor has instructed you otherwise. Never skip a dose just because you feel better. If you grow tired of the taste, ask your pharmacist to suggest a different product. • The gel form of this product is superior to the tablet or wafer forms and should be used unless you have been specifically directed to use a tablet or wafer. • Exact generic equivalents of this product may not be available. However, your pharmacist may be able to suggest a similar product that can save you money.

Preferred: *This product offers an effective combination of recommended ingredients.*

Komed acne preparation

Manufacturer: Barnes-Hind Pharmaceuticals, Inc.
Dosage Form/Ingredients: Lotion: isopropyl alcohol, 25%; salicylic acid, 2%; sodium thiosulfate, 8%; unspecified quantities of camphor, colloidal alumina, and menthol
Use: Treatment of acne
Side Effects: Allergy; local irritation
Warnings: Do not get this product in or near the eyes. • If the condition worsens or if skin irritation develops, stop using this product and consult your physician.
Comments: Wash area gently with warm water and pat dry before applying this product.

Fair: *Products containing more effective ingredients are available.*

Lactinex diarrhea remedy

Manufacturer: Hynson, Westcott & Dunning
Dosage Forms/Ingredients: Granules, Tablet: unspecified quantities of lactobacillus acidophilus and lactobacillus bulgaricus
Use: For the treatment of common diarrhea; for the treatment of oral ulcers
Warnings: This product or any other product for diarrhea should not be used to self-medicate without first consulting a doctor if the person is under age three or over age 60, has a history of asthma, heart disease, peptic ulcer, or is pregnant. • Diarrhea should stop in two to three days. If it persists longer, or recurs frequently or in the presence of high fever, call your doctor and be sure to tell him of any drugs you are taking.
Comments: Be sure to drink at least eight glasses of water each day while taking this product. • The granules should be added to cereal or other foods, or milk before taking. • This product contains live bacteria that work to re-establish the normal bacteria in the intestine. • Store this product in the refrigerator. • While this diarrhea remedy is highly recommended by many doctors and pharmacists, several glasses of milk or some yogurt each day may work just as well. • See "Canker Sore and Fever Blister Remedies" for information on using this product to treat oral ulcers.

Fair: *Adding milk or yogurt to your diet may work just as well as this product in the treatment of common diarrhea.*

Lanacane hemorrhoidal preparation

Manufacturer: Combe Incorporated

Dosage Form/Ingredients: Cream: benzocaine, 6%; resorcinol, 2%; unspecified quantity of chlorothymol

Use: For relief from pain, burning, and itching of hemorrhoids and other irritated anorectal tissue

Side Effects: Irritation

Warnings: Sensitization (continued itching and redness) may occur with long-term and repeated use. • Certain ingredients in this product may cause an allergic reaction; do not use for longer than seven days at a time unless your doctor has advised you otherwise. • Never self-medicate for hemorrhoids if pain is continuous or throbbing, if bleeding or itching is excessive, or if you feel a large pressure within the rectum. • Discontinue use if irritation (pain, itching, or swelling) or rash occurs; consult your pharmacist.

Comments: Hemorrhoidal (pile) preparations relieve itching, reduce pain and inflammation, and check bleeding, but they do not heal, dry up, or give lasting relief from hemorrhoids.

Acceptable: Although generally we prefer a hemorrhoidal discomfort preparation that contains hydrocortisone, this product will also provide some relief.

Liquiprin analgesic

Manufacturer: Norcliff Thayer Inc.

Dosage Form/Ingredient: Liquid (content per 2.5 ml, or one dropperful): acetaminophen, 120 mg

Use: For the relief of discomforts and fever following immunizations, or of colds or "flu"

Side Effects: When taken in overdose: Blood disorders; rash

Warnings: This product should not be taken by persons with certain blood disorders; or with heart, lung, liver, or kidney disease without a doctor's approval. • When taken in overdose, acetaminophen is more toxic than aspirin. The dosage instructions listed on the package should be followed carefully; toxicity may occur in adults or children with repeated doses. • This product is intended for children. Be sure to keep it out of their reach when not in use.

Comments: Acetaminophen does not relieve inflammation, so if pain is caused by swelling or inflammation, it should not be used. Aspirin is better. • Generic substitutes for this product are available and may save you money. Ask your pharmacist for assistance.

Preferred: We recommend this product because it contains a single effective ingredient.

Maalox, Maalox #1, Maalox #2 antacids

Manufacturer: William H. Rorer, Inc.

Dosage Forms/Ingredients: Maalox: Suspension (content per teaspoon): aluminum hydroxide, 225 mg; magnesium hydroxide, 200 mg; sodium, 2.5 mg. Maalox #1: Tablet: aluminum hydroxide, 200 mg; magnesium hydroxide, 200 mg; sodium, 0.8 mg. Maalox #2: Tablet: aluminum hydroxide, 400 mg; magnesium hydroxide, 400 mg; sodium, 1.8 mg

Use: For relief from acid indigestion, heartburn, and/or sour stomach

Side Effects: Constipation; diarrhea; dizziness; mouth irritation;

nausea; rash; abdominal discomfort; vomiting

Warnings: Persons with kidney disease should not use these products. In persons with kidney disease, repeated (daily) use of these products may cause nausea, vomiting, depressed reflexes, or breathing difficulties. • Long-term (several weeks) use of these products may lead to intestinal obstruction and dehydration. Phosphate depletion may occur, leading to weakness, loss of appetite, and eventually bone pain. Phosphate depletion may be prevented by drinking at least one glass of milk a day. • Do not take these products within two hours of a dose of a tetracycline antibiotic. • Consult your physician or pharmacist before taking these products if you are already taking iron, a vitamin-mineral product, chlorpromazine, phenytoin, digoxin, quinidine, or warfarin, or if you are unsure of the type and contents of the medications you are taking. • Never self-medicate with these products if your symptoms occur regularly (two or three or more times a month). Consult your doctor if the symptoms are worse than usual, if you have chest pains or feel "tightness" in the chest, or if you are sweating or short of breath. In fact, we do not recommend self-treatment for severe attacks of heartburn, indigestion, or stomach upset in any circumstances. If you do decide that your symptoms are mild enough to warrant self-medication, limit treatment to two weeks. If symptoms persist, consult your doctor.

Comments: To prevent constipation, drink at least eight glasses of water a day. If constipation persists, consult your doctor or pharmacist. • These products must be taken exactly as directed on the label, unless your doctor has instructed you otherwise. Never skip a dose just because you feel better. If you grow tired of the taste, ask your pharmacist to suggest a different product. • The suspension form of these products is superior to the tablet forms and should be used unless you have been specifically directed to use a tablet. • Exact generic equivalents of these products may not be available. However, your pharmacist may be able to suggest similar products that can save you money.

Preferred: *These products offer an effective combination of recommended ingredients.*

Maalox Plus antacid and antiflatulent

Manufacturer: William H. Rorer, Inc.

Dosage Forms/Ingredients: Liquid (content per teaspoon): aluminum hydroxide, 225 mg; magnesium hydroxide, 200 mg; simethicone, 25 mg; sodium, 2.5 mg. Tablet: dried aluminum hydroxide gel, 200 mg; magnesium hydroxide, 200 mg; simethicone, 25 mg; sodium, 1.4 mg

Use: For relief of acid indigestion, heartburn, and/or sour stomach when accompanied by painful gas symptoms

Side Effects: Constipation; diarrhea; dizziness; mouth irritation; nausea; rash; abdominal discomfort; vomiting

Warnings: Persons with kidney disease should not use this product. In persons with kidney disease, repeated (daily) use of this product may cause nausea, vomiting, depressed reflexes, or breathing difficulties. • Long-term (several weeks) use of this product may lead to intestinal obstruction and dehydration. Phosphate depletion may occur, leading to weakness, loss of appetite, and eventually bone pain. Phosphate depletion may be prevented by drinking at least one glass of milk a day. • Do not take this product within two hours of a dose of a tetracycline antibiotic. • Consult your physician or pharmacist before taking this product if your are already taking iron, a vitamin-mineral product, chlorpromazine, phenytoin, digoxin, quinidine, or warfarin, or if you are unsure of the type and contents of the medications you are taking. • Never self-medicate with this product if your symptoms occur regularly (two or three or more times a month). Consult your doctor if the symptoms are worse than usual, if you have chest pains or feel "tightness" in the chest, or if you are sweating or short of breath. In fact, we do not recommend self-treatment for severe attacks of heartburn, indigestion, or stomach upset in any circumstances. If you do decide that your symptoms are mild enough to warrant self-medication, limit treatment to two weeks. If symptoms persist, consult your doctor.

Comments: To prevent constipation, drink at least eight glasses of water a day. If constipation persists, consult your doctor or pharmacist. • This product must be taken exactly as directed on the label, unless your doctor has instructed you otherwise. Never skip a dose just because you feel better. If you grow tired of the taste, ask your pharmacist to suggest a different product. • The liquid form of this product is superior to the tablet form and should be used unless you have been specifically directed to use the tablet. • Exact generic equivalents of this product may not be available. However, your pharmacist may be able to suggest a similar product that can save you money. • Simethicone is included to relieve bloating and gas formation; this ingredient makes it easier for you to eliminate gas by belching and passing flatus. If you do not suffer from bloating and gas pains, use a product without simethicone. You will probably save money.

Acceptable: Generally, we consider it preferable to treat acid indigestion and flatulence (gas) separately rather than with a combination product.

Measurin analgesic

Manufacturer: Breon Laboratories, Inc.
Dosage Form/Ingredient: Timed-release tablet: aspirin, 650 mg
Use: For the relief of pain of headache, temporary relief of minor arthritic pain, discomforts and fever of colds and "flu," menstrual cramps, muscle aches and pains, toothache, inflammation, fever
Side Effects: Dizziness; mental confusion; nausea and vomiting; ringing in the ears; slight blood loss; sweating
Warnings: Persons with kidney disease, asthma, hay fever, or other allergies should be extremely careful about using this product. The product may interfere with the treatment of gout. This product may cause an increased bleeding tendency and should not be taken by persons with a history of bleeding, peptic ulcer, or stomach bleeding. If you have any of these conditions, consult your doctor or pharmacist before using this medication. • Do not use this product if you are consuming alcohol, or taking methotrexate, oral anticoagulants, oral antidiabetics, probenecid, steroids, and/or sulfinpyrazone; if you are unsure of the type or contents of your medications, ask your doctor or pharmacist. • The dosage instructions listed on the package should be followed carefully; toxicity may occur in adults or children with repeated doses. • This product should not be crushed or chewed. It must be swallowed whole.
Comments: This product's sustained release form may not be worth the extra cost. • Generic substitutes for this product are available and may save you money. Ask your pharmacist for assistance.

Fair: This is an overpriced version of aspirin. The sustained release form may not justify the product's cost.

Medi-Quik antiseptic and burn remedy

Manufacturer: Lehn & Fink Products Company

Dosage Forms/Ingredients: Aerosol spray, Pump spray: benzalkonium chloride, 0.1%; ethyl alcohol, 38%; lidocaine, 2.5%

Use: For the relief of pain from sunburn and other minor burns, minor cuts, scrapes, poison ivy, and insect bites

Side Effects: Allergy; local irritation

Warnings: Do not use this product on deep wounds or serious burns. • Do not use this product on large areas of the body because it is possible that a toxic amount of medication may be absorbed. • Discontinue use if irritation (rash, itching, or swelling) or pain appears. Consult your physician. • The fluid in burn blisters helps healing of underlying tissue. Blisters should not be broken. If you have blisters that are extremely large or painful, contact your doctor. • The aerosol spray is flammable; do not use it while you are smoking or near a fire. Avoid inhalation and keep away from eyes.

Comments: To relieve burn pain, take aspirin and cool the burned area. • If itching is intolerable, we recommend the use of a "wet soak" once daily. See the chapter "Buying, Storing, and Using Drugs" for directions. • Consult your doctor or pharmacist if you have any questions concerning the use of this product.

Acceptable: Greater relief can be achieved with a product containing 20 percent benzocaine.

Mentholatum Deep Heating muscular pain remedy

Manufacturer: The Mentholatum Company

Dosage Forms/Ingredients: Lotion: menthol, 6%; methyl salicylate, 20%. Ointment: menthol, 6%; methyl salicylate, 12.7%; unspecified quantities of eucalyptus oil and turpentine oil

Use: Used externally to temporarily relieve pain in muscles and other areas

Side Effects: Allergic reactions (rash, itching, soreness); local irritation; local numbness

Warnings: This product is for external use only. • Do not use it on broken or irritated skin, or on large areas of the body; keep it away from the eyes. • If the pain in muscles or other areas persists, call your doctor. • While you are using this product, avoid exposure to direct sunlight, heat lamp, or sun lamp. • Discontinue use and consult your pharmacist if irritation (rash, itching, or swelling) or pain occurs. • Before using this product on a child under 12 years of age, consult your doctor. • Children might be attracted to the smell of this product; it should be stored safely out of their reach. • If a child swallows some of this product, call your doctor immediately. • Be sure to rub the lotion vigorously into the skin, but do not rub in the ointment.

Preferred: The methyl salicylate in the lotion form of this product provides an effective treatment for the temporary relief of muscle pain.

Acceptable: The additional ingredients in the ointment form make it less desirable.

Mercurochrome first-aid product

Manufacturer: Becton Dickinson

Dosage Form/Ingredient: Liquid: merbromin, 2%

Use: To disinfect minor burns, cuts, and scrapes on skin

Side Effects: Allergic reactions (rash, itching, soreness); local irritation

Warnings: Do not swallow this product or get it in the eyes. • Keep it out of the reach of children.

Fair: More effective products are available.

Merthiolate (thimerosal) tincture first-aid product

Manufacturer: Eli Lilly and Company
Dosage Form/Ingredients: Liquid: thimerosal, 0.1% in alcohol
Use: To disinfect minor burns, cuts, and scrapes on skin
Side Effects: Burning; itching; stinging. If swallowed may cause abdominal cramping; diarrhea; nausea; vomiting.
Warnings: Do not swallow this product or get it in the eyes. • Keep out of the reach of children.
Comments: This product is not as effective a skin disinfectant as iodine tincture. • This product is also available in a water solution; thimerosal in water does not burn or sting as much, but it is even less effective as a disinfectant than thimerosal in alcohol.

Acceptable: This product is less effective for the use specified than iodine tincture.

Metamucil laxative

Manufacturer: Searle Consumer Products
Dosage Forms/Ingredients: Instant mix (content per packet): psyllium hydrophilic mucilloid, 3.6 gm; unspecified quantities of citric acid and sodium bicarbonate. Regular powder: dextrose, 50%; psyllium hydrophilic mucilloid, 30%
Use: For relief of constipation
Side Effects: None, when used as directed
Warnings: Persons with high fever (100° F or more), black or tarry stools, nausea, vomiting, abdominal pain, intestinal ulcers, intestinal obstruction, fecal obstruction, or difficulty in swallowing; children under age three; and pregnant women should not use this product unless directed by a doctor. • The instant mix form should not be used by people on low-salt diets. • Do not use this product when constipation is caused by megacolon or other diseases of the intestine, or hypothyroidism. • Excessive use (daily for a month or more) of this product may cause diarrhea, vomiting, and loss of certain blood electrolytes. • Never self-medicate with this product if constipation lasts longer than two weeks, or if the medication does not produce a laxative effect within a week. • Limit use to seven days unless directed otherwise by your doctor; this product may cause laxative-dependence (addiction) if used for a longer time.
Comments: Evacuation may not occur for 12 to 72 hours. • This product must be mixed in water or juice before taking; an eight-ounce glass of water should be consumed immediately afterwards.

Preferred: Used as directed, bulk-forming laxatives like this are safe and effective.

Microsyn acne preparation

Manufacturer: Syntex Laboratories, Inc.
Dosage Form/Ingredients: Lotion: resorcinol, 2%; salicylic acid, 2%; sodium thiosulfate, 8%; isopropyl alcohol, 25%; unspecified quantities of camphor, colloidal alumina, and menthol

Use: Treatment of acne

Side Effects: Allergy; local irritation

Warnings: Do not get this product in or near the eyes. • If the condition worsens or if skin irritation develops, stop using this product and consult your physician.

Comments: Wash area gently with warm water and pat dry before applying this product.

Fair: Products containing more effective ingredients are available.

Modane Bulk laxative

Manufacturer: Warren-Teed Laboratories

Dosage Form/Ingredients: Powder: psyllium hydrophilic mucilloid, 50%; dextrose, 50%

Use: For relief of constipation

Side Effects: None, when used as directed

Warnings: Persons with high fever (100° F or more), black or tarry stools, nausea, vomiting, abdominal pain, intestinal ulcers, intestinal obstruction, fecal obstruction, or difficulty in swallowing; children under age three; and pregnant women should not use this product unless directed by a doctor. • Do not use this product when constipation is caused by megacolon or other diseases of the intestine, or hypothyroidism. • Excessive use (daily for a month or more) of this product may cause diarrhea, vomiting, and loss of certain blood electrolytes. • Never self-medicate with this product if constipation lasts longer than two weeks, or if the medication does not produce a laxative effect within a week. • Limit use to seven days unless directed otherwise by your doctor; this product may cause laxative-dependence (addiction) if used for a longer time.

Comments: Evacuation may not occur for 12 to 72 hours. • This product must be mixed in water or juice before taking; an eight-ounce glass of water should be consumed immediately afterwards.

Preferred: Used as directed, bulk-forming laxatives like this are safe and effective.

Modane, Modane Mild laxatives

Manufacturer: Warren-Teed Laboratories

Dosage Forms/Ingredients: Modane: Liquid (content per teaspoon): alcohol, 5%; danthron, 37.5 mg. Tablet: danthron, 75 mg. Modane Mild: Tablet: danthron, 37.5 mg

Use: For relief of constipation

Side Effects: Excess loss of fluid; griping (cramps); mucus in feces

Warnings: Persons with a high fever (100° F or more), black or tarry stools, nausea, vomiting, abdominal pain; pregnant women; and children under the age of three should not use these products unless directed to do so by a doctor. • Do not use these products when constipation is caused by megacolon or other diseases of the intestine, or hypothyroidism. • Excessive use (daily for a month or more) of these products may cause diarrhea, vomiting, and loss of certain blood electrolytes. • Hypokalemia may impair the effectiveness of these products. • Never self-medicate with these products if constipation lasts longer than two weeks, or if the medication does not produce a laxative effect within a week. • Limit use to seven days unless directed otherwise by a doctor since this product may cause laxative-dependence (addiction) if used for a longer time.

Comments: Evacuation may occur within six to twelve hours. • These products may discolor the urine.

Acceptable: We prefer bulk-forming laxatives; however, these products are also effective.

Multicebrin nutritional supplement

Manufacturer: Eli Lilly and Company
Dosage Form/Ingredients: Capsule: vitamin A, 10,000 IU; vitamin D, 400 IU; vitamin E, 6.6 IU; ascorbic acid, 75 mg; thiamine hydrochloride, 3 mg; riboflavin, 3 mg; niacin, 25 mg; pyridoxine hydrochloride, 1.2 mg; cyanocobalamin, 3 mcg; pantothenic acid, 5 mg
Use: To supplement the diet
Side Effects: None
Warnings: If large doses are taken, this product may interfere with the results of urine tests. If your urine is being tested, inform your doctor and/or pharmacist that you are taking this product. • This product contains ingredients that accumulate and are stored in the body. The recommended dose should not be exceeded for long periods (several weeks to months) except by doctor's orders.
Comments: Dietary deficiencies of vitamins are uncommon in the United States. Most people who have vitamin deficiencies should be under a doctor's care, and they should not be self-medicating with OTC vitamin products. If you choose to take supplemental vitamins, choose a generic product to save money. Ask your pharmacist for assistance.

Acceptable: If you choose to take a vitamin supplement, this is an acceptable product.

Murine eyedrops

Manufacturer: Abbott Laboratories
Dosage Form/Ingredients: Drop: benzalkonium chloride, 0.01%; edetate disodium, 0.05%; unspecified quantities of methylcellulose, sodium phosphate, potassium chloride, and sodium chloride
Use: To lubricate dry eyes
Side Effects: Allergic reactions (rash, itching, soreness); local irritation; momentary blurred vision
Warnings: Do not use this product for more than two days without checking with your doctor. • Use this product only for minor eye irritations. • Do not touch the dropper or bottle top to the eye or other tissue because contamination of the solution will result. • The use of more than one eye product at a time may cause severe irritation to the eye.
Comments: This product works best when used correctly. Refer to the instructions for eye products in the chapter, "Buying, Storing, and Using Drugs."

Acceptable: This product offers an acceptable treatment for the lubrication of dry eyes.

Murine Plus decongestant eyedrops

Manufacturer: Abbott Laboratories
Dosage Form/Ingredients: Drop: tetrahydrozoline hydrochloride, 0.05%; edetate disodium, 0.1%; benzalkonium chloride, 0.01%
Use: For relief of minor eye irritation and redness
Side Effects: Allergic reactions (rash, itching, soreness); local irritation; momentary blurred vision

Warnings: Do not use this product if you have glaucoma. • Do not use this product for more than two consecutive days without checking with your doctor. • Keep this product out of the reach of children. If swallowed, this drug is likely to cause overstimulation in children. Call your doctor immediately if this product is accidentally swallowed. • Do not touch the dropper or bottle top to the eye or other tissue because contamination of the solution will result. • Use this product only for minor eye irritations. • The use of more than one eye product at a time may cause severe irritation to the eye.

Comments: This product works best when used correctly. Refer to the instructions on eye products in the chapter, "Buying, Storing, and Using Drugs."

Acceptable: This product offers a satisfactory treatment for the relief of minor eye irritation.

Myadec nutritional supplement

Manufacturer: Parke-Davis

Dosage Form/Ingredients: Tablet: vitamin A, 10,000 IU; vitamin D, 400 IU; vitamin E, 30 IU; vitamin C, 250 mg; folic acid, 0.4 mg; thiamine, 10 mg; riboflavin, 10 mg; niacin (as niacinamide), 100 mg; vitamin B_6, 5 mg; vitamin B_{12}, 6 mcg; pantothenic acid, 20 mg; iodine, 150 mcg; iron, 20 mg; magnesium, 100 mg; copper, 2 mg; zinc, 20 mg; manganese, 1.25 mg

Use: To supplement the diet

Side Effects: Constipation; diarrhea; nausea; stomach pain

Warnings: This product should not be used by persons who have active peptic ulcer or ulcerative colitis. • Alcoholics and persons who have chronic liver or pancreatic disease should use this product with special caution; such persons may have enhanced iron absorption and are therefore more likely than others to experience iron toxicity. • The minerals in this product interact with oral tetracycline antibiotics and reduce the absorption of the antibiotics. If you are currently taking tetracycline, consult your doctor or pharmacist before taking this product. If you are unsure of the type or contents of your medications, ask your doctor or pharmacist. • Accidental iron poisoning is common in children; be sure to keep this product safely out of their reach. • This product contains ingredients that accumulate and are stored in the body. The recommended dose should not be exceeded for long periods (several weeks to months) except by doctor's orders. • If two or more tablets are taken daily, this product may interfere with the results of urine tests. If your urine is being tested, inform your doctor and/or pharmacist that you are taking this product. • Because of its iron content, this product may cause constipation, diarrhea, nausea or stomach pain. These symptoms usually disappear or become less severe after two to three days. Taking your dose with food or milk may help minimize these side effects. If they persist, ask your pharmacist to recommend another product. • This product contains vitamin B_6 (pyridoxine) in an amount great enough that it may interact with levodopa (L-dopa). If you are currently taking L-dopa, check with your doctor before taking this product.

Comments: Black, tarry stools are a normal consequence of iron therapy. If your stools are not black and tarry, this product may not be working for you. Ask your pharmacist to recommend another product. • Most people do not require the high dosages of the ingredients contained in this product. In fact, dietary deficiencies of vitamins are uncommon in the United States. Most people who have vitamin deficiencies should be under a doctor's care, and they should not be self-medicating with OTC vitamin products. If you choose to take supplemental vitamins, choose a generic product to save money. Ask your pharmacist for assistance.

Acceptable: *If you choose to take a vitamin supplement, this is an acceptable product.*

Mycitracin first-aid product

Manufacturer: The Upjohn Company
Dosage Form/Ingredients: Ointment (content per gram): bacitracin, 500 units; neomycin sulfate, 3.5 mg; polymyxin B sulfate, 5,000 units
  Use: To prevent infection from cuts and abrasions; to treat impetigo
  Side Effects: Allergic reactions (rash, itching, soreness); local irritation
  Warnings: Diabetics and persons with impaired circulation should not use this product. • If the condition seems to get worse while using this product, call your doctor at once. • If the infection does not clear up in four or five days, consult your doctor or pharmacist.
  Comments: Apply this product at least three times daily to maintain effectiveness. • If using this product to treat impetigo, apply it with a cotton-tipped applicator. Do not touch the cotton part with your fingers after applying the medication. Wash your hands thoroughly after applying medication to impetigo sores.

Preferred: *This product is effective for the uses specified.*

Mylanta, Mylanta II antacids and antiflatulents

Manufacturer: Stuart Pharmaceuticals
Dosage Forms/Ingredients: Mylanta: Suspension (content per teaspoon), Tablet: aluminum hydroxide, 200 mg; magnesium hydroxide, 200 mg; simethicone, 20 mg; sodium, < 0.7 mg. Mylanta II: Suspension (content per teaspoon), Tablet: aluminum hydroxide, 400 mg; magnesium hydroxide, 400 mg; simethicone, 30 mg; sodium, < 1.4 mg
  Use: For relief of acid indigestion, heartburn, and/or sour stomach when accompanied by painful gas symptoms
  Side Effects: Constipation; diarrhea; dizziness; mouth irritation; nausea; rash; abdominal discomfort; vomiting
  Warnings: Persons with kidney disease should not use these products. In persons with kidney disease, repeated (daily) use of these products may cause nausea, vomiting, depressed reflexes, or breathing difficulties. • Long-term (several weeks) use of these products may lead to intestinal obstruction and dehydration. Phosphate depletion may occur, leading to weakness, loss of appetite, and eventually bone pain. Phosphate depletion may be prevented by drinking at least one glass of milk a day. • Do not take these products within two hours of a dose of a tetracycline antibiotic. • Consult your physician or pharmacist before taking these products if you are already taking iron, a vitamin-mineral product, chlorpromazine, phenytoin, digoxin, quinidine, or warfarin, or if you are unsure of the type and contents of the medications you are taking. • Never self-medicate with these products if your symptoms occur regularly (two or three or more times a month). Consult your doctor if the symptoms are worse than usual, if you have chest pains or feel "tightness" in the chest, or if you are sweating or short of breath. In fact, we do not recommend self-treatment for severe attacks of heartburn, indigestion, or stomach upset in any circumstances. If you do decide that your symptoms are mild enough to warrant self-medication, limit treatment to two weeks. If symptoms persist, consult your doctor.
  Comments: To prevent constipation, drink at least eight glasses of

water a day. If constipation persists, consult your doctor or pharmacist. •
These products must be taken exactly as directed on the label, unless
your doctor has instructed you otherwise. Never skip a dose just because
you feel better. If you grow tired of the taste, ask your pharmacist to suggest a different product. • The suspension forms of these products are
superior to the tablet forms and should be used unless you have been
specifically directed to use a tablet. • Exact generic equivalents of these
products may not be available. However, your pharmacist may be able to
suggest similar products that can save you money. • Simethicone is included to relieve bloating and gas formation; this ingredient makes it
easier for you to eliminate gas by belching and passing flatus. If you do
not suffer from bloating and gas pains, use a product without
simethicone. You will probably save money.

*Acceptable: Generally, we consider it preferable to treat acid indigestion
and flatulence (gas) separately rather than with a combination product.*

Mylicon, Mylicon-80 antiflatulents

Manufacturer: Stuart Pharmaceuticals
Dosage Forms/Ingredient: Mylicon: Chewable tablet, Drop (content per
0.6 ml): simethicone, 40 mg. Mylicon-80: Chewable tablet: simethicone,
80 mg
Use: For symptomatic relief of flatulence and excessive, pain-causing
gas in the digestive tract
Side Effects: Minor nausea and vomiting (rare)
Warnings: Self-treatment of severe or repeated attacks of flatulence is
not recommended. If you do self-treat, limit therapy to two weeks, and call
your doctor if symptoms persist.
Comments: This product works by helping gas bubbles in the stomach
and intestines to burst; thus the gas is freed and is eliminated more easily
by belching or passing flatus. • The tablets should be chewed thoroughly
before being swallowed. • Simethicone is also available in tablet form as
Silain antiflatulent (A. H. Robins Company). Silain contains 50 mg
simethicone per tablet.

*Acceptable: The FDA considers simethicone safe and effective as an
antiflatulent.*

Nature's Remedy laxative

Manufacturer: Norcliff Thayer Inc.
Dosage Form/Ingredients: Tablet (regular and candy-coated): aloe, 100
mg; cascara sagrada, 150 mg
Use: For relief of constipation
Side Effects: Excess loss of fluid; griping (cramps); mucus in feces
Warnings: Persons with a high fever (100° F or more), black or tarry
stools, nausea, vomiting, abdominal pain; pregnant women; and children
under the age of three should not use this product when constipation is
caused by megacolon or other diseases of the intestine, or hypothyroidism. • Excessive use (daily for a month or more) of these products may
cause diarrhea, vomiting, and loss of certain blood electrolytes. • Never
self-medicate with this product if constipation lasts longer than two
weeks, or if the medication does not produce a laxative effect within a
week. • Limit use to seven days unless directed otherwise by a doctor
since this product may cause laxative-dependence (addiction) if used for
a longer time.

Comments: This product may discolor the urine. • Evacuation may occur within six to twelve hours. • The candy-coated tablet may be attractive to children; be sure to keep it out of their reach.

Acceptable: We prefer bulk-forming laxatives; however, this product is also effective.

Neoloid laxative

Manufacturer: Lederle Laboratories Div., American Cyanamid Company
Dosage Form/Ingredient: Emulsion: castor oil, 36.4%
Use: For relief of isolated occurrences of constipation
Side Effects: Excess loss of fluid; griping (cramps); mucus in feces
Warnings: Persons with a high fever (100° F or more), black or tarry stools, nausea, vomiting, abdominal pain; pregnant women; and children under the age of three should not use this product unless directed to do so by a doctor. • Do not use this product when constipation is caused by megacolon or other diseases of the intestine, or hypothyroidism. • Excessive use (daily for a month or more) of these products may cause diarrhea, vomiting, and loss of certain blood electrolytes. • Limit use to one dose per each infrequent occurrence of constipation. Castor oil is generally not recommended for treatment of chronic constipation.
Comments: Evacuation may occur within six to twelve hours.

Acceptable: If use of this product is restricted as described above, this product is acceptable.

Neo-Polycin first-aid product

Manufacturer: Dow Pharmaceuticals
Dosage Form/Ingredients: Ointment (content per gram): bacitracin, 400 units; neomycin sulfate, 3.5 mg; polymyxin B sulfate, 5,000 units
Use: To prevent infection from cuts and abrasions; to treat impetigo
Side Effects: Allergic reactions (rash, itching, soreness); local irritation
Warnings: Diabetics and persons with impaired circulation should not use this product. • If the condition seems to get worse while using this product, call your doctor at once. • If the infection does not clear up in four or five days, consult your doctor or pharmacist.
Comments: Apply this product at least three times daily to maintain effectiveness. • If using this product to treat impetigo, apply it with a cotton-tipped applicator. Do not touch the cotton part with your fingers after applying the medication. Wash your hands thoroughly after applying medication to impetigo sores.

Preferred: This product is effective for the uses specified.

Neosporin first-aid product

Manufacturer: Burroughs Wellcome Co.
Dosage Form/Ingredients: Ointment (contents per gram): bacitracin, 400 units; neomycin sulfate, 3.5 mg; polymyxin B sulfate, 5,000 units; unspecified quantity of white petrolatum
Use: To prevent infection from cuts and abrasions; to treat impetigo
Side Effects: Allergic reactions (rash, itching, soreness); local irritation
Warnings: Diabetics and persons with impaired circulation should not use this product. • If the condition seems to get worse while using this product, call your doctor at once. • If the infection does not clear up in four or five days, consult your doctor or pharmacist.
Comments: Apply this product at least three times daily to maintain effectiveness. • If using this product to treat impetigo, apply it with a

cotton-tipped applicator. Do not touch the cotton part with your fingers after applying the medication. Wash your hands thoroughly after applying medication to impetigo sores.

Preferred: *This product is effective for the uses specified.*

Neo-Synephrine Compound Decongestant cold remedy

Manufacturer: Winthrop Laboratories

Dosage Form/Ingredients: Tablet: phenylephrine hydrochloride, 5 mg; thenyldiamine hydrochloride, 7.5 mg; acetaminophen, 150 mg; caffeine, 15 mg

Use: For relief of nasal congestion, fever, aches, pains, and general discomfort due to colds

Side Effects: Anxiety; blurred vision; chest pain; confusion; constipation; dry mouth; difficult and painful urination; dizziness; drowsiness; headache; increased blood pressure; insomnia; loss of appetite; mild stimulation; nausea; nervousness; palpitations; rash; reduced sweating; tension; tremor; vomiting. In overdose: Blood disorders; rash

Warnings: This product should be used with special caution by the elderly or debilitated, and by persons who have asthma, diabetes, an enlarged prostate, glaucoma (certain types), heart disease, high blood pressure, kidney disease, liver disease, obstructed bladder, obstructed intestine, lung disease, certain blood disorders, peptic ulcer, or thyroid disease. If you have any of these conditions, consult your doctor before taking this product. It should not be used by pregnant or nursing women, or be given to newborn or premature infants. • This product may cause drowsiness. Do not take it if you must drive, operate heavy machinery, or perform other tasks requiring mental alertness. To prevent oversedation, avoid the use of alcohol or other drugs that have sedative properties. • This product interacts with alcohol, guanethidine, monoamine oxidase inhibitors, sedative drugs, and tricyclic antidepressants. If you are currently taking any drugs of these types, check with your doctor before taking this product. If you are unsure of the type or contents of your medications, ask your doctor or pharmacist. • Because this product reduces sweating, avoid excessive work or exercise in hot weather. • When taken in overdose, acetaminophen is more toxic than aspirin. Follow dosage instructions carefully.

Comments: Many other conditions (some serious) mimic the common cold. If symptoms persist beyond one week, or if they occur regularly without regard to season, consult your doctor. • The effectiveness of this product may diminish after being taken regularly for seven to ten days; consult your pharmacist about substituting another medication if this product begins to lose its effectiveness for you. • Chew gum or suck on ice chips or a piece of hard candy to relieve dryness of the mouth.

Unacceptable: *The caffeine included in this product has no value in treatment of the conditions specified.*

Neo-Synephrine Intranasal nasal decongestant

Manufacturer: Winthrop Laboratories

Dosage Forms/Ingredients: Drop: phenylephrine hydrochloride, 0.125%, 0.25%, 0.5%, or 1%. Jelly: phenylephrine hydrochloride, 0.5%. Nasal spray: phenylephrine hydrochloride, 0.25% or 0.5%. Mentholated nasal spray: phenylephrine hydrochloride, 0.5%; unspecified quantity of aromatics

Use: For temporary relief of nasal congestion due to colds, sinusitis, hay fever, or other upper respiratory allergies

173

Side Effects: Blurred vision; burning, dryness of nasal mucosa; increased nasal congestion or discharge; sneezing, and/or stinging; dizziness; drowsiness; headache; insomnia; nervousness; palpitations; slight increase in blood pressure; stimulation; tremor

Warnings: This product should not be used by persons who have glaucoma (certain types). • It should be used with special caution by persons who have diabetes, advanced hardening of the arteries, heart disease, high blood pressure, or thyroid disease. If you have any of these conditions, consult your doctor before using this product. • This product interacts with monoamine oxidase inhibitors, thyroid preparations, and tricyclic antidepressants. If you are currently taking any drugs of these types, check with your doctor before taking this product. If you are unsure of the type or contents of your medications, ask your doctor or pharmacist.

Comments: To avoid side effects such as burning, sneezing, or stinging, and a "rebound" increase in nasal congestion and discharge, do not exceed the recommended dose, and do not use this product for more than three or four continuous days. • This product should not be used by more than one person; sharing the dispenser may spread infection. • This product works best when it is used correctly. Refer to the instructions for the use of nasal sprays and drops in the chapter on "Buying, Storing, and Using Drugs." • Many nasal drops or sprays on the market contain oxymetazoline hydrochloride. This drug has a duration of action of about 12 hours, and because it needs to be used less often, it is less likely to cause "rebound" nasal congestion during use. Therefore, we recommend a product containing oxymetazoline hydrochloride rather than this product, which does not contain the ingredient. • The spray form of this product, although slightly more expensive than the drop and jelly, is preferred for adult use. Nasal spray penetrates far back into the nose, covering the nasal area more completely, and is more convenient to use. The drop is preferable for administration to children. The mentholated spray contains aromatic substances which add no therapeutic value; you may like the aroma.

Acceptable: Although we prefer a product containing oxymetazoline hydrochloride, this product also offers an effective formula for treating the condition specified.

Nervine sleep aid

Manufacturer: Miles Laboratories, Inc.

Dosage Form/Ingredient: Capsule-shaped tablet: pyrilamine maleate, 25 mg

Use: To induce drowsiness and assist in falling asleep

Side Effects: Blurred vision; confusion; constipation; difficult urination; dizziness; drowsiness; dry mouth and respiratory passages; headache; insomnia; low blood pressure; nausea; nervousness; palpitations; rash; restlessness; vomiting. Children may react with primary symptoms of excitement: convulsions; flushed skin; nervousness; tremors; twitching of muscles; uncoordinated movements

Warnings: Persons with asthma, diabetes, glaucoma (certain types), heart disease, high blood pressure, kidney disease, liver disease, thyroid disorders, certain types of peptic ulcer, enlarged prostate, obstructed bladder, or obstructed intestine; pregnant and nursing women; children under 12 years of age; and elderly or debilitated persons should not take this medication. • This product may interact with other drugs. If you are currently taking any medication, do not use this product without first consulting your doctor. • This product also interacts with alcohol, so avoid

alcohol or other central nervous system sedatives while you are using it. •
Since its purpose is to make you sleepy, do not use it while driving,
operating heavy machinery, or performing other tasks that require you to
be mentally alert. • Tolerance to this product may develop; do not increase the recommended dose unless your doctor recommends you to do
so. • Insomnia may be a symptom of serious illness. Seek your doctor's
advice if your sleeplessness continues, and do not take this product for
more than two weeks without consulting your doctor.

Comments: This product may cause dryness of the mouth. To reduce
this feeling, chew gum or suck on ice chips or a piece of hard candy. •
There is probably no need to purchase this drug. You would be better advised to try to find and correct the cause of your insomnia. A glass of
warm milk and a soak in a hot tub may work just as well as this product. •
Many OTC sleep aids are very similar. If you wish to use one, look for a
generic equivalent at a cheaper price. Ask your pharmacist for
assistance.

Unacceptable: *We consider that OTC sleep aids should not be taken
without the advice of a doctor.*

No Doz stimulant

Manufacturer: Bristol-Myers Products
Dosage Form/Ingredient: Tablet: caffeine, 100 mg
Use: To produce a temporary increase in mental alertness
Side Effects: Increased urination. In larger than the recommended
dose: Irregular heartbeat; nervousness; upset stomach; insomnia
Warnings: Do not take this product if you have heart disease, kidney
disease, blood vessel disease, or a nervous disorder.
Comments: No Doz stimulant may cause increased alertness in parts
of the brain and decreased ability in others. • If you take No Doz regularly
for two weeks, you will become tolerant to it and consequently the effectiveness decreases. • We do not recommend the use of this or any other
OTC stimulant. You can get the same effect by drinking coffee, tea, or
colas. If you regularly need a stimulant, you should see your doctor as
something serious may be wrong.

Unacceptable: *We do not recommend the use of any OTC stimulant product. Coffee, tea, or a cola drink will be equally effective. We consider this
product overpriced.*

Noskote sunscreen

Manufacturer: Coppertone Company
Dosage Form/Ingredients: Cream: unspecified quantities of oxybenzone and homosalate
Use: To prevent sunburn, premature aging of the skin, and skin cancer
caused by overexposure to sunlight; to protect persons with sun sensitive
skin, or those taking photo-sensitizing drugs, against sun toxicity
Side Effects: Occasional irritation; rash
Warnings: Avoid prolonged exposure to the sun, especially if you are
sensitive to it. • Do not use this product in or around the eyes. • Discontinue use and consult your pharmacist if irritation (pain, itching, or swelling) or rash appears. • Follow the directions given on the package,
especially regarding frequency of use. Be sure to reapply after swimming
or excessive exercise.

Comments: If you are unsure whether this is the proper sunscreen agent for you, refer for clarification to the section on sunscreen products in this book. If you still have questions, ask your pharmacist or doctor. • This product may stain certain types of clothing.

Not Evaluated: The manufacturer fails to provide sufficient information about the formulation of this product on which to base an evaluation.

Novahistine cold and allergy remedy

Manufacturer: Dow Pharmaceuticals
Dosage Forms/Ingredients: Liquid (content per teaspoon): phenylpropanolamine hydrochloride, 18.7 mg; chlorpheniramine maleate, 2 mg; alcohol, 5%. Tablet: phenylpropanolamine hydrochloride, 18.7 mg; chlorpheniramine maleate, 2 mg
Use: For relief of nasal congestion due to colds and upper respiratory allergies
Side Effects: Anxiety; blurred vision; chest pain; confusion; constipation; dry mouth; difficult and painful urination; dizziness; drowsiness; headache; increased blood pressure; insomnia; loss of appetite; mild stimulation; nausea; nervousness; palpitations; rash; reduced sweating; tension; tremor; vomiting
Warnings: This product should be used with special caution by the elderly or debilitated, and by persons who have asthma, diabetes, an enlarged prostate, glaucoma (certain types), heart disease, high blood pressure, kidney disease, liver disease, obstructed bladder, obstructed intestine, peptic ulcer, or thyroid disease. If you have any of these conditions, consult your doctor before taking this product. It should not be used by pregnant or nursing women, or be given to newborn or premature infants. • This product may cause drowsiness. Do not take it if you must drive, operate heavy machinery, or perform other tasks requiring mental alertness. To prevent oversedation, avoid the use of alcohol or other drugs that have sedative properties. • This product interacts with alcohol, guanethidine, monoamine oxidase inhibitors, sedative drugs, and tricyclic antidepressants. If you are currently taking any drugs of these types, check with your doctor before taking this product. If you are unsure of the type or contents of your medications, ask your doctor or pharmacist. • Because this product reduces sweating, avoid excessive work or exercise in hot weather.
Comments: Many other conditions (some serious) mimic the common cold. If symptoms persist beyond one week, or if they occur regularly without regard to season, consult your doctor. • The effectiveness of this product may diminish after being taken for seven to ten days; consult your pharmacist about substituting a different product if this product begins to lose its effectiveness for you. • Chew gum or suck on ice chips or a piece of hard candy to reduce mouth dryness.

Acceptable: We prefer single-ingredient products rather than combination antihistamine-decongestant products like this one.

Novahistine DMX cough remedy

Manufacturer: Dow Pharmaceuticals
Dosage Form/Ingredients: Liquid (content per teaspoon): dextromethorphan hydrobromide, 10 mg; pseudoephedrine hydrochloride, 30 mg; guaifenesin, 100 mg; alcohol, 10%
Use: For temporary relief of cough and nasal congestion due to colds

or "flu"; to convert a dry, nonproductive cough to a productive, phlegm-producing cough

Side Effects: Drowsiness; mild stimulation; nausea; vomiting; blurred vision; palpitations; flushing; nervousness; dizziness; insomnia

Warnings: This product should be used with special caution by children under two years of age, and by persons who have diabetes, heart disease, high blood pressure, or thyroid disease. In these situations, consult your doctor before taking this product. • This product interacts with guanethidine and monoamine oxidase inhibitors; if you are currently taking any drugs of these types, check with your doctor before taking this product. If you are unsure of the type or contents of your medications, ask your doctor or pharmacist. • If your cough persists, or is accompanied by high fever, consult your doctor promptly. • Do not use this product to treat chronic coughs, such as those from smoking or asthma. • Do not use this product to treat productive (hacking) coughs that produce phlegm.

Comments: If you require an expectorant, you need more moisture in your environment. Drink eight to ten glasses of water daily. The use of a vaporizer or humidifier may also be beneficial. • Many other conditions (some serious) mimic the common cold. If symptoms persist beyond one week or if they occur regularly without regard to season, consult your doctor.

Fair: This product contains a decongestant, an ingredient not directly related to treatment of a cough. Products containing more appropriate ingredients are available.

Novahistine Expectorant cough remedy

Manufacturer: Dow Pharmaceuticals

Dosage Form/Ingredients: Liquid (content per teaspoon): codeine phosphate, 10 mg; guaifenesin, 100 mg; phenylpropanolamine hydrochloride, 18.75 mg; alcohol, 7.5%

Use: For temporary relief of cough, nasal congestion, and other symptoms of colds or "flu"; to convert a dry, nonproductive cough to a productive phlegm-producing cough

Side Effects: Anxiety; blurred vision; chest pain; confusion; constipation; diarrhea; dizziness; drowsiness; headache; heartburn; increased blood pressure; insomnia; loss of appetite; nausea; nervousness; palpitations; rash; severe abdominal pain; sore throat; tension; tremor; vomiting

Warnings: This product should be used with special caution by the elderly or debilitated, and by persons who have asthma or respiratory disease, diabetes, an enlarged prostate, glaucoma (certain types), heart disease, high blood pressure, kidney disease, obstructed bladder, obstructed intestine, peptic ulcer, or thyroid disease. In these situations, consult your doctor before taking this product. • This product should not be given to newborns or premature infants, or taken by pregnant women. • This product may cause drowsiness. Do not take it if you must drive, operate heavy machinery, or perform other tasks requiring mental alertness. To prevent oversedation, avoid the use of alcohol or other drugs that have sedative properties. • This product interacts with alcohol, guanethidine, monoamine oxidase inhibitors, sedative drugs, and tricyclic antidepressants. If you are currently taking any drugs of these types, check with your doctor before taking this product. If you are unsure of the type or contents of your medications, ask your doctor or pharmacist. • Because this product contains codeine, it has the potential for abuse and must be used with caution. It usually should not be taken for more than seven to ten days. Tolerance may develop quickly, but do not increase the dose without consulting your doctor. • Do not use this product to treat chronic coughs, such as those from smoking or asthma. • Do not use this product to treat productive (hacking) coughs that produce phlegm. • If your cough persists, or is accompanied by high fever, consult your doctor promptly.

Comments: Many other conditions (some serious) mimic the common cold. If symptoms persist beyond one week or if they occur regularly without regard to season, consult your doctor. • If you require an expectorant, you need more moisture in your environment. Drink eight to ten glasses of water daily. The use of a vaporizer or humidifier may also be beneficial. • Chew gum or suck on ice chips or a piece of hard candy to reduce mouth dryness. • Over-the-counter sale of this product may not be permitted in some states.

Fair: *This product contains a decongestant, an ingredient not directly related to the treatment of a cough. Products containing more appropriate ingredients are available.*

Noxzema Medicated antiseptic and burn remedy

Manufacturer: Noxell Corporation
Dosage Forms/Ingredients: Cream, Lotion: phenol, less than 0.5%
Use: For temporary relief of pain of sunburn and other minor burns, minor cuts, scrapes, poison ivy, insect bites, skin irritation, and chapping
Side Effects: Allergy; local irritation
Warnings: Do not use this product on broken skin or on large areas of the body because it is possible that a toxic amount of medication may be absorbed. • Discontinue use if irritation (rash, itching, or swelling) or pain appears. Consult your physician. • The fluid in burn blisters helps healing of underlying tissue. Blisters should not be broken. If you have blisters that are extremely large or painful, contact your doctor.
Comments: To relieve burn pain, take aspirin and cool the burned area. • If itching is intolerable, we recommend the use of a "wet soak" once daily. See the chapter "Buying, Storing, and Using Drugs" for directions. • Remember that creams and lotions that are put on serious (second- or third-degree) burns will have to be taken off before definitive treatment can be given. Consult your doctor or pharmacist if you have any questions concerning the use of this product.
Fair: *Phenol is a less effective pain reliever than benzocaine and other local anesthetics.*

NP-27 athlete's foot and jock itch remedy

Manufacturer: Norwich-Eaton Pharmaceuticals
Dosage Forms/Ingredients: Cream: 8-hydroxyquinoline benzoate, 2.5%; unspecified quantities of salicylic acid, benzoic acid, eucalyptol, thymol, menthol, methyl, and propylparaben. Liquid: undecylenate acid, 10%; isopropyl alcohol, 56%. Powder: salicylic acid, 1.5%; unspecified quantities of boric acid, propylparaben, benzoic acid, dichlorophene, eucalyptol, thymol, menthol, and chlorothymol. Aerosol powder: zinc undecylenate, 20%; alcohol, 20.5%
Use: For the treatment of athlete's foot and jock itch
Side Effects: Allergy; local irritation
Warnings: Diabetics should not use this product without first consulting a physician; persons with impaired circulation should not use the

liquid form without consulting a physician. • Do not apply this product to mucous membranes, scraped areas, or to large areas of skin. • If your condition worsens, or if irritation occurs, stop using this product and consult your pharmacist. • When using the aerosol form of this product, be careful not to inhale any of the powder. • Check with your doctor before using this product on a child. Some doctors believe that children under 12 do not get athlete's foot, and a rash appearing between the toes of such an individual may be dermatitis or some other condition that this product would not treat.

Comments: Some lesions take months to heal, so it is important not to stop treatment to soon. • If foot lesions are consistently a problem, check the fit of your shoes. • Wash your hands thoroughly after applying this product. • The cream and liquid forms of this product are more effective than the powders; the best action of the powders may be in drying the infected area. • When using the liquid form of this product, pour some of the liquid into a separate container for each use; this will prevent contamination of the contents of the bottle. • The liquid form may sting temporarily after application. • The aerosol powder may be more expensive than the other forms of this product; check prices before paying for convenience you do not need.

Acceptable: Although we prefer a tolnaftate product, the liquid and aerosol powder forms of this product contain undecylenic acid, which is also a satisfactory treatment for athlete's foot.

Not evaluated: We cannot evaluate the cream and powder forms because the manufacturer fails to specify quantities of the ingredients.

NTZ nasal decongestant

Manufacturer: Winthrop Laboratories

Dosage Forms/Ingredients: Drop, Spray: phenylephrine hydrochloride, 0.5%; thenyldiamine hydrochloride, 0.1%; benzalkonium chloride, 1:5000

Use: For temporary relief of nasal congestion due to colds, sinusitis, hay fever, or other upper respiratory allergies

Side Effects: Blurred vision; burning, dryness of nasal mucosa; increased nasal congestion or discharge; sneezing, and/or stinging; dizziness; drowsiness; headache; insomnia; nervousness; palpitations; slight increase in blood pressure; stimulation

Warnings: This product should not be used by persons who have glaucoma (certain types). • It should be used with special caution by persons who have diabetes, advanced hardening of the arteries, heart disease, high blood pressure, or thyroid disease. If you have any of these conditions, consult your doctor before using this product. • This product interacts with monoamine oxidase inhibitors, thyroid preparations, and tricyclic antidepressants. If you are currently taking any drugs of these types, check with your doctor before taking this product. If you are unsure of the type or contents of your medications, ask your doctor or pharmacist.

Comments: To avoid side effects such as burning, sneezing, or stinging, and a "rebound" increase in nasal congestion and discharge, do not exceed the recommended dose, and do not use this product for more than three or four continuous days. • This product should not be used by more than one person; sharing the dispenser may spread infection. • This product works best when it is used correctly. Refer to the instructions for the use of nasal sprays and drops in the chapter on "Buying, Storing, and Using Drugs." • Many nasal drops or sprays on the market contain oxymetazoline hydrochloride. This drug has a duration of action of about 12 hours, and because it needs to be used less often, it is less likely to cause "rebound" nasal congestion during use. Therefore, we recommend a product containing oxymetazoline hydrochloride rather than this product, which does not contain the ingredient. • Although slightly more expensive than the drop, the spray form of this product is preferred for adult use. Nasal spray penetrates far back into the nose, covering the nasal area more completely, and is more convenient to use. The drop is preferable for administration to children.

Fair: *The antihistamine (thenyldiamine hydrochloride) in this product is unlikely to be effective for this use.*

Nujol laxative

Manufacturer: Plough, Inc.
Dosage Form/Ingredient: Liquid: mineral oil, 100%
Use: For relief of constipation; as a stool softener
Side Effects: Rectal irritation
Warnings: Persons with high fever (100° F or more), black or tarry stools, nausea, vomiting, or abdominal pain; children under age six; and pregnant women should not use this product unless directed by a doctor. • Do not use this product when constipation is caused by megacolon or other diseases of the intestine, or hypothyroidism. • Excessive use (daily for a month or more) of this product may cause diarrhea, vomiting, and loss of certain blood electrolytes. • A type of pneumonia may occur after prolonged (more than two months) and repeated (daily) use. • Never self-medicate with this product if constipation lasts longer than two weeks, or if the medication does not produce a laxative effect within a week. Limit use to seven days; this product may cause laxative-dependence (addiction) if used for a longer period. • This product is referred to as a stool softener and is recommended for relief of constipation when the stool is hard and dry. Do not take another stool softener product at the same time as you are taking this product. • Mineral oil may interfere with the absorption of vitamins A and D, calcium, and phosphate.
Comments: This laxative is best taken at bedtime; it should not be taken at mealtime. • If this product leaks through the rectum, the dose should be reduced until this symptom disappears. • Evacuation may occur within six to eight hours after taking this product.

Acceptable: *This product is an acceptable stool softener laxative. However, you may be able to save money by using a generic form of mineral oil instead.*

Nupercainal hemorrhoidal preparations

Manufacturer: CIBA Pharmaceutical Company
Dosage Forms/Ingredients: Suppository: dibucaine, 2.5 mg; unspecified quantities of cocoa butter, bismuth subgalate, and zinc oxide. Ointment: dibucaine, 1%
Use: For relief of pain, burning, and itching of hemorrhoids and other irritated anorectal tissues
Side Effects: Irritation
Warnings: Sensitization (continued itching and redness) may occur with long-term and repeated use. • Certain ingredients in this product may cause an allergic reaction; do not use for longer than seven days at a time unless your doctor has advised you otherwise. • The suppository is not recommended for external hemorrhoids or bleeding internal hemorrhoids. Use the ointment form. Use caution when inserting applicator. • Never self-medicate for hemorrhoids if pain is continuous or throbbing, if

bleeding or itching is excessive, or if you feel a large pressure within the rectum. • Discontinue use if irritation (pain, itching, or swelling) or rash occurs; consult your pharmacist.

Comments: Hemorrhoidal (pile) preparations relieve itching, reduce pain and inflammation, and check bleeding, but they do not heal, dry up, or give lasting relief from hemorrhoids. • Hemorrhoidal suppositories work best when they are used correctly. Refer to the instructions for their use in the chapter "Buying, Storing, and Using Drugs."

Acceptable: Although generally we prefer a hemorrhoidal discomfort preparation that contains hydrocortisone, this product will also provide some relief.

Nupercainal local anesthetic and burn remedy

Manufacturer: Ciba Pharmaceutical Company

Dosage Forms/Ingredient: Cream: dibucaine, 0.5%. Ointment: dibucaine, 1%

Use: For temporary relief of pain of sunburn and other minor burns, minor cuts, scrapes, poison ivy, insect bites, skin irritation, and chapping

Side Effects: Allergic rash; local irritation; stinging

Warnings: Do not use this product on broken skin or on large areas of the body because it is possible that a toxic amount of medication may be absorbed. • Discontinue use if irritation (rash, itching, or swelling) or pain appears. Consult your physician. • The fluid in burn blisters helps healing of underlying tissue. Blisters should not be broken. If you have blisters that are extremely large or painful, contact your doctor. • Do not use this product in or near the eyes. • Contact your doctor or pharmacist if this product does not bring relief within three or four days.

Comments: To relieve burn pain, take aspirin and cool the burned area. • If itching is intolerable, we recommend the use of a "wet soak" once daily. See the chapter "Buying, Storing, and Using Drugs" for directions. • Remember that ointments and creams that are put on serious (second- or third-degree) burns will have to be taken off before definitive treatment can be given. • Consult your doctor or pharmacist if you have any questions concerning the use of this product.

Acceptable: Greater relief of pain can be achieved with a product containing 20 percent benzocaine.

NyQuil cough remedy

Manufacturer: Vicks Health Care Division, Richardson-Merrell Inc.

Dosage Form/Ingredients: Liquid (content per 2 tablespoons): dextromethorphan hydrobromide, 15 mg; ephedrine sulfate, 8 mg; doxylamine succinate, 7.5 mg; acetaminophen, 600 mg; alcohol, 25%

Use: For relief of cough, nasal congestion, fever, aches, and pains due to colds or "flu"

Side Effects: Anxiety; blurred vision; chest pain; confusion; constipation; dry mouth; difficult and painful urination; dizziness; drowsiness; headache; increased blood pressure; insomnia; loss of appetite; mild stimulation; nausea; nervousness; palpitations; rash; reduced sweating; tension; tremor; vomiting. In overdose: Blood disorders; rash

Warnings: This product should be used with special caution by the elderly or debilitated, and by persons who have asthma, diabetes, an enlarged prostate, glaucoma (certain types), heart disease, high blood pressure, kidney disease, liver disease, obstructed bladder, obstructed intestine, lung disease, certain blood disorders, peptic ulcer, or thyroid disease. In these situations, consult your doctor before taking this product. It should not be used by pregnant or nursing women or be given to newborn or premature infants. • This product may cause drowsiness. Do not take it if you must drive, operate heavy machinery, or perform other tasks requiring mental alertness. To prevent oversedation, avoid the use of alcohol or other drugs that have sedative properties. • This product interacts with alcohol, guanethidine, monoamine oxidase inhibitors, sedative drugs, and tricyclic antidepressants. If you are currently taking any drugs of these types, check with your doctor before taking this product. If you are unsure of the type or contents of your medications, ask your doctor or pharmacist. • Because this product reduces sweating, avoid excessive work or exercise in hot weather. • If your cough persists or is accompanied by high fever, consult your doctor promptly. • When taken in overdose, acetaminophen is more toxic than aspirin. Follow dosage instructions carefully.

Comments: Many other conditions (some serious) mimic the common cold. If symptoms persist beyond one week, or if they occur regularly without regard to season, consult your doctor. • The effectiveness of this product may diminish after being taken regularly for seven to ten days; consult your pharmacist about substituting another medication if this product begins to lose its effectiveness for you. • Chew gum or suck on ice chips or a piece of hard candy to relieve mouth dryness.

Unacceptable: This product contains an analgesic, an antihistamine, a decongestant, and a cough suppressant. We believe to treat a cough you should choose a single-action cough remedy.

Nytol sleep aid

Manufacturer: Block Drug Company, Inc.

Dosage Form/Ingredient: Tablet: pyrilamine maleate, 25 mg. Capsule: pyrilamine maleate, 50 mg

Use: To induce drowsiness and assist in falling asleep

Side Effects: Blurred vision; confusion; constipation; difficult urination; dizziness; drowsiness; dry mouth and respiratory passages; headache; insomnia; low blood pressure; nausea; nervousness; palpitations; rash; restlessness; vomiting. Children may react with primary symptoms of excitement: convulsions; flushed skin; nervousness; tremors; twitching of muscles; uncoordinated movements

Warnings: Persons with asthma, diabetes, glaucoma (certain types), heart disease, high blood pressure, kidney disease, liver disease, thyroid disorders, certain types of peptic ulcer, enlarged prostate, obstructed bladder, or obstructed intestine; pregnant and nursing women; children under 12 years of age; and elderly or debilitated persons should not take this medication. • This product may interact with other drugs. If you are currently taking any medication, do not use this product without first consulting your doctor. • This product also interacts with alcohol, so avoid alcohol or other central nervous system sedatives while you are using it. • Since its purpose is to make you sleepy, do not use it while driving, operating heavy machinery, or performing other tasks that require you to be mentally alert. • Tolerance to this product may develop; do not increase the recommended dose unless your doctor recommends you to do so. • Insomnia may be a symptom of serious illness. Seek your doctor's advice if your sleeplessness continues, and do not take this product for more than two weeks without consulting your doctor.

Comments: This product may cause dryness of the mouth. To reduce this feeling, chew gum or suck on ice chips or a piece of hard candy. • There is probably no need to purchase this drug. You would be better advised to try to find and correct the cause of your insomnia. A glass of warm milk and a soak in a hot tub may work just as well as this product. • Many OTC sleep aids are very similar. If you wish to use one, look for a generic equivalent at a cheaper price. Ask your pharmacist for assistance.

Unacceptable: We consider that OTC sleep aids should not be taken without the advice of a doctor.

Ocusol decongestant eyedrops

Manufacturer: Norwich-Eaton Pharmaceuticals
Dosage Form/Ingredients: Drop: phenylephrine hydrochloride, 0.02%; unspecified quantities of benzalkonium chloride, boric acid, methylcellulose, tetrahydrozoline, sodium borate, and sodium chloride
Use: For relief of minor eye irritation and redness
Side Effects: Allergic reactions (rash, itching, soreness); local irritation; momentary blurred vision
Warnings: Do not use this product if you have glaucoma. • This product contains boric acid, which many medical authorities believe should not be used because it is toxic. • Do not use this product for more than two consecutive days without checking with your doctor. • Keep this product out of the reach of children. • If swallowed, this drug is likely to cause overstimulation in children. Call your doctor immediately if this product is accidentally swallowed. • Do not touch the dropper or bottle top to the eye or other tissue because contamination of the solution will result. • Use this product only for minor eye irritations. • The use of more than one eye product at a time may cause severe irritation to the eye.
Comments: This product works best when used correctly. Refer to the instructions on eye products in the chapter "Buying, Storing, and Using Drugs."

Unacceptable: We cannot recommend the use of this product because it contains boric acid, which many medical authorities believe to be toxic.

One-A-Day nutritional supplement

Manufacturer: Miles Laboratories, Inc.
Dosage Form/Ingredients: Tablet: vitamin A, 5000 IU; vitamin E, 15 IU; vitamin C, 60 mg; folic acid, 0.4 mg; thiamine, 1.5 mg; riboflavin, 1.7 mg; niacin, 20 mg; vitamin B_6, 2 mg; vitamin B_{12}, 6 mcg; vitamin D, 400 IU; pantothenic acid, 10 mg
Use: To supplement the diet
Side Effects: None
Warnings: This product contains vitamin B_6 (pyridoxine) in an amount great enough that it may interact with levodopa (L-dopa). If you are currently taking L-dopa, check with your doctor before taking this product. • If large doses are taken, this product may interfere with the results of urine tests. If your urine is being tested, inform your doctor and/or pharmacist that you are taking this product. • This product contains ingredients that accumulate and are stored in the body. The recommended dose should not be exceeded for long periods (several weeks to months) except by doctor's orders.
Comments: Dietary deficiencies of vitamins are uncommon in the United States. Most people who have vitamin deficiencies should be under a doctor's care, and they should not be self-medicating with OTC

vitamin products. If you choose to take supplemental vitamins, choose a generic product to save money. Ask your pharmacist for assistance.

Acceptable: *If you choose to take a vitamin supplement, this is an acceptable product.*

One-A-Day Plus Iron nutritional supplement

Manufacturer: Miles Laboratories, Inc.

Dosage Form/Ingredients: Tablet: vitamin A, 5000 IU; vitamin E, 15 IU; vitamin C, 60 mg; folic acid, 0.4 mg; thiamine, 1.5 mg; riboflavin, 1.7 mg; niacin, 20 mg; vitamin B_5, 10 mg; vitamin B_6, 2 mg; vitamin B_{12}, 6 mcg; vitamin D, 400 IU; iron, 18 mg

Use: To supplement the diet

Side Effects: Constipation; diarrhea; nausea; stomach pain

Warnings: This product should not be used by persons who have active peptic ulcer or ulcerative colitis. • Alcoholics and persons who have chronic liver or pancreatic disease should use this product with special caution; such persons may have enhanced iron absorption and are therefore more likely than others to experience iron toxicity. • The iron in this product interacts with oral tetracycline antibiotics and reduces the absorption of the antibiotics. If you are currently taking tetracycline, consult your doctor or pharmacist before taking this product. If you are unsure of the type or contents of your medications, ask your doctor or pharmacist. • Accidental iron poisoning is common in children; be sure to keep this product safely out of their reach. • This product contains ingredients that accumulate and are stored in the body. The recommended dose should not be exceeded for long periods (several weeks to months) except by doctor's orders. • If large doses are taken daily, this product may interfere with the results of urine tests. If your urine is being tested, inform your doctor and/or pharmacist that you are taking this product. • Because of its iron content, this product may cause constipation, diarrhea, nausea or stomach pain. These symptoms usually disappear or become less severe after two to three days. Taking your dose with food or milk may help minimize these side effects. If they persist, ask your pharmacist to recommend another product. • This product contains vitamin B_6 (pyridoxine) in an amount great enough that it may interact with levodopa (L-dopa). If you are currently taking L-dopa, check with your doctor before taking this product.

Comments: Black, tarry stools are a normal consequence of iron therapy. If your stools are not black and tarry, this product may not be working for you. Ask your pharmacist to recommend another product. • Dietary deficiencies of vitamins are uncommon in the United States. Most people who have vitamin deficiencies should be under a doctor's care, and they should not be self-medicating with OTC vitamin products. If you choose to take supplemental vitamins, choose a generic product to save money. Ask your pharmacist for assistance.

Acceptable: *If you choose to take a vitamin supplement, this is an acceptable product.*

One-A-Day Plus Minerals nutritional supplement

Manufacturer: Miles Laboratories, Inc.

Dosage Form/Ingredients: Tablet: vitamin A, 5000 IU; vitamin E; 15 IU; vitamin C, 60 mg; folic acid, 0.4 mg; thiamine, 1.5 mg; riboflavin, 1.7 mg; niacin, 20 mg; vitamin B_6, 2 mg; vitamin B_{12}, 6 mcg; vitamin D, 400 IU; pantothenic acid, 10 mg; iron, 18 mg; calcium, 100 mg; phosphorus, 100 mg;

iodine, 150 mcg; magnesium, 100 mg; copper, 2 mg; zinc, 15 mg
Use: To supplement the diet
Side Effects: Constipation; diarrhea; nausea; stomach pain
Warnings: This product should not be used by persons who have active peptic ulcer or ulcerative colitis. • Alcoholics and persons who have chronic liver or pancreatic disease should use this product with special caution; such persons may have enhanced iron absorption and are therefore more likely than others to experience iron toxicity. • The minerals in this product interact with oral tetracycline antibiotics and reduce the absorption of the antibiotics. If you are currently taking tetracycline, consult your doctor or pharmacist before taking this product. If you are unsure of the type or contents of your medications, ask your doctor or pharmacist. • Accidental iron poisoning is common in children; be sure to keep this product safely out of their reach. • This product contains ingredients that accumulate and are stored in the body. The recommended dose should not be exceeded for long periods (several weeks to months) except by doctor's orders. • If large doses are taken daily, this product may interfere with the results of urine tests. If your urine is being tested, inform your doctor and/or pharmacist that you are taking this product. • Because of its iron content, this product may cause constipation, diarrhea, nausea or stomach pain. These symptoms usually disappear or become less severe after two to three days. Taking your dose with food or milk may help minimize these side effects. If they persist, ask your pharmacist to recommend another product. • This product contains vitamin B_6 (pyridoxine) in an amount great enough that it may interact with levodopa (L-dopa). If you are currently taking L-dopa, check with your doctor before taking this product.
Comments: Black, tarry stools are a normal consequence of iron therapy. If your stools are not black and tarry, this product may not be working for you. Ask your pharmacist to recommend another product. • Dietary deficiencies of vitamins are uncommon in the United States. Most people who have vitamin deficiencies should be under a doctor's care, and they should not be self-medicating with OTC vitamin products. If you choose to take supplemental vitamins, choose a generic product to save money. Ask your pharmacist for assistance.
Acceptable: If you choose to take a vitamin supplement, this is an acceptable product.

Ornacol cough remedy

Manufacturer: Menley & James Laboratories
Dosage Forms/Ingredients: Capsule: dextromethorphan hydrobromide, 30 mg; phenylpropanolamine hydrochloride, 25 mg. Liquid (content per teaspoon): dextromethorphan hydrobromide, 15 mg; phenylpropanolamine hydrochloride, 12.5 mg; alcohol, 8%
Use: For temporary relief of cough and nasal congestion due to colds or "flu"
Side Effects: Drowsiness; mild stimulation; nausea; vomiting; blurred vision; palpitations; flushing; nervousness; dizziness; insomnia
Warnings: This product should be used with special caution by children under two years of age, and by persons who have diabetes, heart disease, high blood pressure, or thyroid disease. In these situations, consult your doctor before taking this product. • This product interacts with guanethidine and monoamine oxidase inhibitors. If you are currently taking any drugs of these types, check with your doctor before taking this product. If you are unsure of the type or contents of your medications,

ask your doctor or pharmacist. • If your cough persists, or is accompanied by high fever, consult your doctor promptly. • Do not use this product to treat chronic coughs, such as from smoking or asthma. • Do not use this product to treat productive (hacking) coughs that produce phlegm.

Acceptable: This product contains a cough suppressant and a decongestant. We prefer a cough remedy that contains only one ingredient directly related to treating the cough.

Ornade 2 for Children cold and allergy remedy

Manufacturer: Smith Kline & French Laboratories

Dosage Form/Ingredients: Liquid (content per teaspoon): phenylpropanolamine hydrochloride, 12.5 mg; chlorpheniramine maleate, 2 mg; alcohol, 5%

Use: For relief of nasal congestion due to colds and upper respiratory allergies

Side Effects: Anxiety; blurred vision; chest pain; confusion; constipation; dry mouth; difficult and painful urination; dizziness; drowsiness; headache; increased blood pressure; insomnia; loss of appetite; mild stimulation; nausea; nervousness; palpitations; rash; reduced sweating; tension; tremor; vomiting

Warnings: This product should not be given to newborn or premature infants or pregnant women. This product should be used with special caution by persons who have asthma, diabetes, an enlarged prostate, glaucoma (certain types), heart disease, high blood pressure, kidney disease, obstructed bladder, obstructed intestine, peptic ulcer, or thyroid disease. If your child has any of these conditions, consult your doctor before administering this product. • This product interacts with alcohol, guanethidine, monoamine oxidase inhibitors, sedative drugs, and tricyclic antidepressants. If your child is currently taking any drugs of these types, check with your doctor before administering this product. If you are unsure of the type or contents of your child's medications, ask your doctor or pharmacist. • This product may cause drowsiness. Do not take it if you must drive, operate heavy machinery, or perform other tasks requiring mental alertness. To prevent oversedation, avoid the use of alcohol or other drugs that have sedative properties.

Comments: Many other conditons (some serious) mimic the common cold. If symptoms persist beyond one week, or if they occur regularly without regard to season, consult your doctor. • The effectiveness of this product may diminish after being taken regularly for seven to ten days; consult your pharmacist about substituting another product containing a different antihistamine if this product begins to lose its effectiveness for your child. • Have your child chew gum or suck on ice chips or a piece of hard candy to reduce mouth dryness.

Acceptable: We prefer single-ingredient products rather than combination antihistamine-decongestant products like this one.

Ornex cold remedy

Manufacturer: Menley & James Laboratories

Dosage Form/Ingredients: Capsule: phenylpropanolamine hydrochloride, 18 mg; acetaminophen, 325 mg

Use: For relief of nasal congestion, fever, aches, pains, and general discomfort due to colds

Side Effects: Mild to moderate stimulation; nausea; vomiting. In overdose: Blood disorders; rash

Warnings: This product should be used with special caution by persons who have diabetes, heart, thyroid, lung, liver, or kidney disease, high blood pressure, or anemia. If you have any of these conditions, consult your doctor before taking this product. • This product interacts with alcohol, guanethidine, monoamine oxidase inhibitors, sedative drugs, and tricyclic antidepressants. If you are currently taking any drugs of these types, check with your doctor before taking this product. If you are unsure of the type or contents of your medications, ask your doctor or pharmacist. • This product should not be given to newborn or premature infants or taken by pregnant or nursing women. • When taken in overdose, acetaminophen is more toxic than aspirin. Follow dosage instructions carefully.

Comments: Many other conditions (some serious) mimic the common cold. If symptoms persist beyond one week, or if they occur regularly without regard to season, consult your doctor. • The effectiveness of this product may diminish after being taken regularly for seven to ten days; consult your pharmacist about substituting another medication if this product begins to lose its effectiveness for you.

Acceptable: We prefer single-ingredient products rather than combination analgesic-decongestant products like this one.

Oxy-5, Oxy-10 acne preparations

Manufacturer: Norcliff Thayer Inc.

Dosage Form/Ingredient: Oxy-5: Lotion: benzoyl peroxide, 5%. Oxy-10: Lotion: benzoyl peroxide, 10%

Use: Treatment of acne

Side Effects: Allergy; local irritation

Warnings: Do not get these products in or near the eyes. • Persons having a known sensitivity to benzoyl peroxide should not use these products. • While using these products, do not use harsh, abrasive cleansers. • If excessive redness or peeling occurs, reduce the frequency of your use of these products. • Avoid exposure to heat lamps and sunlamps, as well as prolonged exposure to sunlight, when using these products. • These products may be especially active on fair-skinned people. • If the condition worsens or if skin irritation develops, stop using these products and contact your physician.

Comments: Wash the affected area gently with warm water and pat dry before applying these products. • There may be a slight transitory stinging or burning sensation on initial application of these products. • These products may damage certain fabrics including rayon.

Preferred: Benzoyl peroxide has been shown to be the most effective ingredient in acne preparations.

Oxy-Scrub acne preparation

Manufacturer: Norcliff Thayer Inc.

Dosage Form/Ingredient: Abrasive cleansing granules: unspecified quantity of sodium tetraborate decahydrate (abradant) particles; soapless base

Use: Treatment of acne

Side Effects: Allergy; local irritation

Warnings: Do not get this product in or near the eyes. • If the condition worsens or if skin irritation develops, stop using this product and consult your physician.

Comments: This product is to be used instead of soap. Apply to wet face and massage into skin for one to two minutes; rinse thoroughly.

Not Evaluated: We cannot evaluate this product because the manufacturer fails to supply sufficient information about its ingredients.

Parepectolin diarrhea remedy

Manufacturer: William H. Rorer, Inc.

Dosage Form/Ingredients: Liquid (content per 2 tablespoons): alcohol, 0.69%; kaolin, 5.5 gm; pectin, 162 mg; powdered opium, 15 mg (equivalent to 3.7 ml paregoric)

Use: For the treatment of common diarrhea

Side Effects: Blurred vision, constipation after long-term use (seven days to two months); coughing and sore throat; difficult urination; dizziness; drowsiness; dry mouth; faintness; fever; flushing of face; headaches; loss of appetite; mental confusion; nervousness; palpitations; sedation; skin rash; warm skin; weakness

Warnings: Persons with glaucoma, myasthenia gravis, and certain types of heart, liver, or kidney disease should not use this product. • This product or any other product for diarrhea should not be used to self-medicate without first consulting a doctor if the person is under age three or over age 60, has a history of asthma, thyroid or lung disease, peptic ulcer, or is pregnant. • Avoid excessive use of alcohol, tranquilizers, or any drug that sedates the nervous system. In any case, if you are already taking drugs, do not take this product until you have first checked with your doctor or pharmacist. • Diarrhea should stop in two to three days. If it persists longer, recurs frequently or in the presence of high fever, call your doctor.

Comments: Be sure to drink at least 8 glasses of water each day while you are taking this product. • This product contains a narcotic, but when used as directed, you need not worry about addiction to it. • Over-the-counter sale of this product may not be permitted in some states.

Acceptable: The ingredients in this product are safe and may be effective for you.

Pediaquil cough remedy for children

Manufacturer: Phillips Roxane Laboratories, Inc.

Dosage Form/Ingredients: Liquid (content per teaspoon): phenylephrine hydrochloride, 2.5 mg; guaifenesin, 50 mg; alcohol, 5%

Use: For temporary relief of cough and nasal congestion due to colds or "flu"

Side Effects: Mild stimulation; nausea; vomiting; blurred vision; palpitations; nervousness; dizziness; flushing; insomnia

Warnings: This product should be used with special caution by children under two years of age, and by persons who have diabetes, heart disease, high blood pressure, or thyroid disease. If your child is under two years of age, or has any of these conditions, consult his doctor before using this product. • This product interacts with guanethidine and monoamine oxidase inhibitors. If your child is currently taking any drugs of these types, check with his doctor before using this product. If you are unsure of the type or contents of his medications, ask his doctor or your pharmacist. • If coughing persists, or is accompanied by high fever, take the child to a doctor promptly. • Do not use this product to treat chronic coughs, such as those from smoking or asthma. • Do not use this product to treat productive (hacking) coughs that produce phlegm.

Comments: If your child requires an expectorant, he needs more moisture in his environment. Have your child drink eight to ten glasses of water daily. The use of a vaporizer or humidifier may also be beneficial.

Fair: This product contains a decongestant and an expectorant. If you want to relieve your child's cough, choose a product containing only a cough suppressant.

Pepto-Bismol diarrhea remedy

Manufacturer: Norwich-Eaton Pharmaceuticals
Dosage Forms/Ingredient: Liquid (content per 2 tablespoons): bismuth subsalicylate, 527 mg. Chewable tablet: bismuth subsalicylate, 300 mg
Use: For the treatment of common diarrhea
Side Effects: Constipation after long-term use (seven days to two months)
Warnings: This product or any other product for diarrhea should not be used to self-medicate without first consulting a doctor if the person is under age three or over age 60, has a history of asthma, heart disease, peptic ulcer, or is pregnant. If you are taking other drugs, do not take this product until you have first checked with your doctor or pharmacist. • Diarrhea should stop in two to three days. If it persists longer, recurs frequently or in presence of high fever, call your doctor.
Comments: Be sure to drink at least eight glasses of water each day while you are taking this product. • This product is believed by some to relieve nausea and vomiting. However, its value for the relief of these symptoms has never been shown. • This product may discolor the feces and tongue.

Fair: We feel that diarrhea remedies containing kaolin and pectin are preferable to those with this ingredient.

Percogesic analgesic

Manufacturer: Endo Laboratories, Inc.
Dosage Form/Ingredients: Tablet: acetaminophen, 325 mg; phenyltoloxamine citrate, 30 mg
Use: For the relief of pain of headache, toothache, sprains, muscular aches, menstruation; for the relief of discomforts and fever of colds; for temporary relief of minor aches and pains of arthritis and rheumatism
Side Effects: Anxiety; blurred vision; chest pain; confusion; constipation; difficult and painful urination; dizziness; drowsiness; dry mouth and respiratory passages; headache; insomnia; loss of appetite; nausea; nervousness; palpitations; rash; reduced sweating; restlessness; tremor; tension; vomiting. When taken in overdose: Blood disorders; rash
Warnings: This product should be used with special caution by the elderly or debilitated, and by persons who have asthma, diabetes, enlarged prostate, certain blood disorders, glaucoma (certain types), heart disease, lung disease, high blood pressure, kidney or liver disease, obstructed bladder, obstructed intestine, or peptic ulcer. If you have any of these conditions, consult your doctor before taking this product. • It should not be taken by pregnant women or given to newborn or premature infants. • This product interacts with alcohol, guanethidine, monoamine oxidase inhibitors, sedative drugs, and tricyclic antidepressants. If you are currently taking any drugs of these types, check with your doctor before taking this product. If you are unsure of the type or contents of

your medications, ask your doctor or pharmacist. • Because this product reduces sweating, avoid excessive work or exercise in hot weather. • When taken in overdose, this product is more toxic than aspirin. The dosage instructions listed on the package should be followed carefully; toxicity may occur in adults or children with repeated doses. • This product may cause drowsiness. Do not take it if you must drive, operate heavy machinery, or perform other tasks requiring mental alertness. • To prevent oversedation, avoid the use of alcohol or other drugs that have sedative properties.

Comments: Acetaminophen does not relieve inflammation, so if pain is caused by swelling or inflammation, it should not be used. Aspirin is better. • Chew gum or suck on ice chips or a piece of hard candy to reduce mouth dryness. • This product may not work as well after seven to ten days as it did when you began taking it. Consult your pharmacist about using another product if the effectiveness of this medication diminishes.

Fair: It has not been proven that a combination of ingredients is more effective than an equivalent dose of aspirin or acetaminophen taken alone.

Peri-Colace laxative

Manufacturer: Mead Johnson Co., Pharmaceutical Division

Dosage Forms/Ingredients: Capsule: casanthranol, 30 mg; docusate sodium, 100 mg. Syrup (content per teaspoon): casanthranol, 10 mg; docusate sodium, 20 mg

Use: For relief of constipation; as a stool softener

Side Effects: Excess loss of fluid; griping (cramps); mucus in feces

Warnings: Persons with a high fever (100° F or more), black or tarry stools, nausea, vomiting, abdominal pain; pregnant women; and children under the age of three should not use this product unless directed to do so by a doctor. • Do not use this product when constipation is caused by megacolon or other diseases of the intestine, or hypothyroidism. • Excessive use (daily for a month or more) of these products may cause diarrhea, vomiting, and loss of certain blood electrolytes. • Never self-medicate with this product if constipation lasts longer than two weeks, or if the medication does not produce a laxative effect within a week. • Limit use to seven days unless directed otherwise by a doctor since this product may cause laxative-dependence (addiction) if used for a longer time. • An ingredient in this product is referred to as a stool softener. This product is recommended for relief of constipation only when the stool is hard and dry. Do not take another product containing mineral oil at the same time as you are taking this product.

Comments: This product may discolor the urine. Evacuation may occur within six to twelve hours. • Take the syrup form of this product in one-half glass of milk or fruit juice to help mask the taste.• Although an exact generic equivalent of this item may not be available, very similar products are. Ask your pharmacist if you can save money by purchasing another item.

Acceptable: This product is an acceptable combination stimulant-stool softener laxative.

Pertussin 8-Hour Cough Formula cough remedy

Manufacturer: Chesebrough-Ponds Inc.

Dosage Form/Ingredients: Liquid (content per 4 teaspoons): dextromethorphan hydrobromide, 30.5 mg; alcohol, 9.5%

Use: For temporary relief of cough due to colds or minor throat and bronchial irritations

Side Effects: Drowsiness; nausea; vomiting

Warnings: Do not give this product to children under six years of age. • If your cough persists, or is accompanied by high fever, consult your doctor promptly. • This product interacts with monoamine oxidase inhibitors; if you are currently taking any drugs of this type, check with your doctor before taking this product. If you are unsure of the type or contents of your medications, ask your doctor or pharmacist. • Do not use this product to treat chronic coughs, such as from smoking or asthma. • Do not use this product to treat productive (hacking) coughs that produce phlegm.

Preferred: *Dextromethorphan hydrobromide has been proven effective as a cough suppressant.*

Phillips' Milk of Magnesia laxative and antacid

Manufacturer: Glenbrook Laboratories

Dosage Form/Ingredient: Suspension (content per two tablespoons): magnesium hydroxide, 7.75%; peppermint oil, 1.14 mg. Tablet: unspecified quantities of magnesium hydroxide and peppermint oil

Use: For relief of constipation and symptoms associated with gastric hyperacidity

Side Effects: Diarrhea; nausea

Warnings: Persons with kidney disease should not use this product. In persons with kidney disease, repeated (daily) use may cause nausea, vomiting, depressed reflexes, and breathing difficulties. • Persons with a high fever (100° F or more), black or tarry stools, nausea, vomiting, abdominal pain; pregnant women; and children under the age of three should not use this product unless directed to do so by a doctor. • Do not use this product when constipation is caused by megacolon or other diseases of the intestine, or hypothyroidism. • Excessive use (daily for a month or more) of these products may cause diarrhea, vomiting, and loss of certain blood electrolytes. • Never self-medicate for constipation with this product if the problem lasts longer than two weeks, or if the medication does not produce a laxative effect within a week. • For constipation, limit use to seven days unless directed otherwise by a doctor since this product may cause laxative-dependence (addiction) if used for a longer time. • Do not take this product within two hours of a dose of a tetracycline antibiotic. • Consult your physician or pharmacist before taking this product if you are already taking iron, a vitamin-mineral product, chlorpromazine, phenytoin, digoxin, or quinidine, or if you are unsure of the type and contents of the medications you are taking. • Never self-medicate with this product for acid indigestion if your symptoms occur regularly (two or three or more times a month). Consult your doctor if the symptoms are worse than usual, if you have chest pains or feel "tightness" in the chest, or if you are sweating or short of breath. In fact, we do not recommend self-treatment for severe attacks of heartburn, indigestion, or stomach upset in any circumstances. If you do decide that your symptoms are mild enough to warrant self-medication, limit therapy to two weeks, then call your doctor if symptoms persist.

Comments: Because evacuation may occur within 30 to 60 minutes after using this product, try to take it at a convenient time. An eight-ounce glass of water should be taken with each dose. • As an antacid, this product works best when taken one hour after meals or at bedtime, unless you are directed otherwise by your doctor or pharmacist. • The liquid form of this product is superior to the tablet form, and should be used unless you have been specifically directed to use the tablet.

Acceptable: The liquid form of this product is an acceptable saline laxative.

Not Evaluated: The manufacturer fails to supply sufficient information on the tablet form on which to base an evaluation.

pHisoAc acne preparation

Manufacturer: Winthrop Laboratories

Dosage Form/Ingredients: Cream: colloidal sulfur, 6%; resorcinol, 1.5%; alcohol, 10%

Use: Treatment of acne

Side Effects: Allergy; local irritation

Warnings: Do not get this product in or near the eyes. • If the condition worsens or if skin irritation develops, stop using this product and consult your physician.

Comments: Wash area gently with warm water and pat dry before applying this product.

Fair: Products containing more effective ingredients are available.

pHisoDerm acne preparation

Manufacturer: Winthrop Laboratories

Dosage Form/Ingredients: Liquid cleanser: unspecified quantities of sodium octoxynol 3 sulfonate, white petrolatum, petrolatum, lanolin, lanolin alcohol, sodium benzoate, octoxynol 1, methylcellulose, and lactic acid

Use: Treatment of acne

Side Effects: Allergy; local irritation

Warnings: Do not get this product in or near the eyes. • If the condition worsens or if skin irritation develops, stop using this product and consult your physician.

Comments: This product is to be used instead of soap. Apply to wet face and massage into skin for one to two minutes; rinse thoroughly.

Not Evaluated: We cannot evaluate this product because the manufacturer fails to supply sufficient information about its ingredients.

Polysporin first-aid product

Manufacturer: Burroughs Wellcome Co.

Dosage Form/Ingredients: Ointment (content per gram): bacitracin, 500 units; polymyxin B sulfate, 10,000 units; unspecified quantity of white petrolatum

Use: To prevent infection from cuts and abrasions; to treat impetigo

Side Effects: Allergic reactions (rash, itching, soreness); local irritation

Warnings: Diabetics and persons with impaired circulation should not use this product. • If the condition seems to get worse while using this product, call your doctor at once. • If the infection does not clear up in four or five days, consult your doctor or pharmacist.

Comments: Apply this product at least three times daily to maintain effectiveness. • If using this product to treat impetigo, apply it with a cotton-tipped applicator. Do not touch the cotton part with your fingers after applying the medication. Wash your hands thoroughly after applying medication to impetigo sores.

Preferred: This product is effective for the uses specified.

Poly-Vi-Sol nutritional supplement

Manufacturer: Mead Johnson Co., Nutritional Division

Dosage Forms/Ingredients: Chewable tablet: vitamin A, 2500 IU; vitamin D, 400 IU; vitamin E, 15 IU; vitamin C, 60 mg; folic acid, 0.3 mg; thiamine, 1.05 mg; riboflavin, 1.2 mg; niacin, 13.5 mg; vitamin B_6, 1.05 mg; vitamin B_{12}, 4.5 mcg. Drop (content per 1.0-ml dropper): vitamin A, 1500 IU; vitamin D, 400 IU; vitamin E, 5 IU; vitamin C, 35 mg; thiamine, 0.5 mg; riboflavin, 0.6 mg; niacin, 8 mg; vitamin B_6, 0.4 mg; vitamin B_{12}, 2 mcg

Use: To supplement the diet

Side Effects: None

Warnings: If large doses are taken, this product may interfere with the results of urine tests. If your urine is being tested, inform your doctor and/or pharmacist that you are taking this product. • This product contains ingredients that accumulate and are stored in the body. The recommended dose should not be exceeded for long periods (several weeks to months) except by doctor's orders.

Comments: Chewable tablets should never be referred to as "candy" or as "candy-flavored" vitamins. Your child may take you literally and swallow toxic amounts. • Dietary deficiencies of vitamins are uncommon in the United States. Most people who have vitamin deficiencies should be under a doctor's care, and they should not be self-medicating with OTC vitamin products. If you choose to take supplemental vitamins, choose a generic product to save money. Ask your pharmacist for assistance.

Acceptable: If you choose to take a vitamin supplement, this is an acceptable product.

Predictor urine test for pregnancy

Manufacturer: Whitehall Laboratories

Product Form: Test tube and testing materials

Use: To test urine for determination of pregnancy

Comments: Use only a urine sample that has been freshly collected in the morning. • For accurate results, follow package directions carefully. The test tube must be left undisturbed and unvibrated for two hours, and must be kept away from heat and direct sunlight. • Read the results between two and three hours after starting the test. If a brown ring forms in the bottom of the test tube, you should assume that you are pregnant. Consult your doctor. • Test results may be interfered with if the urine contains a large quantity of protein, or if the patient is taking medication. • This test is highly accurate unless it is performed earlier than nine days after the date on which the first missed menstrual period would have begun. • A refill kit is available for use with this set. You need the original stand that comes with the complete kit to use the refill.

Acceptable: Pregnancy test kits are convenient, but may not be economical. A positive result indicates that you should see a doctor, and he will probably want to confirm the result. You are likely to pay for two tests.

Preparation H hemorrhoidal preparations

Manufacturer: Whitehall Laboratories

Dosage Forms/Ingredients: Ointment, Suppository: live yeast cell derivative supplying 2,000 units of skin respiratory factor (content per ounce of ointment); phenylmercuric nitrate 1: 10,000; shark liver oil, 3%.

Medicated cleansing pad: witch hazel, 50%; glycerin, 10%; triton, 0.05%; methylparaben, 0.1%

Use: For relief of pain, burning, and itching of hemorrhoids and other irritated anorectal tissues

Side Effects: Irritation

Warnings: Sensitization (continued itching and redness) may occur with long-term and repeated use. • Certain ingredients in this product may cause an allergic reaction; do not use for longer than seven days at a time unless your doctor has advised you otherwise. • The suppository is not recommended for external hemorrhoids or bleeding internal hemorrhoids. Use the ointment form. Use caution when inserting applicator. • Never self-medicate for hemorrhoids if pain is continuous or throbbing, if bleeding or itching is excessive, or if you feel a large pressure within the rectum. • Discontinue use if irritation (pain, itching, or swelling) or rash occurs; consult your pharmacist.

Comments: Hemorrhoidal (pile) preparations relieve itching, reduce pain and inflammation, and check bleeding, but they do not heal, dry up, or give lasting relief from hemorrhoids. • Hemorrhoidal suppositories work best when they are used correctly. Refer to the instructions for their use in the chapter "Buying, Storing, and Using Drugs."

Acceptable: *Although generally we prefer a hemorrhoidal discomfort preparation that contains hydrocortisone, this product will also provide some relief.*

Presun 15, Presun 8, Presun 8 Creamy, Presun Lip Protection, Presun 4 sunscreens

Manufacturer: Westwood Pharmaceuticals Inc.

Dosage Forms/Ingredients: Presun 15: Lotion: PABA, 5%; padimate O, 5%; oxybenzone, 3%; SD alcohol 40, 58%. Presun 8: Lotion, Gel: PABA, 5%; SD alcohol 40, 55%. Presun 8 Creamy: Lotion: PABA, 5%; SD alcohol 40, 15%. Presun 4: Lotion: padimate O, 4%; SD alcohol 40, 10%. Presun Lip Protection: Lipstick: padimate O, 4%

Use: To prevent sunburn, premature aging of the skin, and skin cancer caused by overexposure to sunlight; to protect persons with sun sensitive skin, or those taking photo-sensitizing drugs, against sun toxicity

Side Effects: Occasional irritation; rash

Warnings: Avoid prolonged exposure to the sun, especially if you are sensitive to it. • Do not use this product if you are allergic to benzocaine, procaine, sulfa drugs, thiazide diuretics (water pills or high blood pressure medication), or certain dyes. If you are unaware of the nature of the medications you are taking, ask your doctor or pharmacist. • Do not use this product in or around the eyes. • Discontinue use and consult your pharmacist if irritation (pain, itching, or swelling) or rash appears. • Follow the directions given on the package, especially regarding frequency of use. Be sure to reapply after swimming or excessive exercise.

Comments: If you are unsure whether this is the proper sunscreen agent for you, refer for clarification to the section on suncreen products in this book. If you still have questions, ask your pharmacist or doctor. • This product may stain certain types of clothing.

Preferred: *The ingredients in this product offer effective protection against sunburn.*

Primatene M asthma remedy

Manufacturer: Whitehall Laboratories

Dosage Form/Ingredients: Tablet: ephedrine hydrochloride, 24 mg;

pyrilamine maleate, 16.6 mg; theophylline, 130 mg

Use: For control of bronchial asthma

Side Effects: Anxiety; blurred vision; chest pain; confusion; constipation; dizziness; drowsiness; dry mouth and respiratory passages; increased blood pressure; increased frequency of urination; insomnia; loss of appetite; nausea; nervousness; palpitations; rash; reduced sweating; restlessness; tension; tremors; urinary retention; vomiting. Children may react with primary symptoms of excitement: convulsions; flushed skin; nervousness; tremors; twitching of muscles; and uncoordinated movements

Warnings: Overdose may result in convulsions, coma, and cardiovascular collapse. • While taking this product, avoid the use of sedative drugs or alcohol, guanethidine, monoamine oxidase inhibitors, or tricyclic antidepressants. If you are taking any medication of these types, or if you are unsure of the type of medication you are taking, consult your doctor or pharmacist. • Persons with persistent coughs, high blood pressure, diabetes, or heart or thyroid disease should consult a doctor before using this product. • Repeated use of this product may cause nausea and vomiting, depressed reflexes, and breathing difficulties in people with kidney disease. • Asthma is too serious a condition to be routinely self-treated. Asthmatics should be under a doctor's care. Be sure to tell your doctor that you are taking this, or any other OTC asthma remedy. • Because this product reduces sweating, avoid excessive work or exercise in hot weather. • This product may cause drowsiness. Do not take it if you must drive, operate heavy machinery, or perform other tasks requiring mental alertness.

Comments: The effectiveness of this product may diminish after being taken regularly for seven to ten days. Consult your pharmacist about substituting another product containing a different active ingredient if this product begins to lose its effectiveness for you. • Chew gum or suck on ice chips or a piece of hard candy to reduce mouth dryness.

Fair: This product contains pyrilamine maleate, which is an antihistamine. We do not recommend the use of asthma remedies which contain an antihistamine.

Primatene P asthma remedy

Manufacturer: Whitehall Laboratories

Dosage Form/Ingredients: Tablet: ephedrine hydrochloride, 24 mg; phenobarbital, 8 mg; theophylline, 130 mg

Use: For control of bronchial asthma

Side Effects: Anxiety; blurred vision; chest pain; confusion; constipation; dizziness; drowsiness; dry mouth and respiratory passages; increased blood pressure; increased frequency of urination; insomnia; loss of appetite; nausea; nervousness; palpitations; rash; reduced sweating; restlessness; tension; tremors; urinary retention; vomiting. Children may react with primary symptoms of excitement: convulsions; flushed skin; nervousness; tremors; twitching of muscles; and uncoordinated movements

Warnings: Overdose may result in convulsions, coma, and cardiovascular collapse. • While taking this product, avoid the use of sedative drugs or alcohol, guanethidine, monoamine oxidase inhibitors, or tricyclic antidepressants. If you are taking any medication of these types, or if you are unsure of the type of medication you are taking, consult your doctor or pharmacist. • Repeated use of this product may cause nausea and vomiting, depressed reflexes, and breathing difficulties in people with kidney disease. • Asthma is too serious a condition to be routinely self-treated. Asthmatics should be under a doctor's care. Be sure to tell your doctor that you are taking this, or any other OTC asthma remedy. • Because this product reduces sweating, avoid excessive work or exercise in hot weather.

Comments: The effectiveness of this product may diminish after being taken regularly for seven to ten days. Consult your pharmacist about substituting another product containing a different active ingredient if this product begins to lose its effectiveness for you. • Chew gum or suck on ice chips or a piece of hard candy to reduce mouth dryness. • Over-the-counter sale of this product may not be permitted in some states. Do not worry about addiction to this product if you follow directions for use.

Fair: The phenobarbital in this product probably has no beneficial effect. It also may depress the respiratory system and potentially cause underventilation.

Privine nasal decongestant

Manufacturer: CIBA Pharmaceutical Company

Dosage Forms/Ingredients: Drop, Nasal spray: naphazoline hydrochloride, 0.05%; benzalkonium chloride, 1:5000

Use: For temporary relief of nasal congestion due to colds, sinusitis, hay fever, or other upper respiratory allergies

Side Effects: Blurred vision; burning, dryness of nasal mucosa; increased nasal congestion or discharge; sneezing, and/or stinging; dizziness; drowsiness; headache; insomnia; nervousness; palpitations; slight increase in blood pressure; stimulation

Warnings: This product should not be used by persons who have glaucoma (certain types). • It should be used with special caution by persons who have diabetes, advanced hardening of the arteries, heart disease, high blood pressure, or thyroid disease. If you have any of these conditions, consult your doctor before using this product. • This product interacts with monoamine oxidase inhibitors, thyroid preparations, and tricyclic antidepressants. If you are currently taking any drugs of these types, check with your doctor before taking this product. If you are unsure of the type or contents of your medications, ask your doctor or pharmacist.

Comments: To avoid side effects such as burning, sneezing, or stinging, and a "rebound" increase in nasal congestion and discharge, do not exceed the recommended dose, and do not use this product for more than three or four continuous days. • This product should not be used by more than one person; sharing the dispenser may spread infection. • This product works best when it is used correctly. Refer to the instructions for the use of nasal sprays and drops in the chapter on "Buying, Storing, and Using Drugs." • Many nasal drops or sprays on the market contain oxymetazoline hydrochloride. This drug has a duration of action of about 12 hours, and because it needs to be used less often, it is less likely to cause "rebound" nasal congestion during use. Therefore, we recommend a product containing oxymetazoline hydrochloride rather than this product, which does not contain the ingredient. • The spray form of this product, although slightly more expensive than the drop, is preferred for adult use. The spray penetrates far back into the nose, covering the nasal area more completely, and is more convenient to use. The drop is preferable for administration to children. • Do not transfer the contents of this product into an atomizer that has aluminum parts because the drug may decompose and lose its effectiveness. • If the solution becomes discolored, it should be discarded.

Acceptable: Although we prefer a product containing oxymetazoline hydrochloride, this product also offers an effective formula for treating the conditions specified.

Prolamine appetite suppressant

Manufacturer: Thompson Medical Company, Inc.

Dosage Form/Ingredients: Capsule: phenylpropanolamine hydrochloride, 35 mg; caffeine, 140 mg

Use: As an aid in dietary control

Side Effects: Blurred vision; diarrhea; nausea; dizziness; drowsiness; headache; increase in blood pressure, blood sugar, heart rate, and thyroid activity; insomnia; nervousness; palpitations. In larger than the recommended dose: Irregular heartbeat; nasal dryness; upset stomach

Warnings: Persons with heart disease, high blood pressure, diabetes, kidney or thyroid disease; children under 16 years of age; and pregnant or nursing women should not use this product. Consult your doctor for recommendations. • This product interacts with alcohol, guanethidine, monoamine oxidase inhibitors, sedative drugs, and tricyclic antidepressants. If you are currently taking any of these drugs, or if you are unsure of the type or contents of your medications, consult your doctor or pharmacist before taking this product. • Avoid taking this drug while using a decongestant. • Avoid continuous use for longer than three months. • Discontinue use if you experience rapid pulse, dizziness, or palpitations.

Comments: During the first week of therapy with this product, expect increased frequency of urination. • Many medical authorities believe that the ingredient phenylpropanolamine does not help in weight-loss programs. However, the FDA Review Panel has reported that it is effective. • If you want to use this product, remember that you become tolerant to any beneficial effects after a couple of weeks. After each two weeks of use, stop for one week, then resume use. • The primary value in a product of this nature is in following the caloric reduction plan that goes with it.

Fair: This product contains caffeine, which does not contribute to permanent weight loss and may worsen side effects such as nervousness.

P.V.M. appetite suppressant

Manufacturer: The J. B. Williams Company, Inc.

Dosage Form/Ingredient: Capsule: phenylpropanolamine hydrochloride, 75 mg

Use: As an aid in dietary control

Side Effects: Blurred vision; diarrhea; nausea; dizziness; drowsiness; headache; increase in blood pressure, blood sugar, heart rate, and thyroid activity; insomnia; nervousness; palpitations. In larger than the recommended dose: irregular heartbeat; nasal dryness; upset stomach

Warnings: Persons with heart disease, high blood pressure, diabetes, kidney or thyroid disease; children under 16 years of age; and pregnant or nursing women should not use this product. Consult your doctor for recommendations. • This product interacts with alcohol, guanethidine, monoamine oxidase inhibitors, sedative drugs, and tricyclic antidepressants. If you are currently taking any of these drugs, or if you are unsure of the type or contents of your medications, ask your doctor or pharmacist before taking this product. • Avoid taking this drug while using a decongestant. • Avoid continuous use for longer than three months. • Discontinue use if you experience rapid pulse, dizziness, or palpitations.

Comments: During the first week of therapy with this product, expect increased frequency of urination. • Many medical authorities believe that the ingredient phenylpropanolamine does not help in weight-loss programs. However, the FDA Review Panel has reported that it is effective. • If you want to use this product, remember that you become tolerant to any beneficial effects after a couple of weeks. After each two weeks of use, stop for one week, then resume use. • The primary value in a product of this nature is in following the caloric reduction plan that goes with it. • This is a sustained release product. To avoid sleep disturbance, do not take it less than 12 hours before bedtime.

Acceptable: This product is preferable to other available dietary aids because it uses a single effective ingredient.

Rhulicream poison ivy/poison oak remedy

Manufacturer: Lederle Laboratories Div., American Cyanamid Company
Dosage Form/Ingredients: Ointment: benzocaine, 1%; camphor, 0.3%; isopropyl alcohol, 8.8%; menthol, 0.7%; zirconium oxide, 1%
Use: For relief of itching and pain of poison ivy or oak, insect bites, mild sunburn, or other minor skin irritations
Side Effects: Allergic reactions (rash, itching, soreness); local irritation
Warnings: Do not apply this product to extensive or raw, oozing areas of the skin, or use for a prolonged time, except as directed by a physician. • Do not use near the eyes, on mucous membranes, on genitalia, or on infected areas. • Discontinue use and consult your pharmacist if irritation (pain, itching, or swelling) or rash occurs. • Avoid scratching, which may cause irritation and secondary infection.

Comments: Before applying the medication, soak the area in warm water or apply wet towels for five to ten minutes; dry gently by patting with a soft towel and then apply medication. • If itching is intolerable and this product does not relieve it sufficiently, we recommend the use of a "wet soak." In fact, a wet soak may work well enough that you do not need to use this product at all. For more information about how to apply a wet soak, refer to the chapter, "Buying, Storing, and Using Drugs."

Unacceptable: We do not recommend the use of poison ivy/poison oak remedies that contain zirconium oxide. They may cause severe irritation.

Rhulihist poison ivy/poison oak remedy

Manufacturer: Lederle Laboratories Div., American Cyanamid Company
Dosage Form/Ingredients: Lotion: benzocaine, 1%; calamine, 3%; camphor, 0.1%; menthol, 0.1%; tripelennamine hydrochloride, 1%; zirconium oxide, 1%
Use: For relief of itching and pain of poison ivy and oak, insect bites, mild sunburn, and minor skin irritations
Side Effects: Allergic reactions (rash, itching, soreness); local irritation
Warnings: Do not apply this product to extensive or raw, oozing areas of the skin, or use for a prolonged time, except as directed by a physician. • Do not use near the eyes, on mucous membranes, on genitalia, or on infected areas. • Discontinue use and consult your pharmacist if irritation (pain, itching, or swelling) or rash occurs. • Avoid scratching, which may cause irritation and secondary infection.

Comments: Before applying the medication, soak the area in warm water or apply wet towels for five to ten minutes; dry gently by patting with a soft towel and then apply medication. • If itching is intolerable and this product does not relieve it sufficiently, we recommend the use of a "wet soak." In fact, a wet soak may work well enough that you do not need to use this product at all. For more information about how to apply a wet soak, refer to the chapter, "Buying, Storing, and Using Drugs."

Unacceptable: We do not recommend the use of poison ivy/poison oak remedies that contain zirconium oxide. They may cause severe irritation.

Riopan antacid

Manufacturer: Ayerst Laboratories
Dosage Forms/Ingredients: Chewable tablet, Suspension (content per teaspoon), Tablet: magaldrate, 480 mg; sodium, 0.3 mg
Use: For relief from acid indigestion, heartburn, and/or sour stomach
Side Effects: Abdominal discomfort; constipation; diarrhea; dizziness; mouth irritation; nausea; rash; vomiting
Warnings: Persons with kidney disease should not use this product. In persons with kidney disease, repeated daily use of this product may cause nausea, vomiting, depressed reflexes, and breathing difficulties. • Long-term (several weeks) use of this product may lead to intestinal obstruction and dehydration. Phosphate depletion may occur, leading to weakness, loss of appetite, and eventually bone pain. Phosphate depletion may be prevented by drinking at least one glass of milk a day. • Do not take this product within two hours of a dose of a tetracycline antibiotic. • Consult your physician or pharmacist before taking this product if you are already taking iron, a vitamin-mineral product, chlorpromazine, phenytoin, digoxin, quinidine, or warfarin, or if you are unsure of the type and contents of the medications you are taking. • Never self-medicate with this product if your symptoms occur regularly (two or three or more times a month). Consult your doctor if the symptoms are worse than usual, if you have chest pains or feel "tightness" in the chest, or if you are sweating or short of breath. In fact, we do not recommend self-treatment for severe attacks of heartburn, indigestion, or stomach upset in any circumstances. If you do decide that your symptoms are mild enough to warrant self-medication, limit therapy to two weeks. If symptoms persist, consult your doctor.
Comments: To prevent constipation, drink at least eight glasses of water a day. If constipation persists, consult your doctor or pharmacist. • This product must be taken exactly as directed on the label, unless your doctor has instructed you otherwise. Never skip a dose just because you feel better. If you grow tired of the taste, ask your pharmacist to suggest a different product. • The suspension form of this product is superior to the tablet form and should be used unless you have been specifically directed to use the tablet. • The sodium content of this product is low. This makes it more desirable than other antacids for people on a low salt diet.

Acceptable: Products containing magaldrate may be less potent antacids than those containing other combinations of magnesium and aluminum hydroxide. In addition, we generally consider it preferable to treat the symptoms of acid indigestion and flatulence (gas) separately.

Riopan Plus antacid and antiflatulent

Manufacturer: Ayerst Laboratories
Dosage Forms/Ingredients: Liquid (content per teaspoon): magaldrate,

400 mg; simethicone, 20 mg; sodium, < 0.7 mg. Chewable tablet: magaldrate, 480 mg; simethicone, 20 mg; sodium, < 0.7 mg

Use: Relief of acid indigestion, heartburn, and/or sour stomach when accompanied by painful gas symptoms

Side Effects: Abdominal discomfort; constipation; diarrhea; dizziness; mouth irritation; nausea; rash; vomiting

Warnings: Persons with kidney disease should not use this product. In persons with kidney disease, repeated daily use of this product may cause nausea, vomiting, depressed reflexes, and breathing difficulties. • Long-term (several weeks) use of this product may lead to intestinal obstruction and dehydration. Phosphate depletion may occur, leading to weakness, loss of appetite, and eventually bone pain. Phosphate depletion may be prevented by drinking at least one glass of milk a day. • Do not take this product within two hours of a dose of a tetracycline antibiotic. • Consult your physician or pharmacist before taking this product if you are already taking iron, a vitamin-mineral product, chlorpromazine, phenytoin, digoxin, quinidine, or warfarin, or if you are unsure of the type and contents of the medications you are taking. • Never self-medicate with this product if your symptoms occur regularly (two or three or more times a month). Consult your doctor if the symptoms are worse than usual, if you have chest pains or feel "tightness" in the chest, or if you are sweating or short of breath. In fact, we do not recommend self-treatment for severe attacks of heartburn, indigestion, or stomach upset in any circumstances. If you do decide that your symptoms are mild enough to warrant self-medication, limit therapy to two weeks. If symptoms persist, contact your doctor.

Comments: To prevent constipation, drink at least eight glasses of water a day. If constipation persists, consult your doctor or pharmacist. • This product must be taken exactly as directed on the label, unless your doctor has instructed you otherwise. Never skip a dose just because you feel better. If you grow tired of the taste, ask your pharmacist to suggest a different product. • The liquid form of this product is superior to the tablet form and should be used unless you have been specifically directed to use the tablet. • While exact generic equivalents of this product may not be available, products that are very similar are. Consult your pharmacist. You may be able to save money. • Simethicone is included to relieve bloating and gas formation; this ingredient makes it easier for you to eliminate gas by belching and passing flatus. If you do not suffer from bloating and gas pains, use a product without simethicone. You will probably save money.

Acceptable: Products containing magaldrate are less potent antacids than those containing other combinations of magnesium and aluminum. In addition, we generally consider it preferable to treat acid indigestion and flatulence (gas) separately rather than with a combination product.

Robitussin A-C cough remedy

Manufacturer: A. H. Robins Company

Dosage Form/Ingredients: Liquid (content per one teaspoon): codeine phosphate, 10 mg; guaifenesin, 100 mg; alcohol, 3.5%

Use: For temporary relief of cough due to colds or "flu"; to convert a dry nonproductive cough to a productive, phlegm-producing cough

Side Effects: Constipation; nausea; vomiting; slight drying of respiratory passages

Warnings: This product should be used with caution by persons who have asthma or other respiratory diseases. If you have such a condition, consult your doctor before taking this product. • Because this product contains codeine, it has the potential for abuse and must be used with caution. It usually should not be taken for more than seven to ten days. Tolerance may develop quickly, but do not increase the dose without consulting your doctor. • This product interacts with alcohol, guanethidine, monoamine oxidase inhibitors, sedative drugs, and tricyclic antidepressants. If you are currently taking any drugs of these types, check with your doctor before taking this product. If you are unsure of the type or contents of your medications, ask your doctor or pharmacist. • If your cough persists, or is accompanied by high fever, consult your doctor promptly. • Do not use this product to treat chronic coughs, such as from smoking or asthma. • Do not use this product to treat productive (hacking) coughs that produce phlegm.

Comments: If you require an expectorant, you need more moisture in your environment. Drink eight to ten glasses of water daily. The use of a vaporizer or humidifier may also be beneficial. Over-the-counter sale of this product may not be permitted in some states.

Preferred: The codeine in this product has been proven effective as a cough suppressant.

Robitussin cough remedy

Manufacturer: A. H. Robins Company
Dosage Form/Ingredients: Liquid (content per teaspoon): guaifenesin, 100 mg; alcohol, 3.5%
Use: To convert a dry nonproductive cough to a productive, phlegm-producing cough
Side Effects: Nausea; vomiting
Warnings: Do not give this product to children under two years of age unless directed otherwise by your doctor. • If your cough persists, or is accompanied by high fever, consult your doctor promptly. •Do not use this product to treat chronic coughs, such as from smoking or asthma. • Do not use this product to treat productive (hacking) coughs that produce phlegm.

Comments: If you require an expectorant, you need more moisture in your environment. Drink eight to ten glasses of water daily. The use of a vaporizer or humidifier may also be beneficial.

Acceptable: It has yet to be proven that guaifenesin is effective as a cough remedy. However, it is safe, and future studies may prove its effectiveness.

Robitussin-DM Cough Calmers cough remedy

Manufacturer: A. H. Robins Company
Dosage Form/Ingredients: Lozenge: dextromethorphan hydrobromide, 7.5 mg; guaifenesin, 50 mg
Use: For temporary suppression or relief of cough due to colds or "flu," to convert a dry, nonproductive cough to a productive, phlegm-producing cough
Side Effects: Drowsiness; nausea; vomiting
Warnings: Do not give this product to children under six without consulting a doctor. • This product interacts with monoamine oxidase inhibitors. If you are currently taking any drugs of this type, check with your doctor before taking this product. If you are unsure of the type or contents of your medications, ask your doctor or pharmacist. • Do not use

this product to treat chronic coughs, as from smoking or asthma, or to treat productive (hacking) coughs that produce phlegm. • If your cough persists, or is accompanied by a high fever, consult your doctor promptly.

Comments: If you require an expectorant, you need more moisture in your environment; drink eight to ten glasses of water daily. The use of a humidifier or vaporizor may also be beneficial. • This product may provide greater relief of coughing, and it will help soothe a raspy throat better if you lie down while it dissolves in your mouth.

Acceptable: Dextromethorphan hydrobromide is an effective cough suppressant. Although guaifenesin has not been proven effective, it is safe to use and future studies may prove its effectiveness.

Robitussin-DM cough remedy

Manufacturer: A. H. Robins Company

Dosage Form/Ingredients: Liquid (content per teaspoon): dextromethorphan hydrobromide, 15 mg; guaifenesin, 100 mg; alcohol, 1.4%

Use: For temporary relief of cough due to colds or "flu"; to convert a dry, nonproductive cough to a productive, phlegm-producing cough

Side Effects: Drowsiness; nausea; vomiting

Warnings: Do not give this product to children under six without consulting a doctor. • This product interacts with monoamine oxidase inhibitors. If you are currently taking any drugs of this type, check with your doctor before taking this product. If you are unsure of the type or contents of your medications, ask your doctor or pharmacist. • Do not use this product to treat chronic coughs, as from smoking or asthma, or to treat productive (hacking) coughs that produce phlegm. • If your cough persists, or is accompanied by a high fever, consult your doctor promptly.

Comments: If you require an expectorant, you need more moisture in your environment; drink eight to ten glasses of water daily. The use of a humidifier or vaporizor may also be beneficial.

Acceptable: Dextromethorphan hydrobromide is an effective cough suppressant. Although guaifenesin has not been proven effective, it is safe to use and future studies may prove its effectiveness.

Robitussin-PE cough remedy

Manufacturer: A. H. Robins Company

Dosage Form/Ingredients: Liquid (content per teaspoon): guaifenesin, 100 mg; pseudoephedrine hydrochloride, 30 mg; alcohol, 1.4%

Use: For temporary relief of cough and nasal congestion due to colds or "flu"; to convert a dry, nonproductive cough to a productive, phlegm-producing cough

Side Effects: Mild stimulation; nausea; vomiting; dry mouth; nervousness; insomnia; restlessness; blurred vision; dizziness; palpitations

Warnings: This product should be used with special caution by children under two years of age, and by persons who have diabetes, heart disease, high blood pressure, or thyroid disease. In these situations, consult your doctor before taking this product. • This product interacts with guanethidine and monoamine oxidase inhibitors. If you are currently taking any drugs of these types, check with your doctor before taking this product. If you are unsure of the type or contents of your medications, ask your doctor or pharmacist. • If your cough persists, or is accompanied by high fever, consult your doctor promptly. • Do not use this product to treat chronic coughs, such as from smoking or asthma. • Do not use this product to treat productive (hacking) coughs that produce phlegm.

Comments: If you require an expectorant, you need more moisture in your environment. Drink eight to ten glasses of water daily. The use of a vaporizer or humidifier may also be beneficial.

Fair: This product contains an expectorant and a decongestant. We suggest you choose a product containing only a cough suppressant if you want to relieve a cough.

Rolaids antacid

Manufacturer: American Chicle
Dosage Form/Ingredients: Tablet: dihydroxyaluminum sodium carbonate, 334 mg; sodium, 53 mg
Use: For relief of acid indigestion, heartburn, and/or sour stomach
Side Effects: Constipation
Warnings: Persons with kidney disease or those on a salt-free diet should not use this product. In persons with kidney disease, repeated (daily) use of this product may cause nausea, vomiting, depressed reflexes, or breathing difficulties. • Long-term (several weeks) use of this product may lead to intestinal obstruction and dehydration. Phosphate depletion may occur, leading to weakness, loss of appetite, and eventually bone pain. Phosphate depletion may be prevented by drinking at least one glass of milk a day. • Do not take this product within two hours of a dose of a tetracycline antibiotic. • Consult your physician or pharmacist before taking this product if you are already taking iron, a vitamin-mineral product, chlorpromazine, phenytoin, digoxin, quinidine, or warfarin, or if you are unsure of the type and contents of the medications you are taking. • Never self-medicate with this product if your symptoms occur regularly (two or three or more times a month). Consult your doctor if the symptoms are worse than usual, if you have chest pains or feel "tightness" in the chest, or if you are sweating or short of breath. In fact, we do not recommend self-treatment for severe attacks of heartburn, indigestion, or stomach upset in any circumstances. If you do decide that your symptoms are mild enough to warrant self-medication, limit treatment to two weeks. If symptoms persist, consult your doctor.
Comments: To prevent constipation, drink at least eight glasses of water a day. If constipation persists, consult your doctor or pharmacist. • This product must be taken exactly as directed on the label, unless your doctor has instructed you otherwise. Never skip a dose just because you feel better. If you grow tired of the taste, ask your pharmacist to suggest a different product.

Acceptable: Products containing more effective ingredients are available. The high sodium content of this product may make it unsuitable for some users.

RVP, RVPlus, RVPaba sunscreens

Manufacturer: Elder Pharmaceuticals
Dosage Forms/Ingredients: RVP: Ointment: surfactants, 2.5%; unspecified quantities of red petrolatum, paraben, and lanolin free. RVPlus: Ointment: red petrolatum, 30%; unspecified quantity of microcrystalline titanium-coated mica platelets. RVPaba: Lipstick: PABA, 5%; unspecified quantity of red petrolatum
Use: To prevent sunburn, premature aging of the skin, and skin cancer caused by overexposure to sunlight; to protect persons with sun sensitive skin, or those taking photo-sensitizing drugs, against sun toxicity

Side Effects: Occasional irritation; rash

Warnings: Avoid prolonged exposure to the sun, especially if you are sensitive to it. • Do not use this product if you are allergic to benzocaine, procaine, sulfa drugs, thiazide diuretics (water pills or high blood pressure medication), or certain dyes. If you are unaware of the nature of the medications you are taking, ask your doctor or pharmacist. • Do not use this product in or around the eyes. • Discontinue use and consult your pharmacist if irritation (pain, itching, or swelling) or rash appears. • Follow the directions given on the package, especially regarding frequency of use. Be sure to reapply after swimming or excessive exercise.

Comments: If you are unsure whether this is the proper sunscreen agent for you, refer for clarification to the section on sunscreen products in this book. If you still have questions, ask your pharmacist or doctor. • This product may stain certain types of clothing.

Preferred: *The ingredients in the lipstick form of this product offer effective protection against sunburn.*

Not Evaluated: *The manufacturer fails to provide sufficient information about the formulation of the ointment forms of this product on which to base an evaluation.*

St. Joseph Children's cold remedy

Manufacturer: Plough, Inc.

Dosage Form/Ingredient: Chewable tablet: phenylpropanolamine hydrochloride, 3.125 mg; aspirin, 81 mg

Use: To reduce fever, relieve nasal congestion and minor aches and pains due to colds and "flu"

Side Effects: Blurred vision; dizziness; drowsiness or stimulation; dry mouth; headache; insomnia; nervousness; nausea; palpitations; ringing in the ears; slight blood loss; slight increase in blood pressure; vomiting

Warnings: This product should be used with special caution by persons who have diabetes, heart disease, high blood pressure, peptic ulcer, bleeding or stomach bleeding, gout, asthma, or thyroid disease. If your child has any of these conditions, consult your doctor before administering this product. • This product should not be given to newborn or premature infants, or taken by pregnant or nursing women. • This product interacts with alcohol, ammonium chloride, guanethidine, methotrexate, monoamine oxidase inhibitors, oral anticoagulants, oral antidiabetics, probenecid, sedative drugs, steroids, sulfinpyrazone, tricyclic antidepressants, and vitamin C. If your child is currently taking any drugs of these types, check with your doctor before administering this product. If you are unsure of the type or contents of your child's medications, ask your doctor or pharmacist. • The dosage instructions listed on the package should be followed carefully; toxicity may occur in adults or children with repeated doses. • Be sure to keep the tablets out of the reach of your children between doses.

Comments: Many other conditions (some serious) mimic the common cold. If symptoms persist beyond one week, or if they occur regularly without regard to season, consult your doctor. • The effectiveness of this product may diminish after being taken regularly for seven to ten days; consult your pharmacist about substituting another medication if this product begins to lose its effectiveness for your child. • Generic versions of this product are available and may save you money. Consult your pharmacist. • Have your child chew gum or suck on ice chips to reduce mouth dryness.

Senokot laxative

Manufacturer: The Purdue Frederick Company

Dosage Forms/Ingredients: Granules (content per teaspoon): senna concentrate, 326 mg. Liquid (content per teaspoon): senna concentrate extract, 218 mg; alcohol, 7%. Suppository: senna concentrate, 652 mg. Tablet: senna concentrate, 187 mg

Use: For relief of constipation

Side Effects: Excess loss of fluid; griping (cramps); mucus in feces

Warnings: Persons with a high fever (100° F or more), black or tarry stools, nausea, vomiting, abdominal pain; pregnant women; and children under the age of three should not use this product unless directed to do so by a doctor. • Do not use this product when constipation is caused by megacolon or other diseases of the intestine, or hypothyroidism. • Excessive use (daily for a month or more) of this product may cause diarrhea, vomiting, and loss of certain blood electrolytes. • Never self-medicate with this product if constipation lasts longer than two weeks, or if the medication does not produce a laxative effect within a week. • Limit use to seven days unless directed otherwise by a doctor since this product may cause laxative-dependence (addiction) if used for a longer time.

Comments: This product may discolor the urine. • Evacuation may occur within six to twelve hours. • The granular form of this product may be taken plain, mixed with liquids, or sprinkled on food.

Acceptable: We prefer bulk-forming laxatives; however, this product is also effective.

Serutan laxative

Manufacturer: The J. B. Williams Company, Inc.

Dosage Forms/Ingredient: Granules: vegetable hemicellulose derived from Plantago Ovata, 39%. Powder: vegetable hemicellulose derived from Plantago Ovata, 45%

Use: For relief of constipation

Side Effects: None, when used as directed

Warnings: Persons with high fever (100° F or more), black or tarry stools, nausea, vomiting, abdominal pain, intestinal ulcers, intestinal obstruction, fecal obstruction, or difficulty in swallowing; children under age three; and pregnant women should not use this product unless directed by a doctor. • Do not use this product when constipation is caused by megacolon or other diseases of the intestine, or hypothyroidism. • Excessive use (daily for a month or more) of this product may cause diarrhea, vomiting, and loss of certain blood electrolytes. • Never self-medicate with this product if constipation lasts longer than two weeks, or if the medication does not produce a laxative effect within a week. • Limit use to seven days unless directed otherwise by your doctor; this product may cause laxative-dependence (addiction) if used for a longer time.

Comments: Evacuation may not occur for 12 to 72 hours. • This product must be mixed in water or juice before taking; an eight-ounce glass of water should be consumed immediately afterwards.

Preferred: Used as directed, single-ingredient bulk-forming laxatives like this are safe and effective.

Silence Is Golden cough remedy

Manufacturer: Bristol-Myers Products

Dosage Form/Ingredients: Liquid (content per teaspoon): dextromethorphan hydrobromide, 10 mg; honey flavor

Use: For temporary relief of coughs due to colds, the "flu," or minor throat and bronchial irritations

Side Effects: Drowsiness; nausea; vomiting

Warnings: Do not give this product to children under six years of age. • If your cough persists, or is accompanied by high fever, consult your doctor promptly. • This product interacts with monoamine oxidase inhibitors. If you are currently taking any drugs of this type, check with your doctor before taking this product. If you are unsure of the type or contents of your medications, ask your doctor or pharmacist. • Do not use this product to treat chronic coughs, such as from smoking or asthma. • Do not use this product to treat productive (hacking) coughs that produce phlegm.

Preferred: *This product contains dextromethorphan hydrobromide which has been proven effective as a cough suppressant.*

Sinarest cold and allergy remedy

Manufacturer: Pharmacraft Division, Pennwalt Corporation

Dosage Forms/Ingredients: Tablet: acetaminophen, 325 mg; chlorpheniramine maleate, 2 mg; phenylpropanolamine hydrochloride, 18.7 mg. Extra-strength tablet: acetaminophen, 500 mg; chlorpheniramine maleate, 2 mg; phenylpropanolamine hydrochloride, 18.7 mg

Use: For relief of nasal congestion, fever, aches, pains, and general discomfort due to colds and upper respiratory allergies

Side Effects: Anxiety; blurred vision; chest pain; confusion; constipation; dry mouth; difficult and painful urination; dizziness; drowsiness; headache; increased blood pressure; insomnia; loss of appetite; mild stimulation; nausea; nervousness; palpitations; rash; reduced sweating; tension; tremor; vomiting. In overdose: Blood disorders; rash

Warnings: This product should be used with special caution by the elderly or debilitated, and by persons who have asthma, diabetes, an enlarged prostate, glaucoma (certain types), heart disease, high blood pressure, kidney disease, liver disease, lung disease, certain blood disorders, obstructed bladder, obstructed intestine, peptic ulcer, or thyroid disease. If you have any of these conditions, consult your doctor before taking this product. It should not be used by pregnant or nursing women, or be given to newborn or premature infants. • This product may cause drowsiness. Do not take it if you must drive, operate heavy machinery, or perform other tasks requiring mental alertness. To prevent oversedation, avoid the use of alcohol or other drugs that have sedative properties. • This product interacts with alcohol, guanethidine, monoamine oxidase inhibitors, sedative drugs, and tricyclic antidepressants. If you are currently taking any drugs of these types, check with your doctor before taking this product. If you are unsure of the type or contents of your medications, ask your doctor or pharmacist. • Because this product reduces sweating, avoid excessive work or exercise in hot weather. • When taken in overdose, acetaminophen is more toxic than aspirin. Follow dosage instructions carefully.

Comments: Many other conditions (some serious) mimic the common cold. If symptoms persist beyond one week, or if they occur regularly without regard to season, consult your doctor. • The effectiveness of this product may diminish after being taken regularly for seven to ten days; consult your pharmacist about substituting another medication if this product begins to lose its effectiveness for you. • Chew gum or suck on ice chips or a piece of hard candy to relieve mouth dryness.

Acceptable: We prefer single-ingredient products rather than combination analgesic-decongestant-antihistamine products like this one.

Sine-Aid analgesic

Manufacturer: McNeil Consumer Products Company

Dosage Form/Ingredients: Tablet: acetaminophen, 325 mg; phenylpropanolamine hydrochloride, 25 mg

Use: For the relief of sinus headache pain and pressure caused by sinusitis

Side Effects: When taken in overdose: Blood disorders; mild to moderate stimulation; nausea; vomiting

Warnings: Persons with high blood pressure, kidney or liver disease, heart disease, lung disease, diabetes, certain blood disorders, or thyroid disease should be extremely careful about using this product. If you have any of these conditions, consult your doctor or pharmacist before using this medication. • Do not use this product if you are consuming alcohol, or if you are currently taking antidepressants, and/or monoamine oxidase inhibitors; if you are unsure of the type or contents of your medications, ask your doctor or pharmacist. • When taken in overdose this product is more toxic than aspirin. The dosage instructions listed on the package should be followed carefully; toxicity may occur in adults or children with repeated doses.

Comments: Acetaminophen does not relieve inflammation, so if pain is caused by swelling or inflammation, it should not be used. Aspirin is better. • The effectiveness of this product may diminish after being taken regularly for seven to ten days; consult your pharmacist about substituting another medication if this product begins to lose its effectiveness for you.

Acceptable: Generally we prefer single-ingredient products rather than combination decongestants-analgesics like this.

Sine-Off cold and allergy remedy (tablet)

Manufacturer: Menley & James Laboratories

Dosage Form/Ingredients: Tablet: chlorpheniramine maleate, 2 mg; phenylpropanolamine hydrochloride, 18.75 mg; aspirin, 325 mg

Use: To relieve nasal congestion, fever, aches, pains, and general discomfort due to colds or upper respiratory allergies

Side Effects: Anxiety; blurred vision; chest pain; confusion; constipation; difficult and painful urination; dizziness; drowsiness; dry mouth; headache; increased blood pressure; insomnia; loss of appetite; mild stimulation; nausea; nervousness; palpitations; rash; reduced sweating; ringing in the ears; slight blood loss; tension; tremor; vomiting

Warnings: This product should be used with special caution by the elderly or debilitated, and by persons who have asthma, diabetes, enlarged prostate, glaucoma (certain types), heart disease, high blood pressure, kidney disease, liver disease, obstructed bladder, obstructed intestine, peptic ulcer, bleeding or stomach bleeding, gout, or thyroid disease. If you have any of these conditions, consult your doctor before taking this product. It should not be used by pregnant or nursing women, or be given to newborn or premature infants. • This product may cause drowsiness. Do not take it if you must drive, operate heavy machinery, or perform other tasks requiring mental alertness. To prevent oversedation, avoid the use of alcohol or other drugs that have sedative properties. • This product interacts with alcohol, ammonium chloride, guanethidine, methotrexate, monoamine oxidase inhibitors, oral anticoagulants, oral antidiabetics, probenecid, sedative drugs, steroids, sulfinpyrazone, tricyclic antidepressants, and vitamin C. If you are currently taking any drugs of these types, check with your doctor before taking this product. If you are unsure of the type or contents of your medications, ask your doctor or pharmacist. • Because this product reduces sweating, avoid excessive work or exercise in hot weather. • The dosage instructions listed on the package should be followed carefully; toxicity may occur in adults or children with repeated doses.

Comments: Many other conditions (some serious) mimic the common cold. If symptoms persist beyond one week or if they occur regularly without regard to season, consult your doctor. • The effectiveness of this product may diminish after being taken for seven to ten days; consult your pharmacist about substituting another product if this one begins to lose its effectiveness for you. • Chew gum or suck on ice chips or a piece of hard candy to reduce mouth dryness.

Acceptable: *We prefer single-ingredient products rather than combination analgesic-antihistamine-decongestant products like this one.*

Sine-Off cold and allergy remedy (extra strength tablet)

Manufacturer: Menley and James Laboratories
Dosage Form/Ingredients: Extra strength tablet: chlorpheniramine maleate, 2 mg; phenylpropanolamine hydrochloride, 18.75 mg; acetaminophen, 500 mg
Use: For relief of nasal congestion, fever, aches, pains, and general discomfort due to colds and upper respiratory allergies
Side Effects: Anxiety; blurred vision; chest pain; confusion; constipation; dry mouth; difficult and painful urination; dizziness; drowsiness; headache; increased blood pressure; insomnia; loss of appetite; mild stimulation; nausea; nervousness; palpitations; rash; reduced sweating; tension; tremor; vomiting. In overdose: Blood disorders; rash
Warnings: This product should be used with special caution by the elderly or debilitated, and by persons who have asthma, diabetes, an enlarged prostate, glaucoma (certain types), heart disease, high blood pressure, kidney disease, liver disease, lung disease, certain blood disorders, obstructed bladder, obstructed intestine, peptic ulcer, or thyroid disease. If you have any of these conditions, consult your doctor before taking this product. It should not be used by pregnant or nursing women, or be given to newborn or premature infants. • This product may cause drowsiness. Do not take it if you must drive, operate heavy machinery, or perform other tasks requiring mental alertness. To prevent oversedation, avoid the use of alcohol or other drugs that have sedative properties. • This product interacts with alcohol, guanethidine, monoamine oxidase inhibitors, sedative drugs, and tricyclic antidepressants. If you are currently taking any drugs of these types, check with your doctor before taking this product. If you are unsure of the type or contents of your medications, ask your doctor or pharmacist. • Because this product reduces sweating, avoid excessive work or exercise in hot weather. • When taken in overdose, acetaminophen is more toxic than aspirin. Follow dosage instructions carefully.
Comments: Many other conditions (some serious) mimic the common

cold. If symptoms persist beyond one week, or if they occur regularly without regard to season, consult your doctor. • The effectiveness of this product may diminish after being taken regularly for seven to ten days; consult your pharmacist about substituting another medication if this product begins to lose its effectiveness for you. • Chew gum or suck on ice chips or a piece of hard candy to relieve mouth dryness.

Acceptable: We prefer single-ingredient products rather than combination analgesic-decongestant-antihistamine products like this one.

Sine-Off Once-A-Day nasal decongestant

Manufacturer: Menley & James Laboratories
Dosage Form/Ingredients: Nasal spray: xylometazoline hydrochloride, 0.1%; thimerosal, 0.001%; unspecified quantities of menthol, eucalyptol, camphor, and methyl salicylate
Use: For temporary relief of nasal congestion due to colds, sinusitis, hay fever, or other upper respiratory allergies
Side Effects: Blurred vision; burning, dryness of nasal mucosa; increased nasal congestion or discharge; sneezing, and/or stinging; dizziness; drowsiness; headache; insomnia; nervousness; palpitations; slight increase in blood pressure; stimulation
Warnings: This product should not be used by persons who have glaucoma (certain types). • It should be used with special caution by persons who have diabetes, advanced hardening of the arteries, heart disease, high blood pressure, or thyroid disease. If you have any of these conditions, consult your doctor before using this product. • This product interacts with monoamine oxidase inhibitors, thyroid preparations, and tricyclic antidepressants. If you are currently taking any drugs of these types, check with your doctor before taking this product. If you are unsure of the type or contents of your medications, ask your doctor or pharmacist.
Comments: To avoid side effects such as burning, sneezing, or stinging, and a "rebound" increase in nasal congestion and discharge, do not exceed the recommended dose, and do not use this product for more than three or four continuous days. • This product should not be used by more than one person; sharing the dispenser may spread infection. • This product works best when it is used correctly. Refer to the instructions for the use of nasal sprays in the chapter on "Buying, Storing, and Using Drugs." • The long-acting ingredient in this product has a decongestant action that may last up to 12 hours. Because it needs to be administered only twice a day, this product is less likely to cause "rebound" congestion than nasal products containing different ingredients.

Acceptable: Although we prefer a product containing oxymetazoline hydrochloride, this product also offers an effective long-acting formula for treating the conditions specified.

Sinex Long-Acting nasal decongestant

Manufacturer: Vicks Health Care Division, Richardson-Merrell Inc.
Dosage Form/Ingredients: Nasal spray: xylometazoline hydrochloride, 0.1%; thimerosal, 0.001%
Use: For temporary relief of nasal congestion due to colds, sinusitis, hay fever, or other upper respiratory allergies
Side Effects: Blurred vision; burning, dryness of nasal mucosa; increased nasal congestion or discharge; sneezing, and/or stinging; dizziness; drowsiness; headache; insomnia; nervousness; palpitations; slight increase in blood pressure; stimulation

Warnings: This product should not be used by persons who have glaucoma (certain types). • It should be used with special caution by persons who have diabetes, advanced hardening of the arteries, heart disease, high blood pressure, or thyroid disease. If you have any of these conditions, consult your doctor before using this product. • This product interacts with monoamine oxidase inhibitors, thyroid preparations, and tricyclic antidepressants. If you are currently taking any drugs of these types, check with your doctor before taking this product. If you are unsure of the type or contents of your medications, ask your doctor or pharmacist.

Comments: To avoid side effects such as burning, sneezing, or stinging, and a "rebound" increase in nasal congestion and discharge, do not exceed the recommended dose, and do not use this product for more than three or four continuous days. • This product should not be used by more than one person; sharing the dispenser may spread infection. • This product works best when it is used correctly. Refer to the instructions for the use of nasal sprays in the chapter on "Buying, Storing, and Using Drugs." • The long-acting ingredient in this product has a decongestant action that may last up to 12 hours. Because it needs to be administered only twice a day, this product is less likely to cause "rebound" congestion than nasal products containing different ingredients.

Acceptable: Although we prefer a product containing oxymetazoline hydrochloride, this product also offers an effective long-acting formula for treating the conditions specified.

Sinex nasal decongestant

Manufacturer: Vicks Health Care Division, Richardson-Merrell Inc.

Dosage Form/Ingredients: Nasal spray: phenylephrine hydrochloride, 0.5%; cetylpyridinium chloride, 0.04%; thimerosal, 0.001%; unspecified quantities of menthol, eucalyptol, camphor, and methyl salicylate

Use: For temporary relief of nasal congestion due to colds, sinusitis, hay fever, or other respiratory allergies

Side Effects: Blurred vision; burning, dryness of nasal mucosa; increased nasal congestion or discharge; sneezing, and/or stinging; dizziness; drowsiness; headache; insomnia; nervousness; palpitations; slight increase in blood pressure; stimulation

Warnings: This product should not be used by persons who have glaucoma (certain types). • It should be used with special caution by persons who have diabetes, advanced hardening of the arteries, heart disease, high blood pressure, or thyroid disease. If you have any of these conditions, consult your doctor before using this product. • This product interacts with monoamine oxidase inhibitors, thyroid preparations, and tricyclic antidepressants. If you are currently taking any drugs of these types, check with your doctor before taking this product. If you are unsure of the type or contents of your medications, ask your doctor or pharmacist.

Comments: To avoid side effects such as burning, sneezing, or stinging, and a "rebound" increase in nasal congestion and discharge, do not exceed the recommended dose, and do not use this product for more than three or four continuous days. • This product should not be used by more than one person; sharing the dispenser may spread infection. • This product works best when it is used correctly. Refer to the instructions for the use of nasal sprays in the chapter on "Buying, Storing, and Using Drugs." • Many nasal drops or sprays on the market contain oxymetazoline hydrochloride. This drug has a duration of action of about 12 hours, and because it needs to be used less often, it is less likely to cause "rebound" nasal congestion during use. Therefore, we recommend a product containing oxymetazoline hydrochloride over this product, which does not contain the ingredient. • This spray contains aromatic substances which add no therapeutic value; you may like the aroma.

Acceptable: Although we prefer a product containing oxymetazoline hydrochloride, this product also offers an effective formula for treating the conditions specified.

Sinutab cold and allergy remedy

Manufacturer: Warner-Lambert Company

Dosage Forms/Ingredients: Tablet: acetaminophen, 325 mg; phenylpropanolamine hydrochloride, 25 mg; phenyltoloxamine citrate, 22 mg. Extra strength tablet: acetaminophen, 500 mg; phenylpropanolamine hydrochloride, 25 mg; phenyltoloxamine citrate, 22 mg. Extra strength capsule: acetaminophen, 500 mg; phenylpropanolamine hydrochloride, 18.75 mg; chlorpheniramine maleate, 2 mg

Use: For relief of nasal congestion, fever, aches, pains, and general discomfort due to colds and upper respiratory allergies

Side Effects: Anxiety; blurred vision; chest pain; confusion; constipation; dry mouth; difficult and painful urination; dizziness; drowsiness; headache; increased blood pressure; insomnia; loss of appetite; mild stimulation; nausea; nervousness; palpitations; rash; reduced sweating; tension; tremor; vomiting. In overdose: Blood disorders; rash

Warnings: This product should be used with special caution by the elderly or debilitated, and by persons who have asthma, diabetes, enlarged prostate, glaucoma (certain types), heart disease, high blood pressure, kidney disease, liver disease, lung disease, certain blood disorders, obstructed bladder, obstructed intestine, peptic ulcer, or thyroid disease. If you have any of these conditions, consult your doctor before taking this product. It should not be used by pregnant or nursing women, or be given to newborn or premature infants. • This product may cause drowsiness. Do not take it if you must drive, operate heavy machinery, or perform other tasks requiring mental alertness. To prevent oversedation, avoid the use of alcohol or other drugs that have sedative properties. • This product interacts with alcohol, guanethidine, monoamine oxidase inhibitors, sedative drugs, and tricyclic antidepressants. If you are currently taking any drugs of these types, check with your doctor before taking this product. If you are unsure of the type or contents of your medications, ask your doctor or pharmacist. • Because this product reduces sweating, avoid excessive work or exercise in hot weather. • When taken in overdose, acetaminophen is more toxic than aspirin. Follow dosage instructions carefully.

Comments: Many other conditions (some serious) mimic the common cold. If symptoms persist beyond one week, or if they occur regularly without regard to season, consult your doctor. • The effectiveness of this product may diminish after being taken regularly for seven to ten days; consult your pharmacist about substituting another medication if this product begins to lose its effectiveness for you. • Chew gum or suck on ice chips or a piece of hard candy to relieve dryness of the mouth.

Acceptable: We prefer single-ingredient products rather than combination analgesic-decongestant-antihistamine products like this one.

Sinutab Long-Lasting nasal decongestant

Manufacturer: Warner-Lambert Company

Dosage Form/Ingredient: Nasal spray: xylometazoline hydrochloride, 0.1%; unspecified quantity of benzalkonium chloride

Use: For temporary relief of nasal congestion due to colds, sinusitis, hay fever, or other upper respiratory allergies

Side Effects: Blurred vision; burning, dryness of nasal mucosa; increased nasal congestion or discharge; sneezing, and/or stinging; dizziness; drowsiness; headache; insomnia; nervousness; palpitations; slight increase in blood pressure; stimulation

Warnings: This product should not be used by persons who have glaucoma (certain types). • It should be used with special caution by persons who have diabetes, advanced hardening of the arteries, heart disease, high blood pressure, or thyroid disease. If you have any of these conditions, consult your doctor before using this product. • This product interacts with monoamine oxidase inhibitors, thyroid preparations, and tricyclic antidepressants. If you are currently taking any drugs of these types, check with your doctor before taking this product. If you are unsure of the type or contents of your medications, ask your doctor or pharmacist.

Comments: To avoid side effects such as burning, sneezing, or stinging, and a "rebound" increase in nasal congestion and discharge, do not exceed the recommended dose, and do not use this product for more than three or four continuous days. • This product should not be used by more than one person; sharing the dispenser may spread infection. • This product works best when it is used correctly. Refer to the instructions for the use of nasal sprays in the chapter on "Buying, Storing, and Using Drugs." • The long-acting ingredient in this product has a decongestant action that may last up to 12 hours. Because it needs to be administered only twice a day, this product is less likely to cause "rebound" congestion than nasal products containing different ingredients.

Acceptable: Although we prefer a product containing oxymetazoline hydrochloride, this product also offers an effective long-acting formula for treating the conditions specified.

Sinutab-II cold and allergy remedy

Manufacturer: Warner-Lambert Company

Dosage Form/Ingredients: Tablet: acetaminophen, 325 mg; phenylpropanolamine hydrochloride, 25 mg

Use: For relief of nasal congestion, fever, aches, pains, and general discomfort due to colds or upper respiratory allergies

Side Effects: Mild to moderate stimulation; nausea; vomiting. In overdose: Blood disorders; rash

Warnings: This product should be used with special caution by persons who have diabetes, heart, lung, liver, or kidney disease, high blood pressure, certain blood disorders, or thyroid disease. If you have any of these conditions, consult your doctor before taking this product. • This product interacts with alcohol, guanethidine, monoamine oxidase inhibitors, sedative drugs, and tricyclic antidepressants. If you are currently taking any drugs of these types, check with your doctor before taking this product. If you are unsure of the type or contents of your medications, ask your doctor or pharmacist. • This product should not be given to newborn or premature infants or taken by pregnant or nursing women. • When taken in overdose, acetaminophen is more toxic than aspirin. Follow dosage instructions carefully.

Comments: Many other conditions (some serious) mimic the common cold. If symptoms persist beyond one week, or if they occur regularly without regard to season, consult your doctor. • The effectiveness of this product may diminish after being taken regularly for seven to ten days;

consult your pharmacist about substituting another medication if this product begins to lose its effectiveness for you.

Acceptable: We prefer single-ingredient products rather than combination analgesic-decongestant products like this one.

Sleep-Eze sleep aid

Manufacturer: Whitehall Laboratories
Dosage Form/Ingredient: Tablet: pyrilamine maleate, 25 mg
Use: To induce drowsiness and assist in falling asleep
Side Effects: Blurred vision; confusion; constipation; difficult urination; dizziness; drowsiness; dry mouth and respiratory passages; headache; insomnia; low blood pressure; nausea; nervousness; palpitations; rash; restlessness; vomiting. Children may react with primary symptoms of excitement: convulsions; flushed skin; nervousness; tremors; twitching of muscles; uncoordinated movements
Warnings: Persons with asthma, diabetes, glaucoma (certain types), heart disease, high blood pressure, kidney disease, liver disease, thyroid disorders, certain types of peptic ulcer, enlarged prostate, obstructed bladder, or obstructed intestine; pregnant and nursing women; children under 12 years of age; and elderly or debilitated persons should not take this medication. • This product may interact with other drugs. If you are currently taking any medication, do not use this product without first consulting your doctor. • This product also interacts with alcohol, so avoid alcohol or other central nervous system sedatives while you are using it. • Since its purpose is to make you sleepy, do not use it while driving, operating heavy machinery, or performing other tasks that require you to be mentally alert. • Tolerance to this product may develop; do not increase the recommended dose unless your doctor recommends you to do so. • Insomnia may be a symptom of serious illness. Seek your doctor's advice if your sleeplessness continues, and do not take this product for more than two weeks without consulting your doctor.
Comments: This product may cause dryness of the mouth. To reduce this feeling, chew gum or suck on ice chips or a piece of hard candy. • There is probably no need to purchase this drug. You would be better advised to try to find and correct the cause of your insomnia. A glass of warm milk and a soak in a hot tub may work just as well as this product. • Many OTC sleep aids are very similar. If you wish to use one, look for a generic equivalent at a cheaper price. Ask your pharmacist for assistance.

Unacceptable: We consider that OTC sleep aids should not be taken without the advice of a doctor.

Solarcaine antiseptic and burn remedy

Manufacturer: Plough, Inc.
Dosage Forms/Ingredients: Cream: benzocaine, 1%; triclosan, 0.2%. Aerosol spray: benzocaine, 0.75%; isopropyl alcohol, 24%; triclosan, 0.02%. Pump spray: benzocaine, 2%; isopropyl alcohol, 31%; phenol, 0.3%; triclosan, 0.1%
Use: For temporary relief of pain of sunburn and other minor burns, minor cuts, scrapes, poison ivy, insect bites, skin irritation, and chapping
Side Effects: Allergy; local irritation
Warnings: Do not use this product on broken skin or on large areas of

the body because it is possible that a toxic amount of medication may be absorbed. • Discontinue use if irritation (rash, itching, or swelling) or pain appears. Consult your physician. • The fluid in burn blisters helps healing of underlying tissue. Blisters should not be broken. If you have blisters that are extremely large or painful, contact your doctor. • The aerosol spray is flammable; do not use it while you are smoking or near a fire. Avoid inhalation and keep away from eyes.

Comments: To relieve burn pain, take aspirin and cool the burned area. • If itching is intolerable, we recommend the use of a "wet soak" once daily. See the chapter "Buying, Storing, and Using Drugs" for directions. • Remember that creams that are put on serious (second- or third-degree) burns will have to be taken off before definitive treatment can be given. • Consult your doctor or pharmacist if you have any questions concerning the use of this product.

Acceptable: Greater relief can be achieved with a product containing a higher concentration of benzocaine.

Sominex sleep aid

Manufacturer: The J. B. Williams Company, Inc.
Dosage Form/Ingredient: Tablet: pyrilamine maleate, 25 mg
Use: To induce drowsiness and assist in falling asleep
Side Effects: Blurred vision; confusion; constipation; difficult urination; dizziness; drowsiness; dry mouth and respiratory passages; headache; insomnia; low blood pressure; nausea; nervousness; palpitations; rash; restlessness; vomiting. Children may react with primary symptoms of excitement: convulsions; flushed skin; nervousness; tremors; twitching of muscles; uncoordinated movements
Warnings: Persons with asthma, diabetes, glaucoma (certain types), heart disease, high blood pressure, kidney disease, liver disease, thyroid disorders, certain types of peptic ulcer, enlarged prostate, obstructed bladder, or obstructed intestine; pregnant and nursing women; children under 12 years of age; and elderly or debilitated persons should not take this medication. • This product may interact with other drugs. If you are currently taking any medication, do not use this product without first consulting your doctor. • This product also interacts with alcohol, so avoid alcohol or other central nervous system sedatives while you are using it. • Since its purpose is to make you sleepy, do not use it while driving, operating heavy machinery, or performing other tasks that require you to be mentally alert. • Tolerance to this product may develop; do not increase the recommended dose unless your doctor recommends you to do so. • Insomnia may be a symptom of serious illness. Seek your doctor's advice if your sleeplessness continues, and do not take this product for more than two weeks without consulting your doctor.
Comments: This product may cause dryness of the mouth. To reduce this feeling, chew gum or suck on ice chips or a piece of hard candy. • There is probably no need to purchase this drug. You would be better advised to try to find and correct the cause of your insomnia. A glass of warm milk and a soak in a hot tub may work just as well as this product. • Many OTC sleep aids are very similar. If you wish to use one, look for a generic equivalent at a cheaper price. Ask your pharmacist for assistance.

Unacceptable: We consider that OTC sleep aids should not be taken without the advice of a doctor.

Stresscaps nutritional supplement

Manufacturer: Lederle Laboratories Div., American Cyanamid Company
Dosage Form/Ingredients: Capsule: thiamine mononitrate, 10 mg; riboflavin, 10 mg; pyridoxine hydrochloride, 2 mg; cyanocobalamin, 6 mcg; ascorbic acid, 300 mg; niacinamide, 100 mg; calcium pantothenate, 20 mg
Use: To supplement the diet
Side Effects: None
Warnings: This product contains vitamin B$_6$ (pyridoxine) in an amount great enough that it may interact with levodopa (L-dopa). If you are currently taking L-dopa, check with your doctor before taking this product. • This product may interfere with the results of urine tests. If your urine is being tested, inform your doctor and/or pharmacist that you are taking this product.
Comments: Dietary deficiencies of vitamins are uncommon in the United States. Most people who have vitamin deficiencies should be under a doctor's care, and they should not be self-medicating with OTC vitamin products. If you choose to take supplemental vitamins, choose a generic product to save money. Ask your pharmacist for assistance. • Do not be misled by the name of this product; there is no proof that high doses of B and C vitamins will prevent or relieve stress.

Acceptable: If you choose to take a vitamin supplement, this is an acceptable product.

Stresstabs 600 nutritional supplement

Manufacturer: Lederle Laboratories Div., American Cyanamid Company
Dosage Form/Ingredients: Tablet: dl-alpha tocopheryl acetate, 30 IU; L-ascorbic acid, 600 mg; thiamine mononitrate, 15 mg; riboflavin, 15 mg; niacinamide, 100 mg; pyridoxine hydrochloride, 5 mg; cyanocobalamin, 12 mcg; calcium pantothenate, 20 mg
Use: To supplement the diet
Side Effects: None
Warnings: This product contains vitamin B$_6$ (pyridoxine) in an amount great enough that it may interact with levodopa (L-dopa). If you are currently taking L-dopa, check with your doctor before taking this product. • This product may interfere with the results of urine tests. If your urine is being tested, inform your doctor and/or pharmacist that you are taking this product.
Comments: Dietary deficiencies of vitamins are uncommon in the United States. Most people who have vitamin deficiencies should be under a doctor's care, and they should not be self-medicating with OTC vitamin products. If you choose to take supplemental vitamins, choose a generic product to save money. Ask your pharmacist for assistance. • Do not be misled by the name of this product; there is no proof that high doses of B and C vitamins will prevent or relieve stress.

Acceptable: If you choose to take a vitamin supplement, this is an acceptable product.

Stri-Dex acne preparation

Manufacturer: Lehn & Fink Products Co., Div. of Sterling Drug, Inc.
Dosage Form/Ingredients: Medicated pad: alcohol, 28%; salicylic acid, 0.5%
Use: Treatment of acne
Side Effects: Allergy; local irritation

Warnings: Do not get this product in or near the eyes. • If the condition worsens or if skin irritation develops, stop using this product and consult your physician.

Comments: Wash area gently with warm water and pat dry before applying this product.

Fair: Products containing more effective ingredients are available.

Stri-Dex B.P. acne preparation

Manufacturer: Lehn & Fink Products Co., Div. of Sterling Drug, Inc.
Dosage Form/Ingredient: Cream: benzoyl peroxide, 10%
Use: Treatment of acne
Side Effects: Allergy; local irritation
Warnings: Do not get this product in or near the eyes. • Persons having a known sensitivity to benzoyl peroxide should not use this product. • While using this product, do not use harsh, abrasive cleansers. • If excessive redness or peeling occurs, reduce the frequency of this product's use. • Avoid exposure to heat lamps and sunlamps, as well as prolonged exposure to sunlight, when using this product. • This product may be especially active on fair-skinned people. • If the condition worsens or if skin irritation develops, stop using this product and consult your physician.

Comments: Wash the affected area gently with warm water and pat dry before applying this product. • There may be a slight transitory stinging or burning sensation on initial application of this product. • This product may damage certain fabrics including rayon.

Preferred: Benzoyl peroxide has been shown to be the most effective ingredient in acne preparations.

Sudafed cold remedy

Manufacturer: Burroughs Wellcome Co.
Dosage Forms/Ingredients: Liquid (content per teaspoon): pseudoephedrine hydrochloride, 30 mg. Tablet: pseudoephedrine hydrochloride, 30 mg, 60 mg
Use: For relief of nasal congestion and other symptoms of the common cold
Side Effects: Blurred vision; dizziness; drowsiness or stimulation; headache; insomnia; nervousness; nausea; palpitations; slight increase in blood pressure; vomiting
Warnings: This product should be used with special caution by persons who have diabetes, heart disease, high blood pressure, or thyroid disease. If you have any of these conditions, consult your doctor before taking this product. • This product interacts with alcohol, guanethidine, monoamine oxidase inhibitors, sedative drugs, and tricyclic antidepressants. If you are currently taking any drugs of these types, check with your doctor before taking this product. If you are unsure of the type or contents of your medications, ask your doctor or pharmacist.

Comments: Many other conditions (some serious) mimic the common cold. If symptoms persist beyond one week, or if they occur regularly without regard to season, consult your doctor. • The effectiveness of this product may diminish after being taken regularly for seven to ten days; consult your pharmacist about substituting another medication if this product begins to lose its effectiveness for you.

Preferred: This product is pure decongestant; it is very effective and it is reasonably priced. It's our treatment of choice for the common cold.

216

Sudafed Plus cold remedy

Manufacturer: Burroughs Wellcome Co.

Dosage Forms/Ingredients: Liquid (content per teaspoon): pseudoephedrine hydrochloride, 30 mg; chlorpheniramine maleate, 2 mg. Tablet: pseudoephedrine hydrochloride, 60 mg; chlorpheniramine maleate, 4 mg

Use: For relief of nasal congestion due to colds and upper respiratory allergies

Side Effects: Anxiety; blurred vision; chest pain; confusion; constipation; dry mouth; difficult and painful urination; dizziness; drowsiness; headache; increased blood pressure; insomnia; loss of appetite; mild stimulation; nausea; nervousness; palpitations; rash; reduced sweating; tension; tremor; vomiting

Warnings: This product should be used with special caution by the elderly or debilitated, and by persons who have asthma, diabetes, enlarged prostate, glaucoma (certain types), heart disease, high blood pressure, kidney disease, liver disease, obstructed bladder, obstructed intestine, peptic ulcer, or thyroid disease. If you have any of these conditions, consult your doctor before taking this product. It should not be used by pregnant or nursing women, or be given to newborn or premature infants. • This product may cause drowsiness. Do not take it if you must drive, operate heavy machinery, or perform other tasks requiring mental alertness. To prevent oversedation, avoid the use of alcohol or other drugs that have sedative properties. • This product interacts with alcohol, guanethidine, monoamine oxidase inhibitors, sedative drugs, and tricyclic antidepressants. If you are currently taking any drugs of these types, check with your doctor before taking this product. If you are unsure of the type or contents of your medications, ask your doctor or pharmacist. • Because this product reduces sweating, avoid excessive work or exercise in hot weather.

Comments: Many other conditions (some serious) mimic the common cold. If symptoms persist beyond one week, or if they occur regularly without regard to season, consult your doctor. • The effectiveness of this product may diminish after being taken for seven to ten days; consult your pharmacist about substituting a product with another antihistamine if this product begins to lose its effectiveness for you. • Chew gum or suck on ice chips or a piece of hard candy to reduce mouth dryness.

Acceptable: We prefer single-ingredient products rather than combination antihistamine-decongestant products like this one.

Sulforcin acne preparation

Manufacturer: Owen Laboratories

Dosage Form/Ingredients: Lotion: alcohol, 11.65%; resorcinol, 2%; colloidal sulfur, 5%

Use: Treatment of acne

Side Effects: Allergy; local irritation

Warnings: Do not get this product in or near the eyes. • If the condition worsens or if skin irritation develops, stop using this product and consult your physician.

Comments: Wash area gently with warm water and pat dry before applying this product.

Fair: Products containing more effective ingredients are available.

Sundown Sunblock Ultra Protection, Sundown Maximal Protection, Sundown Extra Protection, Sundown Moderate Protection sunscreens

Manufacturer: Johnson & Johnson

Dosage Forms/Ingredients: Sunblock Ultra Protection: Lotion: padimate O, 7%; octyl salicylate, 5%; oxybenzone, 4%. Maximal Protection: Lotion: padimate O, 7%; octylsalicylate, 5%; oxybenzone, 2%; alcohol, 8.6%. Extra Protection: Lotion: padimate O, 5.3%; oxybenzone, 1.75%. Moderate Protection: Lotion: padimate O, 3.8%; alcohol

Use: To prevent sunburn, premature aging of the skin, and skin cancer caused by overexposure to sunlight; to protect persons with sun sensitive skin, or those taking photo-sensitizing drugs, against sun toxicity

Side Effects: Occasional irritation; rash

Warnings: Avoid prolonged exposure to the sun, especially if you are sensitive to it. • Do not use this product if you are allergic to benzocaine, procaine, sulfa drugs, thiazide diuretics (water pills or high blood pressure medication), or certain dyes. If you are unaware of the nature of the medications you are taking, ask your doctor or pharmacist. • Do not use this product in or around the eyes. • Discontinue use and consult your pharmacist if irritation (pain, itching, or swelling) or rash appears. • Follow the directions given on the package, especially regarding frequency of use. Be sure to reapply after swimming or excessive exercise.

Comments: If you are unsure whether this is the proper sunscreen agent for you, refer for clarification to the section on sunscreen products in this book. If you still have questions, ask your pharmacist or doctor. • This product may stain certain types of clothing.

Preferred: *The ingredients in this product offer effective protection against sunburn.*

Super Odrinex appetite suppressant

Manufacturer: Fox Pharmacal, Inc.

Dosage Form/Ingredients: Tablet: phenylpropanolamine hydrochloride, 25 mg; caffeine, 100 mg

Use: As an aid in dietary control

Side Effects: Blurred vision; diarrhea; nausea; dizziness; drowsiness; headache; increase in blood pressure, blood sugar, heart rate, and thyroid activity; insomnia; nervousness; palpitations. In larger than the recommended dose: Irregular heartbeat; nasal dryness; upset stomach

Warnings: Persons with heart disease, high blood pressure, diabetes, kidney or thyroid disease; children under 16 years of age; and pregnant or nursing women should not use this product. Consult your doctor for recommendations. • This product interacts with alcohol, guanethidine, monoamine oxidase inhibitors, sedative drugs, and tricyclic antidepressants. If you are currently taking any of these drugs, or if you are unsure of the type or contents of your medications, consult your doctor or pharmacist before taking this product. • Avoid taking this drug while using a decongestant. • Avoid continuous use for longer than three months. • Discontinue use if you experience rapid pulse, dizziness, or palpitations.

Comments: During the first week of therapy with this product, expect increased frequency of urination. • Many medical authorities believe that the ingredient phenylpropanolamine does not help in weight-loss programs. However, the FDA Review Panel has reported that it is effective. • If you want to use this product, remember that you become tolerant to any beneficial effects after a couple of weeks. After each two weeks of use, stop for one week, then resume use. • The primary value in a product of this nature is in following the caloric reduction plan that goes with it.

Fair: This product contains caffeine, which does not contribute to permanent weight loss and may worsen side effects such as nervousness.

Surfak laxative

Manufacturer: Hoechst-Roussel Pharmaceuticals Inc.
Dosage Form/Ingredient: Capsule: docusate calcium, 50 mg, 240 mg
Use: For relief of constipation; as a stool softener
Side Effects: Mild, transitory cramping pains; nausea; rash
Warnings: Persons with high fever (100° F or more), black or tarry stools, nausea, vomiting, or abdominal pain; children under age three; and pregnant women should not use this product unless directed by a doctor. • Do not use this product when constipation is caused by megacolon or other diseases of the intestine, or hypothyroidism. • Excessive use (daily for a month or more) of this product may cause diarrhea, vomiting, and loss of certain blood electrolytes. • Never self-medicate with this product if constipation lasts longer than two weeks, or if the medication does not produce a laxative effect within a week. • Limit use to seven days unless directed otherwise by your doctor; this product may cause laxative-dependence (addiction) if used for a longer period. • This product is referred to as a stool softener. It is recommended for relief of constipation when the stool is hard and dry. Do not take another product containing a stool softener at the same time as you are taking this product.
Comments: Evacuation may occur within 72 hours. • Although an exact generic equivalent of this item may not be available, very similar products are. Ask your pharmacist if you can save money by purchasing another item.

Acceptable: This product is an acceptable stool softener laxative.

Tedral asthma remedy

Manufacturer: Warner-Chilcott Company
Dosage Forms/Ingredients: Elixir (content per teaspoon): ephedrine hydrochloride, 6 mg; phenobarbital, 2 mg; theophylline anhydrous, 32.5 mg; alcohol, 15%. Suspension (content per teaspoon): ephedrine hydrochloride, 12 mg; phenobarbital, 4 mg; theophylline anhydrous, 65 mg. Tablet: ephedrine hydrochloride, 24 mg; phenobarbital, 8 mg; theophylline anhydrous, 130 mg
Use: For control of bronchial asthma
Side Effects: Anxiety; blurred vision; chest pain; confusion; constipation; dizziness; drowsiness; dry mouth and respiratory passages; increased blood pressure; increased frequency of urination; insomnia; loss of appetite; nausea; nervousness; palpitations; rash; reduced sweating; restlessness; tension; tremors; urinary retention; vomiting. Children may react with primary symptoms of excitement: convulsions; flushed skin; nervousness; tremors; twitching of muscles; and uncoordinated movements
Warnings: Overdose may result in convulsions, coma, and cardiovascular collapse. • While taking this product, avoid the use of sedative drugs or alcohol, guanethidine, monoamine oxidase inhibitors, or tricyclic antidepressants. If you are taking any medication of these types, or if you are unsure of the type of medication you are taking, con-

sult your doctor or pharmacist. • Repeated use of this product may cause nausea and vomiting, depressed reflexes, and breathing difficulties in people with kidney disease. • Asthma is too serious a condition to be routinely self-treated. Asthmatics should be under a doctor's care. Be sure to tell your doctor that you are taking this, or any other OTC asthma remedy. • Because this product reduces sweating, avoid excessive work or exercise in hot weather.

Comments: The effectiveness of this product may diminish after being taken regularly for seven to ten days. Consult your pharmacist about substituting another product containing a different active ingredient if this product begins to lose its effectiveness for you. • Chew gum or suck on ice chips or a piece of hard candy to reduce mouth dryness. • Over-the-counter sale of this product may not be permitted in some states. • Do not worry about addiction to this product if you follow directions for use.

Fair: The phenobarbital in this product probably has no beneficial effect. It also may depress the respiratory system and potentially cause underventilation.

Teldrin allergy remedy

Manufacturer: Menley & James Laboratories

Dosage Forms/Ingredient: Timed-release capsule: chlorpheniramine maleate, 8 mg. Maximum strength timed-release capsule: chlorpheniramine maleate, 12 mg

Use: For relief of symptoms of hay fever and other upper respiratory allergies

Side Effects: Anxiety; blurred vision; chest pain; confusion; constipation; difficult and painful urination; dizziness; drowsiness; dry mouth; headache; increased blood pressure; insomnia; loss of appetite; mild stimulation; nausea; nervousness; palpitations; rash; reduced sweating; tension; tremor; vomiting

Warnings: This product should be used with special caution by the elderly or debilitated, and by persons who have asthma, diabetes, enlarged prostate, glaucoma (certain types), heart disease, high blood pressure, kidney disease, liver disease, obstructed bladder, obstructed intestine, peptic ulcer, or thyroid disease. If you have any of these conditions, consult your doctor before taking this product. It should not be used by pregnant or nursing women, or be given to newborn or premature infants. • This product may cause drowsiness. Do not take it if you must drive, operate heavy machinery, or perform other tasks requiring mental alertness. To prevent oversedation, avoid the use of alcohol or other drugs that have sedative properties. • This product interacts with alcohol, guanethidine, monoamine oxidase inhibitors, sedative drugs, and tricyclic antidepressants. If you are currently taking any drugs of these types, check with your doctor before taking this product. If you are unsure of the type or contents of your medications, ask your doctor or pharmacist. • Because this product reduces sweating, avoid excessive work or exercise in hot weather. • This product has sustained action; never increase the recommended dose or take it more frequently than directed. A serious overdose could result.

Comments: The effectiveness of this product may diminish after being taken regularly for seven to ten days; consult your pharmacist about substituting another product containing a different antihistamine if this product begins to lose its effectiveness for you. • Chew gum or suck on ice chips or a piece of hard candy to reduce mouth dryness. • Products equivalent to this one are available and vary widely in cost. Check prices; you may save money by comparison shopping.

Preferred: *Chlorpheniramine maleate is probably the most effective antihistamine, and it is inexpensive. It is our treatment of choice for the symptoms of upper respiratory allergies.*

Tempra analgesic

Manufacturer: Mead Johnson Co., Nutritional Division
Dosage Forms/Ingredients: Drop (content per drop): acetaminophen, 60 mg; alcohol, 10%. Syrup (content per teaspoon): acetaminophen, 120 mg; alcohol, 10%
Use: For the relief of discomfort and fever following immunizations, or of colds or "flu"
Side Effects: When taken in overdose: Blood disorders; rash
Warnings: This product should not be taken by persons with certain blood disorders or with heart, lung, liver, or kidney disease without a doctor's approval. • When taken in overdose, this product is more toxic than aspirin. The dosage instructions listed on the package should be followed carefully; toxicity may occur with repeated doses. • This product is intended for children. Be sure to keep it out of their reach when not in use.
Comments: Acetaminophen does not relieve inflammation, so if pain is caused by swelling or inflammation, it should not be used. Aspirin is better. • Generic substitutes for this product are available and may save you money. Ask your pharmacist for assistance.
Preferred: *We recommend this product because it contains a single effective ingredient.*

Tes-Tape urine test for glucose

Manufacturer: Eli Lilly and Company
Product Form: Paper tape in roll
Use: To test urine for glucose
Comments: Do not use this product if the tape has turned brown. • Be certain to remind your doctor and pharmacist of any over-the-counter item or prescription drug you are taking. It may affect this test. • Test only freshly collected urine. • Keep the container tightly closed and store in a dry place out of the sun. Do not refrigerate. • Do not keep the tape immersed in urine longer than the directions state. • Compare the color quickly to the chart on the package. Read the color in a bright light. • Before reading the color, touch the tape to the side of the container to remove excess liquid.
Preferred: *This test is effective for the specified purpose, and offers good value for the money.*

Thera-Combex H-P nutritional supplement

Manufacturer: Parke-Davis
Dosage Form/Ingredients: Capsule: ascorbic acid, 500 mg; thiamine mononitrate, 25 mg; riboflavin, 15 mg; pyridoxine hydrochloride, 10 mg; cyanocobalamin, 5 mcg; nicotinamide, 100 mg; *dl*-panthenol, 20 mg
Use: To supplement the diet
Side Effects: None
Warnings: This product contains vitamin B_6 (pyridoxine) in an amount great enough that it may interact with levodopa (L-dopa). If you are cur-

rently taking L-dopa, check with your doctor before taking this product. •
This product may interfere with the results of urine tests. If your urine is
being tested, inform your doctor and/or pharmacist that you are taking
this product.

Comments: Dietary deficiencies of vitamins are uncommon in the
United States. Most people who have vitamin deficiencies should be
under a doctor's care, and they should not be self-medicating with OTC
vitamin products. If you choose to take supplemental vitamins, choose a
generic product to save money. Ask your pharmacist for assistance.

*Acceptable: If you choose to take a vitamin supplement, this is an accept-
able product.*

Theragran nutritional supplement

Manufacturer: E. R. Squibb & Sons, Inc.

Dosage Form/Ingredients: Tablet: vitamin A, 10,000 IU; vitamin D, 400
IU; vitamin E, 15 IU; ascorbic acid, 200 mg; thiamine, 10 mg; riboflavin, 10
mg; niacin, 100 mg; pyridoxine hydrochloride, 5 mg; cyanocobalamin, 5
mcg; pantothenic acid, 20 mg

Use: To supplement the diet

Side Effects: None

Warnings: This product contains vitamin B_6 (pyridoxine) in an amount
great enough that it may interact with levodopa (L-dopa). If you are currently taking L-dopa, check with your doctor before taking this product. •
If large doses are taken, this product may interfere with the results of
urine tests. If your urine is being tested, inform your doctor and/or pharmacist that you are taking this product. • This product contains ingredients that accumulate and are stored in the body. The recommended
dose should not be exceeded for long periods (several weeks to months)
except by doctor's orders.

Comments: Dietary deficiencies of vitamins are uncommon in the
United States. Most people who have vitamin deficiencies should be
under a doctor's care, and they should not be self-medicating with OTC
vitamin products. If you choose to take supplemental vitamins, choose a
generic product to save money. Ask your pharmacist for assistance.

*Acceptable: If you choose to take a vitamin supplement, this is an accept-
able product.*

Theragran-M nutritional supplement

Manufacturer: Squibb Pharmaceutical Co.

Dosage Form/Ingredients: Tablet: copper, 2 mg; zinc, 1.5 mg, manganese, 1 mg; iodine, 0.15 mg; vitamin A, 10,000 IU; vitamin D, 400 IU; vitamin
E, 15 IU; ascorbic acid, 200 mg; thiamine, 10 mg; riboflavin, 10 mg; niacin,
100 mg; pyridoxine hydrochloride, 5 mg; cyanocobalamin, 5 mcg; pantothenic acid, 20 mg; iron, 12 mg; magnesium, 65 mg

Use: To supplement the diet

Side Effects: Constipation; diarrhea; nausea; stomach pain

Warnings: This product should not be used by persons who have active
peptic ulcer or ulcerative colitis. • Alcoholics and persons who have
chronic liver or pancreatic disease should use this product with special
caution; such persons may have enhanced iron absorption and are
therefore more likely than others to experience iron toxicity. • The
minerals in this product interact with oral tetracycline antibiotics and
reduce the absorption of the antibiotics. If you are currently taking tetracycline, consult your doctor or pharmacist before taking this product.

If you are unsure of the type or contents of your medications, ask your doctor or pharmacist. • Accidental iron poisoning is common in children; be sure to keep this product safely out of their reach. • This product contains ingredients that accumulate and are stored in the body. The recommended dose should not be exceeded for long periods (several weeks to months) except by doctor's orders. • If large doses are taken daily, this product may interfere with the results of urine tests. If your urine is being tested, inform your doctor and/or pharmacist that you are taking this product. • Because of its iron content, this product may cause constipation, diarrhea, nausea or stomach pain. These symptoms usually disappear or become less severe after two to three days. Taking your dose with food or milk may help minimize these side effects. If they persist, ask your pharmacist to recommend another product. • This product contains vitamin B_6 (pyridoxine) in an amount great enough that it may interact with levodopa (L-dopa). If you are currently taking L-dopa, check with your doctor before taking this product.

Comments: Black, tarry stools are a normal consequence of iron therapy. If your stools are not black and tarry, this product may not be working for you. Ask your pharmacist to recommend another product. • Dietary deficiencies of vitamins are uncommon in the United States. Most people who have vitamin deficiencies should be under a doctor's care, and they should not be self-medicating with OTC vitamin products. If you choose to take supplemental vitamins, choose a generic product to save money. Ask your pharmacist for assistance.

Acceptable: If you choose to take a vitamin supplement, this is an acceptable product.

Tinactin athlete's foot and jock itch remedy

Manufacturer: Schering Corporation
Dosage Forms/Ingredients: Cream, Aerosol powder, Solution, Powder: tolnaftate, 1%
Use: For the treatment of athlete's foot and jock itch
Side Effects: Allergy; local irritation
Warnings: Diabetics and other persons with impaired circulation should not use this product without first consulting a physician. • Do not apply this product to mucous membranes. • If your condition worsens, or if irritation occurs, stop using this product and consult your pharmacist. • When using the aerosol form of this product, be careful not to inhale any of the powder. • Check with your doctor before using this product on a child. Some doctors believe that children under the age of 12 do not get athlete's foot, and that a rash appearing between a child's toes may be dermatitis or some other condition that this product would not relieve.

Comments: Some lesions take months to heal, so it is important not to stop treatment too soon. • If foot lesions are consistently a problem, check the fit of your shoes. • Wash your hands thoroughly after applying this product. • The cream and solution forms of this product are preferable to the powders for effectiveness; the best action of the powders may be in drying the infected area. • When using the solution form of this product, avoid contaminating the contents of the bottle; squeeze some of the solution into a separate container for each use. • The powder aerosol may be more expensive than the other forms of this product; check prices before paying for convenience you do not need.

Preferred: This product contains tolnaftate, which is the treatment of choice for athlete's foot and other fungal skin infections. Tolnaftate products were formerly sold only with a doctor's prescription, but are now available OTC.

Topex acne preparation

Manufacturer: Vicks Toiletry Products Division, Richardson-Merrell, Inc.
Dosage Form/Ingredient: Lotion: benzoyl peroxide, 10%
Use: Treatment of acne
Side Effects: Allergy; local irritation
Warnings: Do not get this product in or near the eyes. • Persons having a known sensitivity to benzoyl peroxide should not use this product. • While using this product, do not use harsh, abrasive cleansers. • If excessive redness or peeling occurs, reduce the frequency of this product's use. • Avoid exposure to heat lamps and sunlamps, as well as prolonged exposure to sunlight, when using this product. • This product may be especially active on fair-skinned people. • If the condition worsens or if skin irritation develops, stop using this product and consult your physician.
Comments: Wash the affected area gently with warm water and pat dry before applying this product. • There may be a slight transitory stinging or burning sensation on initial application of this product. • This product may damage certain fabrics including rayon.
Preferred: *Benzoyl peroxide has been shown to be the most effective ingredient in acne preparations.*

Triaminic Expectorant cough remedy

Manufacturer: Dorsey Laboratories
Dosage Form/Ingredients: Liquid (content per teaspoon): phenylpropanolamine hydrochloride, 12.5 mg; guaifenesin, 100 mg; alcohol, 5%
Use: For temporary relief of cough and nasal congestion due to colds or "flu"; to convert a dry, nonproductive cough to a productive, phlegm-producing cough.
Side Effects: Mild stimulation; nausea; vomiting; blurred vision; palpitations; flushing; nervousness; dizziness; insomnia
Warnings: This product should be used with special caution by children under two years of age, and by persons who have diabetes, heart disease, high blood pressure, or thyroid disease. In these situations, consult your doctor before taking this product. • This product interacts with guanethidine and monoamine oxidase inhibitors. If you are currently taking any drugs of these types, check with your doctor before taking this product. If you are unsure of the type or contents of your medications, ask your doctor or pharmacist. • Do not use this product to treat chronic coughs, such as those from smoking or asthma. • Do not use this product to treat productive (hacking) coughs that produce phlegm. • If your cough persists, or is accompanied by a high fever, consult your doctor promptly.
Comments: If you require an expectorant, you need more moisture in your environment. Drink eight to ten glasses of water daily. The use of a vaporizer or humidifier may also be beneficial.
Acceptable: *This product contains a decongestant and an expectorant. We suggest you choose a product containing only a cough suppressant to relieve a cough.*

Triaminic Expectorant with Codeine cough remedy

Manufacturer: Dorsey Laboratories
Dosage Form/Ingredients: Liquid (content per teaspoon): codeine

phosphate, 10 mg; guaifenesin, 100 mg; phenylpropanolamine hydrochloride, 12.5 mg; pheniramine maleate, 6.25 mg; pyrilamine maleate, 6.25 mg; alcohol, 5%

Use: For temporary relief of cough, nasal congestion, and other symptoms of colds or "flu"; to convert a dry, nonproductive cough to a productive phlegm-producing cough

Side Effects: Anxiety; blurred vision; chest pain; confusion; constipation; diarrhea; difficult and painful urination; dizziness; drowsiness; dry mouth; headache; heartburn; increased blood pressure; nasal congestion; nausea; nervousness; palpitations; rash; reduced sweating; severe abdominal pain; sore throat; tension; tremor; vomiting

Warnings: This product should be used with special caution by the elderly or debilitated, and by persons who have asthma or respiratory disease, diabetes, an enlarged prostate, glaucoma (certain types), heart disease, high blood pressure, kidney disease, obstructed bladder, obstructed intestine, peptic ulcer, or thyroid disease. In these situations, consult your doctor before taking this product. • This product should not be given to newborns or premature infants, or taken by pregnant women. • This product may cause drowsiness. Do not take it if you must drive, operate heavy machinery, or perform other tasks requiring mental alertness. To prevent oversedation, avoid the use of alcohol or other drugs that have sedative properties. • This product interacts with alcohol, guanethidine, monoamine oxidase inhibitors, sedative drugs, and tricyclic antidepressants. If you are currently taking any drugs of these types, check with your doctor before taking this product. If you are unsure of the type or contents of your medications, ask your doctor or pharmacist. • Because this product reduces sweating, avoid excessive work or exercise in hot weather. • Because this product contains codeine, it has the potential for abuse and must be used with caution. It usually should not be taken for more than seven to ten days. Tolerance may develop quickly, but do not increase the dose without consulting your doctor. • Do not use this product to treat chronic coughs, such as those from smoking or asthma. • Do not use this product to treat productive (hacking) coughs that produce phlegm. • If your cough persists, or is accompanied by high fever, consult your doctor promptly.

Comments: Many other conditions (some serious) mimic the common cold. If symptoms persist beyond one week or if they occur regularly without regard to season, consult your doctor. • If you require an expectorant, you need more moisture in your environment. Drink eight to ten glasses of water daily. The use of a vaporizer or humidifier may also be beneficial. • Chew gum or suck on ice chips or a piece of hard candy to reduce mouth dryness. • Over-the-counter sale of this product may not be permitted in some states.

Unacceptable: *The combination of ingredients in this product—a suppressant, an expectorant, a decongestant and two antihistamines—is illogical for treatment of a cough.*

Triaminicin cold and allergy remedy

Manufacturer: Dorsey Laboratories

Dosage Form/Ingredients: Tablet: phenylpropanolamine hydrochloride, 25 mg; chlorpheniramine maleate, 2 mg; aspirin, 450 mg; caffeine, 30 mg

Use: To relieve nasal congestion, fever, aches, pains, and general discomfort due to colds or upper respiratory allergies

Side Effects: Anxiety; blurred vision; chest pain; confusion; constipation; difficult and painful urination; dizziness; drowsiness; dry mouth;

headache; increased blood pressure; insomnia; loss of appetite; mild stimulation; nausea; nervousness; palpitations; rash; reduced sweating; ringing in the ears; slight blood loss; tension; tremor; vomiting

Warnings: This product should be used with special caution by the elderly or debilitated, and by persons who have asthma, diabetes, an enlarged prostate, glaucoma (certain types), heart disease, high blood pressure, kidney disease, liver disease, obstructed bladder, obstructed intestine, peptic ulcer, bleeding or stomach bleeding, gout, or thyroid disease. If you have any of these conditions, consult your doctor before taking this product. It should not be used by pregnant or nursing women, or given to newborn or premature infants. • This product may cause drowsiness. Do not take it if you must drive, operate heavy machinery, or perform other tasks requiring mental alertness. To prevent oversedation, avoid the use of alcohol or other drugs that have sedative properties. • This product interacts with alcohol, ammonium chloride, guanethidine, methotrexate, monoamine oxidase inhibitors, oral anticoagulants, oral antidiabetics, probenecid, sedative drugs, steroids, sulfinpyrazone, tricyclic antidepressants, and vitamin C. If you are currently taking any drugs of these types, check with your doctor before taking this product. If you are unsure of the type or contents of your medications, ask your doctor or pharmacist. • Because this product reduces sweating, avoid excessive work or exercise in hot weather. • The dosage instructions listed on the package should be followed carefully; toxicity may occur in adults or children with repeated doses.

Comments: Many other conditions (some serious) mimic the common cold. If symptoms persist beyond one week or if they occur regularly without regard to season, consult your doctor. • The effectiveness of this product may diminish after being taken for seven to ten days; consult your pharmacist about substituting another product if this one begins to lose its effectiveness for you. • Chew gum or suck on ice chips or a piece of hard candy to reduce mouth dryness.

Unacceptable: *The caffeine included in this product has no value in treatment of the conditions specified.*

Trind cough remedy

Manufacturer: Mead Johnson Co., Nutritional Division

Dosage Form/Ingredients: Liquid (content per teaspoon): guaifenesin, 50 mg; phenylephrine hydrochloride, 2.5 mg; acetaminophen, 120 mg; alcohol, 15%

Use: For temporary relief of cough, nasal congestion, fever, aches, and pains due to colds or "flu"; to convert a dry, nonproductive cough to a productive, phlegm-producing cough

Side Effects: Drowsiness; mild stimulation; nausea; vomiting; blurred vision; palpitations; flushing; nervousness; dizziness; insomnia. In overdose: Blood disorders; rash

Warnings: This product should be used with special caution by children under three years of age, and by persons who have diabetes, heart disease, high blood pressure, lung disease, liver disease, kidney disease, blood disorders (certain types), or thyroid disease. In these situations, consult your doctor before taking this product. • This product interacts with guanethidine and monoamine oxidase inhibitors. If you are currently taking any drugs of these types, check with your doctor before taking this product. If you are unsure of the type or contents of your medications, ask your doctor or pharmacist. • Pregnant women should not take this product, and it should not be given to newborn or premature infants. •

When taken in overdose, acetaminophen is more toxic than aspirin. Follow dosage instructions carefully. • If your cough persists, or is accompanied by high fever, consult your doctor promptly. • Do not use this product to treat chronic coughs such as those from smoking or asthma, or to treat productive (hacking) coughs that produce phlegm.

Comments: If you require an expectorant, you need more moisture in your environment; drink eight to ten glasses of water daily. The use of a vaporizer or humidifier may also be beneficial. • The effectiveness of this product may diminish after it has been taken regularly for seven to ten days; consult your pharmacist about substituting another product if this product begins to lose its effectiveness for you. • Many other conditions (some serious) mimic the common cold. If symptoms persist beyond one week, or if they occur regularly without regard to season, consult your doctor.

Fair: This product contains ingredients—a decongestant and an analgesic—not directly related to treatment of a cough. Products containing more appropriate ingredients are available.

Trind-DM cough remedy

Manufacturer: Mead Johnson Co., Nutritional Division

Dosage Form/Ingredients: Liquid (content per teaspoon): phenylephrine hydrochloride, 2.5 mg; dextromethorphan hydrobromide, 7.5 mg; quaifenesin, 50 mg; acetaminophen, 120 mg; alcohol, 15%

Use: For temporary relief of cough, nasal congestion, fever, aches, and pains due to colds or "flu"; to convert a dry, nonproductive cough to a productive, phlegm-producing cough

Side Effects: Drowsiness; mild stimulation; nausea; vomiting; blurred vision; palpitations; flushing; nervousness; dizziness; insomnia. In overdose: Blood disorders; rash

Warnings: This product should be used with special caution by children under three years of age, and by persons who have diabetes, heart disease, high blood pressure, or thyroid disease. In these situations, consult your doctor before taking this product. • This product interacts with guanethidine and monoamine oxidase inhibitors. If you are currently taking any drugs of these types, check with your doctor before taking this product. If you are unsure of the type or contents of your medications, ask your doctor or pharmacist. • Pregnant women should not take this product, and it should not be given to newborn or premature infants. • When taken in overdose, acetaminophen is more toxic than aspirin. Follow dosage instructions carefully. • If your cough persists, or is accompanied by high fever, consult your doctor promptly. • Do not use this product to treat chronic coughs such as those from smoking or asthma, or to treat productive (hacking) coughs that produce phlegm.

Comments: If you require an expectorant, you need more moisture in your environment; drink eight to ten glasses of water daily. The use of a vaporizer or humidifier may also be beneficial. • The effectiveness of this product may diminish after it has been taken regularly for seven to ten days; consult your pharmacist about substituting another product if this product begins to lose its effectiveness for you. • Many other conditions (some serious) mimic the common cold. If symptoms persist beyond one week, or if they occur regularly without regard to season, consult your doctor.

Unacceptable: The combination of ingredients in this product—a decongestant, a suppressant, an expectorant, and an analgesic—is illogical for treatment of a cough.

Tucks hemorrhoidal preparation

Manufacturer: Parke-Davis

Dosage Forms/Ingredients: Medicated pad: benzalkonium chloride USP, 0.003%; glycerin, 10%; witch hazel, 50%; unspecified quantity of methylparaben. Cream, Ointment: witch hazel, 50%

Use: For relief of discomfort of hemorrhoids, anorectal wounds, episiotomies, and other superficial irritations

Side Effects: Irritation

Warnings: Sensitization (continued itching and redness) may occur with long-term and repeated use. • Certain ingredients in this product may cause an allergic reaction; do not use for longer than seven days at a time unless your doctor has advised you otherwise. • Never self-medicate for hemorrhoids if pain is continuous or throbbing, if bleeding or itching is excessive, or if you feel a large pressure within the rectum. • Discontinue use if irritation (pain, itching, or swelling) or rash occurs; consult your pharmacist.

Comments: Hemorrhoidal (pile) preparations relieve itching, reduce pain and inflammation, and check bleeding, but they do not heal, dry up, or give lasting relief from hemorrhoids.

Acceptable: Although generally we prefer a hemorrhoidal discomfort preparation that contains hydrocortisone, this product will also provide some relief.

Tums antacid

Manufacturer: Norcliff Thayer Inc.

Dosage Form/Ingredient: Tablet: calcium carbonate, 500 mg

Use: For relief of acid indigestion, heartburn, and/or sour stomach

Side Effects: Constipation

Warnings: Persons with kidney disease or hypercalcemia (an excess of calcium in the blood), or those drinking large quantities of milk should not use this product. • Do not take this product within two hours of a dose of a tetracycline antibiotic. • Consult your physician or pharmacist before taking this product if you are already taking iron, a vitamin-mineral product, chlorpromazine, phenytoin, digoxin, quinidine, or warfarin, or if you are unsure of the type and contents of the medications you are taking. • Never self-medicate with this product if your symptoms occur regularly (two or three or more times a month). Consult your doctor if the symptoms are worse than usual, if you have chest pains or feel "tightness" in the chest, or if you are sweating or short of breath. In fact, we do not recommend self-treatment for severe attacks of heartburn, indigestion, or stomach upset in any circumstances. If you do decide that your symptoms are mild enough to warrant self-medication, remember that this product is safe and effective only when used on an occasional basis. Repeated use over several weeks may result in "rebound acidity," which causes increased acid production and makes your symptoms worse instead of better.

Comments: This product must be taken exactly as directed on the label, unless your doctor has instructed you otherwise.

Acceptable: This product's potential for rebound acidity makes it unsuitable for some users.

2/G cough remedy

Manufacturer: Dow Pharmaceuticals

Dosage Form/Ingredients: Liquid (content per teaspoon): guaifenesin, 100 mg; alcohol, 3.5%

Use: For temporary relief of cough due to colds or "flu"; to convert a dry, nonproductive cough to a productive, phlegm-producing cough

Side Effects: Nausea; vomiting

Warnings: Do not give this product to children under two years of age unless directed to do so by your doctor. • If your cough persists or is accompanied by high fever, consult your doctor promptly. • Do not use this product to treat chronic coughs, such as from smoking or asthma. • Do not use this product to treat productive (hacking) coughs that produce phlegm.

Comments: If you require an expectorant, you need more moisture in your environment. Drink eight to ten glasses of water daily. The use of a vaporizer or humidifier may also be beneficial.

Acceptable: It has yet to be proven that guaifenesin is effective as a cough remedy. However, it is safe, and future studies may prove its effectiveness.

2/G-DM cough remedy

Manufacturer: Dow Pharmaceuticals

Dosage Form/Ingredients: Liquid (content per teaspoon): dextromethorphan hydrobromide, 15 mg; guaifenesin, 100 mg; alcohol, 5%

Use: For temporary relief of cough due to colds or "flu"; to convert a dry, nonproductive cough to a productive, phlegm-producing cough

Side Effects: Drowsiness; nausea; vomiting

Warnings: Do not give this product to children under six without consulting a doctor. • This product interacts with monoamine oxidase inhibitors. If you are currently taking any drugs of this type, check with your doctor before taking this product. If you are unsure of the type or contents of your medications, ask your doctor or pharmacist. • Do not use this product to treat chronic coughs, as from smoking or asthma, or to treat productive (hacking) coughs that produce phlegm. • If your cough persists, or is accompanied by a high fever, consult your doctor promptly.

Comments: If you require an expectorant, you need more moisture in your environment; drink eight to ten glasses of water daily. The use of a humidifier or vaporizor may also be beneficial.

Acceptable: Dextromethorphan is an effective cough suppressant. Although guaifenesin has not been proven effective, it is safe to use, and future studies may confirm its effectiveness.

Tylenol analgesic

Manufacturer: McNeil Consumer Products Company

Dosage Forms/Ingredient: Chewable tablet: acetaminophen, 80 mg. Drop (content per 0.6 ml, or one dropperful): acetaminophen, 60 mg. Elixir (content per teaspoon): acetaminophen, 120 mg. Tablet, Capsule: acetaminophen, 325 mg

Use: For the relief of pain of headache, toothache, sprains, muscular aches, menstruation; for relief of discomforts and fever following immunizations or of colds or "flu"; for temporary relief of minor aches and pains of arthritis and rheumatism

Side Effects: When taken in overdose: Blood disorders; rash

Warnings: This product should not be taken by persons with certain blood disorders or with heart, lung, liver or kidney disease without a doctor's approval. • When taken in overdose, this product is more toxic than aspirin. The dosage instructions listed on the package should be followed carefully; toxicity may occur in adults or children with repeated doses. •

The chewable tablets, drops, and elixir forms of this product are intended for use by children. Be sure to keep the products out of their reach when not in use.

Comments: The drops and elixir forms are 7 percent alcohol. • Acetaminophen does not relieve inflammation, so if pain is caused by swelling or inflammation, it should not be used. Aspirin is better. • Generic substitutes for this product are available and may save you money. Ask your pharmacist for assistance.

Preferred: *We recommend this product because it contains a single effective ingredient.*

Tylenol Extra Strength analgesic

Manufacturer: McNeil Consumer Products Company

Dosage Forms/Ingredient: Capsule, Tablet: acetaminophen, 500 mg. Liquid (content per tablespoon): acetaminophen, 500 mg; alcohol, 8.5%

Use: For the relief of pain of headache, toothache, sprains, muscular aches, menstruation; for the relief of discomforts and fever of colds or "flu"; for temporary relief of minor aches and pains of arthritis and rheumatism

Side Effects: When taken in overdose: Blood disorders; rash

Warnings: This product should not be taken by persons with certain blood disorders, or with kidney, heart, lung, or liver disease without a doctor's approval. • When taken in overdose, this product is more toxic than aspirin. The dosage instructions listed on the package should be followed carefully; toxicity may occur in adults or children with repeated doses.

Comments: The liquid form of this product is 8½ percent alcohol. • Acetaminophen does not relieve inflammation, so if pain is caused by swelling or inflammation, it should not be used. Aspirin is better.

Preferred: *This product contains a single ingredient, which is an effective analgesic.*

Unicap M nutritional supplement

Manufacturer: The Upjohn Company

Dosage Form/Ingredients: Tablet: vitamin A, 5000 IU; vitamin D, 400 IU; vitamin E, 15 IU; vitamin C, 60 mg; folic acid, 0.4 mg; thiamine, 1.5 mg; riboflavin, 1.7 mg; niacin, 20 mg; vitamin B_1, 2 mg; vitamin B_{12}, 6 mcg; pantothenic acid, 10 mg; iodine, 150 mcg; iron, 18 mg; copper, 2 mg; zinc, 15 mg; manganese, 1 mg; potassium, 5 mg

Use: To supplement the diet

Side Effects: Constipation; diarrhea; nausea; stomach pain

Warnings: This product should not be used by persons who have an active peptic ulcer or ulcerative colitis. • Alcoholics and persons who have chronic liver or pancreatic disease should use this product with special caution; such persons may have enhanced iron absorption and are therefore more likely than others to experience iron toxicity. • The minerals in this product interact with oral tetracycline antibiotics and reduce the absorption of the antibiotics. If you are currently taking tetracyline, consult your doctor or pharmacist before taking this product. If you are unsure of the type or contents of your medications, ask your doctor or pharmacist. • Accidental iron poisoning is common in children; be sure to keep this product safely out of their reach. • This product contains ingredients that accumulate and are stored in the body. The recommended dose should not be exceeded for long periods (several weeks to months) except by doctor's orders. • If large doses are taken daily, this product may interfere with the results of urine tests. If your urine is being tested, inform your doctor and/or pharmacist that you are taking this product. • Because of its iron content, this product may cause constipation, diarrhea, nausea or stomach pain. These symptoms usually disappear or become less severe after two to three days. Taking your dose with food or milk may help minimize these side effects. If they persist, ask your pharmacist to recommend another product. • This product contains vitamin B_6 (pyridoxine) in an amount great enough that it may interact with levodopa (L-dopa). If you are currently taking L-dopa, check with your doctor before taking this product.

Comments: Black, tarry stools are a normal consequence of iron therapy. If your stools are not black and tarry, this product may not be working for you. Ask your pharmacist to recommend another product. • Dietary deficiencies of vitamins are uncommon in the United States. Most people who have vitamin deficiencies should be under a doctor's care, and they should not be self-medicating with OTC vitamin products. If you choose to take supplemental vitamins, choose a generic product to save money. Ask your pharmacist for assistance.

Acceptable: If you choose to take a vitamin supplement, this is an acceptable product.

Unicap Multivitamin nutritional supplement

Manufacturer: The Upjohn Company
Dosage Forms/Ingredients: Capsule, Chewable tablet: vitamin A, 5000 IU; vitamin D, 400 IU; vitamin E, 15 IU; vitamin C, 60 mg; folic acid, 0.4 mg; thiamine, 1.5 mg; riboflavin, 1.7 mg; niacin, 20 mg; vitamin B_6, 2 mg; vitamin B_{12}, 6 mcg
Use: To supplement the diet
Side Effects: None
Warnings: This product contains vitamin B_6 (pyridoxine) in an amount great enough that it may interact with levodopa (L-dopa). If you are currently taking L-dopa, check with your doctor before taking this product. • If large doses are taken, this product may interfere with the results of urine tests. If your urine is being tested, inform your doctor and/or pharmacist that you are taking this product. • This product contains ingredients that accumulate and are stored in the body. The recommended dose should not be exceeded for long periods (several weeks to months) except by doctor's orders.
Comments: Chewable tablets should never be referred to as "candy" or as "candy-flavored" vitamins. Your child may take you literally and swallow toxic amounts. • Dietary deficiencies of vitamins are uncommon in the United States. Most people who have vitamin deficiencies should be under a doctor's care, and they should not be self-medicating with OTC vitamin products. If you choose to take supplemental vitamins, choose a generic product to save money. Ask your pharmacist for assistance.

Acceptable: If you choose to take a vitamin supplement, this is an acceptable product.

Unicap T nutritional supplement

Manufacturer: The Upjohn Company
Dosage Form/Ingredients: Tablet: vitamin A, 5000 IU; vitamin D, 400 IU; vitamin E, 15 IU; vitamin C, 300 mg; folic acid, 0.4 mg; thiamine, 10 mg; riboflavin, 10 mg; niacin, 100 mg; vitamin B_6, 6 mg; vitamin B_{12}, 18 mcg;

pantothenic acid, 10 mg; iodine, 150 mcg; iron, 18 mg; copper, 2 mg; zinc, 15 mg; manganese, 1 mg; potassium, 5 mg

Use: To supplement the diet

Side Effects: Constipation; diarrhea; nausea; stomach pain

Warnings: This product should not be used by persons who have an active peptic ulcer or ulcerative colitis. • Alcoholics and persons who have chronic liver or pancreatic disease should use this product with special caution; such persons may have enhanced iron absorption and are therefore more likely than others to experience iron toxicity. • The minerals in this product interact with oral tetracycline antibiotics and reduce the absorption of the antibiotics. If you are currently taking tetracyline, consult your doctor or pharmacist before taking this product. If you are unsure of the type or contents of your medications, ask your doctor or pharmacist. • Accidental iron poisoning is common in children; be sure to keep this product safely out of their reach. • This product contains ingredients that accumulate and are stored in the body. The recommended dose should not be exceeded for long periods (several weeks to months) except by doctor's orders. • If two or more tablets are taken daily, this product may interfere with the results of urine tests. If your urine is being tested, inform your doctor and/or pharmacist that you are taking this product. • Because of its iron content, this product may cause constipation, diarrhea, nausea or stomach pain. These symptoms usually disappear or become less severe after two to three days. Taking your dose with food or milk may help minimize these side effects. If they persist, ask your pharmacist to recommend another product. • This product contains vitamin B_6 (pyridoxine) in an amount great enough that it may interact with levodopa (L-dopa). If you are currently taking L-dopa, check with your doctor before taking this product.

Comments: Black, tarry stools are a normal consequence of iron therapy. If your stools are not black and tarry, this product may not be working for you. Ask your pharmacist to recommend another product. • Dietary deficiencies of vitamins are uncommon in the United States. Most people who have vitamin deficiencies should be under a doctor's care, and they should not be self-medicating with OTC vitamin products. If you choose to take supplemental vitamins, choose a generic product to save money. Ask your pharmacist for assistance.

Acceptable: If you choose to take a vitamin supplement, this is an acceptable product.

Unisom Nighttime sleep aid

Manufacturer: Leeming/Paquin, Division of Pfizer Inc.

Dosage Form/Ingredient: Tablet: doxylamine succinate, 25 mg

Use: To induce drowsiness and assist in falling asleep

Side Effects: Blurred vision; confusion; constipation; diarrhea, difficult urination; dizziness; drowsiness; dry mouth; headache; insomnia; low blood pressure, nasal congestion; nausea; nervousness; palpitations; rash; rash from exposure to sunlight; reduced sweating; restlessness; severe abdominal cramping; sore throat; vomiting

Warnings: Persons with asthma, diabetes, glaucoma (certain types), heart disease, high blood pressure, kidney disease, liver disease, thyroid disorders, certain types of peptic ulcer, enlarged prostate, obstructed bladder, or obstructed intestine; pregnant and nursing women; children under 12 years of age; and elderly or debilitated persons should not take this medication. • This product may interact with other drugs. If you are currently taking any medication, do not use this product without first consulting your doctor. • This product also interacts with alcohol, so avoid alcohol or other central nervous system sedatives while you are using it. • Since its purpose is to make you sleepy, do not use it while driving, operating heavy machinery, or performing other tasks that require you to be mentally alert. • Tolerance to this product may develop; do not increase the recommended dose unless your doctor recommends you to do so. • Insomnia may be a symptom of serious illness. Seek your doctor's advice if your sleeplessness continues, and do not take this product for more than two weeks without consulting your doctor.

Comments: This product may cause dryness of the mouth. To reduce this feeling, chew gum or suck on ice chips or a piece of hard candy. • There is probably no need to purchase this drug. You would be better advised to try to find and correct the cause of your insomnia. A glass of warm milk and a soak in a hot tub may work just as well as this product. • Many OTC sleep aids are very similar. If you wish to use one, look for a generic equivalent at a cheaper price. Ask your pharmacist for assistance.

Unacceptable: We consider that OTC sleep aids should not be taken without the advice of a doctor.

Vanoxide acne preparation

Manufacturer: Dermik Laboratories, Inc.
Dosage Form/Ingredients: Lotion: benzoyl peroxide, 5%; chlorhydroxyquinoline, 0.25%
Use: Treatment of acne
Side Effects: Allergy; local irritation; light yellow stains on skin
Warnings: Do not get this product in or near the eyes. • Persons having a known sensitivity to benzoyl peroxide or chlorhydroxyquinoline should not use this product. • While using this product, do not use harsh, abrasive cleansers. • If excessive redness or peeling occurs, reduce the frequency of this product's use. • Avoid exposure to heat lamps and sunlamps, as well as prolonged exposure to sunlight, when using this product. • This product may be especially active on fair-skinned people. • If the condition worsens or if skin irritation develops, stop using this product and contact your physician.
Comments: Wash the affected area gently in warm water and pat dry before applying this product. • There may be a slight transitory stinging or burning sensation on initial application of this product. • This product may damage certain fabrics including rayon.

Acceptable: Generally, we prefer a benzoyl peroxide product which does not contain other ingredients.

Vanquish analgesic

Manufacturer: Glenbrook Laboratories
Dosage Form/Ingredients: Caplet: aspirin, 227 mg; acetaminophen, 194 mg; caffeine, 33 mg; dried aluminum hydroxide gel, 25 mg; magnesium hydroxide, 50 mg
Use: For the relief of pain of headache, toothache, sprains, muscular aches, menstruation; for the relief of discomforts and fever of colds or "flu"; for temporary relief of minor aches and pains of arthritis and rheumatism
Side Effects: Dizziness; mental confusion; nausea and vomiting; ringing in the ears; slight blood loss; sweating

Warnings: Persons with heart, lung, liver, or kidney disease; certain blood disorders; asthma; hay fever; or other allergies should be extremely careful about using this product. The product may interfere with the treatment of gout. This product may cause an increased bleeding tendency and should not be taken by persons with a history of bleeding, peptic ulcer, or stomach bleeding. If you have any of these conditions, consult your doctor or pharmacist before using this medication. • Do not use this product if you are consuming alcohol, or taking methotrexate, oral anticoagulants, oral antidiabetics, probenecid, steroids, and/or sulfinpyrazone; if you are unsure of the type or contents of your medications, ask your doctor or pharmacist. • When taken in overdose, this product is more toxic than plain aspirin. The dosage instructions listed on the package should be followed carefully; toxicity may occur in adults or children with repeated doses.

Comments: Magnesium interacts with tetracycline antibiotics. There may not be enough magnesium in this product to cause any problem, but if you are taking a tetracycline antibiotic in addition to this product, separate the dosages by at least two hours. • Pain-relief tablets, such as this product, that contain salts of magnesium or aluminum are known as buffered tablets. Such products dissolve faster than unbuffered products, but there is no evidence that they relieve pain faster or better than those products that do not contain buffers. Buffered tablets may be less likely to cause gastric upset in some people. • There is no evidence that combinations of ingredients are more effective than similar doses of a single-ingredient product. • The caffeine in this product may have a slight stimulant effect but has no pain-relieving value.

Unacceptable: Caffeine has never been proven to have any pain-relieving value.

Vaseline Hemorr-Aid hemorrhoidal preparation

Manufacturer: Chesebrough-Pond's Inc.
Dosage Form/Ingredients: Ointment: white petrolatum, 100%
Use: For relief of pain, burning, and itching of hemorrhoids and other irritated anorectal tissue
Side Effects: Irritation
Warnings: Sensitization (continued itching and redness) may occur with long-term and repeated use. • Never self-medicate for hemorrhoids if pain is continuous or throbbing, if bleeding or itching is excessive, or if you feel a large pressure within the rectum.
Comments: Hemorrhoidal (pile) preparations relieve itching, reduce pain and inflammation, and check bleeding, but they do not heal, dry up, or give lasting relief from hemorrhoids. • It is doubtful that this product is worth the money, since it is basically the same as the lower-priced Vaseline petroleum jelly.

Unacceptable: This product is basically an over-priced version of Vaseline petroleum jelly.

Vicks cough remedy

Manufacturer: Vicks Health Care Division, Richardson-Merrell, Inc.
Dosage Form/Ingredients: Liquid (content per tablespoon): dextromethorphan hydrobromide, 10.5 mg; guaifenesin, 75 mg; sodium citrate, 600 mg; alcohol, 5%
Use: For temporary relief of cough due to colds or "flu"; to convert a dry, nonproductive cough to a productive, phlegm-producing cough

Side Effects: Drowsiness; nausea; vomiting

Warnings: Do not give this product to children under two years of age unless directed otherwise by your doctor. • This product interacts with monoamine oxidase inhibitors; if you are currently taking any drugs of this type, check with your doctor before taking this product. If you are unsure of the type or contents of your medications, ask your doctor or pharmacist. • Do not use this product to treat chronic coughs, such as those from smoking or asthma. • Do not use this product to treat productive (hacking) coughs that produce phlegm. • If your cough persists, or is accompanied by high fever, consult your doctor promptly.

Comments: If you require an expectorant, you need more moisture in your environment. Drink eight to ten glasses of water daily. The use of a vaporizer or humidifier may also be beneficial. • Many other conditions (some serious) mimic the common cold. If symptoms persist beyond one week or if they occur regularly without regard to season, consult your doctor.

Acceptable: This product contains an effective cough suppressant and two expectorants (neither of which have been proven effective). We suggest you look for a product that contains a single effective ingredient.

Vicks DayCare cold remedy

Manufacturer: Vicks Health Care Division, Richardson-Merrell, Inc.

Dosage Form/Ingredients: Liquid (content per two tablespoons); acetaminophen, 650 mg; dextromethorphan hydrobromide, 20 mg; phenylpropanolamine hydrochloride, 25 mg; alcohol, 10%

Use: For relief of nasal congestion, fever, coughing, aches, pains, and general discomfort due to colds or "flu"

Side Effects: Mild to moderate stimulation; nausea; vomiting, drowsiness. In overdose: Blood disorders; rash

Warnings: This product should be used with special caution by persons who have diabetes, heart, liver, kidney, or lung disease, certain blood disorders, high blood pressure, or thyroid disease. If you have any of these conditions, consult your doctor before taking this product. • This product interacts with alcohol, guanethidine, monoamine oxidase inhibitors, sedative drugs, and tricyclic antidepressants. If you are currently taking any drugs of these types, check with your doctor before taking this product. If you are unsure of the type or contents of your medications, ask your doctor or pharmacist. • This product should not be given to newborn or premature infants, or taken by pregnant or nursing women. • When taken in overdose, acetaminophen is more toxic than aspirin. Follow dosage instructions carefully. • This product may cause drowsiness. Do not take it if you must drive, operate heavy machinery, or perform other tasks requiring mental alertness. To prevent oversedation, avoid the use of alcohol or other drugs that have sedative properties. • If your cough persists or is accompanied by high fever, consult your doctor promptly.

Comments: Many other conditions (some serious) mimic the common cold. If symptoms persist beyond one week, or if they occur regularly without regard to season, consult your doctor. • The effectiveness of this product may diminish after being taken regularly for seven to ten days; consult your pharmacist about substituting another medication if this product begins to lose its effectiveness for you.

Acceptable: We prefer single-ingredient products rather than combination analgesic-decongestant-cough suppressant products like this one.

Vicks Inhaler nasal decongestant

Manufacturer: Vicks Health Care Division, Richardson-Merrell Inc.

Dosage Form/Ingredients: Inhaler: I-Desoxyephedrine, 50 mg; unspecified quantity of aromatics

Use: For temporary relief of nasal congestion due to colds, sinusitis, hay fever, or other upper respiratory allergies

Side Effects: Blurred vision; burning, dryness of nasal mucosa; increased nasal congestion or discharge; sneezing, and/or stinging; dizziness; drowsiness; headache; insomnia; nervousness; palpitations; slight increase in blood pressure; stimulation

Warnings: This product should not be used by persons who have glaucoma (certain types). • It should be used with special caution by persons who have diabetes, advanced hardening of the arteries, heart disease, high blood pressure, or thyroid disease. If you have any of these conditions, consult your doctor before using this product. • This product interacts with monoamine oxidase inhibitors, thyroid preparations, and tricyclic antidepressants. If you are currently taking any drugs of these types, check with your doctor before taking this product. If you are unsure of the type or contents of your medications, ask your doctor or pharmacist.

Comments: To avoid side effects such as burning, sneezing, or stinging, and a "rebound" increase in nasal congestion and discharge, do not exceed the recommended dose, and do not use this product for more than three or four continuous days. • This product should not be used by more than one person; sharing the dispenser may spread infection. • This product works best when it is used correctly. Refer to the instructions for the use of nasal inhalers in the chapter on "Buying, Storing, and Using Drugs." • Many topical decongestants on the market contain oxymetazoline hydrochloride. This drug has a duration of action of about 12 hours, and because it needs to be used less often, it is less likely to cause "rebound" nasal congestion during use. Therefore, we recommend a product containing oxymetazoline hydrochloride rather than this product, which does not contain the ingredient.

Fair: Products containing better ingredients are available.

Vicks Vaporub muscular pain remedy

Manufacturer: Vicks Health Care Division, Richardson-Merrell, Inc.

Dosage Form/Ingredients: Ointment: mixture of camphor, cedar leaf oil, eucalyptus oil, menthol, nutmeg oil, turpentine oil, 14%; petrolatum base

Use: Used externally to temporarily relieve pain in muscles and other areas

Side Effects: Allergic reactions (rash, itching, soreness); local irritation; local numbness

Warnings: This product is for external use only. • Do not use it on broken or irritated skin, or on large areas of the body; keep it away from the eyes. • If the pain in muscles or other areas persists, call your doctor. • Discontinue use and consult your pharmacist if irritation (rash, itching, or swelling) or pain occurs. • Children might be attracted to the smell of this product; when not in use it should be stored safely out of their reach.

Comments: Traditionally, this product was used in the treatment of colds. It was rubbed on the patient's chest or used in a vaporizer to "ease breathing." There is little objective evidence to support either use. If you do decide to apply it on your chest to ease breathing, be careful not to rub vigorously.

Fair: Products containing more effective ingredients are available.

Viro-Med cold remedy (liquid)

Manufacturer: Whitehall Laboratories

Dosage Form/Ingredients: Liquid (content per two tablespoons): acetaminophen, 600 mg; pseudoephedrine hydrochloride, 30 mg; dextromethorphan hydrobromide, 20 mg; sodium citrate, 500 mg; alcohol, 16.63%

Use: For relief of nasal congestion, fever, coughing, aches, pains, and general discomfort due to colds or "flu"

Side Effects: Mild to moderate stimulation; nausea; vomiting, drowsiness. In overdose: Blood disorders; rash

Warnings: This product should be used with special caution by persons who have diabetes, heart, liver, kidney, or lung disease, high blood pressure, certain blood disorders, or thyroid disease. If you have any of these conditions, consult your doctor before taking this product. • This product interacts with alcohol, guanethidine, monoamine oxidase inhibitors, sedative drugs, and tricyclic antidepressants. If you are currently taking any drugs of these types, check with your doctor before taking this product. If you are unsure of the type or contents of your medications, ask your doctor or pharmacist. • This product should not be given to newborn or premature infants, or taken by pregnant or nursing women. • When taken in overdose, acetaminophen is more toxic than aspirin. Follow dosage instructions carefully. • This product may cause drowsiness. Do not take it if you must drive, operate heavy machinery, or perform other tasks requiring mental alertness. To prevent oversedation, avoid the use of alcohol or other drugs that have sedative properties. • If your cough persists or is accompanied by high fever, consult your doctor promptly.

Comments: Many other conditions (some serious) mimic the common cold. If symptoms persist beyond one week, or if they occur regularly without regard to season, consult your doctor. • The effectiveness of this product may diminish after being taken regularly for seven to ten days; consult your pharmacist about substituting another medication if this product begins to lose its effectiveness for you.

Acceptable: *We prefer single-ingredient products rather than combination analgesic-decongestant-cough suppressant products like this one.*

Viro-Med cold remedy (tablet)

Manufacturer: Whitehall Laboratories

Dosage Form/Ingredients: Tablet: aspirin, 324 mg; chlorpheniramine maleate, 1 mg; pseudoephedrine hydrochloride, 15 mg; dextromethorphan hydrobromide, 7.5 mg; guaifenesin, 50 mg

Use: To relieve nasal congestion, fever, coughing, aches, pains, and general discomfort due to colds or "flu"

Side Effects: Anxiety; blurred vision; chest pain; confusion; constipation; difficult and painful urination; dizziness; drowsiness; dry mouth; headache; increased blood pressure; insomnia; loss of appetite; mild stimulation; nausea; nervousness; palpitations; rash; reduced sweating; ringing in the ears; slight blood loss; tension; tremor; vomiting

Warnings: This product should be used with special caution by the elderly or debilitated, and by persons who have asthma, diabetes, an enlarged prostate, glaucoma (certain types), heart disease, high blood pressure, kidney disease, liver disease, obstructed bladder, obstructed intestine, peptic ulcer, bleeding or stomach bleeding, gout, or thyroid disease. If you have any of these conditions, consult your doctor before taking this product. • It should not be used by pregnant or nursing women, or be given to newborn or premature infants. • This product may cause drowsiness. Do not take it if you must drive, operate heavy machinery, or perform other tasks requiring mental alertness. To prevent oversedation, avoid the use of alcohol or other drugs that have sedative properties. • This product interacts with alcohol, ammonium chloride, guanethidine, methotrexate, monoamine oxidase inhibitors, oral anticoagulants, oral antidiabetics, probenecid, sedative drugs, steroids, sulfinpyrazone, tricyclic antidepressants, and vitamin C. If you are currently taking any drugs of these types, check with your doctor before taking this product. If you are unsure of the type or contents of your medications, ask your doctor or pharmacist. • Because this product reduces sweating, avoid excessive work or exercise in hot weather. • The dosage instructions listed on the package should be followed carefully; toxicity may occur in adults or children with repeated doses. • If your cough persists or is accompanied by high fever, consult your doctor promptly.

Comments: Many other conditions (some serious) mimic the common cold. If symptoms persist beyond one week, or if they occur regularly without regard to season, consult your doctor. • The effectiveness of this product may diminish after being taken for seven to ten days; consult your pharmacist about substituting another product if this product begins to lose its effectiveness for you. • Chew gum or suck on ice chips or a piece of hard candy to reduce mouth dryness.

Unacceptable: This product contains an analgesic, an antihistamine, a decongestant, a cough suppressant, and an expectorant. We believe you should treat your symptoms individually rather than take a product with this many different actions.

Visine decongestant eyedrops

Manufacturer: Leeming/Pacquin, Division of Pfizer Inc.

Dosage Form/Ingredients: Drop: benzalkonium chloride, 0.01%; disodium edetate, 0.1%; tetrahydrozoline hydrochloride, 0.05%; unspecified quantities of boric acid, sodium borate, and sodium chloride

Use: For relief of minor eye irritation and redness

Side Effects: Allergic reactions (rash, itching, soreness); local irritation; momentary blurred vision

Warnings: Do not use this product if you have glaucoma. • This product contains boric acid, which many medical authorities believe should not be used because it is toxic. • Do not use this product for more than two consecutive days without checking with your doctor. • Keep this product out of the reach of children. • If swallowed, this drug is likely to cause overstimulation in children. Call your doctor immediately if this product is accidentally swallowed. • Do not touch the dropper or bottle top to the eye or other tissue because contamination of the solution will result. • Use this product only for minor eye irritations. • The use of more than one eye product at a time may cause severe irritation to the eye.

Comments: This product works best when used correctly. Refer to the instructions on eye products in the chapter, "Buying, Storing, and Using Drugs."

Unacceptable: We cannot recommend the use of this product because it contains boric acid, which many medical authorities believe to be toxic.

vitamin A (retinol) nutritional supplement

Manufacturer: Various

Dosage Forms: Capsule, Tablet: common strengths include 5,000, 10,000, 25,000, and 50,000 IU

Use: To supplement the diet

Side Effects: None

Warnings: Large doses of vitamin A can cause loss of appetite and hair; intense headaches; dry, flaky skin; blurred vision; inflammation of the optic nerve; eye damage; brain or liver damage; and lymph node and spleen enlargement. There is no reason to take vitamin A supplements unless you have a true vitamin-A deficiency, which only your doctor can diagnose. • Vitamin A can accumulate and be stored in the body. Do not exceed recommended doses over long periods (several weeks to months) except by a doctor's orders. • In spite of claims, there is no proof that taking vitamin A supplements will prevent or cure dry or wrinkled skin, respiratory diseases, visual defects, or eye diseases.

Comments: Vitamin A is readily available in liver, yellow-orange fruits and vegetables, dark green leafy vegetables, whole milk, vitamin-A-fortified skim milk, butter, and margarine. Many ready-to-eat breakfast cereals are also fortified with vitamin A. • Oral supplementation with vitamin A is not an effective treatment for acne, but topical application of one form, retinoic acid, has been used effectively against acne.

Unacceptable: Vitamin A is potentially toxic. Self-medication with vitamin A can be dangerous; only a doctor can diagnose a vitamin-A deficiency.

vitamin B₁ (thiamine) nutritional supplement

Manufacturer: Various

Dosage Forms: Liquid, Tablet: common strengths include 5, 10, 25, 50, 100, 250, and 500 mg

Use: To supplement the diet

Side Effects: None

Comments: Vitamin B₁ is present in tiny amounts in most foods. Enriched and whole-grain cereal products, and meat, especially pork, are good sources of the vitamin. An ordinary mixed diet is sufficient to prevent severe deficiency of vitamin B₁, and severe deficiency of this vitamin rarely occurs in the Western world nowadays. A subclinical deficiency—occurring when the amount of vitamin B₁ in the diet is barely adequate—could occur, however, with a less-than-well-balanced diet. A subclinical deficiency does not produce symptoms, but it can be confirmed by blood or urine tests. • There is some evidence that if you require vitamin B₁ supplementation you will also need supplements of other B vitamins. Therefore, there is probably no reason to take plain vitamin B₁ supplements unless your doctor specifically prescribes it for vitamin B₁ deficiency (beriberi)—a disease that only he or she can diagnose. • In spite of claims, there is no proof that taking supplements of vitamin B₁ will give you increased energy, stimulate your appetite, or reduce fatigue, nor will it be effective in the prevention or treatment of dermatitis, multiple sclerosis, neuritis, or mental disorders.

Fair: Unless your doctor has prescribed B₁ supplementation for you, there is probably no reason to use this product.

vitamin B₂ (riboflavin) nutritional supplement

Manufacturer: Various

Dosage Form: Tablet: common strengths include 5, 10, 25, 50, and 100 mg

Use: To supplement the diet

Side Effects: None

Comments: Vitamin B₂ is readily available in milk and dairy products, meats, green leafy vegetables, and in enriched bread and cereal products.

Most Americans get sufficient vitamin B$_2$ in their diets to prevent deficiency without the use of supplementation via tablets. A medical examination is required to determine the existence of a B vitamin deficiency, and there is some evidence that if you require vitamin B$_2$ supplementation you will also need supplements of the other B vitamins. Therefore, there is probably no reason to take plain vitamin B$_2$ supplements unless your doctor specifically prescribes it for a deficiency state that only he or she can diagnose. • In spite of claims, there is no proof that taking large amounts of B vitamins will prevent or cure various diseases such as glaucoma, cataracts, night blindness, diabetes, peptic ulcer, or vaginitis, nor will it relieve stress. • If you take large doses of vitamin B$_2$, your urine may become bright yellow in color.

Fair: Unless your doctor has prescribed B$_2$ supplementation for you, there is probably no reason to use this product.

vitamin B$_3$ (nicotinic acid) nutritional supplement

Manufacturer: Various

Dosage Forms: Capsule, Liquid, Tablet: common strengths include 50, 100, and 150 mg

Use: To correct nicotinic acid (niacin) deficiency; lower blood cholesterol levels; improve blood circulation

Side Effects: Dizziness; dryness of skin; flushing and warmth; headache; itching; nausea; palpitations; tingling in fingers and toes; vomiting; activation of peptic ulcers

Warnings: This product should be used cautiously by people who have diabetes, glaucoma, liver disease, or peptic ulcer, and by pregnant women. Be sure your doctor knows you are taking this product if you have any of these conditions.

Comments: Nicotinic acid is also known as niacin. • If you are taking this product to correct a niacin deficiency, consider taking niacinamide instead. Niacinamide does not cause as many side effects, but it may not lower blood cholesterol. • Flushing, dizziness, and feelings of warmth usually go away after several days of continuous therapy. • To avoid dizziness or light-headedness when you stand, contract and relax the muscles of your legs for a few minutes before rising. Do this by pushing one foot against the floor while raising the other slightly, alternating feet so that you are "pumping" your legs in a pedaling motion. • Nicotinic acid is present in meat, peanuts, beans, peas, and enriched grains. An ordinary, well-balanced diet is sufficient to prevent a deficiency of nicotinic acid (pellagra), and a deficiency of this vitamin rarely occurs in the United States. There is some evidence that if you require nicotinic acid supplementation, you will also need supplements of other B vitamins. Therefore, there is probably no reason to take nicotinic acid alone unless your doctor prescribes it for you.

Fair: Unless your doctor has prescribed B$_3$ supplementation for you, there is probably no reason to use this product.

vitamin B$_5$ (pantothenic acid) nutritional supplement

Manufacturer: Various

Dosage Form: Tablet: common strengths include 10, 30, 100, and 218 mg

Use: To supplement the diet

Side Effects: In high doses (more than 100 mg taken several times daily): occasional diarrhea

Comments: Since pantothenic acid is manufactured in the body and is available in most foods, deficiency is unlikely. Yeast, liver, eggs and milk are good sources. A deficiency has never been noted in humans. Therefore, there is probably no reason to take this item unless your doctor prescribes it for you. • Do not be taken in by claims that pantothenic acid will prevent hair from turning gray or falling out; will treat arthritis, allergy, mental sluggishness; or improve your sex life. It will do none of these.

Fair: *Unless your doctor has prescribed B_5 supplementation for you, there is probably no reason to use this product.*

vitamin B_6 (pyridoxine) nutritional supplement

Manufacturer: Various
Dosage Forms: Tablet, Timed-release capsule: common strengths are 5, 10, 25, 50, 100, 200, and 500 mg
Use: To supplement the diet
Warnings: Large doses (200 to 300 mg) of vitamin B_6 taken daily for over a month have produced a temporary dependency, and unpleasant reactions have occurred when dosage was stopped. • Large doses of vitamin B_6 interfere with the drug levodopa (L-dopa), used in the treatment of Parkinson's disease. If you are taking L-dopa, avoid taking vitamin B_6 supplements and do not eat excessive quantities of foods that are rich in the vitamin.
Comments: Vitamin B_6 is found in all foods; bananas, lima beans, meats, potatoes, and whole-grain cereals are especially rich sources. Most Americans get sufficient vitamin B_6 in their diets to prevent deficiency without the use of supplementation via tablets or capsules. A medical examination is required to determine the existence of a B vitamin deficiency, and there is some evidence that if you require vitamin B_6 supplementation you will also need supplements of the other B vitamins. Therefore, there is probably no reason to take plain vitamin B_6 supplements unless your doctor specifically prescribes it for a deficiency state that only he or she can diagnose, or for use in conjunction with the prescription drug isoniazid. (Vitamin B_6 is frequently prescribed with isoniazid to reduce side effects from the latter drug.) • In spite of claims, there is no proof that taking supplements of vitamin B_6 will reduce the morning sickness of pregnancy, nor will it be effective in the prevention or treatment of kidney stones, migraine headaches, or hemorrhoids.

Fair: *Unless your doctor has prescribed B_6 supplementation for you, there is probably no reason to use this product.*

vitamin B_{12} (cyanocobalamin) nutritional supplement

Manufacturer: Various
Dosage Forms: Capsule, Tablet: common strengths are 10, 25, 50, 100, and 250 mcg
Use: To supplement the diet
Side Effects: None
Comments: Dietary deficiencies of vitamin B_{12} are practically never seen; the body requires only minute amounts daily, and the liver stores small amounts of the vitamin as well. Vitamin B_{12} is found only in animal foods—meats (especially liver), seafood, egg yolk, and cheese, for example—so strict vegetarians (those who eat no eggs or cheese, and do not drink milk) should supplement their diets with B_{12}. • It is important to note that pernicious anemia, resulting from vitamin B_{12} deficiency, is not

caused by a lack of the vitamin in the diet. People with pernicious anemia suffer from a disease that makes them incapable of absorbing vitamin B_{12}, even though it is present in their diets. Oral supplements of the vitamin will not cure them, because they cannot absorb the supplements, unless another medication is taken at the same time. To effectively treat pernicious anemia, vitamin B_{12} must be injected. Therefore, there is no reason to take oral vitamin B_{12} supplements unless you are a strict vegetarian. • In spite of claims, there is no proof that taking supplements of vitamin B_{12} will give you increased energy or ensure mental health.

Fair: Only strict vegetarians need to take B_{12} orally.

vitamin C (ascorbic acid) nutritional supplement

Manufacturer: Various
Dosage Forms: Capsule, Chewable tablet, Drop, Liquid, Tablet, Wafer: common strengths are 25, 50, 100, 250, and 500 mg
Use: To supplement the diet
Side Effects: None
Warnings: The use of megadoses (4 grams or more daily) of vitamin C has been associated with the formation of kidney stones in some people. If you have a predisposition to kidney stones, do not take massive doses of vitamin C. • A few people have complained of abdominal discomfort, cramps, and diarrhea after taking large doses of this vitamin. However, the effects apparently occur in only a small percentage of the people who take megadoses of vitamin C. • If you take massive doses of this vitamin for an extended period of time, you may become conditioned to the increased intake and develop symptoms of vitamin C deficiency (scurvy) if you discontinue or reduce the dosage. • Large doses of vitamin C may counteract the effect of oral anticoagulant drugs and may interfere with urine and blood tests, causing errors in the diagnosis of disease. If you are taking vitamin C, be sure to inform your doctor and pharmacist of the fact. • Vitamin C may interfere with some of the common over-the-counter urinalysis tests for determining blood glucose levels. If you use these urine-testing products, consult your doctor or pharmacist about your concurrent use of vitamin C.
Comments: Vitamin C is readily available in fruits (especially citrus fruits) and vegetables. Most Americans get sufficient vitamin C in their diets to prevent deficiency without the use of OTC supplements. • Take your dose of vitamin C with at least a full glass of water, and drink eight to ten glasses of water daily. • In spite of claims, there is no proof that taking supplemental vitamin C will prevent colds or reduce their seriousness. Vitamin C is not effective in the treatment of hardening of the arteries, allergies, mental illness, corneal ulcers, blood clots, or pressure sores. • Although the concentration of vitamin C in the blood of smokers is lower than that of nonsmokers, it is still within normal range, and smokers who eat an adequate diet do not need vitamin C supplements. • Time-release forms of vitamin C offer no therapeutic advantage and are likely to cost more than other dosage forms.

Fair: Unless your doctor has prescribed C supplementation for you, there is probably no reason to use this product.

vitamin D (calciferol) nutritional supplement

Manufacturer: Various
Dosage Forms: Capsule, Drop, Tablet: common strengths are 400, 8000, 25,000, and 50,000 IU (international units)

Use: To supplement the diet

Side Effects: None

Warnings: Excess amounts of vitamin D cause absorption of abnormally large amounts of calcium, which become deposited in body tissues. Irreversible damage to the kidneys or lungs may result, or irregular heartbeats and abnormal nervous activity may occur, leading to cardiac arrhythmias and to convulsions and death. Never take a vitamin supplement containing more than 400 IU of vitamin D per dose. • Always keep vitamin D supplements out of the reach of children.

Comments: Although fish liver oils and some fish are the only naturally occurring foods containing significant amounts of vitamin D, many ready-to-eat breakfast cereals and all the milk sold commercially in this country are fortified with vitamin D. Furthermore, humans manufacture their own vitamin D when exposed to direct sunlight or ultraviolet light from a sunlamp. Because of the hazards of vitamin D overdose, there is no reason to take vitamin D supplements unless you have a true vitamin D deficiency, which only your doctor can diagnose. Children and young adults under the age of 22, and pregnant and nursing women should drink three to four glasses of fortified milk daily to meet their requirements for vitamin D; people over the age of 22 (whose bone development is complete) are able to meet their daily requirements by exposure to sunlight. If you are seldom exposed to sunshine by reason of occupation, living habits, or mode of dress, you should probably drink fortified milk regularly to ensure an adequate intake. • In spite of claims, there is no proof that taking supplemental vitamin D will prevent or cure arthritis or nervousness.

Unacceptable: *Vitamin D is potentially toxic. Self-medication with vitamin D can be dangerous; only a doctor can diagnose a vitamin D deficiency.*

vitamin E (tocopherol)
nutritional supplement

Manufacturer: Various

Dosage Forms: Capsule, Chewable tablet, Drop, Liquid: common strengths are 30, 50, 100, 200, 400, 600, 800, and 1000 IU (international units)

Use: To supplement the diet

Side Effects: None

Warnings: Some people taking more than 400 IU of vitamin E daily for long periods have suffered nausea, intestinal distress, fatigue, and other flu-like symptoms.

Comments: There is no evidence of even marginal vitamin E deficiency in the American people. Vitamin E is readily available in vegetable and seed oils, and to a lesser extent, in meats, cereal and dairy products, and vegetables. Supplemental vitamin E is advised only when a doctor determines that there is evidence of a deficiency or risk of deficiency in a newborn baby (a circumstance that occasionally occurs, but is easily diagnosed), or in a patient suffering from diseases that inhibit absorption of the vitamin. • In spite of the abundance of claims made for it, there is no proof that vitamin E is effective in the prevention, treatment, or cure of conditions including acne, aging, bee stings, liver spots on the hands, bursitis, diaper rash, frostbite, heart attacks, labor pains, miscarriage, muscular dystrophy, poor posture, sexual impotence, sterility, infertility, sunburn, or scarring. If you accept the unfounded claims for vitamin E and use the vitamin to treat a physical condition yourself, the delay in getting proper medical treatment might have serious consequences.

Unacceptable: There is no proven medical value in supplementing your diet with vitamin E.

Vivarin stimulant

Manufacturer: J. B. Williams Co., Inc.
Dosage Form/Ingredients: Tablet: caffeine, 200 mg; dextrose, 150 mg
Use: To produce a temporary increase in mental alertness
Side Effects: Increased urination. In larger than the recommended dose: Irregular heartbeat; nervousness, upset stomach; insomnia
Warnings: Do not take this product if you have heart disease, blood vessel disease, kidney disease, or a nervous disorder.
Comments: Vivarin stimulant may cause increased alertness in parts of the brain and decreased ability in others. • Vivarin contains dextrose, which provides calories that must be counted by the diabetic. • If you take Vivarin regularly for two weeks, you will become tolerant to it, and consequently the effectiveness decreases. • We do not recommend the use of this or any other OTC stimulant. You can get the same effect by drinking coffee, tea, or colas. If you regularly need a stimulant, you should see your doctor as something serious may be wrong.

Unacceptable: We do not recommend the use of any OTC stimulant. Coffee, tea, or a cola drink will be equally effective. We consider this product overpriced.

Wyanoid hemorrhoidal preparations

Manufacturer: Wyeth Laboratories
Dosage Forms/Ingredients: Suppository: ephedrine sulfate, 3 mg; belladonna extract, 15 mg; unspecified quantities of boric acid, zinc oxide, bismuth oxyiodide, bismuth subcarbonate, Peruvian balsam, cocoa butter, and beeswax. Ointment: benzocaine, 2%; boric acid, 18%; ephedrine sulfate, 0.1%; Peruvian balsam, 1%; zinc oxide, 5%
Use: For relief of pain, itching, and burning of hemorrhoids and other irritated anorectal tissue
Side Effects: Irritation
Warnings: Sensitization (continued itching and redness) may occur with long-term and repeated use. • Certain ingredients in this product may cause an allergic reaction; do not use for longer than seven days at a time unless your doctor has advised you otherwise. • These products contain boric acid, which many medical authorities believe should not be used because it is toxic. Follow the directions on the package carefully. • The suppository is not recommended for external hemorrhoids or bleeding internal hemorrhoids. Use the ointment form. Use caution when inserting applicator. • Never self-medicate for hemorrhoids if pain is continuous or throbbing, if bleeding or itching is excessive, or if you feel a large pressure within the rectum. • Discontinue use if irritation (pain, itching, or swelling) or rash occurs; consult your pharmacist.
Comments: Hemorrhoidal (pile) preparations relieve itching, reduce pain and inflammation, and check bleeding, but they do not heal, dry up, or give lasting relief from hemorrhoids. • Hemorrhoidal suppositories work best when they are used correctly. Refer to the instructions for their use in the chapter "Buying, Storing, and Using Drugs."

Unacceptable: These products contain boric acid, which many medical authorities believe to be toxic.

zinc oxide rash remedy

Manufacturer: Various
Dosage Form/Ingredient: Ointment: zinc oxide, 20%
Use: For relief of skin irritation; to protect against diaper rash
Side Effects: Allergy; local irritation (rare)
Warnings: Discontinue use if irritation (pain, itching, or swelling) or rash appears. Consult your pharmacist.
Comments: This product is not intended for use on puncture wounds, serious burns, or cuts. • If this product is being used to control intolerable itching, we recommend that you also try a wet soak, as is described in the chapter, "Buying, Storing, and Using Drugs." You may find that a wet soak is sufficient for relief of itching, and that you do not need this product at all. • Zinc oxide is also available as a paste. Consult your pharmacist about which of the dosage forms would be better for you.
Preferred: *Zinc oxide is the treatment of choice for diaper rash.*

Ziradryl poison ivy/poison oak remedy

Manufacturer: Parke-Davis
Dosage Form/Ingredients: Lotion: alcohol, 2%; diphenhydramine hydrochloride, 2%; zinc oxide, 2%
Use: For relief of itching due to poison ivy and poison oak
Side Effects: Allergic reactions (rash, itching, soreness); local irritation
Warnings: Do not apply this product to extensive or raw, oozing areas of the skin, or use for a prolonged time, except as directed by a physician. • Do not use near the eyes, on mucous membranes, on genitalia, or on infected areas. • Discontinue use and consult your pharmacist if irritation (pain, itching, or swelling) or rash occurs. • Avoid scratching, which may cause irritation and secondary infection.
Comments: Before applying the medication, soak the area in warm water or apply wet towels for five to ten minutes; dry gently by patting with a soft towel and then apply medication. • If itching is intolerable and this product does not relieve it sufficiently, we recommend the use of a "wet soak." In fact, a wet soak may work well enough that you do not need to use this product at all. For more information about how to apply a wet soak, refer to the chapter, "Buying, Storing, and Using Drugs."

Fair: *The antihistamine in this product may cause further irritation in susceptible people.*

Index

247

E

Eclipse Lip and Face Protectant sunscreen, 136
Eclipse Original sunscreen, 136
Eclipse Partial Suntan sunscreen, 136
Eclipse Total sunscreen, 136
Ecotrin analgesic, 62, 137
Empirin analgesic, 62, 137
enteric-coated products, 63
Enzactin athlete's foot remedy, 138
e.p.t. urine test for pregnancy, 138
ephedrine, 25–26
Excedrin analgesic, 139
Excedrin P.M. analgesic, 62, 139
Ex-Lax laxative, 56, 140
external analgesics. *See* muscular pain remedies
eyedrops, 51
  administration of, 17
  Isopto Plain, 159
  Murine, 168

F

Femiron nutritional supplements, 140, 141
Feosol nutritional supplement, 142
Fergon nutritional supplement, 142
Fer-In-Sol nutritional supplement, 143
ferrous gluconate nutritional supplement, 144
ferrous sulfate nutritional supplement, 144
first-aid products, 51–53
  Baciguent, 88
  Bactine, 88
  hydrogen peroxide, 156
  iodine tincture, 157
  Mercurochrome, 165
  Merthiolate tincture, 166
  Mycitracin, 170
  Neo-Polycin, 172
  Neosporin, 172
  Polysporin, 192
Fleet Enema laxative, 56, 145
Fletcher's Castoria laxative, 56, 145
Formula 44 Cough Control Discs, 46, 146
Formula 44-D cough remedy, 46, 146
Fostex acne preparation, 147
Fostril acne preparation, 147
4-Way cold remedy, 38, 147
Freezone corn and callus remover, 148

G

Gaviscon antacid, 22, 149
Gaviscon II antacid, 22, 149
Gelusil antacid and antiflatulent, 23, 150
Gelusil-M antacid and antiflatulent, 23, 151
Gelusil II antacid and antiflatulent, 23, 150
generic drugs, 11
Gentz Wipes hemorrhoidal preparation, 152
Geritol nutritional supplements, 152, 153
Gly-Oxide canker sore and fever blister remedy, 154
guaifenesin, 26, 45

H

Haley's M-O laxative, 56, 154
Hazel-Balm hemorrhoidal preparation, 154
Heet muscular pain remedy, 155
hemorrhoidal preparations, 53–54
  Americaine, 78
  Anusol, 82
  Gentz Wipes, 152
  Hazel-Balm, 154
  Lanacane, 162
  Nupercainal, 180
  Preparation H, 193
  Tucks, 228
  Vaseline Hemorr-Aid, 234
  Wyanoid, 244
  See also anal-itch products
Hold cough remedy, 46, 155
hydrocortisone, 53
  See also topical steroids
hydrogen peroxide first-aid product, 156

I

Icy Hot Balm muscular pain remedy, 156
Icy Hot Rub muscular pain remedy, 157
impetigo, treatment of, 52
indications for drug use, 9
Infra-Rub muscular pain remedy, 157
iodine tincture first-aid product, 157
Ionax Foam acne preparation, 158
Ionax Scrub acne preparation, 158
iron supplements, 59
Isopto-Frin decongestant eyedrops, 158
Isopto Plain eyedrops, 159
Ivy Dry Cream poison ivy/poison oak remedy, 159

K

Kaopectate Concentrate diarrhea remedy, 159
Kaopectate diarrhea remedy, 159
Ketostix Strips urine test for ketones, 160
Kolantyl antacid, 23, 160
Komed acne preparation, 161

L

Lactinex diarrhea remedy, 161
Lanacane hemorrhoidal preparation, 162
laxatives, 54–57
  Carter's Little Pills, 98
  Colace, 104
  Correctol, 112
  Dorbane, 129
  Dorbantyl, 130
  Dorbantyl Forte, 129
  Doxidan, 130
  Dulcolax, 135
  Ex-Lax, 140
  Fleet Enema, 145
  Fletcher's Castoria, 145
  Haley's M-O, 154
  Metamucil, 166
  Modane, 167
  Modane Bulk, 167
  Modane Mild, 167
  Nature's Remedy, 171
  Neoloid, 172
  Nujol, 180

vitamin C, 242
vitamin D, 242
vitamin E, 243
NyQuil cough remedy, 46, 181
Nytol sleep aid, 182

O

Ocusol decongestant eyedrops, 183
ointment, application of, 16
One-A-Day nutritional
  supplement, 183
One-A-Day Plus Iron nutritional
  supplement, 184
One-A-Day Plus Minerals
  nutritional supplement, 184
oral inhalers, use of, 17–18, 26–27
Ornacol cough remedy, 46, 185
Ornade 2 for Children cold and
  allergy remedy, 40, 186
Ornex cold remedy, 40, 186
Oxy-5 acne preparation, 187
Oxy-Scrub acne preparation, 187
Oxy-10 acne preparation, 187
oxymetazoline, 33

P

pain relievers, 60–63
  See also analgesics
pantothenic acid. See vitamin B$_5$
  nutritional supplement
paregoric, 50
Parepectolin diarrhea remedy, 188
Pediaquil cough remedy, 48, 188
Pepto-Bismol diarrhea remedy, 189
Percogesic analgesic, 62, 189
Peri-Colace laxative, 56, 190
Pertussin 8-Hour Cough Formula
  cough remedy, 48, 190
pharmacist assistance, 11
phenylpropanolamine hydrochloride, 24
Phillips' Milk of Magnesia laxative,
  56, 191
pHisoAc acne preparation, 192
pHisoDerm acne preparation, 192
poison ivy/poison oak remedies, 64–65
  Caladryl, 97
  calamine lotion, 98
  Ivy Dry Cream, 159
  Rhulicream, 198
  Rhulihist, 198
  Ziradryl, 245
Polysporin first-aid product, 192
Poly-Vi-Sol nutritional supplement,
  193
Predictor urine test for pregnancy,
  193
Preparation H hemorrhoidal
  preparation, 193
Presun 8 sunscreens, 194
Presun 15 sunscreen, 194
Presun 4 sunscreen, 194
Presun Lip Protection sunscreen, 194
Primatene M asthma remedy, 194
Primatene P asthma remedy, 195
Privine nasal decongestant, 196
Prolamine appetite suppressant, 197
P.V.M. appetite suppressant, 197
pyridoxine. See vitamin B$_6$
  nutritional supplement

R

rash remedy, 65
  zinc oxide, 245

rebound congestion, 33
retinol. See vitamin A nutritional
  supplement
Rhulicream poison ivy/poison oak
  remedy, 198
Rhulihist poison ivy/poison oak
  remedy, 198
riboflavin. See vitamin B$_2$
  nutritional supplement
Riopan antacid, 24, 199
Riopan Plus antacid and antiflatulent,
  24, 199
Robitussin cough remedy, 48, 200
Robitussin A-C cough remedy, 48, 201
Robitussin-DM Cough Calmers cough
  remedy, 48, 201
Robitussin-DM cough remedy, 48, 202
Robitussin-PE cough remedy, 48, 202
Rolaids antacid, 24, 203
RVPaba sunscreen, 203
RVPlus sunscreen, 203
RVP sunscreen, 203

S

St. Joseph Children's cold remedy,
  40, 204
Senokot laxative, 56, 205
Serutan laxative, 56, 205
side effects, 9–10
Silain antiflatulent. See Mylicon,
  Mylicon-80 antiflatulents
Silence Is Golden cough remedy, 48,
  206
simethicone, 21
Sinarest cold and allergy remedy, 40,
  206
Sine-Aid analgesic, 62, 207
Sine-Off cold and allergy remedy
  (extra strength tablet), 40, 208
Sine-Off cold and allergy remedy
  (tablet), 40, 207
Sine-Off Once-A-Day nasal
  decongestant, 209
Sinex Long-Acting nasal
  decongestant, 209
Sinex nasal decongestant, 210
Sinutab cold and allergy remedy, 40,
  211
Sinutab Long-Lasting nasal
  decongestant, 211
Sinutab-II cold and allergy remedy,
  40, 212
sleep aids, 65–66
  Compoz, 105
  Nervine, 174
  Nytol, 182
  Sleep-Eze, 213
  Sominex, 214
  Unisom Nighttime, 232
Sleep-Eze sleep aid, 213
sodium bicarbonate, 20
Solarcaine antiseptic and burn
  remedy, 213
Sominex sleep aid, 214
steroids. See anal-itch products,
  topical steroids
stimulants, 66
  No Doz, 175
  Vivarin, 244
storage of drugs, 13
Stresscaps nutritional
  supplement, 215

251